# COVID-19 in Indian Country

Farina King • Wade Davies
Editors

# COVID-19 in Indian Country

Native American Memories and Experiences of the Pandemic

*Editors*
Farina King
The University of Oklahoma
Norman, OK, USA

Wade Davies
The University of Montana
Missoula, MT, USA

ISBN 978-3-031-70183-2     ISBN 978-3-031-70184-9   (eBook)
https://doi.org/10.1007/978-3-031-70184-9

© The Editor(s) (if applicable) and The Author(s), under exclusive license to Springer Nature Switzerland AG 2024

This work is subject to copyright. All rights are solely and exclusively licensed by the Publisher, whether the whole or part of the material is concerned, specifically the rights of translation, reprinting, reuse of illustrations, recitation, broadcasting, reproduction on microfilms or in any other physical way, and transmission or information storage and retrieval, electronic adaptation, computer software, or by similar or dissimilar methodology now known or hereafter developed.
The use of general descriptive names, registered names, trademarks, service marks, etc. in this publication does not imply, even in the absence of a specific statement, that such names are exempt from the relevant protective laws and regulations and therefore free for general use.
The publisher, the authors and the editors are safe to assume that the advice and information in this book are believed to be true and accurate at the date of publication. Neither the publisher nor the authors or the editors give a warranty, expressed or implied, with respect to the material contained herein or for any errors or omissions that may have been made. The publisher remains neutral with regard to jurisdictional claims in published maps and institutional affiliations.

This Palgrave Macmillan imprint is published by the registered company Springer Nature Switzerland AG.
The registered company address is: Gewerbestrasse 11, 6330 Cham, Switzerland

If disposing of this product, please recycle the paper.

*To all those who have walked on in the COVID-19 pandemic*

# Acknowledgments

This collaboration started with coeditor Farina King's Diné family of healers who descend from hataałii, known as "medicine men" and "medicine women," or translated directly as "singer." We acknowledge the generations of Diné and Indigenous healers, including Farina's father, Phillip Lee Smith, M.D., and her deceased grandparents, Red Smith and Johanna Haskeltsie, who have sustained their people through major public health crises. Farina turned to them and their stories for strength during the COVID-19 pandemic. She decided to launch an open-access online syllabus, called "Diné Doctor History Syllabus," to educate the public about histories and lived experiences of Diné facing disease and healing through generations. She sought ways to contextualize and historicize, for a general audience to understand, the disproportionate susceptibility of Diné and Native Americans to COVID-19 or Dikos Nstaaígíí-Náhást'éíts'áadah and ts'ííh niidóóh (disease).

In these efforts, Farina organized a panel for the 2022 annual conference of the Organization of American Historians (OAH) with her father Phillip Smith and sister Heather Tanana, inviting the author of *Healing Ways: Navajo Health Care in the Twentieth Century* (2001), Wade Davies, to chair the session. Farina asked Heather to participate in such conversations because of her work as an active community leader in the Utah State Bar Indian Law Section, which launched the Utah Tribal COVID-19 Relief to support the eight distinct Native Nations of Utah. For the OAH panel, Wade prepared through extensive research of Native American and Diné experiences with disease and specifically COVID-19.

A senior editor of Palgrave Macmillan, an imprint of Spring Nature, at the time, Philip Getz, reached out to Wade and Farina, encouraging them to submit a book proposal about the impacts of COVID-19 in Native American communities. The contributors wholeheartedly thank Philip Getz for his backing of the book in its early stages, including its inception. We appreciate the various editors of Palgrave Macmillan and peer reviewers, beginning with Clifford E. Trafzer, who supported the development of the book.

This collaboration would not have been possible without the 22 authors and the Native American communities with which they work. We thank families and friends who sustain us. We offer special thanks to the Muscogee (Creek) Nation for approving the contributions of their employees RaeLynn Butler and Midge Dellinger to this book. We are also grateful for the artists who shared their work in this book, such as the cover artist Johnnie Diacon of the Muscogee (Creek) Nation. While this book does not represent all the voices and experiences of Native Americans through the COVID-19 pandemic, we appreciate them and hope that this storywork continues.

The coeditors would like to express much gratitude for their families. Wade thanks his wife, Colleen, son Madoc, and daughter Maren. Farina says, "Ahéhee'" ("Thank you"), to all her relatives, especially her husband, Brian, and children, Will, Wes, and Luci, as well as her parents, JoAnn and Phillip, and her Diné kin past, present, and future. Díí Baa Ahééh Niilzin.

# Contents

1 Introduction     1
Farina King and Wade Davies

Part I    Historical Inequities and Pandemics     21

2 The Intersection of the Law and Health: Water (In)security in Indian Country     23
Heather Tanana

3 The Tribal Decline: Fort Hall Reservation and the Influenza Pandemic, 1918–1920     41
Yvette A. Towersap

4 Aunties of Resilience: Decolonization During COVID-19     65
Jennifer Frazee

Part II    Community Well-Being     73

5 A Vigil     75
Farina King

6  Azee'íił'íní Reflections 89
Phillip Lee Smith

7  A Twenty-First Century Pandemic in Indian Country:
The Resilience of the Muscogee (Creek) Nation Against
COVID-19 95
Midge Dellinger and RaeLynn Butler

Part III  Students, Innovative Learning, and Community
Building 119

8  Lived Experiences of Native American College Students
During the COVID-19 Pandemic 121
Amoneeta Beckstein and Tapati Dutta

9  Navigating the Unknown: Lessons Learned from
Sustaining Indigenous Community in Higher Education
During the COVID-19 Pandemic 145
Daniel Piper, Melissa Tehee, Racheal Killgore, and
Erica Ficklin

10  Maawanji'idiwag: They Come Together 161
Chelsea M. Mead

11  Using that Good Tech Medicine: An Indigenous
Autoethnographic Recount of Teaching and Learning
with Elders During COVID-19 179
Kelly Berry

Part IV  Art as Survivance 197

12  Native American Graffiti and Aerosol Muralism of the
Pandemic: Alternative Messaging of Community Well-
Being 199
Gavin A. Healey

| | | |
|---|---|---|
| 13 | Wołí bee: Diné Cultural Arts Amid Pandemics<br>Christine Marie Ami | 219 |
| Part V | Motherhood and Family Wellness | 239 |
| 14 | American Indian Women Combating COVID-19: The Household Disruptor<br>Aresta Tsosie-Paddock and Mary Jo Tippeconnic Fox | 241 |
| 15 | Indigenous Motherhood Resiliency: Adapting Cultural Teachings During COVID-19 Restrictions<br>Natahnee Nuay Winder | 261 |
| 16 | COVID-19 Memory Dreamscapes<br>Shaina A. Nez | 281 |
| 17 | Conclusion<br>Farina King and Wade Davies | 287 |
| Bibliography | | 295 |
| Index | | 319 |

# Notes on Contributors

**Christine Marie Ami** (Diné) holds a Ph.D. in Native American Studies from the University of California, Davis, USA. She is an associate professor at Diné College, where she teaches classes such as Indigenous research methods, traditional ecological knowledge, decolonization and Indigenous resilience, Diné cultural arts business systems, and human/non-human animal relationship building through Diné ways of knowing. She is the former Navajo Cultural Arts Program grant and program manager. She explores Indigenous experiences with epistemological imperialism in academia, culturally grounded curriculum building in higher education, and varying levels of internal colonization within tribal entities. Táchii'nii nilí, Bilagáana yáshchíín, T'ó'aheedl'íínii dabicheii, Bilagáana dabinálí.

**Amoneeta Beckstein** (Aniyunwiya and Jewish Israeli) is an assistant professor of psychology at Fort Lewis College. He is a co-author and editor of *The COVID-19 Pandemic: A Multidisciplinary Approach to Managing Health Challenges* (2021); "Mental wellbeing and boosting resilience to mitigate the adverse consequences of the COVID-19 pandemic: A critical narrative review," *SAGE* Open 12, no. 2 (2022); "The COVID-19 pandemic and mental health in Malaysia: Current treatment and future recommendations," *Malaysian Journal of Public Health Medicine* 20, no. 1 (2021); and "How Indigenous peoples of North America are coping with COVID-19," *Psychreg*, October 13, 2020.

**Kelly Berry** is an enrolled citizen of the Apache Tribe of Oklahoma with affiliations to the Kiowa and Choctaw Nations. He earned his doctoral degree in Educational Leadership at Kansas State University, where he was employed as the Indigenous Initiatives Research Associate in the College of Education. He is a Mellon Impact Postdoctoral Fellow in the Department of Native American Studies at the University of Oklahoma as well as a University Council for Educational Administration Barbara L. Jackson Scholar and a University of Arizona Native Nation's Institute Tribal Governance Fellow. He also served as adjunct faculty at Upper Iowa University.

**RaeLynn Butler** is a citizen of the MCN and is the Acting Secretary of Culture and Humanities at the MCN. She oversees the Tribe's efforts to promote, protect, and preserve Mvskoke and Euchee language, culture, history, arts, and cultural resources. She served as the manager of the Historic and Cultural Preservation Department for nine years and has extensive experience with repatriation and sacred lands protection. RaeLynn earned a Master of Science degree in Botany and Plant Pathology from Purdue University and a Bachelor of Science degree in Environmental Science from Haskell Indian Nations University.

**Wade Davies** is Professor of History at the University of Montana, USA, where he has taught courses in History and Native American Studies for over 20 years. He received his Ph.D. in History from Arizona State University in 1998. His books are *Native Hoops: The Rise of American Indian Basketball, 1895–1970* (University Press of Kansas, 2020); *Healing Ways: Navajo Health Care in the Twentieth Century* (University of New Mexico Press, 2001); *American Indian Sovereignty and Law: An Annotated Bibliography* (coedited with Richmond Clow; Scarecrow, 2009); and *"We Are Still Here": American Indians Since 1890, second edition* (coauthored with Peter Iverson; Wiley Blackwell, 2015). He has also written numerous articles and book chapters related to the history of Diné health care and Native American sporting traditions.

**Midge Dellinger** is of Muscogee, Mexican, and European descent. She is the Oral Historian for the Muscogee (Creek) Nation Historic and Cultural Preservation Department. Preserving and protecting Muscogee culture, tradition, and history is at the core of Midge's oral history work. As a tribal historic preservationist, her research focuses on historical truth-telling and its intersections between Indigenous and US histories. Areas of study are Indigenous boarding school history and the Civil War in Indian Territory. Midge is currently the Native American Representative on the Board of Directors for the Southwest Oral History Association.

**Tapati Dutta** (India) is Assistant Professor and Interim Chair of Public Health at Fort Lewis College (FLC), Colorado. With twenty-five years' experience in Asia, Africa, and the rural-United States, she's a social scientist and inclusion strategist in public health. A first-generation-non-traditional-age-group graduate, and growing up in a hetero-patriarchal background, Dutta champions DEIA-centric initiatives among indigenous, women, BIPOC, and LGBTQ+ communities, as evident from her widely viewed TEDx talk *Life Lessons via Cannibals, Sex Workers & Marginalized People*. Her translational research includes COVID-19 vaccination intentions and behaviors at FLC, and the meaning-making of the Multidimensional Scale of Perceived Social Support among Navajos.

**Erica Ficklin,** MS, is a member of the Tlingit and Oglala Lakota Tribes. She is currently a graduate student in the Combined Clinical & Counseling Psychology program at Utah State University. Erica is from Alabama and received her bachelor's degree from the University of South Alabama. Her work focuses on reducing health disparities among Native communities by emphasizing cultural strengths. She aims to have a career that focuses on raising the well-being of Native peoples and marginalized communities.

**Mary Jo Tippeconnic Fox** (Comanche/Cherokee) is Research Professor of American Indian Studies (AIS), and an affiliate faculty in Gender and Women's Studies (GWS) at the University of Arizona (UArizona), USA. She is the coeditor of the books *American Indian Studies: Native PhD Graduates Gift Their Stories* (2022); *On Indian Ground, the Southwest* (2021); and *Serving Native American Students in Higher Education* (2005). Her recent publications include "Scholar-Activists: Female Native Scholars in American Indian Studies," in Marianne Nielsen and Karen Jarratt Snider, eds., *Indigenous Women and Justice* (2023) and coauthored "Strengthening the Link Between Education Policy, Culturally Responsive Schooling and American Indian and Alaska Native Health," *Journal of Indigenous Early Childhood Education* 1 (2020).

**Jennifer Frazee** a Choctaw citizen, is the director of the Fort Gibson Historic Site and an Adjunct Professor of History at Connors State College, in Oklahoma, who provides support and healing for her community through education and the tending of family histories. She holds a Master's degree in American Studies from Northeastern State University in Tahlequah. In addition to academic paper presentations, she completed her thesis in 2014, titled "A Mansion at the Athens of Indian Territory: Hunter's Home, 1845–1991."

**Gavin A. Healey** is Assistant Professor of Anthropology and Applied Indigenous Studies at Northern Arizona University, USA. His expertise in community-based participatory research and mixed method design aspires to provide agency to individual and community voices with a focus on Native public art, graffiti, and muralism. Gavin's goal is to engage in interdisciplinary discourses using comparative Indigenous and western theoretical applications with contemporary Native art and Native public art as dialectics of place-making. He also works with Native artists and communities as an artist assistant on public murals and curator of museum and gallery exhibitions.

**Racheal Killgore** is a member of the Diné (Navajo) Nation. She is Kinyaa'áanii (The Towering House Clan) born for the White People Clan. Racheal is from Gallup, New Mexico. She is a graduate student in the combined clinical and counseling psychology program at Utah State University. Prior to attending graduate school, she spent several years working in the anti-violence field in her community advocating for victims/survivors of domestic violence and sexual assault. She is very passionate about this work and intends on continuing community work after graduate school.

**Farina King** a citizen of the Navajo Nation, is the Horizon Chair of Native American Ecology and Culture and Associate Professor of Native American Studies at the University of Oklahoma (OU), USA. Her research centers on Native American oral histories, especially among her Diné relatives and connections in Oklahoma. In 2023–2024, she served as the interim department chair of Native American Studies at OU. She received her Ph.D. in History from Arizona State University. She is the author of various publications, including *The Earth Memory Compass: Diné Landscapes and Education in the Twentieth Century* and *Gáamalii dóó Diné: Navajo Latter-Day Saint Experiences in the Twentieth Century*; coauthor with Michael P. Taylor and James R. Swensen of *Returning Home: Diné Creative Works from the Intermountain Indian School*; and coeditor of The Lyda Conley Series on Trailblazing Indigenous Futures with the University Press of Kansas. She is the former president of the Southwest Oral History Association (2021–2022).

**Chelsea M. Mead** is a Professor of American Indigenous Studies and History at Minnesota State University, Mankato. She grew up on the lands of the Potawatomi in Southwest Michigan and now lives and works in the

Dakota homelands of Southern Minnesota. Mead earned her PhD in History at Arizona State University and has been a learner of Anishinaabemowin for almost 20 years. As a historian with a passion for language, her scholarship combines ethnohistory with linguistic anthropology to examine the role Indigenous language initiatives can play in transforming spaces that have historically excluded Indigenous knowledge.

**Shaina A. Nez** is Táchii'nii born for Áshįįhi. She is Senior Lecturer in Creative Writing and English at Diné College. She is a Doctoral Candidate in Justice Studies at Arizona State University. She holds an MFA Degree in Creative Nonfiction from the Institute of American Indian Arts (IAIA), Santa Fe, New Mexico. Her work has appeared in 'A Gathering of Native Voices' (*The Massachusetts Review*), 'Nonwhite and Women: 131 Micro-Essays on Being in the World,' winner of the 2023 Silver IPPY Award of Adult Multicultural Nonfiction, and Issue 14: *Indigenous Ecopoetry* (Green Linden Press).

**Daniel Piper** PhD is a Professional Practice Assistant Professor in the Emma Eccles Jones College of Education & Human Services at Utah State University. He currently serves as the Faculty Advocate in the Mentoring and Encouraging Student Academic Success (MESAS) program for Native American students. His work focuses on Native American language education policy, Indigenous community engaged learning, and community-based language revitalization.

**Phil Lee Smith** MD, MPH is a retired Senior Clinician for the Utah Navajo Health System. He also recently retired as an associate faculty member at the Johns Hopkins Center for American Indian Health, where he worked closely with the center's training team on developing and implementing courses and mentoring students. He previously served as Chair of the Indian Health Service National Institutional Review Board and he remained a member for many years. He is a past director of the IHS Office of Health Programs and past IHS Chief Medical Officer. Smith received his medical degree from the University of Utah, School of Medicine.A Family and Community Medicine physician, he is a fellow of both the American Academy of Family Practice and The American College of Preventive Medicine and Board Certified in both specialties. He is a graduate of the Uniformed Services University School. Dr. Smith grew up on the Navajo reservation and after his medical and residency training, returned to the reservation to serve as a family and emergency medicine physician in various rural sites over several decades before being assigned to his work at the IHS.

**Heather Tanana** is a citizen of the Navajo Nation. She is a visiting professor at the University of California—Irvine School of Law and Associate Faculty with Johns Hopkins University's Center for Indigenous Health. Heather's research interests revolve around the intersection of environmental law, health policy, and tribal sovereignty. Much of her work focuses on tribal water issues, from climate change impacts to Colorado River management. She leads the initiative on Universal Access to Clean Water for Tribal Communities, which seeks to bring awareness to the lack of clean, safe, and reliable drinking water in Indian Country and to make tangible progress on securing water access for all Americans.

**Melissa Tehee** J.D., PhD, is a citizen of the Cherokee Nation and an associate professor of Psychology at Utah State University. She came to USU in 2015 to direct the American Indian Support Project, a program that has trained Native psychologists since 1986. Dr. Tehee is also the Assistant Director of the Mentoring and Encouraging Student Academic Success (MESAS) program for Native Students, a program funded by HHMI Inclusive Excellence. Dr. Tehee's work focuses on multicultural competence, holistic mentorship in higher education, and addressing trauma across the lifespan.

**Yvette A. Towersap** is enrolled in the Shoshone-Bannock Tribes of Fort Hall, Idaho, and is a doctoral student at Montana State University, where she is studying US history and tribal histories. She has a unique background in tribal government relations, consultation, and tribal history. Past historical research efforts have included tribal gender roles in the nineteenth century, the Bannock War and memory studies, nineteenth-century leadership roles, the reduction of the Fort Hall Indian Reservation to create urban communities, and most recently, tribal health histories.

**Aresta Tsosie-Paddock** (Diné) is an assistant professor in the Department of American Indian Studies and Linguistics at the University of Arizona, USA. Her authored or coauthored publications include "Language Landscapes and Native Resilience: Land-Connectivity, Language, and Identity Among Urban American Indians," in *Language and Identity in Contests of Migration and Diaspora* (2022); "An Arizona Legacy: Modern Day Relocation of Diné Peoples," in *The Smoke Signal* 110/111 (2022); "Didiishkall: Putting Forth Effort," in M.L. Blair et al. eds., *American*

*Indian Studies,* (2022); "Cultural Sovereignty and Native in the Age of Western Cultural Immersion" in J.W. Tippeconnic and M.J. Tippeconnic-Fox, eds., *On Indian Ground: The Southwest* (2021).

**Natahnee Nuay Winder** (Duckwater Shoshone Tribe of Nevada) is an assistant professor in the Department of Indigenous Studies at Simon Fraser University and in the School of Public Policy, British Columbia, Canada. She grew up on the Southern Ute reservation and spent the summers with her maternal grandparents. Her mother is Duckwater Shoshone and Pyramid Lake Paiute from Nevada, and her father is Navajo, Southern Ute, and Black from Colorado. She is the coauthor of "Colliding Heartwork: The Space Where Our Hearts Meet and Collide to Process the Boarding School Experience," and "Reflections," in S.J. Minton, ed., *Residential Schools and Indigenous Peoples,* (Routledge, 2020).

# Abbreviations

| | |
|---|---|
| BIA | Bureau of Indian Affairs (previously the OIA, U.S., est. 1824) |
| CARES Act | Coronavirus Aid, Relief, and Economic Security Act (2020) |
| CDC | Centers for Disease Control and Prevention (U.S., est. 1946) |
| EPA | Environmental Protection Agency (U.S., est. 1970) |
| H1N1 | Influenza A virus subtype |
| IAIA | Institute of American Indian Arts |
| IHCIA | Indian Health Care Improvement Act of 1976, reauthorized 2010 |
| IHS | Indian Health Service (U.S., est. 1955) |
| IIJA | Infrastructure Investment and Jobs Act (2021) |
| IRB | Institutional Review Board (institutional, tribal, or university oversight of human subjects research) |
| MCN | Muscogee (Creek) Nation |
| MESAS | Mentoring and Encouraging Student Academic Success program for Native students at Utah State University |
| MMIW | Missing and Murdered Indigenous Women |
| NAS/NAIS | Native American Studies/Native American and Indigenous Studies |
| NPS | National Park Service (U.S., est. 1916) |
| OIA | Office of Indian Affairs (later known as the BIA, U.S., est. 1824) |
| PHS | Public Health Service (U.S., est. 1798) |
| PWAP | Public Works of Art Project (est. 1933) |
| PWI | Predominantly White Institutions (colleges and universities) |
| RIS | Riverside Indian School |

SANSR  Superintendents Annual Narrative and Statistical Reports from Field Jurisdictions of the Bureau of Indian Affairs, MI0II microfilm, Washington, DC: National Archives and Records Service, 1975
SDS    IHS Sanitation Deficiency System
SFC    Sanitation Facilities Construction Program (est. 1959)
UNHS   Utah Navajo Health System
WHO    World Health Organization (est. 1948)

# List of Figures

| | | |
|---|---|---|
| Fig. 2.1 | Navajo Nation Homes without piped water access May 2020. Source: Navajo Safe Water: Protecting You and Your Family's Health, www.navajosafewater.org | 24 |
| Fig. 2.2 | Water hauling on Navajo Nation. Credit: Tara Kerzhner | 38 |
| Fig. 2.3 | Identified SFC program need vs. appropriated funding, 2010–2021. Credit: Heather Tanana | 39 |
| Fig. 3.1 | Summary of epidemics, 1906–1920. Credit: Annual Report, Dr. Wheeler, Section Two, Health section, 21 (M1011-049-0550), *SANSR* | 51 |
| Fig. 3.2 | Monthly data on influenza cases in Fort Hall. Credit: Yvette Towersap | 57 |
| Fig. 5.1 | Farina King with her two sons and Aunt Florence in 2019. Credit: Farina King | 78 |
| Fig. 6.1 | Dr. Phillip Lee Smith. Credit: Farina King | 90 |
| Fig. 7.1 | "Kvlonv Ennokvn (Coronavirus)." Credit: Johnnie Diacon, 2020 | 96 |
| Fig. 7.2 | "Going for Groceries During the Time of the Pandemic." Credit: Johnnie Diacon, 2020 | 100 |
| Fig. 7.3 | "Tribute to the Healthcare Warriors in Indian Country During COVID-19." Credit: Johnnie Diacon, 2020 | 112 |
| Fig. 12.1 | Jaque Fragua (Jemez), "Idle No More." Mural (2014). Undisclosed location. Image courtesy of Jaque Fragua | 201 |
| Fig. 12.2 | Jaque Fragua (Jemez), "People System." Mural (2020). Albuquerque, New Mexico. Image courtesy of Jaque Fragua | 203 |
| Fig. 12.3 | Jaque Fragua (Jemez), "This Is Indian Land." Mural (2016). Los Angeles, California. Image courtesy of Jaque Fragua | 204 |

Fig. 12.4  Ivan Lee (Diné/Navajo), We Will Survive. Mural (2020). Fruitvale, New Mexico. Image courtesy of Kayla Jackson  216

Fig. 13.1  Brent Toadlena, "Traditional Diné Moccasins." White Latigo, Rust Suede, Sterling Silver and Liberty Half Dollar Buttons. *T'áá awołí bee* Exhibit, Diné College, Tsaile, Arizona. credit: Photography by Matthew Bollinger, 2021  222

Fig. 13.2  Sue V. Begay, "Beauty." Wedge Weave, Natural Wool, Natural Dyes. *T'áá awołí bee* Exhibit, Diné College, Tsaile, Arizona. credit: Photography by Matthew Bollinger, 2021  224

Fig. 13.3  Carlon P. Ami II, "Ripples." Sterling Silver, Handmade Graduated Beads, Tufa Cast Pendant, Lapis Lazuli Buttons. *T'áá awołí bee* Exhibit, Diné College, Tsaile, Arizona. credit: Photography by Matthew Bollinger, 2021  224

Fig. 13.4  Tammera Martin, "My Worlds." Commercial Dyed Brown & Brown Wool, Natural Wool, Mixed plant Dyed. *T'áá awołí bee* Exhibit, Diné College, Tsaile, Arizona. credit: Photography by Matthew Bollinger, 2021  225

Fig. 13.5  Bryan J Roessel, "Lightning." Sterling Silver, Tufa Cast. *T'áá awołí bee* Exhibit, Diné College, Tsaile, Arizona. credit: Photography by Matthew Bollinger, 2021  226

Fig. 13.6  Ryan Dodson, "Tobacco Canteen." Sterling Silver, Hand Stamped, Handmade Chain-link, 1860s inspired. *T'áá awołí bee* Exhibit, Diné College, Tsaile, Arizona. credit: Photography by Matthew Bollinger, 2021  227

Fig. 13.7  Christine Ami, "Running with Mud." Hand Processed Clay, Kiln Fired Pot. *T'áá awołí bee* Exhibit, Diné College, Tsaile, Arizona. credit: Photography by Matthew Bollinger, 2021  229

Fig. 13.8  Tavian Nutlouis, "Ch'ééh Digháhii." Shadow Box Bolo, Sterling Silver, Handmade Bolo Tips. *T'áá awołí bee* Exhibit, Diné College, Tsaile, Arizona. credit: Photography by Matthew Bollinger, 2021  232

Fig. 13.9  Brittany Greymountain, "For My Children: Our Robot." Commercial Dyed Brown & Brown Wool, Handspun Wool Warp. *T'áá awołí bee* Exhibit, Diné College, Tsaile, Arizona. credit: Photography by Matthew Bollinger, 2021  232

Fig. 15.1  Traditional kinship system. Credit: Natahnee Nuay Winder  268

Fig. 15.2  Connecting with our medicines  273

Fig. 15.3  *Önöönik(i)*  276

CHAPTER 1

# Introduction

## Farina King and Wade Davies

In March 2020, as COVID-19 ravaged Indigenous communities in one of the first major hotspots of the pandemic, the Seattle Indian Health Board and Abigail Echo-Hawk, a Pawnee Nation citizen and public health researcher, pleaded for support and supplies. The State of Washington and federal contacts responded by sending body bags.[1] Echo-Hawk's photos of the body bags and Indigenous communities' outrage and dismay went viral along with the ongoing disease, while Echo-Hawk asserted: "I'll never accept their body bags for our [Indigenous] people … all I will

---

[1] Nicole Pasia, "When they gave her body bags instead of PPE, she used them to make a healing ribbon dress," *Seattle Times*, April 1, 2021, accessed online, https://www.seattletimes.com/life/when-they-gave-her-body-bags-instead-of-ppe-she-used-them-to-make-a-healing-ribbon-dress/.

F. King (✉)
The University of Oklahoma, Norman, OK, USA
e-mail: farinaking@ou.edu

W. Davies
The University of Montana, Missoula, MT, USA
e-mail: wade.davies@mso.umt.edu

© The Author(s), under exclusive license to Springer Nature Switzerland AG 2024
F. King, W. Davies (eds.), *COVID-19 in Indian Country*, https://doi.org/10.1007/978-3-031-70184-9_1

accept is a world where we are thriving, ever continuing."[2] The delivery of body bags revealed a common but perverse assumption in American society that Native Americans were destined to die.[3] Cherokee scholar Thomas King delineated this notion by defining the "Dead Indian" as one of the stereotypes that have shaped American mentalities and mistreatment of Indigenous peoples. The "Dead Indian" stems from the myths, often accepted as factual narratives, that "Live Indians living today cannot be genuine Indians," relegating the only "Live Indians" to the past.[4] Thus, in 2020, state and federal government officials' assumption that the Seattle Indian Health Board needed body bags for "Dead Indians" perpetuated a twisted sense that Native Americans were inevitably set to die out.

Two and a half years later, during a *60 Minutes* interview on September 18, 2022, President Joseph Biden surprised even his health advisors by declaring off-the-cuff that the COVID-19 pandemic, which had cost the lives of more than a million Americans, was finally "over." Despite drawing criticisms for the offhand nature of his statement, and the fact that less virulent variants of the disease were still circulating widely, the sentiment Biden expressed reaffirmed the prevailing public opinion in the United States that the pandemic crisis had largely passed.

By the fall of 2022, painful memories of the crisis were fading for most Americans, apart from the more unfortunate who had lost loved ones or livelihoods, or still suffered the lingering effects of what had come to be known as "long COVID." Many Native people, at that time, shared a sense of closure and relief with their fellow citizens and a determination to move on with their lives, but for Indian Country[5] on the whole, the COVID-19 crisis could not easily be set to the past. Native Americans had suffered so disproportionately from the pandemic—physically, mentally, socially, and economically—that few had escaped the crisis without experiencing pronounced trauma. They were troubled that deadlier variants of the disease might still emerge and that too little had been done during this

---

[2] Abigail Echo-Hawk cited in Cecilia Nowell, "They Asked for PPE and Got Body Bags Instead—She Turned Them Into a Healing Dress," *Vogue*, February 4, 2021, accessed online, https://www.vogue.com/article/body-bag-native-ribbon-dress.

[3] Lindsay Montgomery, "A Rejoinder to Body Bags: Indigenous Resilience and Epidemic Disease, From COVID-19 to First 'Contact,'" *American Indian Culture and Research Journal* 44, issue 3 (2020): 65.

[4] Thomas King, *The Inconvenient Indian: A Curious Account of Native People in North America* (Toronto: Doubleday Canada, 2012), 64.

[5] "Indian Country" refers to Native Nations and communities in North America.

pandemic to prevent them from again suffering disproportionately in future epidemics. They were particularly distressed about the insufficient actions of federal government agencies charged with promoting Indigenous communities' physical and economic health; including past and present failures to adequately address needs for clean water and thriving ecologies.

Despite the media's increased focus on Indian Country during the COVID-19 pandemic, history showed that public sympathy would quickly dissipate rather than sustain full-scale action.[6] The bureaucratic dismissiveness of the "body bag" incident and fleeting nature of media coverage left Indigenous Americans unsettled and uncertain about the future. Although the threat of this virus has further diminished by 2024, the medical comorbidities, health care deficiencies, and socioeconomic inequities that exacerbated COVID-19's impact persist throughout Indian Country. While many Americans have returned to good health and financial prosperity since the worst days of the pandemic, such a reality is still out of reach for many Native people.

## Hardest Hit

The Centers for Disease Control and Prevention (CDC) has carefully outlined the history of COVID-19 since its outbreak. The agency declared the end of the pandemic on May 11, 2023, but continues to monitor COVID-19 statistics to this day. Scientists confirmed the first U.S. case of COVID-19 on January 20, 2020, in the state of Washington. Ten days later, the CDC confirmed the first U.S. case of transmitting the virus between two people, neither of whom had traveled abroad. On March 11, the World Health Organization officially declared COVID-19 a pandemic after 118,000 cases occurred in 114 countries around the world, resulting in 4291 deaths to that point. By April 10, the U.S. overtook Spain as the leading nation with confirmed COVID-19 cases, with 500,000 people infected and 18,600 confirmed deaths.[7]

---

[6] The Hantavirus Four Corners Outbreak hit the Navajo Nation in 1993, for example, but the nation and Diné were not equipped to face the COVID-19 outbreak over 25 years later. For more about this hantavirus outbreak, see Charles J. Van Hook, "Hantavirus Pulmonary Syndrome—The 25th Anniversary of the Four Corners Outbreak," *Emerging Infectious Diseases* 24, issue 11 (November 2018): 2056–60.

[7] "CDC Museum Covid-19 Timeline," Centers for Disease Control and Prevention: David J. Sencer CDC Museum, last reviewed, March 15, 2023, https://www.cdc.gov/museum/timeline/covid19.html#:~:text=March%2011%2C%202020,declares%20COVID%2D19%20a%20pandemic.

The novel coronavirus SARS-CoV-2, or COVID-19, caused this pandemic, but partisan politics fueled human actions and inactions, hastening its spread. During the early stages of the crisis in 2020, President Donald J. Trump downplayed the disease's impact and discouraged people from following public health guidelines or taking protective measures. Trump even endorsed unproven and harmful treatments for COVID-19, such as taking the drug hydroxychloroquine, and he hosted "superspreader" indoor political rallies with thousands of people before vaccines were widely available, despite advisories warning against large gatherings.[8] In their book, *Pandemic Politics*, Shana Kushner Gadarian, Sara Wallace Goodman, and Thomas B. Pepinsky emphasize that "the partisan politics of American health care exacerbates racial disparities in health access and health outcomes." Such disparities reached epic proportions during the COVID-19 pandemic as partisanship drove human responses.[9] All Americans suffered the dire consequences of executive inactions, falsehoods, and political division, but these outcomes were magnified in some non-white communities and terribly so in Indian Country.

Although COVID-19 spread and affected every human being and ecology around the world, the virus hit many Indigenous peoples of the United States in ways that echoed the ravages of past plagues. As the global health crisis unfolded, many news articles reported the disproportionate number of cases in Native America. The virus then exploded in the Navajo Nation as the pandemic's first wave peaked in the spring of 2020.[10]

---

[8] Kacper Niburski and Oskar Niburski, "Impact of Trump's Promotion of Unproven COVID-19 Treatments and Subsequent Internet Trends: Observational Study," *Journal of Medical Internet Research* vol. 22, 11 (November 2020), accessed online April 20, 2024, https://www.ncbi.nlm.nih.gov/pmc/articles/PMC7685699/; and Shana Kushner Gabarian, Sara Wallace Goodman, and Thomas B. Pepinsky, *Pandemic Politics: The Deadly Toll of Partisanship in the Age of COVID* (Princeton, NJ: Princeton University Press, 2022), 1–2.

[9] Gadarian, Goodman, and Pepinsky, *Pandemic Politics*, 40.

[10] Wilfred F. Denetclaw, Zara K. Otto, Samantha Christie, Estrella Allen, Maria Cruz, Kassandra A. Potter, and Kala M. Mehta, "Diné Navajo Resilience to the COVID-19 Pandemic," *PLOS ONE* 17, 8 (August 2022), accessed online May 14, 2024, https://doi.org/10.1371/journal.pone.0272089. See also Donovan Quintero, "The COVID-19 Outbreak in the Navajo Nation," *American Indian: Magazine of Smithsonian's National Museum of the American Indian* 22, no. 2 (Summer 2021), accessed online January 11, 2024, https://www.americanindianmagazine.org/story/the-covid-19-outbreak-in-the-navajo-nation#:~:text=Addressing%20the%20Navajo%20Nation&text=(As%20of%20mid%2DJune%202021,the%20Navajo%20Nation%20have%20died.).

On May 18, reports stated that the Navajo Nation's cumulative COVID-19 case rate of 2344 per 100,000 residents exceeded that of any other region or state in the country.[11] A week later, on May 26, Navajo Nation officials implemented lockdowns, curfews, stay-at-home orders, masking, and checkpoints to mitigate the further spread of the virus. Reports of COVID-19 cases were also flooding in from throughout the U.S. at this point, including from other Native American communities.[12] Between May and June 2020, about 40% of the approximately 11,000 citizens of the Mississippi Band of Choctaw Indians (MBCI) also tested positive for COVID-19, prompting MBCI Chief Cyrus Ben to stress "that's worse than what we saw in New York City or elsewhere in the U.S."[13]

While many Native Americans relied exclusively on the U.S. Indian Health Service (IHS), which minimized costs for patients, great distances between homes and hospitals in tandem with high gas prices deterred people from taking advantage of it, especially at the height of the pandemic as the underfunded health system witnessed longer wait times and strained resources.[14] Unlike most Americans and the mainstream media who look back on this pandemic as a once-in-a-century-aberration, many Native people understand the calamity that befell them as an acute intensification of an ongoing health crisis they had confronted for centuries, brought about by the enduring legacies of colonization.

Among those described in this anthology, many Native Americans are not surprised by the devastation the virus has wrought on Indigenous populations, as the COVID-19 pandemic fell into a larger pattern of violence against Native Nations. During, and in some ways since the European and Euro-American conquest of Native America, Indigenous peoples have

---

[11] Ely F. Miller, Jacob Neumann, Ye Chen, Abhishek Mallela, Yen Ting Lin, William S. Hlavacek, and Richard G. Posner, "Quantification of early nonpharmaceutical interventions aimed at slowing transmission of Coronavirus Disease 2019 in the Navajo Nation and surrounding states (Arizona, Colorado, New Mexico, and Utah)," *PLOS Global Public Health* 3, 6 (June 21, 2023), accessed online, https://doi.org/10.1371/journal.pgph.0001490.

[12] Mark Walker, "Pandemic Highlights Deep-Rooted Problems in Indian Health Service," *New York Times*, September 29, 2020, accessed online, https://www.nytimes.com/2020/09/29/us/politics/coronavirus-indian-health-service.html.

[13] Cyrus Ben cited in Martha Hostetter and Sarah Klein, "Learning from Pandemic Responses Across Indian Country," September 30, 2020, *Advancing Health Equity*, The Commonwealth Fund, accessed online January 31, 2024, https://www.commonwealthfund.org/publications/2020/sep/learning-pandemic-responses-across-indian-country.

[14] Walker, "Pandemic Highlights," *New York Times*, September 29, 2020.

faced various forms of genocide induced by warfare, rape, forced sterilization, removal, incarceration, dispossession, contamination, and diseases such as smallpox. Several studies have tracked how COVID-19's onslaught on Native Americans correlated with their socioeconomic and health disparities, underscoring how its elevated "death rates among Native Americans serve as a stark reminder of the legacies of historical mistreatment and the continued failure of governments to meet basic needs of this population."[15] Should it be a surprise that Native Americans have been infected and died at higher rates than the general public from the COVID-19 virus? Many may argue it would be a surprise had they not, based on these circumstances.

Statistics portraying the pandemic's disproportionate toll on Indigenous American communities in rates of infection, hospitalization, and death were especially stark in contrast to those for white Americans, with Native people being three times more likely to be hospitalized and twice as likely to die. Inadequate data collection and failures to report by race in many states likely obscured even harsher statistical realities across Indian Country. All told, between the initial outbreak in the spring of 2020 and the end of 2022, nearly 12,000 Native Americans and Alaska Natives are estimated to have died from COVID-related causes.[16]

COVID-19 could have been less deadly across Indian Country if the federal government had provided the best possible medical care to Indigenous communities based on a long-term commitment. As Heather Tanana, a Navajo Nation citizen and legal scholar, details in the opening chapter to this volume, through treaties and statutes during the nineteenth and twentieth centuries, the United States acknowledged its responsibility to provide health care to the citizens of all federally recognized Native Nations in exchange for cessions of vast Indigenous territories.[17] Specific government agencies were then tasked with addressing

---

[15] Katherine Leggat-Barr, Fumiya Uchikoshi, and Noreen Goldman, "COVID-19 risk factors and mortality among Native Americans," *Demographic Research* 45, 39 (November 17, 2021): 1208, accessed online, https://www.demographic-research.org/volumes/vol45/39/45-39.pdf.

[16] The hospitalization rate is an approximate average based on multiple sources. KFF, "COVID-19 Cases, Deaths, and Vaccinations by Race/Ethnicity as of Winter 2022," https://www.kff.org/coronavirus-covid-19/issue-brief/covid-19-cases-deaths-and-vaccinations-by-race-ethnicity-as-of-winter-2022/; Farida B. Ahmad, Jodi A. Ciseski, Jiaquan Xu, and Robert N. Anderson, "COVID-19 Mortality Update—United States, 2022," *CDC Morbidity and Mortality Weekly Report*, https://www.cdc.gov/mmwr/volumes/72/wr/pdfs/mm7218a4-H.pdf; Laura Finley, "State Crime, Native Americans and Covid-19," *State Crime Journal* 10, no. 1, (2021): 53.

[17] Native Nations have historically been known as tribes in the United States.

chronic health disparities among Indigenous peoples, which historically included high infant mortality and infectious disease rates.[18] This responsibility has been held by the IHS since 1955 and is also allocated through federal contracts to nongovernmental and tribally operated health care providers.

Theoretically, the IHS should have been well positioned to respond to the COVID-19 crisis because of the agency's comprehensive health care model, encompassing environmental and other preventive services in concert with hospital care. Without question, the IHS has contributed to improving Indigenous health statistics over time, particularly as measured by dramatically decreased infant mortality rates from 62.5 per every 1000 births in 1955 (2.4 times the national rate) to 7.5 in 2021 (1.4 times the national rate). Such improvements reflect positively on the IHS, but not exclusively so, as they have also resulted from general advances in medical science; determined efforts by Native peoples and tribal governments to pursue the benefits of Western medicine and Indigenous healing ways in combination; and increased involvement of tribal agencies as direct providers of medical care.[19]

However, the IHS's ability to meet its obligations to Native peoples has historically been stunted by persistent funding shortfalls, which ranged annually into the billions of dollars in the years leading up to the COVID-19 pandemic. These deficits have long translated into chronic staffing, equipment, and facility deficiencies that can be experienced particularly acutely during disease outbreaks. Congress delivered partial relief through the 2020 Coronavirus Aid, Relief, and Economic Services (CARES) Act, which provided just over one billion dollars in additional IHS funding, but this came too late to compensate for the long-existing deficiencies that had exacerbated the pandemic crisis in Indian Country.[20]

---

[18] Wade Davies, *Healing Ways: Navajo Health Care in the Twentieth Century* (Albuquerque: University of New Mexico Press, 2001), 86–88, 136, 154–56.

[19] Davies, *Healing Ways*, 86; Danielle M. Ely and Anne K. Driscoll, "Infant Mortality in the United States: Provisional Data from the 2022 Period Linked Birth/Infant Death Rate," *NVSS Vital Statistics Rapid Release*, no. 33 (November 2023), https://www.cdc.gov/nchs.data/vsrr.vsrr033.pdf.

[20] Libby Smith, "Impact of the Coronavirus and Federal Responses on Indigenous Peoples' Health, Security, and Sovereignty," *American Indian Law Review* 45, no. 2 (2021): 312; Aila Hoss and Heather Tanana, "Upholding Tribal Sovereignty and Promoting Tribal Public Health Capacity during the COVID-19 Pandemic," in S. Burris, et al., eds., *Assessing Legal Responses to COVID-19* (Boston: Public Health Law Watch, University of Utah College of Law Research Paper No. 391, 2020), accessed online January 8, 2024, https://ssrn.com/abstract=3675940.

At the time that COVID-19 struck, Indigenous people were also less likely than other Americans to hold private health insurance, which limited their options in seeking care from non-government medical providers. Those who were ineligible for IHS care because they lacked citizenship in a federally recognized Native Nation were thus placed at increased risk of poor health outcomes during the pandemic, as were many of the 70% of Native Americans who resided in cities and typically had less access to the full complement of IHS services.[21] Future studies will reveal more about the health care system's overall effectiveness (both in terms of the IHS and contract providers) during the pandemic, as well as the system's failings. Regardless of those findings, the many thousands of Indigenous people who lost loved ones and other valued community members will still remember the IHS's inability to provide enough hospital beds and ventilators to meet the crisis, as well as other impediments to their receiving the quality care long promised them.[22]

The poor pandemic outcomes in Indigenous communities reflected more than shortcomings in the health care system. Legacies of colonialism also left most of Indian Country highly vulnerable to the ravages of epidemic disease in multifarious ways. Many of these problems stemmed from low socioeconomic status, with Native Americans at the time the pandemic struck experiencing poverty at twice the average national rate. Financial hardship manifested in numerous ways detrimental to the peoples' health. Indigenous households in 2020 were typically more crowded than non-Native households and whether through necessity or family preference were more often multi-generational.

Low socioeconomic status also compelled many Indigenous people to rely on shared transportation to travel to school, work, or to procure necessities, often over great distances. These factors facilitated the communal spread of the virus and placed extremely vulnerable Elders at higher risk. Native households were also far more likely than other American households to lack electricity, internet or telephone service, and indoor

---

[21] Latoya Hill and Samantha Artiga, "Health Coverage among American Indian and Alaska Native and Native Hawaiian and other Pacific Islander Peoples," *KFF*, November 30, 2023, accessed online January 8, 2024, https://www.kff.org/racial-equity-and-health-policy/issue-brief/health-coverage-among-american-indian-and-alaska-native-and-native-hawaiian-and-other-pacific-islander-people/.

[22] Marc A. Emerson, and Teresa Montoya, "Confronting Legacies of Structural Racism and Settler Colonialism to Understand COVID-19 Impacts on the Navajo Nation," *American Journal of Public Health* 111, no. 8 (August 2021): 1465–69; Smith, "Impact of the Coronavirus," 308–09.

plumbing. These privations made it difficult or impossible for people to access telehealth, receive public health updates, schedule medical appointments, effectively work or attend school online, or rely on handwashing to reduce the spread of infection.[23] These factors also negatively affected peoples' incomes or school performance and intensified feelings of isolation, which in turn contributed to mental health problems and already high suicide rates.[24]

None of these challenges were new to Indian Country in 2020, which also meant Indigenous Americans were more likely to suffer from an array of pre-existing health conditions that increased their risk of experiencing poor outcomes during the pandemic. Compared to the overall population, Indigenous Americans in recent decades have been more than eight times as likely to suffer from tuberculosis, nearly twice as likely to die from influenza and pneumonia, and more than three times as likely to die from diabetes, all of which contributed to life expectancies five and a half years lower than the national average.[25] The high prevalence of diabetes, in particular, has been linked to poor nutrition consequent of low household incomes, the historic disruption of Indigenous food ways, and the higher likelihood of Native peoples to live in "food deserts" where sustenance has been severely limited. This problem was particularly acute in the Navajo Nation during the pandemic, with only thirteen grocery stores serving a 27,000-square-mile area nearly the size of Ireland.[26]

Although Indigenous Americans felt as blind-sided by COVID-19 as did other Americans, the crisis was much less of a historical anomaly in Indian Country than elsewhere in the United States. Any new epidemic conjured up trauma in Native communities because of many Indigenous people's tragic familiarity with the scourge of disease. The 500-plus-year

---

[23] Adam Crepelle, "Tribes, Vaccines, and COVID-19: A Look at Tribal Responses to the Pandemic," *Fordham Urban Law Journal* 49, no. 1 (2021): 31–64; Gloria Oladipo, "Native American communities lashed by Covid, worsening chronic inequities," *The Guardian*, May 13, 2021, accessed online February 17, 2022, https://www.theguardian.com/us-news/2021/dec/13/pandemic-challenges-native-american-communities.

[24] Oladipo, "Native American communities lashed by Covid."

[25] CDC, "Health Disparities in HIV, Viral Hepatitis, STDs, and TB," accessed online January 8, 2024, https://www.cdc.gov/nchhstp/healthdisparities/americanindians.html; Indian Health Service, "Mortality Disparity Rates, 2009–2011," https://www.ihs.gov/newsroom/factsheets/disparities/; Crepelle, "Tribes, Vaccines, and COVID-19," 36.

[26] Talha Burki, "COVID-19 among American Indians and Alaska Natives," *The Lancet Infectious Diseases* 21, no. 3 (2021): 325–26; Emerson and Montoya, "Confronting Legacies of Structural Racism," 1465–69.

history of Native relations with non-Natives has always featured disease prominently, beginning with the so-called virgin soil epidemics that may have wiped out the majority of North and South America's Indigenous inhabitants during the early decades of European colonization. Historians no longer share consensus about why foreign pathogens like smallpox and measles wreaked havoc on Indigenous populations in the years after Columbus, nor the precise timelines of these epidemic events. Whereas previous scholars argued that these catastrophes occurred rapidly and resulted primarily from Native peoples' lack of immunity to newly introduced pathogens, more recent studies have argued that high death rates resulted as much, or more so, from the ways colonization magnified the effects of disease over time. Through displacement, genocidal violence, enslavement, and the destruction of natural resources and traditional livelihoods, Europeans after 1492 rendered Native populations far more vulnerable to invasive pathogens.[27]

Whether or how often Europeans and Euro-Americans purposely spread epidemics among Indigenous people remains a subject of scholarly debate. Historians and anthropologists generally do not attribute the preponderance of these calamities to intentional acts, but some argue that numerous localized instances or broader patterns of biological warfare once occurred. Many Indigenous oral traditions also speak of such acts taking place from the early colonial period into the mid-1800s, involving perpetrators of multiple European nationalities, as well as Euro-Americans. Numerous scholars concur that an act of biological warfare did indeed occur in 1763 during what became known as Pontiac's War. This involved a group of British officers and traders scheming to lift the siege of Fort Pitt, located in what is currently Pittsburgh, Pennsylvania, by exposing Native Americans to contaminated blankets from the post hospital to induce a smallpox epidemic among them.[28]

---

[27] Catherine M. Cameron, Paul Kelton, and Alan C. Swedlund, eds., *Beyond Germs: Native Depopulation in North America* (Tucson: University of Arizona Press, 2015).

[28] Barbara Alice Mann, *The Tainted Gift: The Disease Method of Frontier Expansion* (Santa Barbara, CA: ABC Clio, 2009); Elizabeth A. Fenn, "Biological Warfare in Eighteenth-Century North America: Beyond Jeffrey Amherst," *The Journal of American History* 86 (March 2000): 1552–80; Adrienne Mayor, "The Nessus Shirt in the New World: Smallpox Blankets in History and Legend," *The Journal of American Folklore* 108, no. 427 (Winter 1995): 54–77; Gregory Evans Dowd, *Groundless: Rumors, Legends, and Hoaxes on the Early American Frontier* (Baltimore: Johns Hopkins, 2015), 38–62 and 228–47; Philip Ranlet, "The British, the Indians, and Smallpox: What Actually Happened at Fort Pitt in 1763?" *Pennsylvania History: A Journal of Mid-Atlantic Studies* 67, no. 3 (Summer 2000): 427-41.

Throughout the nineteenth and early twentieth centuries, Native Americans also suffered severely as U.S. federal policies of removal and concentration increased their exposure and susceptibility to waves of smallpox, cholera, measles, and influenza that swept across North America. Although these policies were conceived primarily to dispossess Indigenous peoples of their lands, their ill effects on community health were well known to federal authorities. On reservations, people's lost access to nutritious foods, dependence on inadequate government rations, and the forced disruptions of their kinship networks and cultural practices all proved highly detrimental to their physical and mental well-being, thus increasing their vulnerability to infectious diseases. Federal policies that confined Native youth to boarding schools in the late-nineteenth and early-twentieth centuries also exacted a heavy toll, as influenza, tuberculosis, and trachoma ran rampant among students who were crowded together, malnourished, and often traumatized.[29] Prior to the mid-twentieth century establishment of the IHS, the U.S. Office of Indian Affairs did attempt to address high infectious disease rates in Native communities through employing physicians and some particularly dedicated field nurses. These services made some limited headway in combatting infectious diseases, but the federal government failed to appropriate the resources necessary to fully counteract the health disparities its own policies had caused.[30]

The chronic health crisis spanning Indian Country proved disastrous when the Great Influenza pandemic swept the globe from 1918 to 1920, killing more than 50 million people worldwide and foreshadowing some patterns that would later repeat with COVID-19. Native Americans had also been more likely than non-Natives to perish during this influenza pandemic, although to a much greater degree than with COVID-19,

[29] See Preston S. McBride, *A Lethal Education: Institutionalized Negligence, Epidemiology, and Death in Native American Boarding Schools, 1879–1934* (PhD dissertation, University of California, Los Angeles, 2020).

[30] Robert A. Trennert, *White Man's Medicine: Government Doctors and the Navajo, 1863–1955* (Albuquerque: University of New Mexico Press, 1988), ix–x; Brianna Theobald, *Reproduction on the Reservation: Pregnancy, Childbirth, and Colonialism in the Long Twentieth Century* (Chapel Hill: The University of North Carolina Press, 2019), 6 and 42; David Wallace Adams, *Education for Extinction: American Indians and the Boarding School Experience, 1875–1928* (Lawrence: University Press of Kansas, 1995), 124–25 and 131–33. Regarding some early health care successes see Trennert, *White Man's Medicine*; and Clifford E. Trafzer, *Strong Hearts and Healing Hands: Southern California Indians and Field Nurses, 1920–1950* (Tucson: The University of Arizona Press, 2021).

equaling four times the national average. Diné communities in the Navajo Nation (then known as the Navajo Reservation) were among the hardest hit, as would also be the case a century later. In successive waves of influenza beginning in the fall of 1918, large numbers of Diné fell ill and close to 3400 perished out of a total population of about 28,000, sparking mass panic and overwhelming meager Office of Indian Affairs medical services. High mortality rates throughout Indian Country stemmed from some of the same causal factors that would later be behind many COVID-19 deaths, including poor housing conditions, pre-existing health problems, and inadequate medical care. Different characteristics of the involved pathogens, on the other hand, meant that children and young adults proved more vulnerable to the 1918 influenza than they would be to COVID-19, which primarily targeted the older generation.[31] In this book's third chapter, Yvette Towersap, a public intellectual and citizen of the Shoshone-Bannock Tribes from the Fort Hall Indian Reservation, highlights how Shoshone-Bannock memories and experiences of the early-twentieth-century influenza have affected their responses to COVID-19.

## To "Be a Good Relative"

Despite the parallels between the COVID-19 and 1918 Influenza pandemics, certain differences explain why the more recent death rates in Indian Country, though terrible, were lower in comparison. Much of this variance can be explained by the different nature of the two viruses, historic improvements in the health care system, and other societal developments over the intervening century, but the development of effective COVID-19 vaccines played a vital role, as did the high rates at which Native Americans sought those vaccines.

By mid-summer of 2021, Native Americans and Alaska Natives exceeded the vaccination rate for all other racial and ethnic groups, with approximately 39% being fully vaccinated. Despite often distrusting or viewing skeptically health care initiatives promoted by federal agencies,

---

[31] Benjamin R. Brady and Howard M. Bahr, "The Influenza Epidemic of 1918–1920 among the Navajos: Marginality, Morality, and the Implications of Some Neglected Eyewitness Accounts," *The American Indian Quarterly* 38, no. 4 (Fall 2014): 459–91; Trennert, *White Man's Medicine*, 122-2; Dana Hedgpeth, "Native American tribes were already being wiped out. Then the 1918 flu hit," *The Washington Post*, January 27, 2020, accessed online January 8, 2024, https://www.washingtonpost.com/history/2020/09/28/1918-flu-native-americans-coronavirus/.

Indigenous Americans spoke of their obligations not only to protect themselves, but to protect their kin and community by taking any measures necessary to slow the spread of infection. Many Native Americans have also chosen to get vaccinated, even if they are personally concerned about potential side effects, because they feel a strong obligation to protect highly vulnerable Elders and the important cultural knowledge they carry. Speaking to a journalist in early July of 2021, Kerry Hawk Lessard, a descendant of Assiniboine and Shawnee people and the executive director of an eastern Urban Indian Health program, explained that the "language you hear throughout Indian Country is 'be a good relative.'" Indigenous people "do this for the grandmas, do this for the ceremony, do this for the language, because our people are precious ... We already lost a lot. We can't afford to lose more."[32]

Many tribal governments also exhibited this dedication to collective well-being in responding to the pandemic, taking swift actions to ensure that vaccinations were distributed quickly, widely, and strategically. Many exercised their right to obtain vaccines through the IHS rather than states as a more efficient and flexible option. They also determined which groups would receive vaccines first, often prioritizing Elders, knowledge keepers, and language speakers. Tribal health care agencies used social media and messaging from Elders to overcome vaccine hesitancy, appealing to ethics of community responsibility and cultural preservation. The San Carlos Apache Tribe, for one, conducted its outreach in both English and their own language, and endeavored to make the vaccine rollout widely accessible by closely collaborating with the IHS and staging drive-through vaccinations and pop-up clinics.[33]

---

[32] Sukee Bennett, "American Indians have the highest Covid vaccination rate in the US," *Nova*, July 6, 2021, accessed online January 8, 2024, https://www.pbs.org/wgbh/nova/article/native-americans-highest-covid-vaccination-rate-us/; Amanda D. Boyd and Dedra Buchwald, "Factors That Influence Risk Perceptions and Successful COVID-19 Vaccination Communication Campaigns With American Indians," *Science Communication* 44, no. 1 (February 2022): 130–39.

[33] Crepelle, "Tribes, Vaccines, and COVID-19," 44–51; Smith, "Impact of the Coronavirus," 318–19; Raymond Foxworth et al. "COVID-19 Vaccination in American Indians and Alaska Natives—Lessons from Effective Community Response," *The New England Journal of Medicine* 385, no. 26 (2021): 2403–06; Nam Le-Morawa et al., "Effectiveness of a COVID-19 Vaccine Rollout in a Highly Affected American Indian Community, San Carlos Apache Tribe, December 2020-February 2021," *Public Health Reports* 138, sup. 2, (2023): 23s–29s.

Many Native Nations were also quicker and firmer than surrounding state governments in issuing mask mandates, curfews, and lockdowns, thus exercising sovereign authority to protect their citizens. Tribal authorities at Cheyenne River and Oglala took things even further by setting up highway checkpoints against viral spread from surrounding South Dakota where state protective measures were especially lax.[34] During the peak of the pandemic, in the spring of 2020, the Navajo Nation "sent workers home, shuttered offices and non-essential businesses, mandated masks, closed its borders to visitors and enacted curfews."[35] Diné officials also enforced rationing for certain groceries and supplies in high demand.

Hard choices had to be made, with some tribal governments preferring masking and social distancing options in public places and others opting for lockdowns. Those that shut down government offices, local merchants, and casinos (among those that had them) suffered lost revenue for social services and lost income for struggling families as unemployment rates in Indian Country surged past 20% in April 2020. Federal financial support through the CARES Act provided only partial relief to tribal economies hit hard by the pandemic.[36]

Stay-at-home measures also meant that important ceremonies, cultural events (such as powwows), and social gatherings were temporarily suspended, with regrettable consequences in terms of a community's spiritual, social, and economic vitality. Widespread decisions by state and tribal authorities to suspend in-person K-12 schooling and coursework at tribal colleges and universities also presented significant challenges for Indigenous students and families. These were nevertheless all measures that many tribal leaders deemed lesser evils than losing more citizens and cultural knowledge to the pandemic. Nor were tough decisions made in a defeatist mindset. As numerous chapters in this volume attest, tribal leaders, community groups, families, teachers, and others drew on available

---

[34] Crepelle, "Tribes, Vaccines, and COVID-19," 53–58.

[35] Pauly Denetclaw, "Final COVID restrictions lifted on Navajo Nation," *Indian Country Today*, May 9, 2023, accessed online January 31, 2024, https://www.nhonews.com/news/2023/may/09/final-covid-restrictions-lifted-navajo-nation/.

[36] Crepelle, "Tribes, Vaccines, and COVID-19," 59–61; Smith, "Impact of the Coronavirus," 321–23; U.S. Bureau of Labor Statistic, "Unemployment rate for American Indians and Alaska Natives at 7.9 percent in December 2021," January 26, 2022, accessed online January 8, 2024, https://www.bls.gov.opub/ted/2022.

technologies and grassroots solutions to facilitate learning and maintain vital social and spiritual connections even when people could no longer gather in person.

This collection of chapters is timely and, most importantly, helps bring public attention to the ongoing challenges Native Americans face in maintaining physical and economic well-being, as they strive to be *good relatives*. By privileging the voices of Native scholars, as well as those of diverse scholars well-versed in Native American and Indigenous Studies, this volume seeks to better understand why Indian Country suffered disproportionately from this pandemic and place this crisis in a broader historical context. Equally important, these chapters highlight the resilience and creativity of myriad Indigenous communities in responding to crises in ways that have asserted and reinforced their shared values, cultural traditions, and sovereignty. As much as these scholars focus on why, to what extent, and in what ways Native communities suffered so deeply during this pandemic, they also offer stories of perseverance and ingenuity that, we hope, will guide and inspire future communities—Indigenous and non-Native people alike—to act effectively in future epidemics and pandemics.

This volume also emphasizes the vibrancy and importance of Native American and Indigenous Studies (NAIS) as an academic discipline by demonstrating how to take a holistic approach drawn from various subdisciplines. Throughout the pandemic, reporters begged the question, why are Native Americans infected at higher rates than the rest of the country, especially when the Navajo Nation passed New York City as the most infected population in the U.S. per capita. Reporters swarmed for quick answers, not realizing that the NAIS field had already answered them, or at least, many of them, even before the onset of the pandemic. The answers to these questions are complex and require a multidisciplinary approach offered by the field of NAIS, which intertwines history, political science, sociology, anthropology, and more. Even before the onset of the pandemic, NAIS scholars had looked at language retention and revitalization; the effects of urbanization; resource rights—particularly water; food sovereignty; self-government/sovereignty; the history of education in Indian Country; and the history of health care in Indigenous territories. NAIS is a field that addresses real-life issues—including pandemics such as COVID-19—that have affected Native American communities.

## Core Themes

In addition to this introductory chapter and a conclusion, this anthology is broken up into fifteen chapters, which fall into five parts: Historical Inequities and Pandemics; Community Well-Being; Students, Innovative Learning, and Community Building; Art as Survivance; and Motherhood and Family Wellness. Each part begins with an introduction that underscores its main concepts.

Many of the contributing authors of this volume position themselves as central to these accounts of the pandemic, and they express their own feelings of loss, anxiety, triumph, and hope—their first-hand experiences show through, as well as their observations of their students and communities. In many ways, we are all living with the present and recent consequences of the COVID-19 outbreak. While we do not have the critical distance that some scholars might prefer, it is precisely because of this closeness that this book is valuable. The pandemic was personal for everyone, making us value our relationships with others and providing us with new perspectives on what matters most in life.

These chapters capture the emotion and feeling of the moment in ways that a later generation of scholars might find disruptive of objectivity but nevertheless serve as critical sources for present communities looking forward and future scholars looking back. Native communities have experienced these trials more intensely and have had their own ways of responding as the inequities of the pandemic highlighted the gulf between them and other Americans. These first-hand experiences and observations we all share, however, also gave us a more common experience, reminding us of our humanity. This humanity comes through in all the chapters of this book—sometimes very overtly and other times underpinning the discussions. Along these same lines, the reason that so many chapters focus on college environments is that the authors felt compelled to position themselves as a part of this story, and what everyone who contributed to this work shares are our livelihoods as professors, administrators, students, and public intellectuals.

Another common theme that emerges from these chapters is not just resilience but also positive adaptation and silver linings. While many readers might expect that most chapters would concentrate on pain and loss, as well as perseverance, they might be surprised to see a majority of these pieces also honing in on some positive outcomes, both short-term and enduring, that arose from such terrible circumstances. Some authors speak of communities finding new ways to connect using technology and other innovative means; of teachers and staff learning more effective ways to serve students; and other creative adaptations that served not only to meet the immediate challenges and dress the wounds of the pandemic but that may endure as effective strategies for maintaining connections through less trying times to come. In other words, emergency responses transitioned into potentially long-term strategies for proactive change. Beyond this, there are the silver linings that come from people tapping into their internal strengths as individuals and communities, and the growth that comes from realizing that they possessed these abilities. We do not mean to imply that the pandemic was "not all that bad" or worse yet, somehow portray it as a positive experience overall, but these silver linings prominently come through some of these stories and speak not only to Indigenous peoples' resiliency and adaptability but to a general human hopefulness that transcends nationality, race, and ethnicity. This is a story of COVID-19 in Indian Country, but many of the positive and hopeful lessons transcend Indigenous communities.

Multiple authors, in this book, refer to the term "survivance" explicitly, as well as otherwise expressing and exemplifying this concept that Anishinaabe scholar Gerald Vizenor defines as "an active sense of presence, the continuance of native stories, not a mere reaction, or a survivable name."[37] No other term appears as frequently, which speaks to the applicability of survivance to pandemic crises, as well as to the shared terminology that scholars use within Native American and Indigenous Studies despite coming from different disciplinary backgrounds.

Themes of community and kinship run through most of the chapters as well, both in terms of loss and separation and the pain this caused that was arguably more acute than among many other peoples; as well as the innovative means Native people devised together to restore existing communities and forge new surrogate communities. Among others, such surrogate communities developed among students and educators who were otherwise distanced from their established kith and kin. Certain technologies, which in many ways played a role in distancing people, especially considering the impersonal nature of virtual meetings such as via Zoom, were also flipped around and used as tools for good to maintain and build communities. But other means also came to the fore, from billboards and signs, to

---

[37] Gerald Vizenor, *Manifest Manners: Narratives on Postindian Survivance* (Lincoln: University of Nebraska Press, 1999), vii.

care packages and contactless deliveries of necessities. These are stories of Indigenous communities and individuals suffering loss and separation but also stories of group resilience and creativity, reflecting centuries-long efforts of Indigenous peoples to persist amid colonization, genocide, and other forms of loss and dislocation.

## HEALING AND HOPE

After her shock from receiving the body bags for the Seattle Indian Health Board, Abigail Echo-Hawk posted on social media and various platforms about her distress over the mistreatment and violence of this response from their "state and federal partners."[38] The body bags triggered memories of assaults against Indigenous people, including by government and non-government forces that threatened their survival and well-being. Such actions caused harm and exposed how governments were failing to provide essential supplies, such as masks and personal protective equipment (PPE), COVID-19 testing, medicines, and other materials, to combat the virus and protect Indigenous people. Native Americans and their allies shared media posts about the body bags, adding their voices and stories of how U.S. government officials and members of society presumed Indigenous people's ultimate demise with culpable "settler innocence."[39] This American "settler innocence" refers to those who resist and block the recognition of their culpability and responsibility for the violence, destruction, and death that has plagued Indigenous people, including during the COVID-19 pandemic.

Despite these affronts, Echo-Hawk has continued to advocate, seek, and find necessary aid to ensure the health of Indigenous peoples. The Seattle Indian Health Board and Echo-Hawk have worked with urban

---

[38] Pasia, "When they gave her body bags instead of PPE, she used them to make a healing ribbon dress."

[39] See Melissa del Carmen Gomez, "How COVID-19 is Affecting Indigenous Communities," *Voices of Gen-Z*, July 26, 2020, accessed online, https://www.voicesofgenz.com/post-1/how-covid-19-is-affecting-indigenous-communities; F. Evan Nooe, *Aggression and Sufferings: Settler Violence, Native Resistance, and the Coalescence of the Old South* (Tuscaloosa, AL: University of Alabama Press, 2023), 135; Boyd Cothran, *Remembering the Modoc War: Redemptive Violence and the Making of American Innocence* (Chapel Hill: University of North Carolina Press, 2014), 166; and Erik Ortiz, "Native American health center asked for COVID-19 supplies. It got body bags instead," NBC News, May 5, 2020, accessed online, https://www.nbcnews.com/news/us-news/native-american-health-center-asked-covid-19-supplies-they-got-n1200246.

Native Americans who live and traverse but are often overlooked and caught in liminal spaces without support from tribal governments and their homelands. Echo-Hawk made a ribbon dress for healing from one of the body bags in defiance of the "Dead Indian" trope imposed on her and Indigenous people. She wrote on a fold of the dress "a personal mantra: 'I am a tangible manifestation of my ancestors' resiliency," and she used red paint to impress the front of the dress with her handprints three times for Murdered and Missing Indigenous Women (MMIW).[40] Her ribbon dress remains a symbol of not only survival but also ingenuity and hope for Indigenous futurity.

As Laura Harjo, a Muscogee scholar, underscores, futurity is based on how Indigenous ancestors will recognize their children and descendants in the present and future. She clarifies how "futurity is the enactment of theories and practices that activate our ancestors' unrealized possibilities, the act of living out the futures we wish for in a contemporary moment, the creation of the conditions for these futures."[41] They will continue to exist and sustain intergenerational ties, emphasizing how Indigenous peoples live on and never all die. Echo-Hawk asserts that she is "the descendant of genocide survivors. And it is because of their resiliency, and their fight to survive that I can thrive."[42] Indigenous peoples live after 2020 and the COVID-19 pandemic, and they will always remember what they suffered and how stereotypes such as "Dead Indians" became life-threatening dangers in the pandemic. Most importantly, as each of these chapters in this edited volume affirm, Echo-Hawk's ribbon dress and stories of Indigenous experiences through the COVID-19 pandemic reveal the healing power of hope among Indigenous peoples past, present, and future.

**Competing Interests Declaration** The authors have no conflicts of interest to declare that are relevant to the content of this chapter.

---

[40] Pasia, "When they gave her body bags instead of PPE, she used them to make a healing ribbon dress."

[41] Laura Harjo, *Spiral to the Stars: Mvskoke Tools of Futurity* (Tucson: University of Arizona Press, 2019), 5.

[42] Echo-Hawk cited in Cecilia Nowell, "They Asked for PPE and Got Body Bags Instead—She Turned Them Into a Healing Dress."

PART I

# Historical Inequities and Pandemics

COVID-19 became a pandemic, rather than simply an epidemic, because it struck globally, exacting steep costs in lives and livelihoods among people of all nationalities and races. The virus was not, however, entirely indiscriminate. People's histories mattered, as it often hit hardest those communities that had previously suffered ill effects from centuries of colonization, marginalization, and neglect. This was particularly so among Native Americans, as the authors in this section demonstrate.

In the opening chapter, Heather Tanana explains how water insecurity became a leading cause of poor health outcomes among Indigenous Americans during the COVID-19 pandemic, particularly on the Navajo Nation. Lacking basic sanitation or clean water for drinking and washing became "a matter of life or death," which was a dilemma Native people should never have faced given the federal government's treaty and trust obligations to provide tribes "with a permanent, healthy homeland." Federal measures have attempted to address health disparities and water insecurity in Indian country over many decades, but funding shortfalls have undermined these efforts and left Native communities vulnerable to infectious diseases.

Yvette Towersap provides another historical perspective by looking back to the Great Influenza pandemic of 1918, considering its impacts on the Fort Hall community in Idaho and drawing important parallels and contrasts to COVID-19. She attributes the 1918 influenza's particular severity among the Shoshone and Bannock people to poor health and housing conditions resulting from federal assimilation policies coupled with inadequate medical care. Towersap also describes the challenges of accurately representing this past given her people's "customs to avoid speaking of significant sickness." Stories told here of people at Fort Hall visiting influenza victims through hospital windows foreshadow what would occur across the United States during COVID.

Jennifer Frazee then speaks to the toll COVID-19 has taken by reflecting on the life before in her Choctaw community. She recalls experiencing the warmth of kinship as a child, including the foods people lovingly prepared and the assurance of knowing a whole community was looking after its youth. The legacies of colonization nevertheless left people physically vulnerable to disease and tore at families, physically distancing people from each other before disaster struck. Facing this crisis, says Frazee, Indigenous peoples have responded with renewed "commitments to fighting for the survival and success of their people in an echo of the ways of their ancestors."

CHAPTER 2

# The Intersection of the Law and Health: Water (In)security in Indian Country

*Heather Tanana*

*Tó éí iiná át'é* (water is life). Water is critical to survival, necessary for the health, socioeconomic, and cultural needs of any community. Every household in the United States needs and deserves access to clean, reliable, and affordable drinking water. Yet, tribal communities face high rates of water insecurity. More than a half million people—nearly 48% of tribal homes in Native communities across the United States—do not have access to reliable water sources, clean drinking water, or basic sanitation. In comparison, less than 1% of households in the United States lack these facilities. Indeed, Native American households are 19 times more likely to lack indoor plumbing than white households.[1] The Navajo Nation, in particular, experiences severe water insecurity with an estimated 30–40% of households lacking running water and making Navajo residents 67

---

[1] U.S. Water Alliance & Dig Deep, *Closing the Water Access Gap in the United States: A National Action Plan* (2019), 22 and 38.

---

H. Tanana (✉)
University of Irvine School of Law, Irvine, CA, USA
e-mail: htanana@law.uci.edu

© The Author(s), under exclusive license to Springer Nature Switzerland AG 2024
F. King, W. Davies (eds.), *COVID-19 in Indian Country*,
https://doi.org/10.1007/978-3-031-70184-9_2

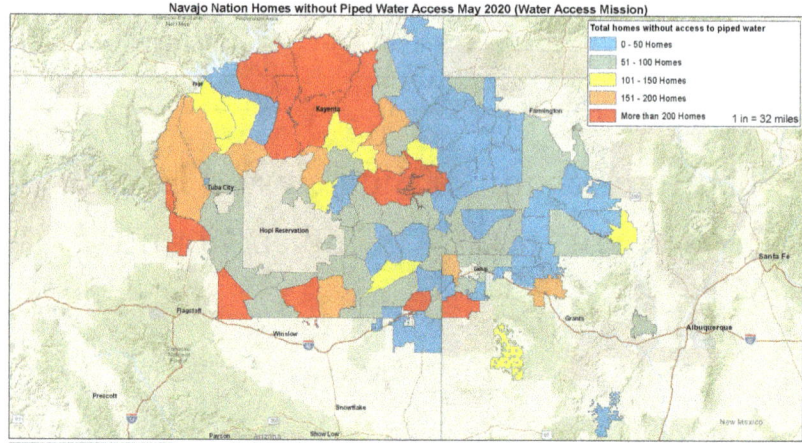

**Fig. 2.1** Navajo Nation Homes without piped water access May 2020. Source: Navajo Safe Water: Protecting You and Your Family's Health, www.navajosafewater.org

times more likely to lack running water than white households.[2] This persistent problem became a matter of life or death during the COVID-19 pandemic (Fig. 2.1).

Media outlets across the world highlighted the virus's disproportionate impact on tribal communities, including the Navajo Nation. During the pandemic, Native Americans experienced higher rates of COVID-19, hospitalization, and death compared with other ethnic groups in the U.S.[3] This disproportionate impact has been attributed to long-standing inequities, such as limited health services, inadequate housing, and lack of infrastructure (including water infrastructure).[4] Testifying before Congress,

---

[2] DigDeep: Navajo Water Project, "About the Project," accessed online, https://www.navajowaterproject.org/project-specifics.

[3] CDC, "Hospitalization, and Death by Race/Ethnicity," accessed online https://www.cdc.gov/coronavirus/2019-ncov/covid-data/investigations-discovery/hospitalization-death-by-race-ethnicity.html.

[4] U.S. Congress, *Hearing on An Unequal Burden: Addressing Racial Health Disparities in the Coronavirus Pandemic Before the Select Subcommittee on the Coronavirus Crisis*, 116th Cong. 3–6 (2020) (written testimony of Fawn Sharp, President of the National Congress of American Indians).

Navajo Nation President Jonathan Nez attributed the high COVID-19 rate among the Navajo Nation largely to the lack of water access. Sanitation and access to running water are important determinants of disease transmission. President Nez also emphasized that "clean water is a sacred and scarce commodity."[5]

These inequities are especially egregious given the federal government's treaty and trust responsibilities to the Navajo Nation (and other tribal nations) in the United States. This chapter explores how past federal policies have contributed to the historical lack of clean water access experienced in Indian Country. First, a background of the special relationship between the federal government and tribal nations is provided, along with a history of the various federal policy eras. The federal government's promise to provide tribes with a permanent, healthy homeland is discussed next. But, the United States' failure to uphold these promises created inequities that left the Navajo Nation vulnerable to COVID-19. Within this context, the experience of the Navajo Nation during the pandemic is examined.

## THE FEDERAL GOVERNMENT AND TRIBAL NATIONS: A SPECIAL RELATIONSHIP

The United States maintains a special relationship with tribal nations defined by power imbalances and unique historic legal arrangements. Native Americans are the original inhabitants of this country; therefore, they predate the formation of the United States. However, adopting the Doctrine of Discovery (an international principle of law), the United States justified colonizing the land and developing domestic laws that maintained an unequal hierarchy. This body of law, referred to as Federal Indian law, defines the unique legal and political status of federally recognized tribes and establishes the relationship between tribes, states, and the federal government.

The foundations of Federal Indian law are grounded in racist beliefs that Native Americans were savages and inferior to white settlers. This racial bias is embedded in foundational U.S. Supreme Court decisions,

---

[5] U.S. Congress, *Addressing the Urgent Needs of Our Tribal Communities: Hearing before the House Committee on Energy and Commerce*, 116th Cong. 7–8 (2020) (statement of Jonathan Nez, President, Navajo Nation).

perpetuating a form of colonial violence that seeks to preserve a white racial dominance.[6] In a series of cases commonly known as the Marshall trilogy, the Supreme Court set the foundations for Federal Indian law. The Marshall trilogy consists of three cases: *Johnson v. M'Intosh*, 21 U.S. 543 (1823); *Cherokee Nation v. Georgia*, 30 U.S. 1 (1831); and *Worcester v. Georgia*, 31 U.S. 515 (1832).

These cases established crucial and sometimes conflicting concepts in the law. They acknowledged tribes' inherent sovereignty to govern their people and land, but with the condition of subservience to the federal government. For example, in *Cherokee Nation v. Georgia*, the court found that the Cherokee Nation and other tribes "have been recognized as sovereign and independent states; possessing both the exclusive right to their territory, and the exclusive right of self-government within that territory." Such sovereignty essentially equates to a tribe's right to govern itself. And yet, tribes are also considered domestic dependent nations, reliant upon the protection of the federal government. "They are dominated domestic because they are within the United States and dependent because they are subject to federal power."[7] As a result, a trust relationship exists between the federal government and tribes, whereby the United States has a duty to act in good faith in its dealings with tribes. This relationship has been compared to that of a guardian and ward, or a trustee and beneficiary, with the federal government carrying trust duties within three broad categories: (1) protection of tribal property held in trust by the United States; (2) protection of the tribal right to self-government; and (3) protection of tribal well-being, including the provision of social, medical, and education services necessary for the survival of the tribes.[8]

---

[6] Joubin Khazaie, "Fanon, Colonial Violence, and Racist Language in Federal American Indian Law," *University of Miami Race and Social Justice Law Review* 12, no. 2 (2022): 297–311.

[7] Cohen's Handbook of Federal Indian Law, ch. 1 (2012).

[8] Kirke Kickingbird and Everett R. Rhoades, "The Relation of Indian Nations to the U.S. Government," in *American Indian Health: Innovations in Health Care Promotion, and Policy*, ed. Everett R. Rhoades (Baltimore, MD: Johns Hopkins University Press, 2000), 61 and 68 (citing American Indian Policy Review Commission, 95th Cong., 1st Sess., Final Rep. (Comm. Print 1977)).

## Federal Indian Policies

Since the formation of the United States, the federal government engaged in a series of federal Indian policies—various laws, regulations, and actions implemented by the federal government concerning tribes and their relationship with the federal government—which have shaped the landscape in Indian Country and had lasting impacts on tribal communities. As a result, the historical and legal background of these policy eras is necessary context for understanding any actions that take place in Indian Country. To that end, a brief summary of the federal Indian policy eras is provided in Table 2.1.[9]

Table 2.1 Federal Indian policy eras

| Federal Indian policy era | Timeframe | Policy goal |
| --- | --- | --- |
| Removal era | 1835–1861 | Forcible relocation of eastern tribes westward to provide tribes with a place to live undisturbed where they could govern themselves and adjust to civilized ways, while opening up land for white settlers |
| Reservation era | 1861–1887 | Confinement of tribes onto reservations to continue opening up land to white settlers and to domesticate Native Americans |
| Allotment & assimilation era | 1871–1928 | Division of tribal lands into individual allotments to civilize and assimilate Native Americans into mainstream American society |
| Indian reorganization era | 1928–1942 | Encouragement of tribal-self-government and tribal governments to promote "good" Indian culture, economic development, and self-determination, subject to approval of the federal government |
| Termination era | 1943–1961 | Termination of the special status of tribes and the trust relationship between tribes and the federal government |
| Self-governance era | 1961–present | Support of tribal management of their own programs and services recognizing a government-to-government relationship between the federal government where tribes are the primary driver of Indian policy through their exercise of inherent sovereign powers |

Credit: Heather Tanana

[9] See generally Justin Blake and Sarah Deer, *Introduction to Tribal Legal Studies* (Lanham, MD: AltaMira Press, 2010), 73–91; and *Cohen's Handbook, supra* note 7, § 1.

For the most part, past federal Indian policies have reduced, diminished, and otherwise harmed Native communities. The majority of these policies sought (1) to remove tribes from their ancestral homelands in order to open up land for white settlers and (2) to "kill the Indian" and assimilate Native Americans into mainstream society. The U.S. Senate has summarized the federal government's historic intentions as follows:

> Beginning with President Washington, the stated policy of the Federal Government was to replace the Indian's culture with our own. This was considered "advisable" as the cheapest and safest way of subduing the Indians, of providing a safe habitat for the country's white inhabitants, of helping the whites acquire desirable land, and of changing the Indian's economy so that he would be content with less land.[10]

These policies have profoundly impacted tribal nations and their members, with severe consequences including the termination of tribal status and erosion of cultural identity. Such actions have left an indelible mark, contributing to a legacy of historical trauma that persists in contemporary times.

Dr. Maria Yellow Horse Brave Heart, an expert in trauma and Indigenous populations, defines historical trauma as the "cumulative emotional and psychological wounding across generations, including the lifespan, which emanates from massive group trauma."[11] Historical trauma has far-reaching effects and has been connected to mental and behavioral health issues. Native communities, having endured historical trauma, grapple with a spectrum of challenges, including heightened rates of depression, anxiety, suicidality, and substance abuse.[12]

It is essential to understand the depth and complexity of historical trauma when working with Native communities. It involves acknowledging the intergenerational impact of past injustices (often stemming from past federal policies) and recognizing the ongoing struggles that result from the disruption of cultural continuity and the deliberate dismantling

---

[10] Bureau of Indian Affairs, Federal Indian Boarding School Initiative Investigative Report 21 (citing S. Rep. No. 91-501, at 143 (1969)).

[11] Maria Yellow Horse Brave Heart et al., "Historical Trauma among Indigenous Peoples of the Americas: Concepts, Research, and Clinical Considerations," *Journal of Psychoactive Drugs* 43, no. 4 (2011): 282–83.

[12] Ibid. 284.

of tribal structures. As demonstrated during the COVID-19 pandemic, this awareness is crucial for developing effective approaches to public health threats.

## Federal Promises

"In exchange for the surrender and reduction of tribal lands and removal and resettlement of approximately one-fifth of Native American tribes from their original lands," the United States entered into hundreds of treaties and made certain promises to promote tribal self-government, support tribal well-being, and protect tribal resources and lands.[13] Notwithstanding changes in the federal Indian policy eras, the federal government has generally recognized the treaty promises made to tribal nations, including the establishment of reservations as permanent homelands and the responsibility to provide health care services to Native Americans.

## A Permanent Homeland

At present, there are 574 federally recognized tribes in the United States. While each tribe is unique and independent, they share a common history of colonization and removal, often onto lands that "were not considered to be located in the most desirable area of the Nation."[14] The Navajo Nation was no exception. In 1849, the federal government entered into a treaty that recognized the Navajo Nation as a tribe under the jurisdiction of the United States and agreed to "designate, settle, and adjust" the boundaries of the Navajo territory.[15] But, during the "Long Walk" of the mid-1860s, the federal government subsequently forced many Navajos to travel hundreds of miles to Bosque Redondo in eastern New Mexico, where they were imprisoned for several years. In 1868, the United States and Navajo Nation entered into a second treaty that "set apart" a

---

[13] U.S. Commission on Civil Rights, *Broken Promises: Continuing Federal Funding Shortfall for Native Americans* (2018), accessed online, https://www.usccr.gov/files/pubs/2018/12-20-Broken-Promises.pdf.

[14] *Arizona v. California*, 373 U.S. 546, 598 (1963).

[15] Treaty between the United States of America and the Navajo Tribe of Indians, Sept. 9, 1849, 9 Stat. 974 (ratified Sept. 24, 1850).

reservation for the "use and occupation of the Navajo tribe."[16] The reservation was intended to be a permanent homeland for the Navajo Nation and its people. Notably, the Navajo reservation ultimately was established within the original, ancestral lands of the Navajos, including the four mountains they consider sacred. But, water is necessary for survival and therefore, a requirement for any homelands to be permanent. This is especially true for lands located in the arid Southwest where water is scarce.

Generally speaking, treaties did not explicitly address the water-related needs of reservations. However, a 1908 Supreme Court ruling, *Winters v. United States*, held that tribes have a reserved right to water sufficient to fulfill the purposes of their reservation, including enough to support the land as a permanent home for present and future generations of the tribe.[17] Aside from treaty promises, the federal government also has an underlying trust responsibility to protect tribal treaty rights, lands, assets, and resources. Combined, federal treaty and trust responsibilities create a federal duty to ensure water security on reservations. Access to a clean, reliable supply of water is required to fulfill the basic standards of living and guarantee a permanent homeland.

Although tribes are entitled to federally reserved water rights, quantifying and securing these rights prove challenging, often requiring significant expenditures of time and money. Nonetheless, the "quantification of water rights is viewed by many as necessary to design and plan adaptation strategies that secure water" for all of the community needs.[18]

Tribal water rights may be quantified through either adjudication (litigation) or negotiated settlements. In adjudications, tribes may choose to have the federal government act as their trustee, protecting and asserting their water rights, or they can waive their tribal sovereign immunity by intervening as party defendants. Since the landmark *Winters* decision, 46 tribes have opted to quantify their water rights through adjudications, a process that on average spans a lengthy 22 years to complete. Given the time-consuming nature of litigation and other associated disadvantages, such as high costs, tribes often lean towards negotiated settlements as a

---

[16] Treaty between the United States of America and the Navajo Tribe of Indians, June 1, 1868, 15 Stat. 667–668 (ratified Aug. 12, 1868).

[17] 207 U.S. 564 (1908).

[18] U.S. Global Change Research Program, "Tribes and Indigenous Peoples," *in Fourth National Climate Assessment, Volume II: Impacts, Risks, and Adaptation in the United States* (2018), 572 and 579.

more favorable alternative. These settlements, also known as Indian or tribal water rights settlements, progress through four distinct phases: pre-negotiation, negotiation, settlement, and implementation. The federal government actively participates in negotiations, aligning with its trust responsibility to tribes by assisting in the assertion of tribal water right claims. Following negotiation, settlements typically require congressional authorization for the terms to be implemented. To date, the federal government has engaged in thirty-nine tribal water rights settlements, thirty-five of which have been congressionally approved.

Even after the quantification of tribal water rights, many tribes encounter challenges in utilizing their water resources due to a lack of funding and infrastructure. This results in what is colloquially termed "paper" water rights, signifying rights on paper rather than actual access to water (referred to as "wet" water rights). Negotiated settlements can play a pivotal role in overcoming these challenges by including funding authorization, and ideally, mandatory appropriations for infrastructure projects that facilitate access and development of tribal water resources. However, settlements come with their own set of disadvantages, including the pressure to relinquish the full extent of their water rights to meet the immediate needs of their community. For example, some tribes have agreed to receive less water or accept a lower priority date than they are entitled to in order to secure much-needed infrastructure development.

In *Arizona v. Navajo Nation*, the U.S. Supreme Court recently held that the federal government did not need to help assess and plan for the Nation's water needs.[19] All of the parties (and the court) agreed that the Navajo Nation has recognized rights to water to support its reservation under the *Winters* doctrine. However, securing and accessing those rights appears to ultimately be on the shoulders of the Tribe.

While negotiated water settlements and the quantification of tribal water rights can serve as catalysts for much-needed water infrastructure projects, they should not be deemed pre-conditions for achieving water security for tribal communities. The federal government bears a distinct responsibility to safeguard tribal health and ensure that reservations have the necessary water to be permanent homelands, as promised. Water security remains a paramount concern for many tribes, including the Navajo Nation. And the federal government holds a central role in promoting

---

[19] *Arizona et al. v. Navajo Nation et al.*, no. 21-1484, slip op. (S. Ct. Jun. 22, 2023).

tribal well-being and protecting tribal futures, which should include clean water access. In recognition of this responsibility, the federal government has established and overseen a diverse array of at least 23 distinct programs through 7 different federal agencies that provide funding and support for tribal water and sanitation projects.[20] One of the primary programs is the Indian Health Service's Sanitation Facilities Construction Program.

## Indian Health Care

Treaties between the United States and tribes not only set aside land as a permanent homeland but also frequently included other provisions related to the well-being of Native Americans. Of the 389 ratified treaties, 31 (12%) contain provisions related to health care.[21] These provisions were not merely symbolic; they embodied the federal government's commitment to advancing tribal welfare and ensuring adequate health care to Native Americans—a duty that is consonant with and required by the federal government's historical and unique legal relationship with tribal nations. Indeed, promoting the health of Native Americans has been recognized by Congress as "the policy of this Nation, in fulfillment of its special trust responsibilities and legal obligations to Indians."[22] Notwithstanding this federal obligation, Native Americans experience vast health disparities compared to other populations. This inequity is historical and stems in large part from the federal government's broken promises over the past 200 years and its failure to fully fund tribal health services.

Initially, the Department of War was responsible for management of tribal affairs. During this period, military physicians provided limited, sporadic care to Native Americans residing near military posts. In 1849, the Department of Interior assumed jurisdiction over tribal matters, including health services, leading to a more organized and systematic approach. Over subsequent decades, the federal government gradually assumed increasing commitments to tribes, typically in the form of providing

---

[20] Heather Tanana et al., *Universal Access to Clean Water for Tribal Communities* (2020), accessed online, https://tribalcleanwater.org/wp-content/uploads/2021/09/WTI-Full-Report-4.20.pdf.

[21] David H. DeJong, *"If You Knew the Conditions": A Chronicle of the Indian Medical Service and American Indian Health Care, 1908-1955* (Lanham, MD: Lexington Books, 2008), 5.

[22] Indian Health Care Improvement Act, 25 U.S.C. § 1602.

physicians and medications. However, these efforts were insufficient, as the ongoing tribal health care needs continued to exceed the available assistance provided by the federal government. Reports on tribal communities have consistently found widespread impoverishment and poor health conditions. The Meriam Report, published in 1928, identified deficiencies in health facilities and equipment as well as a shortage of health professionals. "Taken as a whole practically every activity undertaken by the national government for the promotion of the health of the Indians is below a reasonable standard of efficiency."[23]

Eventually, the administration of Indian health care was transferred from the Department of Interior to the Public Health Service (PHS), and in 1955, the Division of Indian Health was created, now known as the Indian Health Service (IHS). Its mission is "to raise the physical, mental, social, and spiritual health of American Indians and Alaska Natives to the highest level."[24] Based upon a broad definition of health, IHS services include preventative and medical services, community and social well-being, and environmental improvements.

Several federal laws have played pivotal roles in shaping the health and general welfare of Native Americans. The Snyder Act of 1921 was the first major law passed establishing the underlying framework for the Native American healthcare system that exists today. The Act authorized funds for the benefit, care, and assistance of Native Americans, including the employment of physicians and delivery of health services. However, programs established under the Snyder Act were discretionary and subject to Congress actually appropriating funds for use. The Indian Self-Determination and Education Assistance Act of 1975 authorized IHS to allow tribes to assume control over and manage health-related programs and services delivered by IHS. Such agreements, often referred to as 638 contracts and compacts, allowed tribes to tailor health programs and services to their specific community needs. The Indian Health Care Improvement Act (IHCIA) is another important law passed in 1976, and then permanently reauthorized in 2010 as part of the Patient Protection and Affordable Care Act. The IHCIA set forth the following national goals:

---

[23] Lewis Meriam, *The Problem of Indian Administration: Report of a Survey Made at the Request of Honorable Hubert Work, Secretary of the Interior, and Submitted to Him, Feb. 21, 1928* (Baltimore, MD: The Johns Hopkins Press 1928), 189.

[24] Indian Health Service, "About IHS," accessed online, https://www.ihs.gov/aboutihs/.

[T]o provide the resources, processes, and structure that will enable Indian tribes and tribal members to obtain the quantity and quality of health care services and opportunities that will eradicate the health disparities between Indians and the general population of the United States, [and] to provide the quantity and quality of health services which will permit the health status of Indians to be raised to the highest possible level and to encourage the maximum participation of Indians in the planning and management of those services.[25]

Recognizing the intrinsic connection between access to water and public health, Congress authorized the creation of the Sanitation Facilities Construction (SFC) Program in 1959 to support drinking water and sanitation projects in tribal communities.[26] The goal of the SFC Program is to improve the health of Native Americans "by improving the environment in which they live," more specifically, by providing "safe water supplies, adequate means of waste disposal, and other essential sanitation facilities."[27]

As part of the SFC Program, IHS collects data about water supply and sewage disposal for tribal homes and identifies sanitation deficiencies. Deficiencies are categorized by the following levels:

Level I: An Indian tribe or community with a sanitation system which complies with all applicable water supply and pollution control laws, and in which the deficiencies relate to routine replacement, repair, or maintenance needs.

Level II: An Indian tribe or community with a sanitation system which complies with all applicable water supply and pollution control laws, and in which the deficiencies relate to capital improvements that are necessary to improve the facilities in order to meet the needs of such tribe or community for domestic sanitation facilities.

Level III: An Indian tribe or community with a sanitation system which has an inadequate or partial water supply and a sewage disposal facility that does not comply with applicable water supply and pollution control laws, or that has no solid waste disposal facility.

---

[25] 25 U.S.C. § 1601.
[26] Indian Sanitation Facilities Construction Act of 1959, Pub. L. 86–121.
[27] Indian Health Service, et al., *Criteria for the Sanitation Facilities Construction Program* (1999), 1-1, accessed online, https://www.ihs.gov/sites/dsfc/themes/responsive2017/display_objects/documents/Criteria_March_2003.pdf.

Level IV: An Indian tribe or community with a sanitation system which lacks either a safe water supply system or a sewage disposal system.
Level V: An Indian tribe or community that lacks a safe water supply and a sewage disposal system.[28]

Within the Navajo Nation, IHS has identified 349 sanitation deficiency projects. A significant portion of these projects, 109 (31%), are at Level V.[29] In contrast, only 3 (0.8%) of these projects are at Level I. Notably, due to data limitations, the IHS database does not identify every household on the Navajo Nation and, therefore, does not fully reflect the actual need on Navajo Nation.[30]

Notwithstanding the Congressional authorizations to provide health services and support healthy homelands, federal funding shortfalls have undermined federal efforts. IHS (including the SFC Program) has been historically underfunded and understaffed, hindering the federal agency's ability to fulfill its mission and violating fundamental principles of broader treaty and trust responsibilities to tribal nations. "Indeed, when adjusted for inflation and population growth, the IHS budget has remained static in recent decades, with little additional funding available to target the chronic health disparities facing Native communities."[31] The per capita expenditures of IHS amount to only one-third of the federal government's spending per person nationwide on health care. For example, in fiscal year 2017, the IHS allocated a mere $3332 per capita per patient for health services, in stark contrast to the national health care spending of $9207 per person.[32] Such severe underinvestment has also occurred with respect to the SFC Program. The SFC Program end-of-year need in 2020 was

---

[28] See Indian Health Service, *Annual Report to the Congress of the United States on Sanitation Deficiency Levels for Indian Homes and Communities* (2019), 4, accessed online, https://www.ihs.gov/sites/newsroom/themes/responsive2017/display_objects/documents/FY_2019_RTC_Sanitation_Deficiencies_Report.pdf.

[29] Indian Health Service, *FY 2021 Annual Report of Sanitation Deficiency Levels* (Nov. 16, 2021), accessed online, https://www.ihs.gov/sites/dsfc/themes/responsive2017/display_objects/documents/FY_2021_Appendix_Project_Listing.pdf.

[30] U.S. Government Accountability Office, GAO-18-309, *Drinking Water and Wastewater Infrastructure: Opportunities Exist to Enhance Federal Agency Needs Assessment and Coordination on Tribal Projects* (2018), 16–17, 19–20.

[31] Ibid. 67.

[32] National Congress of American Indians, *Reducing Disparities in the Federal Health Care Budget in Fiscal Year 2020 Indian Country Budget Request* (2019), 55, accessed online, https://www.ncai.org/07_NCAI-FY20-Healthcare.pdf.

over $3 billion, but only $196.6 million was appropriated by Congress for fiscal year 2021. Overall, the federal government's efforts have been insufficient to fulfill its promise to protect the health and well-being of Native Americans, resulting in significant health disparities that persist today and far exceed other population groups.[33]

## UNMASKING INEQUITY AND THE COVID-19 PANDEMIC

The COVID-19 pandemic ravaged the Navajo Nation. As reported by the Centers for Disease Control (CDC), the COVID-19 incidence rate among Native Americans was 3.5 times higher than that of white individuals.[34] Once infected, Native American adults also had a higher risk of developing severe illness compared to other demographic groups. The Navajo Nation experienced one of the highest incidence and death rates in the United States, with more than 87,075 positive cases and at least 2224 confirmed deaths.[35] Following the pandemic, the life expectancy of Native Americans dropped from 71.8 years (in 2019) to 65.2 years (end of 2021).[36] At this point, no one on the Navajo Nation has been spared from the effects of the pandemic.

Past federal policies have cast a long shadow, leading to persistent health and socioeconomic disparities faced by Native Americans that made them ill-prepared for the onslaught of the coronavirus pandemic. These disparities are well documented and long-standing. Native Americans suffer higher rates of various chronic diseases, such as heart disease, obesity, and diabetes. They also experience one of the highest poverty rates in the United States.[37] Moreover, historical trauma has adversely affected Native communities and can exacerbate health inequities. For example, historical trauma can produce physiological stress, leading to epigenetic changes

---

[33] *Broken Promises, supra* note 13 at 65.

[34] Sarah M. Hatcher et al., "COVID-19 Among American Indian and Alaska Native Persons—23 States, January 31–July 3, 2020," *Morbidity and Mortality Weekly Report* 69, no. 34 (2020): 1166–67.

[35] Navajo Department of Health, *Dikos Ntsaaígíí-19 (COVID-19)*, accessed online, https://www.ndoh.navajo-nsn.gov/COVID-19 (as of February 1, 2024).

[36] Elizabeth Arias, et al., *Provisional Life Expectancy Estimates for 2021*, Vital Statistics Surveillance Report (2022), accessed online, https://www.cdc.gov/nchs/data/vsrr/vsrr023.pdf.

[37] National Community Reinvestment Coalition, "Racial Wealth Snapshot: Native Americans," accessed online, https://ncrc.org/racial-wealth-snapshot-native-americans/.

affecting health.[38] Other factors prevalent in tribal communities also have been linked to COVID-19 community transmission; specifically household size, shared transportation, and limited access to running water.[39]

During the pandemic, the public was told (1) to wash their hands frequently and (2) to stay home and practice social distancing. But, for those on the Navajo reservation, it was difficult to follow these public health directives due to the widespread water insecurity on the reservation. With over one-third of households lacking piped water delivery, these families must purchase bottled water or haul water, often from long distances. Hauling water is a time-consuming and laborious task. Hauling water is also more expensive. Navajo families pay an estimated 67 times more for hauled water compared to piped water.[40] As a result, families try to conserve water to meet all their needs, from drinking and cooking to cleaning and personal hygiene. The average Navajo resident uses seven gallons of water per day, compared to the average American's use of approximately 90 gallons per day (Fig. 2.2).[41]

The federal government has been aware of the poor water and sanitation conditions on tribal lands for well over a century. The 1928 Meriam Report found: "Sometimes it is difficult even to get enough to drink, so lack of cleanliness of body, clothing and homes is a natural consequence and is found with discouraging frequency."[42] Such continued conditions are unacceptable in light of the federal government's promise that the Navajo Nation would have a permanent and healthy homeland upon which they could thrive. And while the federal government has invested in modern water and sanitation systems as a means of eradicating waterborne diseases and stimulating economic prosperity, the majority of this

---

[38] Melissa Walls, et al., "Stress Exposure and Physical, Mental, and Behavioral Health among American Indian Adults with Type 2 Diabetes," *International Journal of Environmental Research and Public Health* 14, no. 9 (2017): 1074; Teshia G. Arambula Solomon, et al., "The Generational Impact of Racism on Health: Voices from American Indian Communities," *Health Affairs* 41, no. 2 (2022): 281–88.

[39] Hatcher, "COVID-19 Among American Indian and Alaska Native Persons," *supra* note 34, 1167.

[40] Navajo Nation Office of the President and Vice President, "E. Agency Council Rep., President Nez Provides Testimony in Support of Congressional Bills That Will Deliver More Clean Water to Navajo Communities," (June 4, 2022), accessed online, https://opvp.navajo-nsn.gov.

[41] U.S. Water Alliance and Dig Deep, *Closing the Water Gap*, *supra* note 1.

[42] Meriam, *The Problem of Indian Administration*, *supra* note 23.

**Fig. 2.2** Water hauling on Navajo Nation. Credit: Tara Kerzhner

investment bypassed reservations.[43] As a result, the Navajo Nation lacked the necessary water infrastructure, and therefore water access, to protect their communities against a public health threat like COVID-19.

## A Historic Moment

Without a doubt, the COVID-19 pandemic devastated the Navajo Nation, and more so because of systemic inequities rooted in the federal government's failure to uphold treaty promises and its trust responsibility to tribes. However, the pandemic has served as a call to action. One

---

[43] U.S. Congress, *Addressing Tribal Needs Through Innovation and Investment in Water Resources Infrastructures through the U.S. Bureau of Reclamation, Hearing on Energy and Water Development Appropriations for 2022 Before the House Committee on Appropriations and Subcommittee on Energy and Water Development*, 117th Congress (2021), (statement of Bidtah N. Becker, Associate Attorney, Navajo Tribal Utility Authority).

community member, Jeneda Benally, reflected on her hope when speaking with the media that the attention received during the pandemic will lead to positive change: "We need systems that invest in our people, that are not Band-Aid solutions but really, truly invest in the strength and resilience of our people."[44]

Early in his administration, President Joe Biden recommitted the federal government to honoring trust and treaty responsibilities to tribes when the administration acknowledged:

> The United States has made solemn promises to Tribal Nations for more than two centuries. Honoring those commitments is particularly vital now, as our Nation faces crises related to health, the economy, racial justice, and climate change—all of which disproportionately harm Native Americans.[45]

However, due to the Infrastructure Investment and Jobs Act (IIJA), for the first time in its history, the SFC Program received the full amount of funding for its reported need, plus administrative costs. As part of IIJA, the SFC Program will receive $3.5 billion over five years (fiscal years 2022 through 2026) (Fig. 2.3).

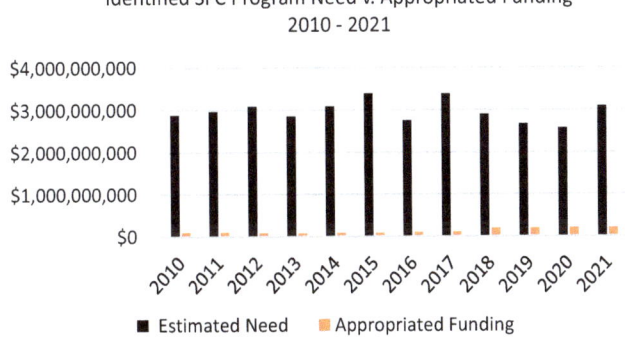

Fig. 2.3 Identified SFC program need vs. appropriated funding, 2010–2021. Credit: Heather Tanana

---

[44] NBC News, "'Hit us at our core': Vulnerable Navajo Nation fears a second COVID-19 wave," (Aug. 3, 2020), accessed online, https://www.nbcnews.com/specials/navajo-nation-fears-second-covid-19-wave/index.html.

[45] Memorandum No. 02075, 86 Fed. Reg. 7,491, 7,491 (Jan. 26, 2021).

Other federal agencies administering tribal programs also received additional funding. The Environmental Protection Agency plays a major role in ensuring that water quality standards are met and oversees the Drinking Water Infrastructure Grant Tribal Set Aside and Clean Water Indian Set Aside programs. These programs provide funding for tribal drinking water and wastewater infrastructure (respectively) and received supplemental funding of approximately $250 million each. Additionally, under the Inflation Reduction Act, the Bureau of Reclamation received $550 million to assist disadvantaged communities in the planning, design, or construction of water projects that will "provide domestic water supplies to communities or households that do not have reliable access to domestic water supplies."[46]

The enforcement of federal treaty and trust responsibilities to promote the health of Native Americans and ensure reservations are permanent homelands is necessary to protect tribes from another pandemic. The recent Congressional funding is the first step in the right direction. Federal policies contributed to conditions that made Native Americans more susceptible to the coronavirus. To ensure that the past does not repeat itself, the federal government must uphold its treaty and trust responsibilities to tribes. This includes protecting tribal public health, which requires clean, safe water access.

**Competing Interests Declaration** The author has no conflicts of interest to declare that are relevant to the content of this chapter.

---

[46] Public Law 117–169, Section 50232.

CHAPTER 3

# The Tribal Decline: Fort Hall Reservation and the Influenza Pandemic, 1918–1920

*Yvette A. Towersap*

### INTRODUCTION

On April 3, 2020, the Shoshone-Bannock Tribes Chairman Ladd Edmo reported to the tribal community the first positive case of COVID-19 on the Fort Hall Reservation, on Facebook Live. With this announcement, the Fort Hall Business Council, the governing body for the Shoshone-Bannock Tribes (hereafter "the Tribes") in southeast Idaho, immediately enacted a stay-at-home order for all reservation residents. Chairman Edmo urged the tribal community to "avoid close contact with sick people, avoid public gatherings, avoid all non-essential travel, and to designate one person to do necessary shopping."[1] The impact of COVID-19 extended to Indian Country as the Fort Hall Reservation residents began the health emergency that impacted their daily life for two years.

---

[1] Facebook Live, April 3, 2020, Shoshone-Bannock Tribes.

## Community Responses to New Health Challenges

As the COVID-19 pandemic quickly progressed, Shoshone-Bannock tribal leaders, health care professionals, and community members encountered twenty-first century challenges to the health and life of the community. Due to the high risk of infection from the air-borne virus, health officials and tribal leaders struggled to ensure the Fort Hall community remained healthy because common activities, such as in-person community or tribal staff meetings were deemed unsafe. Tribal leaders had to communicate with the local tribal community using new media and methods, work closely with an expanded group of health officials to identify and implement safety measures, and as the pandemic advanced, they had to determine how to protect highly vulnerable populations—the tribal elders and fluent speakers of the Shoshone and Bannock languages.

The Fort Hall community responded to COVID-19 in different ways. After decades of reliance on advanced Western medicine, some tribal members returned to their traditional medicines. Others turned to the safety and solitude of the outdoors, while some people stayed at home with extended family members. People reinforced their traditional spirituality with prayers, and all were urged to care for elderly and vulnerable tribal members. Some tribal members resisted medical advice, questioned if COVID-19 was a hoax, refused medications, and declined to wear face masks. As the COVID-19 pandemic evolved, tribal leaders struggled with incorporating health safety measures while sustaining Shoshone and Bannock traditions, as the number of COVID-19 deaths and funerals increased.

## Emergence of a New Virus

A few weeks earlier, in March 2020, the United States federal government recognized the significant risk of this new virus, and had initiated extraordinary efforts to track, monitor, and enact protective measures against what became known as COVID-19. It was a silent, killer virus that did not differentiate among political or reservation boundaries, race, or gender. At this same time, the media reported on previous infectious epidemics, such as the 2009 swine flu and the devastating 1918 influenza virus.[2]

---

[2] The 1918 influenza virus pandemic had many names, including the "Spanish flu," "the Great Influenza epidemic," grippe, and the flu.

## Can History Inform Current Decisions?

I questioned what lessons could be learned from tribal experiences with past infectious diseases that could be applied to the COVID-19 crisis. What was the past medical response, how did the Office of Indian Affairs (OIA) respond, and how did the Indian people react? What was the infection rate in 1918 among Native populations? What differences and similarities exist between the 1918–1920 influenza and the COVID-19 pandemic? As tribal health care and emergency officials developed mitigations and new strategies to communicate with the public, and engaged in active dialogue with local, state, and regional health entities, I wondered how history could inform current decisions. While I knew I might not be able to answer all these questions fully, I found the Shoshone and Bannock historical experiences of the 1918 influenza pandemic to be alarming and thought-provoking.[3] This is the story of the 1918–1920 global influenza pandemic on the Fort Hall Reservation and how the OIA responded. It identifies assimilation-related challenges to the communal Native culture that arose involving health care, education, housing issues, vaccinations, and quarantines, which complicated the delivery of effective health care for local Indian residents. As it turns out, several factors were common to both pandemics.

During the pandemic years from 1918 to 1920, the Bannock and Shoshone people living on the Fort Hall Reservation experienced a rapidly changing lifestyle complicated by an increased risk from the deadly influenza virus. As the global infections from influenza spread and killed millions of people, with no life-saving treatments or vaccinations available, the people of the Fort Hall Reservation also suffered.[4] The survivor story of Louise Truchot, a Shoshone-Chippewa-Cree, who worked as a matron

---

[3] This chapter uses several terms referring to Indians. In the historical documents, it was common to refer to the local Indian people of the Fort Hall Agency and Reservation, as Fort Hall Indians. To be historically accurate, I used the term "Indians" where the sources cite it. The contemporary Tribal government uses the terms Tribal members, or Tribal community when referring to community members for the Fort Hall Reservation. I use "Native American" interchangeably when referring to general non-specific Indian people.

[4] President Woodrow Wilson came down with a case of influenza during the negotiations of the Versailles Treaty, 1919, which ended the First World War, Alfred Crosby, *American's Forgotten Pandemic: The Influenza of 1918* (New York: Cambridge University Press, 1989), 195.

at the Fort Hall Boarding School in 1918, offers a window into the suffering of the Indians of this reservation.[5] Her story also details how people developed survival tactics that could be comparable to COVID-19.

## Assimilation and Viruses

The world suffered through the 1918 pandemic because there were no vaccines available to fight this strain of influenza, and with no effective medical treatments, the influenza virus was dangerous and lethal.[6] The Fort Hall Reservation was outside the authority of state and county health officials, so neighboring communities excluded the reservation community from health care. Some tribal members had the view that many non-Indians thought the people on the Fort Hall Reservation "was just Indians," and therefore, were indifferent to their suffering.[7] But the Native residents of the Fort Hall Reservation suffered more intensely from the 1918 influenza virus due to the assimilative efforts occurring at the same time, and the lack of effective medical services provided by the federal government.

## 1918 Influenza Virus

The influenza virus of 1918 was deadly nationwide and globally. Current scholarship indicates the influenza virus first appeared during the spring of 1918, re-occurred in the spring of 1919, and struck again in 1920.[8] It infected victims rapidly, usually within three days, and occurred in waves.

---

[5] There were several names for the Fort Hall Boarding School including the School Plant or the "big school."

[6] Jeremy Brown, *Influenza: The Hundred-Year Hunt to Cure the Deadliest Disease in History* (New York: Simon & Schuster, 2018), 84. Brown provided a biological and medical analysis of the virus. It was later determined that the H1N1 strain called Influenza A/South Carolina/1/18 was responsible for the influenza virus outbreak.

[7] Clyde Hall, interview on June 4, 2021.

[8] Crosby, *America's Forgotten Pandemic*, 203–204. For more information on the 1918 influenza pandemic at the national level see John Barry's, *The Great Influenza: The Story of the Deadliest Pandemic in History* (New York: Penguin Books, 2005). For state historical papers, please see Leonard J. Arrington, "The Influenza Epidemic of 1918–1919 in Southern Idaho," *Idaho Yesterdays* 32, no. 3 (September 1988): 19–29; HannaLore Hein, "Idaho's Response to the 1918 Influenza Pandemic: ISHS Briefing Paper No. 1" Idaho State Historical Society, August 31, 2020; and Kevin Marsh, "Influenza in Idaho: How the World's Deadliest Pandemic Shaped the Gem State," June 1, 2020.

During September and October, the virus raced across the United States. Wave upon wave of attacks hit regions throughout the nation, including Indian reservations. According to John Barry, the initial American victims were sailors who experienced violent symptoms, with victims suffering severe nosebleeds, bleeding from their ears, and coughing so hard that they ripped their abdominal muscles and rib cartilage. The infected withered in agony or delirium, and had massive headaches and body aches so intense it felt like bones were breaking. Some of the patients developed changing skin colors, with blue skin around their lips or fingertips, and some had darkening skin, to the point of almost turning black.[9] Cities and rural areas were swept up in the waves of the highly contagious virus and hospitals were completely overwhelmed with victims. This virus was so widespread and severe that the 1918 average life expectancy in the United States fell from 51 to 39 years old.[10]

## Impacts on Haskell and Indian Students

Native Americans are often overlooked in historical studies of the 1918 pandemic despite their early involvement. For example, Native American students who attended Haskell Institute, in Lawrence Kansas, in the spring of 1918, were some of the first victims of the influenza virus, with 100–300 students infected, resulting in numerous deaths. Several male students who were interested in military service traveled to the nearby Army base at Camp Funston, Kansas, and became infected. Just as other soldiers moving from base to base spread the deadly influenza virus, so did the Native American students who visited Camp Funston.[11]

## Influenza Impacts on Native Americans

Although Native American reservations had previously experienced epidemics of smallpox, influenza, pneumonia, trachoma, and syphilis, this new influenza virus stood out in how quickly it spread through reservations. As Native Americans traveled from reservation to reservation, they

---

[9] Barry, *The Great Influenza*, 2.
[10] Brown, *Influenza*, 60.
[11] Mikaëla M. Adams, "'A Very Serious and Perplexing Epidemic of Grippe': The Influenza of 1918 at the Haskell Institute," *The American Indian Quarterly* 44, no. 1 (Winter 2020): 1–35.

carried the virus with them. Depending on the tribal practices and travel patterns, influenza impacted reservation populations differently.[12] Despite such variations, Native Americans overall, along with other minority populations, experienced higher mortality rates than other Americans, paralleling what would occur a century later during the COVID-19 pandemic.[13] Between October 1, 1918, and March 31, 1919, the Office of Indian Affairs estimated about 24% of reservation residents nation-wide contracted influenza. From this group, 9% of the victims died, which was a mortality rate four times higher than among the general population of urban communities.[14] Another report indicated that Idaho had an American Indian mortality rate of 11.5%.[15]

### LOCAL RESERVATION RESPONSES TO INFLUENZA

In general, Indian reservations experienced high rates of influenza but received varying responses from local authorities. On the Colville Indian Reservation in Washington State, the Red Cross worked in conjunction with the Indian agencies and local county agencies to reopen an old hospital and to help the local Indians. The county sheriff visited numerous homes with corpses lying in the same room where the remaining living members were too weak and emaciated to bury their dead or to care for themselves. The local Indian police forbade the "indiscriminate visiting of the sick," which saved many lives. The Indians "found that mentholated Okanogan sagebrush was an infallible [*sic*] remedy for the Flu."[16] The

---

[12] Susan Mayer, "Four Pacific Northwest Reservations and the Influenza Pandemic From 1918 to 1919." Master's Thesis, Emporia State University, 2012, 10, 12–14. Mayer studied the Spokane, Nez Perce, Colville, and Yakama reservations.

[13] Crosby, *America's Forgotten Pandemic*, 228.

[14] Crosby, *America's Forgotten Pandemic*, 35.

[15] Tara A. Rowe, "Pocatello and the 1918 Spanish Flu," *Idaho State Journal*, April 10, 2020, accessed online, https://www.idahostatejournal.com/opinion/columns/pocatellos-and-the-1918-spanish-flu/article_639ca612-76f6-5ed2-9fda-afdec3e80d6f.html. This is an opinion column written to compare the 2020 COVID-19 pandemic with the 1918 Influenza pandemic.

[16] Mourning Dove and Jay Miller, editor, *Mourning Dove: A Salishan Autobiography* (Lincoln: University of Nebraska Press, 1990), 190–192. This autobiography included an essay on the Okanagan Indians' fight with the 1918 influenza and how the Red Cross was integral in helping their people.

Colville people nevertheless encountered numerous waves of the flu into the 1930s.[17]

On the Nez Perce Reservation, in Idaho, the Nez Perce people utilized treatments such as ceremonies, sweat lodges, and herbal medicines against the infections.[18] A second wave of flu appeared and lasted until February 1919 and a third wave occurred in May 1919. Again, in January 1920, tribal members were sickened with the flu, with the final wave striking in 1922.[19] Since the Nez Perce population was already struggling with respiratory diseases, a sanitarium was established for children due to a high tuberculosis rate of 75% on the reservation.[20] This sanitarium was the only medical facility for the Nez Perce in Lapwai and it only served those Nez Perce who lived in the immediate vicinity.[21]

## Research Challenges

Researching the history of health care in Fort Hall for this chapter was challenging. The most readily available sources are narrative and statistical annual reports submitted to the Indian Affairs Office by the Fort Hall Agency superintendents and physicians. These reports included sections from agency physicians, who wrote on schools, health, sanitation, and vital statistics, among other topics.

Recognizing the need for oral histories from tribal members, I made local inquiries seeking tribal informants who were willing to share family stories or memories, but this produced few results. One elderly woman over 70 stated, [in her family] "Indians refuse to talk about it, because so many people were sick. Many people died, so they never talked about that flu." Another elderly woman in her eighties indicated, "There was so many people who got sick. People were dying in their tipis and tents." Another elderly individual in her seventies reported her family had not shared family stories with subsequent generations, but she knew people had suffered during the influenza epidemic. Another person heard of "seeing Indians walking around wearing gauze masks. They all stayed away to avoid getting sick." Other tribal members deliberately ignored requests to discuss

---

[17] Mayer, *Four Pacific Northwest Reservations*, 71.
[18] Mayer, *Four Pacific Northwest Reservations*, 61.
[19] Mayer, *Four Pacific Northwest Reservations*, 32.
[20] Mayer, *Four Pacific Northwest Reservations*, 61.
[21] Mayer, *Four Pacific Northwest Reservations*, 59–60.

the timeframe, family impacts, and experiences. Only one individual has shared his family memories for this chapter—a descendant of Louise Truchot.[22] The fact that it has been over 100 years since the 1918 pandemic—combined with tribal family customs to avoid speaking of significant sickness—makes it difficult to accurately reflect individual memories within the community.

## Reservation Time and Space

The Fort Hall reservation was a different place in 1918 than it is today. It was only 51 years earlier that the President of the United States issued the 1867 Executive Order establishing the reservation. Although the U.S. was involved in the First World War, for the people of the Fort Hall Reservation, living and practicing the original traditions, customs, and beliefs of the Shoshone and Bannock people was still the norm. English was not the primary language, as most Fort Hall Indians spoke either the Bannock or Shoshone language. To conduct reservation business with the Indians, the OIA required native language interpreters. Old-style traditional medicines were still used, and they turned to medicine men for curing sickness. Nevertheless, the federal governments' forced assimilation policy was in full swing and Indian kids were being forcibly encouraged to attend public schools, day schools, or boarding schools.

## Assimilation, Cultural Changes, and Federal Policies

Major geopolitical attributes of the Reservation were still in development during the early 1900s. The Fort Hall town site was not yet established, but an Indian hospital had been established in 1902 and, in 1904, the new School Plant was built on the Fort Hall Reservation at a cost of $75,000. Congress authorized the allotment of lands at Fort Hall in 1910 and within four years, the OIA had approved 1863 allotments. Individual families were encouraged to live on their assigned allotments in the outlying areas throughout the Fort Hall Reservation. Approximately 1700 Native Americans were living on the Reservation, with many of them still living in tipis, tents, and some in the traditional wickiups. As late as 1920, rations were still provided, but were limited to those who could not physically

[22] Hall, Interview.

work to support themselves. Cultural changes were slowly being implemented among the Bannock and Shoshone residents.

Assimilation policies were taking a toll on the Fort Hall residents by 1918. Education was an ongoing component of federal efforts to "civilize" Indian children.[23] The 1887 Dawes Act further continued legal efforts to civilize Indians by breaking up tribal land bases into individual allotments with the intent of compelling them to become "agrarian farmers and assimilate into the mainstream."[24] OIA efforts to change Indian peoples' living standards included getting them to accept "white man medicine," live in houses instead of tipis and tents, earn wages if they were men, rather than hunting for subsistence, and educate the children by sending them to either public, day, or boarding schools. The final reduction of the original 1867 Fort Hall Reservation occurred with the 1898 Cession Agreement in which the tribes negotiated to sell land to the United States for the establishment of the town site of Pocatello.[25] The funds the tribes received as a part of the agreement were used to construct the Fort Hall School Plant, so essentially, the tribes paid for their own boarding school.[26] The School Plant later impacted the health of the Fort Hall students.

## Treaty Rights for Health and Medical Care

In accordance with the 1868 Fort Bridger Treaty, health and medical care was a guaranteed right to the Indians, and the US government committed to providing health care and facilities for the Shoshone and Bannock people. Articles III and X of the Fort Bridger Treaty provided guarantees that the United States would provide medical care for the Indians.[27] At that time, the OIA was the primary agency responsible for the health and welfare of the Shoshone and Bannock Indian residents of the Fort Hall Reservation.

---

[23] Colin Calloway, *The Indian History of an American Institution: Native Americans and Dartmouth* (Hanover, NH: Dartmouth College Press, 2010) 1.

[24] Donald Fixico, *Bureau of Indian Affairs*. Landmarks of the American Mosaic (Santa Barbara, CA: ABC-CLIO, 2012), 87–90.

[25] Congress approved it in the Act of 1900.

[26] "Annual Report, 1920," 39, *Superintendents Annual Narrative and Statistical Reports from Field Jurisdictions of the Bureau of Indian Affairs*, (SANSR) MI0II microfilm, Washington, DC: National Archives and Records Service, 1975.

[27] July 3, 1868 Treaty of Fort Bridger, Article III and X. 15 Stat 673.

## Previous Epidemics at Fort Hall

Health-wise, Fort Hall Tribal community members had suffered for decades from epidemics. Indians struggled with infectious diseases, such as trachoma (a highly contagious bacterial infection of the eyes, which can lead to blindness), measles, smallpox, influenza, and tuberculosis. Previous epidemics had frequently occurred in Fort Hall. In 1890, an outbreak of scarlet fever took place at the school with 68 children infected, eight deaths, and within the Indian camps, 38 adults died.[28] A measles outbreak in 1899 also struck the school in Fort Hall, but no deaths occurred as school health officials were able to successfully treat all the afflicted.[29] Physician reports indicate that from June 30, 1906, to June 30, 1920, another 24 epidemics of various diseases occurred (see Fig. 3.1).[30]

Although tuberculosis was the primary deadly disease that afflicted the people of Fort Hall, influenza was a common occurrence throughout the reservation. Historical reports vary when it comes to the disease mortality rate in Fort Hall. Historian Brigham Madsen reported that generally, "Influenza and pneumonia killed more than four times as many Fort Hall Indians in proportion to the deaths of that disease in Idaho. The death rate among the Shoshoni and Bannock was three times the national average."[31] As indicated by the statistics in Fig. 3.1, the health situation on the Fort Hall Reservation was already poor. The lack of physicians and overworked nursing staff along with the general assimilation policies led to increased vulnerability to infections from viruses and to high mortality rates among the Indian people.

## Tribal Distrust of Doctors

The 1918 influenza pandemic collided with the local Native population's high rate of distrust for hospitals, doctors, and schools. In 1880, Fort Hall Indian Agent John Wright sought to implement Captain Richard Pratt's educational model to "kill the Indian, and save the man," by educating

---

[28] John Heaton. "'Bad Medicine': The Shoshone-Bannock Rejection of the First Fort Hall Reservation Boarding School, 1880–1900," *Idaho Yesterdays* 51, no.1 (Spring/Summer 2010), 6–7.

[29] Heaton, "Bad Medicine," 8.

[30] *SANSR*, Annual Report, Dr. Wheeler, Section Two, Health section, 21 (M1011-049-0550).

[31] Brigham Madsen, *The Northern Shoshoni* (Caldwell, ID: Caxton Printers, 1980), 209.

## 3 THE TRIBAL DECLINE: FORT HALL RESERVATION AND THE INFLUENZA...

- 21 -

Section Two.                                                                    Health.

SUMMARY OF EPIDEMICS.
Epidemics of the Fort Hall School
Reservation occuring since June 30, 1906.

| Fiscal Year | Name of Epidemic | No. of School Patients | | | Prevalence on Reservation | | | No. Death on Res. | |
|---|---|---|---|---|---|---|---|---|---|
| | | M. | F. | Total | M. | F. | Total | M. | F. |
| 1907 | ............. | 0 | 0 | 0 | 0 | 0 | 0 | 0 | 0 |
| 1908 | Influenza | 27 | 48 | 75 | 21 | 26 | 47 | 1 | 3 |
| | Measles | 25 | 27 | 52 | 19 | 7 | 26 | 2 | 0 |
| 1909 | Influenza | 9 | 9 | 18 | 29 | 24 | 53 | 5 | 7 |
| | Chickenpox | 15 | 9 | 24 | 2 | 0 | 2 | 0 | 0 |
| | Mumps | 74 | 57 | 131 | 11 | 7 | 18 | 0 | 0 |
| 1910 | Influenza | 21 | 23 | 44 | 33 | 20 | 53 | 2 | 2 |
| | Dysentery | 0 | 0 | 0 | 15 | 5 | 20 | 1 | 0 |
| 1911 | Influenza | 9 | 12 | 21 | 17 | 15 | 32 | 3 | 4 |
| | Chickenpox | 7 | 4 | 11 | 0 | 1 | 1 | 0 | 0 |
| | Measles | 0 | 0 | 0 | 6 | 9 | 15 | 1 | 0 |
| 1912 | Influenza | 15 | 25 | 37 | 20 | 13 | 37 | 3 | 1 |
| | Smallpox | 0 | 0 | 0 | 14 | 4 | 18 | 0 | 0 |
| | Whoopingcough | 0 | 0 | 0 | 13 | 12 | 25 | 3 | 0 |
| 1913 | Influenza | 12 | 25 | 37 | 20 | 13 | 33 | 2 | 3 |
| 1914 | Influenza | 12 | 26 | 28 | 26 | 30 | 56 | 1 | 2 |
| 1915 | Influenza | 16 | 5 | 21 | 26 | 28 | 54 | 0 | 2 |
| | Chickenpox | 13 | 7 | 20 | 1 | 3 | 4 | 0 | 0 |
| 1916 | Influenza | 47 | 34 | 81 | 52 | 26 | 78 | 2 | 6 |
| 1917 | Influenza | 11 | 16 | 27 | 31 | 26 | 57 | 2 | 3 |
| | Measles | 39 | 50 | 89* | 33 | 36 | 69 | 6 | 8 |
| 1918 | Influenza | 15 | 14 | 29 | 38 | 47 | 85 | 3 | 0 |
| | Ger. Measles | 16 | 21 | 37 | 6 | 2 | 8 | 0 | 0 |
| 1919 | Influenza | 5 | 7 | 12 | 88 | 74 | 162 | 18 | 17 |
| 1920 | Influenza | 3 | 4 | 7 | 73 | 59 | 132 | 6 | 6 |
| | Mumps | 12 | 9 | 21 | 1 | 1 | 2 | 0 | 0 |
| | Dysentery | 0 | 0 | 0 | 15 | 14 | 29 | 0 | 0 |
| | Total | 400 | 430 | 830 | 534 | 450 | 984 | 61 | 63 |

* Death at school from measles

SUMMARY EPITOMIZED

| Name Occurrence. | Times | Number Cases | | | Number Deaths | | |
|---|---|---|---|---|---|---|---|
| | | M | F | Total | M | F | Total |
| Influenza | 13 | 597 | 595 | 1192 | 48 | 55 | 103 |
| Measles | 3 | 122 | 129 | 251 | 10 | 8 | 18 |
| Mumps | 2 | 98 | 74 | 172 | 0 | 0 | 0 |
| Ger. Measles | 1 | 22 | 23 | 45 | 0 | 0 | 0 |
| Dysentery | 2 | 30 | 19 | 49 | 1 | 0 | 1 |
| Smallpox | 1 | 14 | 4 | 18 | 0 | 0 | 0 |
| Chickenpox | 3 | 38 | 24 | 62 | 0 | 0 | 0 |
| Whoopingcoug. | 1 | 13 | 12 | 25 | 3 | 0 | 3 |
| Total | | 934 | 880 | 1814 | 62 | 63 | 125 |

**Fig. 3.1** Summary of epidemics, 1906–1920. Credit: Annual Report, Dr. Wheeler, Section Two, Health section, 21 (M1011-049-0550), *SANSR*

local Shoshone and Bannock children in local schools.[32] But the local boarding schools were often unhealthy for students. A scarlet fever epidemic in 1890 occurred at the Fort Hall Boarding School that infected 68 students and killed eight. It also infected and killed 30 people elsewhere

---

[32] Heaton, "Bad Medicine," 2.

on the reservation. In 1884, Fort Hall Agent A.L. Cook reported to the Indian Commissioner that "Indians are averse to sending their children to school, because their medicine-men have told them that the school was 'bad medicine, that those who attended it would die.'" Often, school officials were overwhelmed with sick patients and either forced Indian students to act as nurses, exposing them to infection, or provided no medical help at all.[33] Indian medicine continued to be used, involving medicine men, ceremonial prayers, sweat lodges, and traditional medicines for familiar ailments and conditions. But the new infectious diseases—smallpox, scarlet fever, influenza, trachoma, tuberculosis, syphilis, and pneumonia—overwhelmed the Indian practitioners.

## Quarantine and Vaccination History on the Reservation

Prior to the 1918 influenza pandemic, Fort Hall Reservation Indians had endured various infectious diseases and quarantines that sometimes involved the entire reservation population. In some situations, Shoshone and Bannock individuals traveled to nearby border towns for medical care, outside the knowledge of OIA. In 1912, an Indian mother went to a town doctor to treat her baby who had a skin condition. The town physician was horrified to diagnose the child with smallpox, and immediately quarantined the entire reservation, warning "any Indian leaving the reserve would be placed under arrest." A few days later, four other town doctors examined the baby, and they diagnosed the child with eczema. The quarantine order was lifted.[34] It was unclear if these private town physicians had the official authority to enact reservation-wide quarantines, yet they acted as if they did.

To maintain the general health of the Fort Hall Indians, the OIA had attempted to impose further Western medical services, including a vaccination program for smallpox. But participation was not always voluntary on the part of the Indians. In 1901, for example, a mandatory vaccination was enacted for smallpox. Individual Indians were entitled to $34.50, their share of a $10,000 land payment to the tribe, but Indian

---

[33] Heaton, "Bad Medicine," 7.
[34] Madsen, *The Northern Shoshoni*, 208.

superintendent Caldwell would not allow any Indian resident of the reservation to receive their payment unless they received this vaccination. Although the Indians widely protested, tribal leader Jim Ballard's support for the vaccination program ultimately swayed opinions in favor of the smallpox vaccination effort. As a result of his influence on the Fort Hall community, all but one individual received the vaccination.[35] This effort at mass vaccination reduced the cases of smallpox, as evidenced by Fig. 3.1. If it were not for Jim Ballard's support, the OIA's mandatory vaccination effort would likely have failed.

## Limited Health Services

Compounding the lack of trust, the limited medical staff had been unable to treat all Indian patients, even prior to the 1918 epidemic. Dr. Henry Wheeler was the primary physician from 1907 to 1932, where he oversaw over 2000 Indians, two hospitals, and regularly conducted home visits to patients who lived away from the Fort Hall Agency. He was assisted by only one nurse.[36] The OIA reported that these two people provided most of the medical care during the influenza pandemic of 1918 and beyond.[37] In 1918, Indians had to overcome their suspicion and distrust when Dr. Wheeler and his nurse came to their outlying camps to check on sick people. Knowing the infectiousness of the disease, he advised Indians to enact safety measures. He told them to make personal sacrifices, to wear a face cover, avoid visits to other families or tribal members, refrain from travel, and simply stay home.[38] The effectiveness of his advice is uncertain, but it was undoubtedly difficult for him to persuade the Bannock and Shoshone speakers to follow.

## Assimilation and Infectious Disease

For American Indians overall, two phenomena were occurring simultaneously: the influenza pandemic of 1918–1920 and the age of assimilation. This was when the federal government devoted considerable energy and

[35] Madsen, *The Northern Shoshoni*, 207.
[36] Madsen, *The Northern Shoshoni*, 208.
[37] *SANSR*, Annual Report, 1920, 20.
[38] *SANSR*, Annual Report, 1920, 20.

attention to the country's so-called Indian problem. The 1928 Meriam Report, which examined the general conditions of American Indians in the mid-1920s, concluded that federal Indian programs had been overall failures, and noted the deficiencies in OIA health programs. For example, the report cited the Indian Service's (the employees of the Office of Indian Affairs) failure to collect vital statistics, which prevented efficient planning, development, or operation of a sound public health program for Indians.[39] The Shoshone and Bannock Indians, and other Indian peoples, were still "reeling from these [lifestyle] changes when the virulent new strain of influenza began its deadly global march."[40]

## THE NEW FLU VIRUS HITS IDAHO AND FORT HALL

After escaping the milder first wave of infections that had swept other parts of the country in the spring of 1918, Idaho reported its first infections on September 30, when Canyon County reported cases to the Board of Health. On October 4, the State Board of Health voted that "all indoor public assemblages and places of amusement, excepting public and private schools, be closed at once and remain closed until further orders of the State Board of Health." By October 8, the first cases occurred in southeastern Idaho with 30 reported cases. Once in Pocatello, located immediately adjacent to the Fort Hall Reservation, the virus moved quickly. On October 11, Bannock County had zero cases, but the next day, 25 suspected cases were reported. Smaller waves continued, with the U.S. suffering its last outbreak in late spring of 1920. In southeast Idaho, Pocatello's last cluster of deaths came in the summer 1919.[41]

---

[39] Institute for Government Research, Meriam Report, "The Problem of Indian Administration." February 21, 1928. The Meriam Report. This was a study to examine the conditions of American Indians, including the economies, health, education, and federal government administration of federal programs.

[40] Mikaëla M. Adams. "#COVIDintheSouth: Social Distancing in the Age of Assimilation: The Influenza Pandemic of 1918–1920 in Indian Country," The Center for the Study of the American South, University of North Carolina, Chapel Hill, April 16, 2020, accessed online, https://south.unc.edu/2020/04/16/covidinthesouth-social-distancing-in-the-age-of-assimilation/.

[41] Tara Rowe, "Pocatello and the 1918 'Spanish' flu," *Idaho State Journal*, April 10, 2020.

## State and OIA Responses

The State of Idaho was unprepared for the 1918 influenza outbreak but later created new programs and guidelines.[42] Since the state was organized by counties, all their planning ignored Indian reservations because state law did not apply on reservations. No mandatory reporting to state health officials for reservation health statistics occurred. This jurisdictional gap explained why no information was available regarding influenza's impact on the Fort Hall Reservation in state documents.

On October 11, 1918, OIA Commissioner Cato Sells issued a stringent mass warning via a telegraph to all Indian reservation agents and superintendents. He wrote: "Spanish flu of virulent type spreading over [the] country with alarming rapidity[,] many superintendent [*sic*] reporting serious conditions." Commissioner Sells further recommended specific safety measures for Indian boarding schools to ensure sanitary facilities were available for Indian students, and required regular reports on the reservation health situation. He also directed school staff to "regulate temperature[,] avoid overcrowding[,] enforce isolation or quarantine[,]" and encouraged "all to cease all activities not urgently required so employers are available and other influenza work[,] employing extra help when strictly necessary[.]"[43] The Fort Hall Agency was ill equipped to handle the virus and was unable to meet these OIA demands, as indicated by the 1919 winter influenza statistics. Further, in January 1919, Superintendent H.H. Miller wrote that he is not requesting additional "special epidemic employees" to combat influenza because he did not think it was necessary.[44] Unfortunately, this was in the height of the sickness, and it is unclear if this was the recommendation of Dr. Wheeler.

---

[42] HannaLore Hein, "Idaho's Response to the 1918 Influenza Pandemic: ISHS Briefing Paper No. 1." Idaho State Historical Society, August 31, 2020. Idaho reorganized in 1919 to address these needs. In Idaho, state health authorities did not recognize influenza as a contagious disease, since it was considered a common illness. New rules and regulations were developed to prevent the spread of dangerous, contagious, and infectious diseases, after the state established regional and county health boards.

[43] Telegram from Office of Indian Affairs Commissioner Cato Sells to all Indian agents and superintendents, October 11, 1918.

[44] Letter to Commission of Indian Affairs, from Fort Hall Agency Superintendent H.H. Miller. January 18, 1919.

## 1919, THE DEADLIEST YEAR

In the spring of 1918, the United States encountered the first wave of infections, but Fort Hall avoided being impacted. The second wave of influenza in the fall of 1918, however, did strike Fort Hall with infections and deaths, which extended into the spring of 1919. The 1919 annual reports for the Agency Division (which focused on the outlying Indian camps), recorded the highest ever number of influenza cases, extending back to 1868, when the reservation was established. Since the school was closed, the population of the camps increased, "and where the population is, there illness will be also."[45] The rationale offered by Dr. Wheeler for these differences was that "the patients of the school have the best of care and timely medical attention while the camp patient is frequently his own victim of uncomfortable shelter and improvident manner of living, both of which are the twin birds of prey in illness."[46] It appeared that there was limited communication to the outlying allotment camps, where the majority of the Native people lived.

## INFLUENZA CASES AND MORTALITY

The data provided by the OIA during this time reveal startling and conflicting figures and conclusions, as indicated in Dr. Wheeler's monthly supplemental reports on the influenza cases and deaths in Fig. 3.2. In 1918, he reported 107 total cases of influenza, with 47 men infected, 85 women, and 22 school children. Deaths from influenza in 1918 consisted of nine victims, but since the virus struck Fort Hall at the end of the year, the 1919 data is more revealing. In 1919, a total of 174 total influenza cases were reported, sickening 88 men, 74 women, and 12 school children. A total of 30 individuals died from these infections.[47] This disturbing number of deaths came entirely from the Indian camps since the School Plant was then closed. Note that in Fig. 3.1, the number of deaths

---

[45] *SANSR*, Annual Report, 1919, Health, Agency Division, 84.

[46] *SANSR*, Annual Report, Health, 1920, Dr. Wheeler, 20. He is referring to two major problems occurring at the same time, inadequate medical care and inadequate housing. Influenza cases and death rates of students were only recorded when the school was open.

[47] Monthly letters to Horton H. Miller, Superintendent of Fort Hall Agency, from Dr. Henry Wheeler. October 1918 to September 1919.

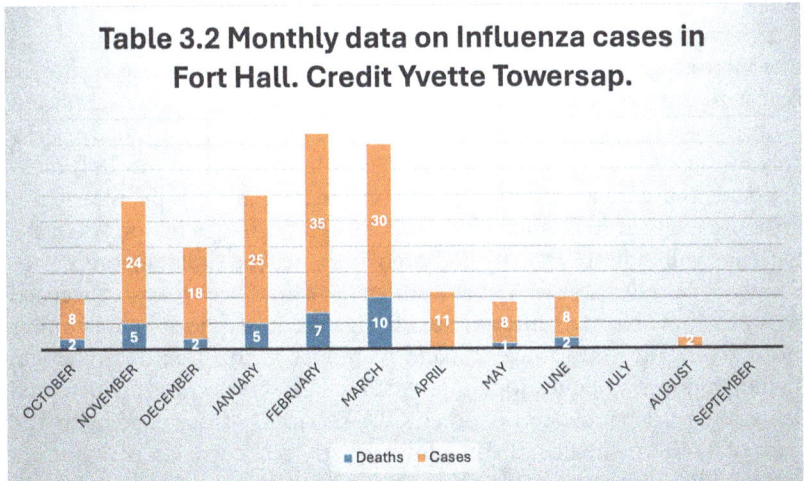

**Fig. 3.2** Monthly data on influenza cases in Fort Hall. Credit: Yvette Towersap

for 1918 to 1919 totals 38, but in Dr. Wheeler's monthly tallies, it shows 34. However, due to the difficulties of traveling on a horse and buggy in winter conditions, it is likely that the numbers changed as more cases were reported, and did not fully account for all influenza victims or deaths in Fort Hall.

Dr. Wheeler reported in 1920 that influenza had "struck Fort Hall 13 of 14 years, infected over a thousand patients, and had 100 deaths (9% death rate)" (see Fig. 3.1). He also noted that this influenza epidemic had a fatality rate that was four times greater than for all the other epidemics combined. Dr. Wheeler was concerned about the high death rate of influenza, and compared it to tuberculosis and measles, noting that "influenza is now more to be dreaded than tuberculosis."[48] He went on to point out that measles epidemics could be severe as well, as in 1917 when 15 people died of that disease, but noted that "measles, unlike influenza, is able to establish immunity … which prevents frequent return of that epidemic."[49]

---

[48] *SANSR*, Annual Report, 1920. Dr. Wheeler, 22.
[49] Ibid.

## Fears of Tribal Extinction

The increasing deaths, in large part attributable to influenza, in combination with a decreasing birth rate, led OIA officials to express significant concerns about "The Tribal Decline" in the years 1917–1920. In 1919 only 59 births were recorded versus 81 deaths.[50] Based on the 1919 census data, the annual agency report concluded that "the people of this Tribe are inclined to be short lived and are approaching a period when the age zone will indicate an early and premature decline simultaneously with a noticeable reduction of Tribal number."[51] Dr. Wheeler was concerned about the possible extinction of the Shoshone and Bannock people unless more assimilative efforts were made to influence tribal cultural change, including domestic education, improved medical services, and an increased delivery and dependence on other OIA services.[52] Combined with the fears of Western medicines, the almost-yearly reoccurrence of influenza and the high death rate made this a reasonable fear.

## Louise Truchot, Survivor

When the first waves of the 1918–1920 influenza hit, the hospitals were overwhelmed.[53] The agency physician repeatedly reported the students who stayed at the School Plant were more likely to not get sick or were able to be isolated in a safe location. Louise Truchot was a local survivor of the global influenza pandemic, and her story was shared by her great-great-grandson, Clyde Hall.[54] Louise was a matron at the School Plant, and several of her family members attended the school at the same time. She witnessed the waves of infections in the fall of 1918, as the school was closed due to sickness as both students and staff became ill. At that time, people wore gauze masks to reduce exposure to the virus, but it was too little, too late. The students were sent home, but they were already exposed, and they carried the sickness with them, and further exposed their families.

Before they closed the school, Louise became sick with the influenza and was quarantined at the school hospital, along with other sick school

---

[50] *SANSR*, Annual Report, 1919, Agency Division, 85.
[51] *SANSR*, Annual Report, 1919, 68.
[52] *SANSR*, Annual Report, Health, 1920, 67.
[53] *SANSR*, Annual Reports 1919, 1920, Schools.
[54] Hall, Transcript, 7.

employees. Her family would visit her through the windows. She told her family "You come to look for me at the windows to know if I was okay." They waved at each other to show she was okay. Food was brought to her until she recovered. None of her family became ill because they isolated themselves at their family ranch. Louise's daughter, Hazel Truchot, remembered, "It was a horrible time. There were lots of families who died, whole families who died."[55] This survivor's lone narrative was the only personal memory offered from the Fort Hall community, which—combined with the numerous individuals who indicated no family memories—only confirms the horrific human experience from the influenza pandemic.

## 1918 Health Mitigation Measures

The OIA realized the drastic implications of this deadly disease and its lethal impact on the local tribal community, but its efforts to mitigate the spread of the virus were mixed. During the pandemic, the OIA encouraged all Indians to quarantine at the various Indian camps, avoid visiting people, and avoid going to the Fort Hall Agency and town. When necessary, influenza victims were isolated at their home dwellings, but many Indians were infected, along with their caregivers. The OIA encouraged continued education at the boarding school and in the Indian camps. The Fort Hall School taught the older girls nursing, hygiene, care of infants and the health and sanitary management of the Indian home.[56] Dr. Wheeler traveled the reservation and camped among its inhabitants, "living like a traveling evangelist, constantly preaching the good news of personal cleanliness to the filthy ungodly." It is difficult to assess the effectiveness of Dr. Wheeler's attempt to spread the "gospel of sanitation among the Indian people of this reservation" because he admitted that "some Indians profit by it, and others appear to listen to it with a painful silence and other endeavors to rebuff it with argument prompted by a crude philosophy."[57] Given the challenges of communicating in three different languages, English, Shoshone, and Bannock, it is highly likely that

---

[55] Hall, Transcriptions, 5–7. The study of oral history and memories is often controversial by non-Indian historians due to a lack of written sources, but Mr. Hall indicated he was told that same story over and over, for years, from his grandmother, Hazel Truchot.

[56] *SANSR*, Annual Report, Health. 1920, 70.

[57] Ibid, 71.

this effort was less successful than Dr. Wheeler claimed. When communicating with Native communities, it is important to remember that words matter, along with tone, and expression, and it is clear that his view of his Native patients was colored by his privilege.

## HOUSING AND DISEASES

Changing Native American housing had been a key goal of federal assimilation policies, but reservation housing nevertheless became a health care problem during periods of infectious diseases. Annual OIA reports included an inventory of housing structures that described poor sanitary conditions and acknowledged that housing was a key health factor for individual Indians in the years during and following the 1918 pandemic. The 1920 inventory counted 50 tepees in use, 250 tents, 65 cabins, 40 frame structures and 5 cottages, totaling 410 Indian dwellings for the Fort Hall Reservation.[58] As described in the 1921 report, more permanent log cabins were only used seasonally.[59] During the pandemic and thereafter there were also a few people still living in wickiups.[60] Indian patients used wickiups as a "retreat for confinement cases and the separation of the sick from the rest of the family and for the aged of the family who desire to be isolated. On account of its small size, it is very limited for the visits of the medical man or any spectators." Dr. Wheeler's report indicated that the moon house was a small tent, used reportedly for sanitary conditions, and was deemed better than a wickiup. OIA reports described tepees as being "inconvenient and insanitary [*sic*]."[61]

Tribal families used moon houses as separate temporary residences for menstruating women, or for women who were completing their 30-day post-birth recovery with their newborn. Traditionally, limited family members can attend to the person staying inside, so adopting the moon

[58] *SANSR*, Annual Reports, 1920, 28.

[59] *SANSR*, Annual Reports, 1921, 22. "Some of them look more like a chicken house with one window and one door and the size could be expressed by saying that they are 7 × 8 feet on the clear inside and only six feet to roof which is covered with dirt. The floor is dirt; the window 2 × 1 feet and the door is large if it is 5 × 2 in size. Like the tent, it must be heated by a stove and it would be warm in winter but it would have but little ventilation. Such is the brief account of the small size of cabin not seldom found on this reservation, yet they serve for shelter mostly in the winter and are abandoned in the summer for the tent or wickeyup."

[60] *SANSR*, Annual Reports 1919, Sanitation.

[61] *SANSR*, Annual Reports, 1920, Sanitation, Housing, 25.

house or the wickiup or even tents to temporarily house sick people was not uncommon. As the OIA pushed local tribal families to transition into more permanent housing, on their newly assigned allotments, Indians gradually adapted by moving into wall tents, or constructing cabins, but still having the familiar wickiup, tent, or tipi immediately adjacent.

The OIA staff regarded Indian housing as problematic, not always recognizing the health advantages of tipis and tents and adjudging the traditional structures as primitive and non-progressive. However, traditional tipis and wickiups had advantages because they were mobile, provided good ventilation, and Indians were accustomed to living in these types of dwellings. Health-wise, in contrast, wood frame structures were often overcrowded, lacked air ventilation, and did not have sanitation amenities. This created a vulnerable situation where multiple generations of family members who lived in one home became sick and easily infected others. This health problem was affirmed in 1900, when Dr. G.M. Bridges reported that "many of the lung-associated ailments were due to the close confinement in school dormitories and in the new frame houses being furnished for Indian families. The Indian home owners were given only one-half a window [due to lack of federal funding] which was set in a solid frame and could not be raised or lowered."[62] Although the students at the Fort Hall Schools were less infected, the outlying Indian camps were greatly affected by the flu virus.[63] As more local Indians tried to live on their new allotments, they still moved from location to location quite frequently, for social and economic purposes, which likely spread the influenza virus. This led to the conflicting perspectives of OIA on housing, as assimilation goals conflicted with both epidemics and pandemics. Even though the OIA was well aware of the dangers of infectious diseases, problems with wood frame cabins, and of their trust responsibility to Native Americans, insufficient funding was allocated to ensure healthy reservation communities.

## Discussion

Understanding the 1918 influenza pandemic and later waves of influenza among Native American communities poses certain challenges for scholars. The medical uncertainty in the early twentieth century, especially in

---

[62] Madsen, *The Northern Shoshoni*, 207–208.
[63] Madsen, *The Northern Shoshoni*, 207.

Indian Country, made it difficult to distinguish the more lethal flu virus from the more common form of influenza. As Fig. 3.1 shows, Dr. Wheeler indicated in his report for the period 1906–1920 that Fort Hall experienced contagious diseases regularly. In fact, infections and deaths from influenza occurred every year, except for 1907. Another question is whether the 1918 influenza virus was the direct cause of many of the deaths attributed to it, or whether these were due to a secondary bacterial pneumonia or other underlying health conditions. An additional reason for uncertainty about deaths during this time was the tribal tradition of not naming infants or recording their birth, until they survived to an older age. As a result, the Fort Hall Agency vital statistics often failed to record younger victims who died during this time.

Conducting research on this 100-year-old viral pandemic was challenging and difficult due to limited and incomplete sources. The lack of oral histories from local victims and their families is a sizable gap in the historical record, but as noted earlier, local families avoid discussing the extreme sickness in their community. The difficulty of exploring this major health event in Idaho is compounded by the lack of victim narratives or compelling evidence. It is hoped with additional informants that the story of the Fort Hall people can be more fully revealed—but respecting the tribal customs of avoiding speaking of that difficult time—it is not likely to occur.

## Lessons Learned for Surviving Future Pandemics

There are both significant comparisons and contrasts between the 1918 and 1920 influenza pandemic and the 2020 COVID-19 pandemic. Both crises inflicted substantial suffering and sorrow, with incredible losses of community members and elders, the carriers of our tribal traditions and activities, and our tribal languages. As the media shared stories about previous pandemics—of health measures taken in 1918, of gauze masks, of food delivery to patients, and lines of makeshift hospital beds filled with sick patients—the COVID-19 experience was eerily similar. COVID-19 temporarily changed tribal activities, but also enabled tribal members to empower themselves. Tribal members embraced making facemasks using tribal-themed materials and digital technology to allow internet communications with each other, and across the Fort Hall community. The Tribes returned to small individual "COVID-19 houses" that resembled wall tents or moon houses, for individuals infected with COVID-19. Our people had to adjust how we conducted traditional activities, from birth to death. But we also emphasized the need to take care of our people, to continue our spiritual ways, or for some, to learn or relearn our spiritual traditions and prayers. Our traditional plant medicines were proven, again, to be valuable, and effective. Yet, we choose to accept the value of contemporary medicines, of vaccinations, and prescribed quarantines, and some of the community adopted other health safety measures, such as wearing masks, washing hands, and social distancing.

Tribal government interactions included active and regular discussions and regular coordination with regional and national Indian Health Service administrators, along with regional and state health agencies. The Fort Hall Business Council regularly consulted with the Idaho governor and congressional delegation representatives and Indian Country supporters to improve federal policy for health care. In comparison, Dr. Wheeler also reached out to the tribal community to advise tribal individuals of health safety measures that were very similar to the COVID epidemic, albeit in a condescending manner. It was uncertain how effective Dr. Wheeler's solo efforts were. Overall, the OIA and later the Indian Health Service did try to protect and help the sick people of Fort Hall in both situations, but combating a global respiratory pandemic was almost overwhelming. Future pandemic communication methods and protocols must be prepared to immediately respond to future infectious diseases.

Many of the 1918 pandemic problems persist and have impacted the 2020 pandemic. Indian housing remains inadequate as we continue to have multiple generations living in one household, increasing the health risks from infectious diseases. Health care services and funding have not increased to sufficiently provide for Indian health and medical needs, and the 2020 pandemic exacerbated these inadequacies. Although on-reservation vaccination rates during the COVID-19 pandemic were higher than off reservation, more efforts are needed to achieve a 100% vaccination rate on the Fort Hall Reservation. Tribal education was also impacted as schools turned to virtual learning, with limited results.

It was ill fated that the 1918 influenza virus struck during major federal policies forcing systemic and cultural change on American Indians. That influenza strain produced devastating impacts by highlighting deficiencies in medical care, housing, health care, safety standards, and the distrust people back then had of non-Indian medicine. As discussed, this 1918 pandemic was not the first epidemic crisis the Fort Hall community had suffered, nor will COVID-19 be the last; future planning to prepare for other epidemics is necessary to protect the community. Tribal communal cultures will not change, but the problem of contagious disease must be thoughtfully planned to overcome future challenges.

Mirroring the 1919 influenza epidemic, just as the Truchot children visited Louise Truchot through the window of the school hospital in 1919, during the COVID-19 epidemic, tribal member families also visited their sick family members through windows and used iPads while they were in the intensive care unit (ICU) at the hospital. In the case of my aunt who was exposed and was deathly sick with COVID-19, compassionate hospital staff allowed family members to enter ICU rooms wearing full-body protection with gowns and respirators, for brief emotional in-person visits with her. Family members offered prayers and blessings to help prepare for her journey into the afterlife. Just as the Truchot children stood outside looking at Louise's hospital room window, 102 years earlier, we also stood in the hospital parking lot in that early morning, but we began the mourning process.

The Tribes recognized the overall community loss of each COVID-19 victim. In 2021, the Tribes held a unique honoring for all the people who succumbed during this time, proclaiming it was important to remember, honor, and offer respect to the victims and families. The victims of the 1918–1920 pandemic should not be forgotten. It is imperative to prepare for future pandemics by remembering and learning from the past sickness and its victims, even though the memories are traumatic and painful. The question of how to address modern pandemics with modern Western science and medicine for tribal communities and reservations is best answered by using contemporary health and medical care in a respectful manner that reinforces, and where possible, engages native beliefs, practices, and communalism.

**Competing Interests Declaration** The author has no conflicts of interest to declare that are relevant to the content of this chapter.

CHAPTER 4

# Aunties of Resilience: Decolonization During COVID-19

*Jennifer Frazee*

The siege of colonization wages war on multiple fronts in Native American communities, one of which has been against means of providing community support. Policies designed to weaken family units have included removal, forced urbanization, ethnocide through boarding schools, and lack of investment and barriers to opportunities for Natives that forced our people to seek careers and futures in regions far from home. The cracks in traditional foundations created by such policies left our people vulnerable to crises such as the COVID-19 pandemic.

When COVID hit, folks who were able to maintain their communities faced the disproportionate dangers of diseases that ravage underserved and underrepresented communities. Because of colonization, those of the Native diaspora were also left to face a deadly virus without the support of family nearby. Even faced with such adversity, however, we exhibited the strength of Nations that have refused to be broken for over 500 years. Our communities' responses during the pandemic illustrate the resilience and skill that enable us to thrive even when the deck is stacked against us. But,

J. Frazee (✉)
Connors State College, Warner, OK, USA
e-mail: jennifer.frazee@history.ok.gov

© The Author(s), under exclusive license to Springer Nature Switzerland AG 2024
F. King, W. Davies (eds.), *COVID-19 in Indian Country*,
https://doi.org/10.1007/978-3-031-70184-9_4

I cannot tell you of COVID in Indian Country without first telling of Indian Country before COVID.

When I was growing up, I spent roughly half a year with my family, still living in the Choctaw community they had built after a removal spanning the 70 years from the 1830s to 1903. My community stamped its legacy into my spirit during the many family and community functions, led and held together by the aunts, when we gathered to care for one another in times of joy and grief. Community was the all-encompassing feeling that shaped my early childhood and one I long and grieve for in turn. Through this experience, I learned we had the good fortune and blessing to have responsibilities and a duty to care for one another, not rights that isolated us from the world. Because of this responsibility to one another, we knew there were just as many people there to help us as we were there to help. And as our people continued the process of rebuilding and carrying on with life, each event and meeting was met with food to sustain us. From Ohoychisba bringing corn to the good humans who helped her when people first began to walk this land to the meal my mother brought to me as I recovered from surgery, food has held a place of importance in the tending of our people.

Perhaps my early life experiences explain why I am so food-driven. This is because most of our gatherings revolve around the love that it is to feed each other and the many ways there are to share affection in the process of feeding and feasting. My cousin, Anson for example would tease his mother, my Aunt Joyce, about her biscuit and how he had to be careful not to drop it or it would crack off a corner of the table, even as he happily ate his fill. The happiness on my grandpa's face when the joyful scent of fresh cooked breakfast brought my brother and sisters quickly from their morning beds. The gratitude I felt for my grandpa when he made salt meat and fry bread for my cousins and I to take into the woods as we explored the day away.

When hardship came, we gathered at the church to lean on one another and eat delicious foods made by family that dealt with their grief by providing sustenance to the ones they loved. Special people who tended to their loved ones' stomachs so their hearts could deal with loss. At times of happiness, we maintained the energy to celebrate with dishes passed down through generations of women and tastes of new recipes excitedly shared. These meals were created from vegetables planted with care and forethought and tended to by loving hands with the intention that they be enjoyed upon harvest by specific people. Perhaps a cousin grew tomatoes because an aunt loved to eat them like apples. Or a brother made sure to sow beans because his sibling enjoyed them in winter soups. It is an equally great feeling to eat food prepared by someone who took time from their day to gather the ingredients because they knew someone coming to the singing loved one recipe or another. They selected items with the intention of caring for the members of the community they would soon see.

My early memories are full of the scent of fish cooked right where they were caught; of savory stews bubbling and chicken fried on wood burning stoves; and moist flavorful cakes, dumplings, beans and ham, pashofa and banaha, laid among the Jell-O and pudding on long tables to serve all who came. With the memory of food come the sounds of us kids, four generations from the 1903 removal, running in delirious happiness through relatives' yards, church grounds, and woods, stopping in camphouses or kitchens to sneak food cooked by aunts two generations from removal and watched over by hungry Elders before we disappeared again. I remember the sounds of singing from the church and conversation from the aunts carrying out the tasks that made a gathering of Choctaws into an experience. I feel the echo of full body laughs that had cousins rocking back and forth against one another, eyes nearly closed with delight in my own bones. Above all, I remember children running around the country safe in the knowledge that all adults there accepted the blessed responsibility of caring for every one of us. I remember hearing the histories and stories—memories being shared and passed on. All in Chahta Anumpa, Choctaw language, woven through with English as they directed us kids to help, gather, and pass on messages. That they had to use English to speak to their kids rather than their first language is one illustration of the colonization that sent us into the pandemic at a disadvantage.

Many of my cousins and I did not speak Chahta. To some that may seem a small thing; after all, the world around us had been created to cater to European American comforts. But language carries tradition, stories, and connections that allow a people to not only survive but thrive. As a young adult, I wondered why none of our parents pushed us to learn our language. Later, I realized that their parents, our grandparents, did not teach them, did not force the issue, or did not have the time. The darker reason, however, was some of our grandparents were the product of boarding schools. My own grandfather attended Carter Seminary in the 1950s, before the Nations took the education of our people back from the European Americans. Schools in that time were designed to erase the Native and replace them with European American beliefs and systems. As our language is our history, the blood that ties our generations and people together, it was one of the first things children were forced to leave behind.

The children of those schools were taught the language was bad, wrong, backward. If they did not listen, they were taught the language would bring them pain. After a time, the teaching left scars of trauma preventing generations from passing on the language to their children. And so the language that carried the continuance of a community, the spirit and strength of the people was not passed on as widely. Fewer of us learned the lessons that guided our ancestors and the reasons for banding together and we became susceptible to the new version of history that did not include our people.

Loss of language was not the only impact of colonization. Concerted efforts to build systems of racism since European arrival resulted in a distinct lack of opportunities for Native families to succeed in the newly created country. Laws that prevented Natives from settling in certain areas, allotment, and the following tricks used to take ever more land allowed for poverty and mental health issues to take root. Long traditions of European Americans who discouraged Natives from participating in society meant better careers and job paths were closed to people who looked like my grandfather. Those same traditions taught people who looked like my aunts the places they belonged in didn't span much further than domestic work or homemaking. There were those who challenged that ideology, but it required an intense fight, knowledge of resources, and always contained the possibility of danger.

My mother's generation did not escape the impact of colonization as generational trauma extracted its payment. Whole groups of her generation moved away from home in search of opportunities, partnerships, and dreams that could not be easily realized were they to stay in their communities. As hers was the first generation not legally required to attend boarding schools, the wish to travel away from the effects those schools had on previous generations and communities under constant siege must have been a powerful lure.

Boarding schools and removal stories taught children to be ashamed of their culture or they would be harmed. Assimilation policies insisted that progress required the old and uncivilized to make way for the new. Parents and grandparents grew afraid of their children being harmed for participating in traditions or defiantly angry at the inhuman behavior of colonizers. For whatever reason, an entire generation was shaken up and scattered, many of them becoming lost in the process. Some found the burden of those traumas too heavy to carry and died trying to rid themselves of the weight of them, leaving their children to be raised by family still living.

Those who moved away had to create new identities without the structure of tradition and community to support them. They had to make the choice for their children while losing out on access to that tradition and community that had sustained our people for generations. They made those decisions out of desperation, for chances of better lives, something new, something more, further rendering communities and cultures. The children of those who moved away had to learn to navigate life feeling unmoored, untethered, as though they did not quite belong. They did not get to hear stories full of traditional lessons, learn the recipes passed down from one hand to another, help maintain each other's homes, babysit for family, carry loads, or learn the language or the thousand other ways a community and member claim one another.

Those who stayed dealt with the loss of family dwindling in size as Elders passed and friends moved away to chase their dreams. They lived with the impacts of racism that meant their parents were denied loans; poverty and self-medication sapped their strength and hope; some professions had doors firmly shut; and safer or progressive neighborhoods were closed to them. They encountered the unique issues that come with being a member of a community that has heavy stereotypes levied against it. One or two Natives may be safe, but a whole community has a strength that terrifies those who wish to eradicate them. Those who stayed watched land that had been promised to their family as long as the grasses grow and the waters flow steadily shrink while their histories were erased and misshapen in the schools their children attended.

And no matter whether one was a child of those that stayed or the child of those who left, with the passing of each person, there was one less lifeline binding the community together. As Elders died, their children lost the anchors that held them to the heart of the community. Since the Elders did not always pass traditions to the next generation, those too began to disappear. Each death meant one less familiar person to anchor the scattered people to the ancestors and the strength that sustained us for centuries. People grew up and life got busy, some of us began to forget and questioned why we should go to this singing or that family reunion. With each loss of an anchor, some of us wondered when we would begin to seem like an interloper rather than a member of that community.

My grandfather died when I was in my teens, and our community closed ranks around us once we came back home to grieve. Even deep in the pain of loss, I could feel the arms of his sisters who loved me that had also loved him. I could talk to the folks who brought him back to life with their stories and memories of him. I saw the faces of my cousins and friends that I hung around with as a kid and they comforted me, joked with me, took my mind off the thought of continuing in a world that contained my grandpa, vmafo, no longer. My people. People that belonged to me and to whom I belonged. But because my family had built a life far away, we did not stay long and over time I lost so much more than just him.

When my aunt died, I was in my late twenties and the group of people my age was a bit smaller. Some of the Elders had passed on and were not there to encourage their children to help us carry on the memory. When we gathered for a family thanksgiving just before the pandemic, I saw fewer of the familiar faces, and only a handful of the kids I'd run around with. Since I'd lost contact over the years without the internet and no phones to keep in touch, I had no idea where their lives had taken them or who they had become. Every year since we moved, more of our people died way too young or left the community in some form because of illness, depression, self-medication, or broken ties. Policies designed to assimilate or eradicate Natives took their toll in ways big and small, seen and unseen, as the systems put in place long ago moved in perpetual motion, undermining our people to this day. Generational trauma, forced poverty, disinformation, and lack of access created the perfect conditions to chip away at a people, each tragedy and disaster swiping more and more into the abyss.

By the time the pandemic hit, we only made the four-hour trip to see family for funerals if we could get time off work and for one family reunion. We were too far away from each other to share strength and had fewer connections to hear from those who needed help. If our Elders were alive, they would have continued to maintain their gardens, cook, sew, and check up on each other, but many of them were long gone. If we had not had to move, we could have been part of the chain that dropped off food on each other's porches, drove sick family members to the doctor, shouldered burdens when others needed a break. We would still be able to undertake the work of nourishing one another with healthy foods grown by loving hands and made into dishes that were a medicine to the body and the soul.

Those of us far away had to isolate in smaller numbers, with three or four households to pick up groceries, or provide other forms of help where once we had a whole community to lean on. When family got sick back home, we had to wait helplessly to hear how they got on from afar. We were not there to help each other translate or understand the news that was coming in or make sense of a world gone crazy overnight. And since U.S. policies designed to disintegrate and eradicate Natives resulted in severely underrepresented and marginalized populations, our communities had very few supports to protect us when the entire nation grasped for supplies and help. Marginalized communities are already purposefully weakened, leaving them with fewer layers of protection. This means when disasters strike, they are usually the first casualties and the Elders and poorest of these groups are the most vulnerable. During the pandemic, we lost Elders in terribly high numbers. Those Elders were the bridge between our past and our future.

The fear and worry that my family might have little protection or few resources became reality when I heard my cousin Anson of the quiet jokes and quick wit, had become ill and was hospitalized. He had diabetes, a disease that is one of the more peculiar results of colonization. With a heavily burdened health care system leaving less access to regular monitoring, it is easy for diabetes to snowball into serious illness. My cousin had fewer family members as the years went by to help maintain all that had been left in his care, and with his parents' and brothers' illnesses and deaths, his health got away from him. He caught an infection that quickly spread, requiring the need for surgery but with COVID-19 raging like wildfire, beds, surgeons, and nurses were all taken up. Eventually, my cousin was transferred to a hospital in Texas, hours away from family. My eldest uncle wore himself out traveling back and forth to Texas in between caring for other sick family members as he was the only one able to by this point in the pandemic.

I made plans to take off work and travel to stay with him as soon as I was released from quarantine, but his release came before mine. I called his hospital at midnight to make sure I would be able to enter the hospital since I'd arrive in the early hours of the morning and was told my cousin had just passed. He was born into a noisy, big, loving community and died all alone and far from those who loved him.

Even his funeral was impacted by signs of change and brokenness. Where once we would have gathered together at our church for the care of our loved ones, both living and dead, for Anson we gathered in a funeral home. The room was barely filled when prior to COVID our family from all around would have been present. The smells of fire, decades-old wooden buildings lovingly maintained, and delicious foods laid out on long tables by the aunts were replaced by quick meals and moments snatched before family had to disperse back to far away homes and to jobs with little or no leave time left after a year of COVID, quarantine, and shutdowns.

COVID disproportionately impacted marginalized communities, but the people of those communities did not just surrender to the inevitable. The impacts of COVID worked as a catalyst, a spark that lit the fire within communities across the globe, to stand up and make changes. Nations took advantage of technology, like businesses and companies, and disseminated lost knowledge to many citizens unable to come home and learn. Those of generations stilted by the diaspora awoke to new ways of connecting to community as traditional knowledge keepers worked to share this important information and history. The biggest impact for me personally is the wide and colorful world that opened up when I began to learn the first language my grandfather ever spoke. The memories of community became clearer and closer; learning my peoples' history in their own words solidified in me a strength that comes from taking hold of the lifeline that connects a descendant to their ancestors. Across all of Turtle Island, Natives were able to overcome adversity and renew or strengthen commitments to fighting for the survival and success of their people in an echo of the ways of their ancestors.

This generation of Native Aunties took the knowledge of their people and began to build community on the internet. When one space closed to them, they opened new avenues for sharing knowledge, lessons, medicine, skills, and trades along with methods of resistance against forces that would harm them. Communities gathered in support of one another, communicating and sharing resources not only between towns in a state but across the nation and eventually the globe. Just a few generations from removal and descendants are showing what it is to be all that our ancestors hoped for.

**Competing Interests Declaration** The author has no conflicts of interest to declare that are relevant to the content of this chapter.

PART II

# Community Well-Being

The COVID-19 pandemic revealed, as many crises through generations, how many Indigenous peoples turn to ancestral teachings and values of community well-being. They have come together to heal, protect, and respect one another, not only as individuals but also as kin that seek healthy relationships with interconnected human and nonhuman relatives in their homelands. In this section, three chapters delve into the voices and relations of community that sustain Native Americans through the darkest times.

Coeditor, Farina King, writes, "A Vigil," which reflects her positionality—"intersecting subjectivities (e.g. class, race, gender, sexuality)" and "personal and professional experiences, beliefs, and values"—by recounting her experiences as a Diné professor at Northeastern State University (NSU) in Tahlequah, homelands of the Cherokee Nation and United Keetoowah Band of Cherokees in Oklahoma.[1] Previously known as the Cherokee National Female Seminary, the Cherokee Nation founded and operated the school, which became one of the institutions of higher learning with the largest populations of Native American college students in the United States. King, a professor of history and Native American Studies, organized a vigil to honor those lost to the pandemic, especially her beloved aunt Florence, which drew attention from local media. King intertwines her experiences with those of her Diné father, Phillip Lee Smith, who at the time was serving as a physician in Monument Valley, the

---

[1] See Liz Atkins and Vicky Duckworth, eds. *Research Methods for Social Justice and Equity in Education* (Cham, Switzerland: Palgrave Macmillan, 2019).

Navajo Nation, where he witnessed and tried to abate mortalities brought by the coronavirus.

Father then follows daughter as Phillip Lee Smith reflects on his work as a "frontline medical provider," or azee'íłʼíní as Diné call a doctor, for the Navajo Nation during the pandemic. He underscores what he learned during that crisis and his prior decades of medical service to Diné and other Indigenous people. Dr. Smith portrays a medical care system (including the IHS) that had the ample experience and well-suited design to address infectious threats in the Navajo Nation but was nevertheless underfunded and outpaced by COVID's intensity in exploiting "the residual high vulnerabilities of the Diné families." There were simply too few hospitals and medical workers to meet the pandemic surge. Dr. Smith also conveys hopeful messages about the power of vaccines and the "patience, kindness, love, and good in people" shown through the depths of the pandemic. "Other infectious pathogens will come into our midst in the future," he concludes. "To address these new challenges, we can learn from the past, plan for the future, and live in the present."

Highlighting oral histories led by and for Muscogee (Creek) citizens, Midge Dellinger and RaeLynn Butler of the Muscogee (Creek) Nation Historic and Cultural Preservation Department share Muscogee voices about the pandemic. Muscogee people, including leaders, remember the Road of Misery, or removal that expelled them from their homelands in the Southeast to present-day Oklahoma in the northeastern part of the state. Muscogee people exerted their resilience through an oral history project that focused on 40 Mvskoke community members to protect their people's knowledge about how they fought against the invisible killer—the virus. Community well-being stems from learning and practicing being a good relative who honors the lives of people through all generations.

# CHAPTER 5

# A Vigil

*Farina King*

In remembrance and honor of nihimá Florence and other victims of Dikos Nstaaígíí-19 (COVID-19).

My father delivered me in the place of "tangled waters," Tó Naneesdizí, at an Indian Health Service (IHS) hospital where he worked as a physician. His hands were the first human touch to my skin. The air, water, and land of our ancestors, Diné Bikéyah, embraced me in my mortal form.[1] My father continued to work for IHS for many years, and then he moved directly from retirement to a full-time position as a senior clinician and family and community medicine physician with the Utah Navajo Health System (UNHS) in Tsé Bii' Nidzisgaii, or Monument Valley, where "the streaks go around in the rocks." He worked with the UNHS health team from 2012 through the COVID-19 pandemic.

My father has shared stories with me throughout my life, inspiring me to write books based on his boarding school and religious experiences, for example. Worrying for my father's life every day of the pandemic, I

---

[1] Diné Bikéyah refers to Navajo lands.

---

F. King (✉)
The University of Oklahoma, Norman, OK, USA
e-mail: farinaking@ou.edu

© The Author(s), under exclusive license to Springer Nature Switzerland AG 2024
F. King, W. Davies (eds.), *COVID-19 in Indian Country*,
https://doi.org/10.1007/978-3-031-70184-9_5

realized how I never focused on his stories as a healer. Whenever I could convince him to spend any of his precious time, taking a break from his pressing work, to answer my questions about his experiences and insights, he would tell me what he could.

My father tried to follow the transformation of the COVID-19 virus as it spread across the earth, initially observing it as a faraway disease problem on the other side of the world that then came to his doorstep. Outbreaks in the Navajo Nation hit quickly, and my father witnessed the infections in the northern region of the reservation where he worked. Most of the infection was mild, but then the elderly and those with diabetes and pulmonary problems started to develop severe respiratory complications, and health providers struggled to find resources to care for them. The deaths started to appear in all our Diné communities. Intensifying this catastrophe was the unknown course of the disease and its impact on subsets of patients, including children, young adults, adults, and the aged, and those with cancer or other comorbidities.

My father silently withheld his feelings of hopelessness and anguish as he watched his patients and relatives, as Diné k'é, die slowly from COVID-19 without access to the needed critical care.[2] The nearest health facilities were 6–7 hours away. One of the darkest moments was when he learned that his beloved older sister Florence, several first cousins, and extended family had succumbed to the virus. Their funerals were cancelled as each died far away from their home in the large cities where they were taken to address their respiratory failures. Many of our Diné relatives were dying far from home all alone with the intensive care teams in big hospitals.

Not realizing my father shared my sentiments, since he continued to press on through the pandemic with resolve, I felt helpless and on the verge of hopelessness, living apart from my parents and beyond the Four Sacred Mountains of Diné Bikéyah. I never did well under stress. Anxieties flamed within me. I am impatient. A fighter. When COVID-19 hit, everything seemed like a waiting game. Waiting for a train wreck in slow motion.

I was in Tahlequah, home of the Cherokee Nation and United Keetoowah Band of Cherokees, teaching and working as a professor of Native American history at a university with one of the largest Native American populations in the country. I am Bilagáana born for the Kinyaa'áanii and Tsinaajini clans of Diné and a Navajo Nation citizen.[3]

---

[2] Diné k'é refers to Navajo kinship and clan relations.

[3] Bilagáana translates as white American, and Kinyaa'áanii means Towering House. Tsinaajini translates as Black-Streaked Woods. Diné introduce ourselves by our clans.

Most of my family lives in our homelands of Diné Bikéyah. The pandemic cut us off from each other. Mom and Dad were on lockdown in the Navajo Nation. My children, husband, and I could not leave Tahlequah. My classes, like everyone else's, moved suddenly from in person to online by March 2020. The pandemic hit like a bag of bricks, even though we saw warnings and red flags. We all thought it could not happen to us—that a pandemic could not happen to us.

It did happen to us, especially striking my Diné relatives and diverse Native American peoples. One of my Diné cousins, Nathan Benally, was one of the earliest ones to warn me and our family. He was a nurse. He sent me messages, warning me and my father and family to prepare by getting supplies and protections such as hazmat suits and face masks. I thought that he was overreacting at the time, but he was one of the few people I knew who demonstrated great foresight. He was right.

As a physician in Navajo Nation, at the time, my father has horror stories of what he witnessed and experienced during the pandemic. But he kept a cool demeanor. Whatever will be, will be. "Que sera, sera." It's not that he did not care. When anyone praised and honored him for being a doctor during the pandemic, calling him a hero, he simply said in a calm but firm voice: "I am not a hero. I just care." Caring meant doing something. He did not stand around and wait. He stood up and served, putting his life continually at risk for others—for Diné people who are some of the most susceptible to COVID-19. But he abetted his fears by telling himself and his loved ones that if he dies, he dies. That is what he meant by whatever will happen, will be.

I was the one who told him that his sister, Florence, was dying of COVID-19. She contracted the disease when an outbreak hit her nursing home in Gallup, a bordertown at the crossroads of Diné, Pueblo, white settlers, and many diverse peoples. They call Gallup a bordertown for bordering the Navajo Nation and other Native Nations. My dear aunt, Florence, died on May 6, 2020, during the earlier waves of the pandemic. I had finished the academic semester that moved entirely online at that point and joined a pod with my in-laws who were not under the same kind of blockade as that of the Navajo Nation. My parents could not go out and no one could go in. And my father was on the frontlines in a UNHS clinic. He moved to telehealth, which relieved the family, but the toll and risks continued to be high. The toll on his mental health skyrocketed, as he tried to support and save his people who are some of the most vulnerable communities in the world to COVID-19 (Fig. 5.1).

**Fig. 5.1** Farina King with her two sons and Aunt Florence in 2019. Credit: Farina King

When my aunt passed away, a dagger of pain stabbed at my heart, mind, and spirit. We could not grieve and mourn together as family. She passed away, without her many loved ones, in a hospital that had limited and filtered visits with only one of her granddaughters, Felicia. But making it all worse was that I was seeing and hearing people who continued to defy wearing masks and mocked the gravity of the pandemic. In an evening, when some of my in-laws gathered and sat around an outdoor fire, one of them started to spurt out how he thought the pandemic was a ploy of China and how wicked that country was.

I glared directly at him and blurted, "That is racist. Stop saying that."

He and other in-laws then looked at me in shock, as if I was wrong for talking back to him that way. I ran away from the group and cried in anger. People were dying. My aunt died and many people like that in-law wanted to blame another country and spread hate.

Hate doesn't heal. Hope and love heal. But that hate of racism, bigotry, and discrimination spurs my anger and rage because it continues to harm. I want to go into warrior mode and fight back to protect my loved ones and any people at risk. It was as if the hate and racism killed my aunt and so many Diné who suffer the intergenerational impacts of violence, dispossession, and injustice. My aunt lived struggling to pay her water and electric bills, taking care of many children—including her grandchildren—into her old age until she could not continue to even care for herself. She was sent to a boarding school from a young age, being taught that Diné bizaad is useless and other such detrimental colonizing curriculum.[4] Like me, my father, and all our relatives, she was the descendant of survivors of the Long Walk—the expulsion and death march of Diné to Hwééłdi, Land of the Suffering, or a concentration camp where the people endured and many of them fell to the most inhumane conditions: impure, contaminated waters; rape and sexual violence; disease; and the US military burning and poisoning their homelands and waters. The US military rounded up families, including Elders and children, like cattle for the slaughter. They tortured them, forcing them to march and wait at the slaughterhouse, Hwééłdi, to linger until they died.[5]

But they didn't all die. They held onto hope. Laura Tohe, a Diné poet, "[believes] it was the mountains that sustained the hearts and spirits of the Diné and helped to bring them back."[6] Those who survived carried hope. They sang, "Shí naashá," with joy and hózhǫ́ as they walked on their return to Diné Bikéyah after four years in bondage.[7]

> Ahala ahalago naashá ghą
> Shí naashá ghą, shí naashá ghą,
> Shí naashá lágo hózhǫ' la.
> Shí naashá ghą, shí naashá ghą,

---

[4] Diné Bizaad means Navajo language.

[5] See Laura Tohe, "Hwéeldi Bééhániih: Remembering the Long Walk," *Wicazo Sa Review* 22, no. 1 (Spring 2007): 77–82.

[6] Tohe, "Hwéeldi Bééhániih," 82.

[7] Hózhǫ́ does not have a direct translation but is a powerful ideal of Diné society and values, which is compared to harmony, beauty, and happiness. Shí naashá means "I am going" or "I am walking around." This Navajo song is referenced in https://web.archive.org/web/20120212211559/; http://www.newworldrecords.org/linernotes/80406.pdf. Charlotte Heth, "Overview," in *The Garland Encyclopedia of World Music*, 366–373. See "Navajo Songs from the Cayon De Chelly liner notes," *New World Records Archived from the original (PDF) on 2012-02-12.*

Shí naashá, ladee hózhǫ'ǫ' lá.
I am going in freedom
I am going, I am going,
I am going in beauty.
I am going, I am going,
I am going, beauty is all around me.[8]

But they also carried soul wounds, because the violence did not stop after they returned to their homelands, which remained under the colonizing power of the United States.[9] The experiences of my father and Aunt Florence at boarding schools attest to that as well as all the struggles that my relatives face, including the monster of COVID-19.

Many Diné refer to COVID-19 or Dikos Nstaaígíí-Náhást'éíts'áadah as a monster, evoking the origins of Diné and the Hero Twins. Ałk'idą́ą́', a long time ago, the twin sons of Asdzą́ą́ Nádleehé, known as Naayéé'neizghání and Tóbájíshchíní, faced and fought monsters that plagued the earth.[10] After defeating one of the fiercest naayéé', or monsters, called Yé'iitsoh, they dispersed the knives from the giant's flint armor in the Four Sacred Directions from East, South, West, to North, saying: "From now on the people of the earth shall use you. The Giant's spirit has departed from you."[11] In a sense, Diné healers have been using knives for medical and health care over generations after the warrior twins, such as Lori Arviso Alvord, who became the first known Diné woman general surgeon in 1994.[12] Diné learn how to take from naayéé' to strengthen and

---

[8] "Navajo Songs from the Cayon De Chelly liner notes."

[9] For more about "soul wounds," see Eduardo Duran, *Healing the Soul Wound: Counseling with American Indians and Other Native Peoples* (New York: Teachers College Press, 2006); and Stefanie L. Gillson and David A. Ross, "From Generation to Generation: Rethinking 'Soul Wounds' and Historical Trauma," *Biol Psychiatry* 86, issue 7 (October 2019): 19–20, accessed online February 1, 2024, https://www.ncbi.nlm.nih.gov/pmc/articles/PMC7557912/#R3.

[10] Asdzą́ą́ Nádleehé refers to Changing Woman who is a revered Diné deity and the mother of all the clans, also known as White Shell Woman or White Bead Woman. The Hero Twins or Warrior Twins are called Naabaahii in Diné bizaad. Their names are Naayéé'neizghání or Slayer of Monsters, and Tóbájíshchíní or Born for Water. Their father is the Sun.

[11] Hastin Tlo'tsi hee (Old Man Buffalo Grass) Sandoval recorded by Aileen O'Bryan in November 1928 in Aileen O'Bryan, *The Diné origin myths of the Navaho Indians [transcribed] by Aileen O'Bryan* (Washington, DC: *Bulletin* of the Smithsonian Institution, Bureau of American Ethnology, 1956), 84.

[12] Lori Arviso Alvord and Elizabeth Cohen Van Pelt, *The Scalpel and the Silver Bear: The First Navajo Woman Surgeon Combines Western Medicine and Traditional Healing* (New York: Bantam Books, 2000).

protect themselves. As knives often derive from the metal forged through intense heat and fire, the resilience and resurgence of Diné since COVID-19 reaffirm how Naayéé'neizghání and Tóbájíshchíní teach us of strength under pressure.

Allie Young, a Diné woman who spearheaded initiatives to Protect the Sacred and disseminate messages of the "Navajo Strong" campaign through media, directly articulates this connection: "The creation story for the Navajo people is one where twin warriors slay monsters that are hurting our people. The virus is another monster that we will overcome. . . . Because of what happened to us throughout history, our people and our population was decimated to 2% now of the entire population, and we have to protect that 2%. And so even one death is a lot for a native community."[13] For me, the individual deaths of my beloved aunt, relatives, and fellow Native Americans, when we are already a minority of minorities because of the violence and horrors of the past and present, led me to organize, talk, create, and sing in honor of our loved ones' lives.

Since I could not mourn with my family, I wondered how many others could not mourn together. At the historically Native American university where I worked, between 2020 and 2021, several students described to me their pain and suffering, considering ways that the pandemic affected them. Other students still joked that the pandemic was a hoax. I initiated programs for COVID-19 relief and student wellness and support, starting a collaboration of wellbeing for the university that included webinars, recorded podcasts, music programs, nature walks, meditation, and fundraising for student needs. Healing centered in these initiatives.

In March 2021, students in my U.S. History survey course completed an exercise of examining primary sources from the 1918 influenza pandemic, considering and comparing their experiences during the COVID-19 pandemic over a century later. Many students mentioned how they could relate to the primary sources from 1918, such as social distancing and using PPE and face masks. A photograph of an emergency hospital serving people infected by the 1918 influenza reminded one Native American student

---

[13] Allie Young cited in Colton Shone and Nathan O'Neal, "How the Navajo People are using culture to fight back against 'Covid Monster,'" Center for Health Journalism, September 15, 2020, accessed online January 27, 2024, https://centerforhealthjournalism.org/our-work/reporting/how-navajo-people-are-using-culture-fight-back-against-covid-monster. Protect the Sacred is an organization that Allie Young founded during the COVID-19 pandemic to support Diné communities.

of his relatives struggling to survive COVID-19 in January 2021. One of his aunts spent seven days in the hospital on high levels of oxygen, and his mother missed 23 days of work. When his grandparents went to the emergency room, his grandmother took the only remaining bed because of her low oxygen levels, while his grandfather had to lay isolated in a waiting room on one of the couches before a bed became available. His grandparents were sick for nearly a full month, and his grandpa lost thirty pounds. His grandma returned two more times to the hospital since they kept releasing her prematurely to make more beds available. Along with the fears and anxieties from worrying about their loved ones and their own health, the separation and cancelation of holiday gatherings also hurt students in multiple ways, but especially on a mental and emotional level.

Another Native American student referred to a historic telegram to the Bureau of Indian Affairs (BIA) addressing how officials were responding to the impacts of the influenza on Native American boarding schools in 1918. As a Native American, she heard stories from her Elders about their experiences in boarding schools, and she related her family history to her own schooling experiences during the COVID-19 pandemic.[14] She recognized how the schoolchildren's separation from family and home and the assault on their Indigenous cultures, languages, and identities intensified during the 1918 pandemic. In the early months of the COVID-19 pandemic, this student and her family avoided meeting in person to protect their relatives, especially their grandparents. She also praised how the tribal government responded quickly to the crisis and provided both medical and residential assistance for all Elders in the region, including transportation to Tahlequah for healthcare and other necessities such as groceries. The two pandemics, to her, tested communities and their resilience. Working with such insightful students from diverse backgrounds in northeastern Oklahoma helped sustain me through the COVID-19 pandemic.

Since mourning is a part of healing, I decided to organize a vigil, on April 19, 2021, just as much for personal reasons because I needed to grieve for my aunt with a collective. I wanted to gather with others to recognize those who walked on and lost the fight against COVID-19. Some people hid and silenced the COVID deaths. They blurred, ignored,

---

[14] The author received permission from the students in her class, in 2021, to share a copy of their reflection assignments about the pandemic with the special collections and library of Northeastern State University in Tahlequah, Oklahoma.

or suppressed statistics and information about reporting COVID-19 cases and mortalities. I wanted to get beyond the numbers and stand, sing, and speak for the people—individual lives and human beings, including my aunt, Florence.

They called her Nááníbaa', which means "She Returns from War." I will never forget the day that I had to tell my father how his beloved sister, bádí[15] Florence, was dying from the coronavirus. I woke up that morning, even before I knew she had walked on, thinking about my aunt and crying. I just knew that she was struggling. Then, my cousin called to tell me that my aunt Florence was getting worse. In tears, my father's voice quivered when he tried to console me: "It's okay to cry. We will see her again." My father, Phillip Smith, joined a Christian church as a young adult, upsetting his Diné father who had hoped that he would follow Diné ancestral ways of healing and ceremony. My father later became a physician, and he has primarily worked in American Indian and Navajo health services. Healing underlies Si'ąh Naagháí Bik'eh Hózhǫ́, which some translate as Diné ideals of "Live a long life in beauty" or "Walk in Beauty," which is a cyclical journey and process of restoring balance and wellbeing. My dad followed a different path to healing than his own father, but he has continued the path of healing and walking in the beauty of our ancestors.[16]

At the sunset of a spring evening, hundreds of miles away from my parents and relatives in Diné Bikéyah, I stood at a microphone outdoors in front of a small group in Tahlequah down the hill from the Sequoyah statue on the university campus. The student government organization and some university administrators were in the audience. I held my hand drum, dedicating a song for the vigil to Aunt Florence: "She did not make it through these outbreaks, and many of us know someone who has passed on. They are in our hearts. It is for them that we gather here, and that is what inspired this event."[17] My hand pounded the drum with a slow, steady rhyme, as I sang the following words with some that I adjusted to honor my aunt and loved ones who passed on:

---

[15] Bádi means his older sister.
[16] Farina King, "Diné Doctor: A Latter-day Saint Story of Healing," *Dialogue: A Journal of Mormon Thought* 54, no. 2 (Summer 2021): 81–85.
[17] Farina King cited in Brian D. King, "Candlelight vigil mourns lives lost during pandemic, especially Natives," *Tahlequah Daily Press*, April 19, 2021, accessed online February 1, 2024, https://www.tahlequahdailypress.com/multimedia/when-i-see-you-again/video_0c7dabb6-a12b-11eb-9079-17b58542b2e0.html.

> When I see you again, it will be sweet like honey on frybread...
> When I see you again, it will be sweet like your Navajo tea...
> When I see you again, it will be sweet like living a dream...
> When I see you again, it will be sweet like an answered prayer.[18]

In those moments, I envisioned my aunt's face and heard her tender voice. Florence's siblings would say that "everybody always favored Florence." In her home, it was common to see bundles of Navajo tea hanging from the ceiling to dry, and as we talked, she took a dried bundle that had been gathered from the land where she dwelled, and she placed it into a pot of hot water to make tea.

I always enjoyed visiting Florence because I loved spending time with her adorable grandchildren and their puppies. She told me, thinking about her children: "I want them to get a good education. I want them to find someone who really cares for them. . . I'm glad for taking care of all these kids, if they finish school and get their own jobs. Now, they got their families to think about. I encourage my children to get an education and take responsibility in their life." My dad remembers sitting with Florence under the stars as children, staring at the night sky in near silence. On some nights, they talked about their dreams. When my dad was in high school, Florence told him about her dreams and regrets. She regretted never finishing school, and she encouraged him to continue his studies. She regretted not being able to drive, which she eventually learned after automatic transmissions were introduced.

In honor of the World War II warriors such as her maternal uncle, Nelson Haskeltsie, who died from battle wounds near Florence, Italy, her mother Johanna called her, Nááanábaa,' which means "She returns from war." She returned from a war against the coronavirus. But the virus was only one struggle that my dear aunt, our mother, faced over her lifetime. She was as constant and peaceful as a gentle river. She continued to flow, to give life and to give of what she could. She cared for children almost all her life. She lived most of her adult life by the red rocks and hills of Iyanbito, "Buffalo Springs." I gave her a necklace with a buffalo pendant in honor of her home, which she wore during the funeral services of her precious son Alexander, who passed away in 2012. She cared for her grandchildren; some of them called her "mother." Of anyone I have ever

---

[18] Farina King cited in King, "Candlelight vigil mourns lives lost during pandemic, especially Natives."

known in my life, she was always there. She was there when you needed her. She was there, as if she was always just waiting for you. She was waiting for you to come and see her, to visit with her. She did not just talk or tell you what to do. She mostly listened. Like a rock, she was strong, still, and constant. You knew where to find her. She would be there for you.

My parents raised my siblings and me miles away from my aunt and relatives, across the country. Growing up, it was a special occasion to see my relatives. But my father always tried to bring us to visit Aunt Florence. I have early memories of entering her house where she lived and raised children for many years. Florence was always surrounded by children. One of my first memories of my relatives that changed my life was visiting Florence with my dad and siblings and noticing one of her grandchildren—a baby in a pack n' play. I recognized then, looking into the deep dark eyes of my baby relative in Florence's home, that I was with family. Every time I was inside her house, I knew that I was with kin. This was our return home, and Florence always welcomed us. Her door was always open to us—to me—years and years after I would return to her. She offered me food when I came. I realized that her children are my relatives, as I returned over and over. Her grandchildren, they are our posterity in the Diné way.

We are family and she instilled a kindness and gentleness in anyone who spent much time with her, no matter how hard and trying their lives had been. When she started to live in the nursing home, we continued to visit her, still greeted by her beautiful, welcoming smile. Her gentle eyes calmed my soul. Sometimes, all I could really say was "I love you," and she would reciprocate that love with a simple, "I love you too." The last time I saw her was a tender mercy.

In early March 2020, on my way rushing to the airport to catch a flight in Albuquerque, I had a strong impression to stop to see Aunt Florence. I was worried that I would miss my flight, and I thought that I would be returning to visit longer only a couple weeks later. I nearly passed the exit to her nursing home before I abruptly changed my mind, realizing that I had to see her, even if just for a moment. I ran into the nursing home to find her in her room, where it was as if she was waiting there to see me. She started to have dementia, but she always looked at me, recognizing me for who I was. She smiled, and as if it was a dream, I hugged her and gave her a bouquet of roses, telling her that I loved her and that I would return soon. She embraced me too, and we said "I love you" in English and in Navajo—"Ayóó áníínishní." I never would have expected that an outbreak of COVID-19 would have forced a lock down of the nursing home. The same virus also cancelled my scheduled return trip, and it hit her nursing home within the following weeks. I never thought that she would get the coronavirus and pass away only a couple months later, and I never envisioned how that moment with her would be my last time to embrace her.

Although the grief and sorrow of her passing is so painful for our family, especially when we could not run and embrace each other as we would have done before the pandemic, our hearts and spirits as family continue to connect and support each other. Florence passed on her love, tenderness, and good heart to our family, her children, and posterity. That was her greatest gift—an open heart of grace and love. She may have been very quiet and subtle, but her constancy touched many in countless ways. She shared treats like pickles and fry bread with passersby and relatives. She gathered Navajo tea to make and give away. She joked and talked with family. She loved to sew and make quilts. She taught those around her through the food, cooking and basic life lessons. She inspired children to become nurses, to pursue their dreams, while she was their rock and foundation. For me, her legacy and gift were her willingness to open the door to me and acknowledge me as family. If she ever wanted or asked for anything, it was for her children, her many children that she dearly loved. Generous, gracious, kind, and patient, that is how I will always remember her, our Florence. One of her grandchildren, Alexandria, said about her: "One thing that I learned from my grandma was to smile when times are hard because that is what she did. You would never catch my grandma crying. She never showed her pain as well and she fought to her fullest." Florence was a warrior, Náánábaa', who fought with kindness and good heart for her family and love. She has returned home from the war, and we will one day reunite and embrace her again.[19]

I thought of Florence as I lit my candle with those who mourned loved ones with me in Tahlequah during the candlelight vigil of 2021. Dr. Charles Knife Chief, a Pawnee physician and bishop of a Latter-day Saint congregation in Tahlequah, dedicated an opening prayer for the vigil and shared some thoughts on his own experiences seeing "week after week, it was getting worse ... how it has evolved and the effect [the pandemic] has

---

[19] Farina King, "They Called Her 'Náánábaa' Or 'She Returns From War,'" COVID-19 Mormon Stories, May 6, 2020, accessed online, February 1, 2024, https://research.cgu.edu/mormonism-migration-project/farina-king/.

had on the worldwide population."[20] Then, a Lakota emeritus professor, Joseph Faulds, spoke of "Mitakuye Oyasin" that we are all relatives "to honor the memory of those we have lost in this pandemic" by trying "to live in such a way to honor both their memory and that part of them which remains present in us."[21] Faulds closed with the following message that resonates with me to this day, as I constantly think of what it means to be a good relative and what the pandemic taught me of that:

> We all live as relatives in this creation, *all*, living together in the mutual context of the earth and sky, and this is true of everyone in our world, of all those we have lost in the pandemic, all those we knew and all those we never met, every single one of the many thousands who together helped make up our world; and most especially this is true and fundamental in relation to those we held close, those we loved and whose loss we felt as an inner wound, yet who remain forever an essential part of who we are. Let us then seek to live in a way worthy of their memory and of that essential echo of their presence which lives on in us, and thus we shall remember them and honor them as yet present in that sacramental sense among the living, and we shall do this by living lives that are, in themselves, memorials to all our beloved dead.[22]

The vigil and these words, like the light of the candles when darkness fell, illuminate the importance and relevance of every life. My aunt and those who have died during the COVID-19 pandemic are more than just numbers to count—they are relatives. As my father and ancestors, including Florence, taught me, the path of hózhǫ́ and a good life begins with care. These teachings are underscored through the vigil to commemorate and remember our loved ones, echoing through generations past, present, and future. We stand together, holding the light just as we did standing side by side with familiar and new faces—all relatives—during the vigil.

**Competing Interests Declaration** The author has no conflicts of interest to declare that are relevant to the content of this chapter.

---

[20] Charles Knife Chief cited in King, "Candlelight vigil."
[21] Joseph Faulds, "In Memoriam: Mitakuye Oyasin," April 19, 2021, Tahlequah, Oklahoma. See also Joseph Faulds cited in King, "Candlelight vigil."
[22] Joseph Faulds, "In Memoriam: Mitakuye Oyasin."

CHAPTER 6

# Azee'ííł'íní Reflections

*Phillip Lee Smith*

In Diné bizaad, the Navajo language, I am called azee'ííł'íní, "the one that makes medicine" or a medical doctor. As I reflect on working as a frontline medical provider and physician for Native American communities prior, during, and after the onset and waning of the COVID-19 pandemic, I have concluded that most people tend to hold a myopic view of the events that transpired.

Professionals working in a service-related industry are all affected in various ways and at different levels and degrees by their daily interactions with people. The teachings and moral values they have gained throughout their lives shape that impact. The influence of my Diné family, my traditional health training from observing my father and his peer healers complemented my formal university, medical school, and residency training. The key elements that played in my mind during and after the pandemic are that we learn from the past, we prepare for the future, and we live in the present. The onslaught of COVID-19 highlighted each setting (Fig. 6.1).

We have learned a lot as medical providers in the Navajo Nation through the years because of the rural and remote settings of our health care for

P. L. Smith (✉)
South Jordan, UT, USA

**Fig. 6.1** Dr. Phillip Lee Smith. Credit: Farina King

people. The Indian Health Service is the principal federal healthcare provider and health advocate for the Navajo Nation. Several health facilities are under the direct management of the Diné government. The Utah Navajo Health clinic where I worked for over 10 years and during the pandemic is a tribal clinic.

The key to addressing COVID-19 in the Navajo Nation was understanding the history of Indian health care and service to Diné. The health care system was built on a foundation of addressing major disease outbreaks among American Indian and Alaska Natives in this country over a century using public health principles while integrating advances in clinical medical care.

Principal health care providers for the Navajo Nation, clinics and hospitals, and public health workers were well-prepared in some aspects of addressing the public health issues related to the COVID-19 pandemic. Providers understood health as addressing the physical, mental, spiritual, social, and emotional well-being of the people and not merely the absence of disease. American Indian healthcare professionals have been working to address the social determinants of health for over 70 years. The framework for the social and community networks in which individuals lived and where communities existed was in place. Partnerships with federal, state, county, and private organizations were in place and functional to various degrees.

But when the pandemic spread, the residual high vulnerabilities of the Diné families were fully exposed to the world. This issue stemmed from the socio-economic and environmental infrastructures' issues that healthcare professionals, including me, have been working on for decades. The lack of potable water, utilities, grocery stores, transportation issues, short staffing of professional personnel in the clinics, and insufficient hospitals are a few of the other factors that came into play. These challenges became quite apparent when the "medical surge" occurred. We found that the few primary care hospitals in the Navajo Nation did not have the capacity to address the critical tertiary clinical care needs of the people.

The past had prepared us to address many of these issues. We had working partnerships with surrounding states with major medical centers, as well as federal and state health agencies to help address some of these concerns. The disaster plan we made in the past came to the forefront. The problem was the disaster, and its impact was real and stayed for a long time.

We had learned in the past to plan for mass communication links in the future. This strategy for addressing prevention and the local community networks came via local radio and TV. Thus, the needed health education on the COVID-19 virus was given in English and Diné bizaad—the Navajo language. We had learned we needed to plan for working with the local tribal government in addressing health risk restrictions on movement and travel advisories. When COVID peaked, this response was all put in place to protect the public.

Yet, when we took a broad view of our work during the peak of the pandemic, we could see that despite our best efforts, many were in vain as our vulnerable Navajo people died and traumatized the living. We were told by the statisticians and Centers for Disease Control and Prevention that the Navajo Nation had one of the highest mortality rates based on our population. But we learned to live in the present as we came to understand the unknown characteristics of the COVID-19 virus better. While noting the high level of incidence and prevalence rates and mortality rates in the Navajo Nation, we also realized many of us survived. We remembered our past experience with some health epidemics and knew we could survive as we cared for each other.

Since the 1940s, the Navajo people had participated in biomedical research involving vaccines for some infectious diseases. We remembered that past, as Diné contributed to scientific research that led to the technology that now prevents infectious diseases. It is too easy to take for granted how commonplace these vaccines are, and what work went into them to render them effective.

When the race to find an effective COVID-19 vaccine commenced, the Navajo Nation partnered with The Johns Hopkins Bloomberg School of Public Health on research involving the efficacy trials of the Pfizer COVID vaccine on the Navajo Reservation. We were elated when the vaccine was deemed effective and approved for emergency use by the Food and Drug Administration, which reviews the safety of drugs and medical products. But the logistics of getting the vaccine to the people and having them accept it was another issue. This concern was addressed through the working health network of the nation, the federal, state, county, and private health associations developed through the years.

The pandemic impacted all aspects of our lives. While we saw the selfishness of some accepting or claiming undeserved credit, puffing deserved credit, and resenting the genuine success of others, we became acutely aware that as a people we really cared for each other. We realized we needed to trust one another and acknowledged that we are part of a world where our actions and thoughts do impact others in our community for good or bad. As a local leader in a small congregation of the Church of Jesus Christ of Latter-day Saints, I helped locals by procuring essentials for daily life, like food and water for many of the residents living in our remote area of the Navajo Nation. We even went into the canyons to obtain wood for warming homes and cooking the meals. And the people from Salt Lake City brought truckloads of firewood from the trees that had been uprooted in an unusual storm that came to their area. This activity allowed me to see patience, kindness, love, and good in people fully expressed. The strength, power, and spiritual fortitude of Diné people were brought forth in living in what was our present. Moral values prevailed as we saw people helping each other, sharing their resources, shedding anxiety about many things, and shedding pride and hypocrisy in human relations. I saw the elements of faith in a higher being, manifested through prayer and acts of charity and love.

There has never been a time like this. This is true because we live in a changing world. Technology has fully altered every aspect of our lives. We must cope with these advances, even the cataclysmic change in a world which our forbearers never dreamed of. While we often focus on the physical aspect of our being, we know that attention needs to be paid to peoples' mental and spiritual health in these changing times.

I feel that our thoughts of tomorrow take up too much of today, often in daydreaming or wishing and longing for a future which will provide comfort and peace. But this will not take the place of living in the present with what is in our life sphere. The experience with the viral pandemic has demonstrated this in all aspects of our lives. Today, I feel this is a day of opportunity that we need to grasp. There is no tomorrow if we do not do something today.

I am optimistic that when we work together, we can do something that seems impossible. Overcoming the seemingly insurmountable was demonstrated by all who helped in addressing the pandemic from its onset to the development of preventative vaccines and public intervention and effective clinical care. We found that knowledge without labor is profitless, whereas knowledge with labor is genius. I am very grateful for the thousands who helped the Navajo Nation and Indian Country cope with the pandemic.

In my overall experience as a medical doctor prior to the onset of the pandemic or working through the pandemic and now looking back in its aftermath, I found the process of planning, gathering, building, helping, preparing, and working—not the completed project—provided the most enduring satisfaction and pleasure in the experience. This is life, living together, working together, and learning together with the imperfections in all of us.

Living in the present, I realize we are not on our own. Our thoughts and subsequent actions affect our world and the lives of others who live with us on this earth that serves as our home. We now know that what happens in far off remote places thousands and thousands of miles away, such as in Wuhan, China, can greatly impact and affect the lives of those who live in the isolated and rural remote Diné community of Oljato, Navajo Nation, in Native America.

Each person has the power to make small but important impacts in their communities, cities, and nations. Other infectious pathogens will come into our midst in the future. To address these new challenges, we can learn from the past, plan for the future, and live in the present. As we do this, we must always remember the simple measures that helped our ancestors survive the infectious diseases from the past. We know them as public health principles to wash your hands, keep social distancing, cover your mouth and nose, and get immunized. These simple actions can often provide greater health protection for the masses than the sterile walls of the guarded buildings, which house the most advanced skills, knowledge, and technology of biomedical science. Remember the ancients who warned us: "It is better to obey, than offer sacrifice."

**Competing Interests Declaration** The author has no conflicts of interest to declare that are relevant to the content of this chapter.

CHAPTER 7

# A Twenty-First Century Pandemic in Indian Country: The Resilience of the Muscogee (Creek) Nation Against COVID-19

*Midge Dellinger and RaeLynn Butler*

## INTRODUCTION

The Muscogee (Creek) Nation Reservation, situated in northeastern Oklahoma, has not been spared the devastation of the COVID-19 pandemic. In early 2020, Muscogee leaders worked quickly and tirelessly in preparation for the impending pandemic. On March 13, 2020, the Muscogee (Creek) Nation (MCN) declared a state of emergency.[1] As a part of their emergency plan, MCN leaders reconfigured daily operating routines to provide employees and citizens the best means of service, safety, and survival from a seemingly unstoppable viral killer. Even with

---

[1] Joshua Slane, *Mvskoke Media*, "Muscogee (Creek) Nation Declares COVID-19 State of Emergency," accessed online August 29, 2023, https://www.mvskokemedia.com/muscogee-creek-nation-declares-COVID-19-state-of-emergency/

---

M. Dellinger (✉) • R. Butler
Muscogee (Creek) Nation Historic and Cultural Preservation Department, Okmulgee, OK, USA
e-mail: ddellinger@muscogeenation.com; raebutler@muscogeenation.com

© The Author(s), under exclusive license to Springer Nature Switzerland AG 2024
F. King, W. Davies (eds.), *COVID-19 in Indian Country*,
https://doi.org/10.1007/978-3-031-70184-9_7

**Fig. 7.1** "Kvlonv Ennokvn (Coronavirus)." Credit: Johnnie Diacon, 2020

such great effort, during the first two years of the pandemic, Mvskoke people suffered, and hundreds lost their lives. Mvskoke men and women, including Elders, ceremonial ground leaders, church pastors, language speakers, and family members, were suddenly gone (Fig. 7.1).

The painful impact of COVID-19 on the Muscogee (Creek) Nation is only one of many significant events the Mvskoke have encountered, as their life experiences and history reveal an existence of trauma and turmoil due to centuries of European encroachment, colonization, and past pandemics. In remembering the story of twenty-first century Mvskoke people and the COVID-19 pandemic, it is critical to recognize how they have suffered yet resisted and survived other harsh and challenging experiences. One such event, the removal of Mvskoke people from their southeastern homelands, continues to have compounding negative impacts on Mvskoke communities, language, culture, and health, and this tragedy still resonates in the hearts and minds of Mvskoke descendants.

Immediately following European encroachment in the sixteenth-century, Mvskoke people began losing their homes and lands. Today, these lands are predominantly the states of Georgia and Alabama. In the late 1820s, due to the unrelenting pressures of the settler population, Mvskoke people began leaving their ancestral homelands. After the passage of the Indian Removal Act in 1830, and continuing into the 1850s, the federal government forcibly removed Mvskoke people from the southeast. Between 1836 and 1837, the bulk of Mvskoke ancestors, 23,000 people, experienced forced displacement and the horrendous extremes of inhumane treatment inflicted by US soldiers. Thousands suffered, and more than 3500 died, and were left behind, on what the Mvskoke call the Road of Misery (Nene Estemerkv), most where they fell. With immense strength, courage, and fortitude, other Mvskoke ancestors overcame their horrid oppression and continued their journey to reestablish their nation on new lands in Indian Territory.

Survivors of the removal period carried our Mvskoke language, culture, and oral tradition with them from the southeast and today oral tradition continues to be an important aspect of storytelling and education for our people. Mvskoke oral traditions passed down through generations have exemplified how Mvskoke people approach life and provide guidance on how to continue their journey forward. As an example, there is a Mvskoke oral tradition remembered from the time of removal:

> Since removal from their southeastern homelands, an unimaginable and traumatic event in the lives of the Mvskoke, there are those Mvskoke ancestors remembered for telling others on their road of misery (nene estemerkv), "don't look back and don't go back; there is nothing there for you now." For the future of the Muscogee (Creek) Nation, these ancestors knew that this was what they had to do; keep looking forward and keep moving forward. These ancestors had the ability, even in their own time of immense grief and suffering, to encourage other Mvskoke peoples to get to their new lands. And while thousands of Mvskoke died during removal, thousands more survived.

It is with the same mindset and ambition given by Mvskoke ancestors to overcome whatever adversity comes their way that the Mvskoke of the twenty-first century battled COVID-19. Throughout the pandemic, Mvskoke people remained powerful, intent, and ever-moving forward, fully engaged in acts of resilience and survival, and they still are today.

This chapter also considers public memory of the COVID-19 pandemic. What do people outside of Indian Country remember about the adverse impact of the pandemic and its ravages on the Indigenous peoples of the United States? In the early months of the pandemic, there was continuous media coverage and reports about COVID-19 worldwide and the burgeoning pandemic. Even so, local and national media sources in the United States provided minimal, if any, news coverage about COVID-19's devastation of Indian Country, including Oklahoma, home to 39 Tribal Nations. Seemingly, the world outside of Indian Country was not paying attention to Indigenous peoples' pandemic hardships and struggles. From an Indigenous perspective, this type of erasure is unfortunately not new. Even so, the experiences of *every* person, community, and nation impacted by COVID-19 are essential to a complete and authentic memory of the pandemic and the historical narrative left in its wake. Indigenous pandemic experiences and lives matter too.

To counter the erasure of Indigenous COVID-19 experiences, the Muscogee (Creek) Nation Historic and Cultural Preservation Department created and performed an oral history project focused on the life experiences of 40 Mvskoke citizens and community members, each sharing their COVID-19 stories. Titled "A Twenty-First Century Pandemic in Indian Country: The Resilience of the Muscogee (Creek) Nation Against Covid-19," this oral history project reveals COVID-19's impact on the Muscogee (Creek) Nation and how Mvskoke people have suffered, yet managed, maneuvered, and survived the pandemic. Since time immemorial, Indigenous peoples have been great practitioners of orality, engaging in oral traditions to perpetuate and protect tribal knowledge and teachings. In 2021, the Muscogee Nation seized the opportunity to ensure that future generations of Mvskoke would have written and oral documentation about how Mvskoke ancestors battled an invisible killer. As shared in this chapter, the Mvskoke voice provides a glimpse into the Mvskoke COVID-19 pandemic story.

## COVID-19 ON THE MUSCOGEE RESERVATION

The Muscogee (Creek) Nation is the fourth largest Tribal Nation in the United States, with an enrollment in 2020, of just over 100,000 citizens. Located in northeastern Oklahoma, the Muscogee (Creek) Nation Reservation consists roughly of 4000+ square miles, including 69 cities and towns, 67 school districts, 23 Mvskoke Community Centers, and 16 active ceremonial grounds. The Mvskoke maintain a multi-million dollar yearly operating budget and they employ over 4000 people. The Muscogee Nation provides healthcare, housing, education, and other critical social services to Mvskoke citizens.

On March 6, 2020, Tulsa County, the most populated county in the Muscogee (Creek) Nation, confirmed the first case of COVID-19 in Oklahoma and on Muscogee Reservation lands.[2] Eleven days later, on March 17, Tulsa County reported its first death due to COVID-19.[3] Soon after, on a daily basis, other residents living across the Muscogee Reservation began falling prey to the unstoppable viral killer. In the Muscogee Nation, hundreds of Mvskoke lives have been lost to COVID-19, with over 300 deaths occurring within the first five months of the pandemic's arrival on reservation lands.[4] This loss is tragic and difficult to accept (Fig. 7.2), especially knowing that Muscogee (Creek) Nation Tribal and health officials began immediately addressing COVID-19's arrival in the United States.

With the MCN Department of Health consisting of three hospitals, eight clinics, and one rehabilitation center, Mvskoke leaders promptly put together what they believed to be a plan of "extreme measures" to prepare for an influx of COVID-19 patients into MCN medical facilities.[5] Multiple operational changes and goals were created by the MCN Department of

---

[2] Tulsa Health Department, accessed online August 31, 2023, https://www.tulsa-health.org/news/tulsa-health-department-reports-first-case-COVID-19
[3] Tulsa Health Department, accessed online August 31, 2023, https://www.tulsa-health.org/news/tulsa-health-officials-confirm-first-COVID-19-death-oklahoma
[4] Lani Hansen, *Mvskoke Media*, "A Third of all Oklahoma COVID-19 Deaths are happening on the MCN Reservation," accessed online August 29, 2023, https://www.mvskokemedia.com/a-third-of-all-COVID-19-deaths-are-happening-on-the-mcn-reservation/
[5] Muscogee (Creek) Nation, Executive Branch, FY2020, 2nd Quarter Report (January, February, March), accessed online August 29, 2023, 6-7, https://www.muscogeenation.com/wp-content/uploads/2022/08/FY20-2nd-Quarterly-Report-Digital-FINAL.pdf

**Fig. 7.2** "Going for Groceries During the Time of the Pandemic." Credit: Johnnie Diacon, 2020

Health, including a Coronavirus Taskforce to work closely with Tribal administrators. Between the end of January and through March 2020, many measures were put into place, such as a "hotline" for patients and employees to screen COVID-19 infection, telehealth appointments, increased hospital bed capacity, and the establishment of a mental health crisis line.[6]

On March 21, 2020, as the incidence of COVID-19 rapidly increased, thousands of MCN employees were sent home to shelter in place. In-person gatherings and daily work routines came to an end. A minimal number of "frontline" workers remained in their offices to continue critical services to Mvskoke citizens, such as Elder support, food distribution, and funeral assistance to those needing to bury family members. The need for cemetery clean-up services catapulted in number throughout the first year of the pandemic and the Muscogee Nation's Cemetery Crew and Tribal Driveways worked in earnest to keep up with the demand of opening up graves and cleaning family cemeteries in preparation for funerals.

[6] Ibid.

The loss of life during the first year hit close to home. The Muscogee (Creek) Nation Historic and Cultural Preservation Department lost two Elders due to complications from COVID-19. The pandemic also disrupted traditional Mvskoke burial practices and needed acts of mourning, including physical contact such as hugs with family members. This caused further trauma as Mvskoke families were prevented from properly grieving the loss of loved ones. Early into the pandemic, this became the new normal. Many lived day to day in fear and isolation waiting for the vaccine to come to the Muscogee (Creek) Nation.

On December 17, 2020, the Muscogee (Creek) Nation began its vaccination process, referring to it as a "mass vaccination plan."[7] Vaccinations started with health care staff, followed by long-term care residents, Mvskoke Elders over 65, and people over age 16 with underlying health conditions.[8] When the vaccine was more readily available, all Mvskoke citizens age 16 and over, and the non-Mvskoke public, became eligible for vaccination.[9] The MCN Health Department provided an aggressive vaccination program to all those residing on the Muscogee Reservation. Mobile units were put into place and taken to rural areas on the reservation. "Pop-up" vaccine clinics appeared throughout the Muscogee Nation and thousands of people were vaccinated. In 2021, the Muscogee Nation offered a $500 incentive to citizens to be vaccinated within a specific deadline.[10] By December of 2022, the MCN Health Department had administered 52,223 vaccines.[11]

As a community partner, the Muscogee (Creek) Nation led the way in providing health care services to Mvskoke and non-Mvskoke people, such as a Monoclonal Antibody Infusion Center built in 2021. In 2022, the Muscogee Nation appointed its first Surgeon General and, in 2023, the Muscogee Nation hired a Public Health Director responsible for the

---

[7] Muscogee (Creek) Nation, Executive Branch, FY2021, 1st Quarter Report (October, November, December, 2020), accessed online August 29, 2023, 7.
https://www.muscogeenation.com/wp-content/uploads/2022/08/FY-2021-1st-Quarterly-Report-Final.pdf
[8] Ibid.
[9] Ibid.
[10] Mvskoke Media, accessed online August 31, 2023, https://www.mvskokemedia.com/national-council-passes-citizen-vaccine-incentive/
[11] Muscogee (Creek) Nation, Executive Branch, FY2023, 1st Quarter Report (October, November, December), accessed online August 29, 2023, 8, https://www.muscogeenation.com/wp-content/uploads/2023/01/FY23-1st-Quarterly-Report.pdf

protection and improvement of health among Mvskoke citizens. Today, the MCN Health Department maintains reliable COVID-19 resources and services for Mvskoke citizens, and keeps a watchful eye on public health trends.

It is evident from the significant pandemic work completed by the Muscogee (Creek) Nation and the MCN Health Department that Mvskoke people will be better prepared for the next pandemic assault. Even so, life is different now for many who survived the pandemic.

## The Oral History Project

One of the many missions of the Muscogee (Creek) Nation Historic and Cultural Preservation Department to preserve the MCN's tangible and intangible cultural heritage. One way to accomplish this mission is by preserving Mvskoke oral traditions and histories. Since time immemorial, the practice of oral tradition has helped Indigenous people protect and perpetuate tribal knowledge and teachings. Today, across Indian Country, this practice remains imperative to the longevity of Indigenous existence.

The Muscogee (Creek) Nation Oral History Program provides a necessary space for Mvskoke oral tradition (passed-down stories embedded in cultural practice) to merge with the use of Western oral history methodology (recorded and archived interviews focusing on first-hand life experiences). The gathering of recorded Mvskoke oral histories generates a critical historical research tool accessible to generations of Mvskoke, and it offers a critical means of retaining the memory of the Mvskoke people and their lived experiences. In January 2021, the Muscogee (Creek) Nation Historic and Cultural Preservation Department began an oral history project, focusing on the voices and life experiences of Mvskoke and the COVID-19 pandemic. Funded by the Andrew W. Mellon Foundation, this two-year project titled "A Twenty-First Century Pandemic in Indian Country: The Resilience of the Muscogee (Creek) Nation Against COVID-19," has gathered oral histories and first-hand knowledge about a ruthless virus and how it has changed life for twenty-first century Mvskoke people, including how they have suffered immense loss, yet endured and overcome extreme adversities created by the pandemic.

At the core of this project are 40 Mvskoke citizens and community members who participated as narrators. Each participant shared their experiences of the COVID-19 pandemic, including personal and Tribal knowledge regarding the virus and its path of destruction. To offer a well-rounded look at COVID-19 on the Muscogee Reservation, narrators came from various occupations, ages, and demographics. For example, narrators for this project include MCN leadership, employees, first responders, Elders, at-large citizens, youth, artists, citizens from rural and urban areas, and non-Mvskoke community members.

The interviews contain emotions of uncertainty, fear, sadness, and grief, as the Mvskoke have lost many people, including community, church, and ceremonial ground leaders. With these losses, an immeasurable amount of knowledge regarding Mvskoke culture, tradition, and language is forever gone. But also, amid a tremendous battle for survival, the narrators for this project give messages of encouragement, hope, gratitude, love, and care for one another, including all living beings. And for any who will listen and learn, there are lessons of determination and survival. Indigenous pandemic experiences have much to teach us all.

## THE MVSKOKE PANDEMIC STORY

How have the Mvskoke of the twenty-first century accomplished acts of resilience and survival against COVID-19? How does daily life continue for Mvskoke and other community members, knowing that COVID-19 remains a lingering threat? And given the loss experienced, how have the Mvskoke created a new "normal" going forward, as they have always done despite a history of traumatic and life-changing events? At the core of the oral history project are questions such as these, and provided in the remainder of this chapter are the thought-provoking responses to these questions and many others, from the perspective and voices of project narrators.

In remembering the early stages of the COVID-19 pandemic, Linda Dellinger, a Mvskoke Elder, sat quietly sheltering at home, processing her understanding and thoughts about COVID-19:

> "The first thing they were saying is it could be very fatal for the Elders. Being an Elder, okay, is this how I am going to die, am I going to die from this virus?"[12] Linda quickly told herself "No, that's not going to be, I'm not going to let that happen."[13]

---

[12] Linda Dellinger, interview by Midge Dellinger, January 27, 2021, Tulsa, Oklahoma, transcript, *A Twenty-First Century Pandemic in Indian Country: The Resilience of the Muscogee (Creek) Nation Against COVID-19*, Muscogee (Creek) Nation National Library and Archives Oral History Collection, https://mvskokenationallibraryarchive.org/digital-heritage/linda-dellinger-interview

[13] Ibid.

RaeLynn Butler, former manager of the MCN Historic and Cultural Preservation Department and current MCN Secretary of Culture and Humanities remembers her thoughts and feelings about being diagnosed with COVID-19 in 2020:

> It feels like a death sentence once you've been told you're positive, because of everything you've seen on the news. And I was really scared to think, could this be—could I die in a week?[14]

Mvskoke citizen Jennifer Handsel remembers the early days of the pandemic and the consistent news reports about the number of people dying from the virus, she states:

> And you'd hear in the news, they were keeping a death tally on CNN, the people that were infected, the people that were dying.[15]

In facing the COVID-19 pandemic on Mvskoke lands, Mvskoke Elder and MCN Council Representative Anna Marshall remembers being in Africa when Ebola swept across the countryside and killed thousands of African residents. In remembering the past pandemic experiences of Mvskoke ancestors, she comments:

> My fear is that Natives are always more susceptible to these unknown viruses and things like that, so I assumed that it would come to Oklahoma. I knew that.[16]

---

[14] RaeLynn Butler, interview by Midge Dellinger, April 17, 2021, Tulsa, Oklahoma, transcript, *A Twenty-First Century Pandemic in Indian Country: The Resilience of the Muscogee (Creek) Nation Against COVID-19*, Muscogee (Creek) Nation National Library and Archives Oral History Collection, https://mvskokenationallibraryarchive.org/digital-heritage/raelynn-butler-interview

[15] Jennifer Handsel, interview by Midge Dellinger, January 27, 2023, Tulsa, Oklahoma, transcript, *A Twenty-First Century Pandemic in Indian Country: The Resilience of the Muscogee (Creek) Nation Against COVID-19*, Muscogee (Creek) Nation National Library and Archives Oral History Collection, https://mvskokenationallibraryarchive.org/digital-heritage/jennifer-handsel-interview

[16] Anna Marshall, interview by Midge Dellinger, May 5, 2021, Tulsa, Oklahoma, transcript, *A Twenty-First Century Pandemic in Indian Country: The Resilience of the Muscogee (Creek) Nation Against COVID-19*, Muscogee (Creek) Nation National Library and Archives Oral History Collection, https://mvskokenationallibraryarchive.org/digital-heritage/representative-anna-marshall-interview

By March 2020, Muscogee (Creek) Nation leadership was fully aware of COVID-19's potential for causing widespread illness and death. Muscogee (Creek) Nation Chief David Hill declared a State of Emergency, and Tribal and health administrators began spending time in a pandemic *war room*. Meeting hour after hour, MCN Tribal and health administrators talked in great detail about how to continue providing care and services to Mvskoke but to do so in the safest way without further spreading the virus among Mvskoke citizens and community members. Oral history interviews with top MCN leaders reveal the weight of human life and Mvskoke existence on their shoulders, but also how the expedient actions of MCN leadership were able to save thousands of lives. Even as the world outside the Muscogee (Creek) Nation was in chaos, Muscogee leaders and people remained steadfast and courageous in their battle against COVID-19.

Shawn Terry, Secretary of the MCN Health Department remembers:

> We started seeing headlines in the newspaper that there was a virus, around January. And then, we watched it start tracking across the world in February. By the time March hit, the first case had landed in the United States. It could have as high as a one percent death rate with this virus and we knew that we had about forty thousand patients in our system, and that if this thing did what it said it would do, we were going to lose about four hundred tribal citizens to this virus. We started laying the groundwork. We knew we had to probably shelter in place for a while, we were going to have to stop the flow of traffic into the tribal service buildings. We have an incredibly good infection control team at Creek Nation Department of Health. And those guys were really on top of this from day one.[17]

On January 4, 2020, David Hill became Chief of the Muscogee (Creek) Nation. He was inaugurated just 16 days before the first case of COVID-19 was detected in the United States. Little did he know, on his inauguration day, that he would quickly become responsible for decisions concerning life-saving measures for 90,000 citizens. With the COVID-19 pandemic steamrolling across the United States, Chief Hill, his cabinet,

---

[17] Shawn Terry, interview by Midge Dellinger, June 24, 2021, Tulsa, Oklahoma, transcript, *A Twenty-First Century Pandemic in Indian Country: The Resilience of the Muscogee (Creek) Nation Against COVID-19*, Muscogee (Creek) Nation National Library and Archives Oral History Collection, https://mvskokenationallibraryarchive.org/digital-heritage/shawn-terry-secretary-health-interview

and the newly created Coronavirus Taskforce kept a vigilant eye on the elusive virus until early March 2020, when it found its way into Oklahoma and the Muscogee (Creek) Nation Reservation.

Chief Hill recalls:

> Me and Mr. Terry had almost daily meetings about it, and we decided to have a health taskforce team, and they just updated me almost daily. And so, we had a meeting twice a week, three times a week, then we went five days a week on what we need to do.[18]

By March 2020, Mvskoke leadership faced the rapidly growing issue of illness within the Muscogee Nation.

Chief Hill remembers:

> I think on March 13, when it actually got too big, the cases, the positivity rate, everywhere, and it actually hit our nation, someone tested positive. And it just kept getting worse every day. So, I think it was March 13 I had to call an emergency, declared it a state of emergency to shut down the complex, which that was a very hard decision to do because we still need to provide services for the citizens.[19]

When Second Chief Del Beaver entered his elected office in January 2020, he vividly remembers the media reporting the existence of COVID-19 in China. He states:

> What does COVID-19 mean? And you saw it spread overseas, you saw it spread over in China. Surely we'll have something by the time it gets to the United States. We'll have something developed. And so, really, it moved so fast. You couldn't get ahead of this thing. At that time, you couldn't believe this is really happening here. People were dying left and right from this. And it just started creeping this way.[20]

---

[18] Chief David Hill, interview by Midge Dellinger, June 1, 2022, Okmulgee, Oklahoma, transcript, *A Twenty-First Century Pandemic in Indian Country: The Resilience of the Muscogee (Creek) Nation Against COVID-19*, Muscogee (Creek) Nation National Library and Archives, https://mvskokenationallibraryarchive.org/digital-heritage/chief-david-hill-interview

[19] Ibid.

[20] Second Chief Del Beaver, interview by Midge Dellinger, June 6, 2022, Okmulgee, Oklahoma, transcript, *A Twenty-First Century Pandemic in Indian Country: The Resilience of the Muscogee (Creek) Nation Against COVID-19*, Muscogee (Creek) Nation National Library and Archives, https://mvskokenationallibraryarchive.org/digital-heritage/second-chief-del-beaver-interview

After the arrival of COVID-19 on Mvskoke lands, Second Chief Beaver recalls:

> We were making decisions that morning where we had to turn and pivot and make another decision that afternoon. You felt like they were life and death decisions that you were making. And at the end of the day, we were talking, how can we keep people alive? And that's a big question, right?[21]

On the topic of pandemic mortality, Chief Hill spoke with great emotion about combating the loss of life due to the COVID-19 virus:

> I didn't want to lose anyone. My goal was to have minimum amount of citizens passing away. That's one of the things that you just didn't know when it was going to happen, who was going to get it. That was tough.[22]

Beginning generations before the COVID-19 pandemic in 2020, Mvskoke oral traditions reveal the coming of a "strong illness" (enokketv yekce). With an innate wisdom and understanding of the world around them and a deep connection to Mother Earth, Indigenous peoples have long been able to make such predictions. Mvskoke descendants today remember the teachings about an illness such as COVID-19, as told by traditional Mvskoke Elders.

From Mvskoke citizen Rebecca Barnett:

> I'm going to tell you when I first heard about the COVID-19. About six months before my mother passed. Sometimes me and my mother would just sit around and talk, and she would tell me stories. And she said the Elders had predicted that there will be an illness that will hit the country. And she said it's going to take a lot of people. And she said, you probably won't see it, but your grandkids will. She said it's going to kill a lot of stecate (the Mvskoke word for Native people). And when this pandemic hit, you know, she's been gone seven years this past July, I think she was talking about this.[23]

---

[21] Ibid.

[22] Chief David Hill, interview by Midge Dellinger.

[23] Rebecca Barnett, interview by Midge Dellinger, October 30, 2021, Tulsa, Oklahoma, transcript, *A Twenty-First Century Pandemic in Indian Country: The Resilience of the Muscogee (Creek) Nation Against COVID-19*, Muscogee (Creek) Nation National Library and Archives, https://mvskokenationallibraryarchive.org/digital-heritage/rebecca-barnett-interview

Mvskoke traditionalist Robin Soweka remembers throughout his life hearing his Elders talk about a coming illness. He recalls:

> Back then, the Elders, they would foretell you some things. And they used to talk about illnesses coming, one of these days you're going to experience it. And I look back at that, what they had told. And to me, it refers to that. I thought back on that and just figured that's what they had been telling us about.[24]

Traditional Mvskoke Elder Melissa Harjo-Moffer remembers hearing since childhood Mvskoke Elders say:

> Things are coming. Things that we never knew would even happen to us. And nobody knew or even thought, twenty years ago, that there was going to be an epidemic.[25]

When asked about personal COVID-19 safety measures, the 40 project narrators spoke about various precautions. While some Mvskoke focused on the doctrines and teachings of Western science, others leaned on their traditional beliefs and practices. Still, others engaged in both. Protective measures included keeping hands clean, wearing a mask, sanitizing everything brought into the house, including groceries, and removing contaminated clothing and shoes before entering their homes, and prayer. Some of the narrators share lessons on the importance of physical and spiritual cleanliness.

From Mrs. Harjo-Moffer:

> Well, you know, when I thought about the pandemic, I thought to myself, at home, when I was a kid, we were always taught to wash your hands. Taught to wash your face as soon as you get up, because in the Muscogee

---

[24] Robin Soweka, interview by Midge Dellinger, April 26, 2022, Okmulgee, Oklahoma, transcript, *A Twenty-First Century Pandemic in Indian Country: The Resilience of the Muscogee (Creek) Nation Against COVID-19*, Muscogee (Creek) Nation National Library and Archives, https://mvskokenationallibraryarchive.org/digital-heritage/robin-soweka-interview

[25] Melissa Harjo-Moffer, interview by Midge Dellinger, June 29, 2021, Okmulgee, Oklahoma, transcript, *A Twenty-First Century Pandemic in Indian Country: The Resilience of the Muscogee (Creek) Nation Against COVID-19*, Muscogee (Creek) Nation National Library and Archives, https://mvskokenationallibraryarchive.org/digital-heritage/melissa-harjo-moffer-interview-part-two

traditional way, we were always told that something comes around you when you're asleep. So, what society was saying to do, wash your hands, this, that, this, that. We had already been practicing it. I always had wipes in my truck. I always had sprays in the house. We were always told that they were dirty and they carried disease. I guess, they're thinking back to De Soto's time, when he came and spread all the disease. We lost half our people. If we had a visitor, a non-Native, I wiped down the house. My mother did, too, when somebody came to the house.[26]

She also states that traditional "full-bloods" had this thing about the non-Natives, the stehvtke (white) people.

As a nursing student during the first two years of the COVID-19 pandemic, Mvskoke citizen Apollonia Piña states:

I follow a lot of science news. I've always been really fascinated by viruses since I was a young person. And reading about it from some legitimate science websites and being like, I think this might turn into a thing.[27]

In her interview, Ms. Piña expresses frustration over people not taking seriously the warning signs given by the medical profession about the adversities of contracting COVID-19 or the safety protocols for non-contraction of the illness; she shares:

It's like you kind of have this feeling of you can see something that is coming into your community and as we know, especially for Brown communities such as Native people, we always get hit worse, disproportionately.[28]

Throughout the pandemic, Ms. Piña worked to help Brown communities understand the many aspects of COVID-19:

I really strive to be a good science communicator, especially for Indigenous and Brown communities.[29]

---

[26] Ibid.
[27] Apollonia Piña, interview by Midge Dellinger, May 25, 2021, Tulsa, Oklahoma, transcript, *A Twenty-First Century Pandemic in Indian Country: The Resilience of the Muscogee (Creek) Nation Against COVID-19*, Muscogee (Creek) Nation National Library and Archives, https://mvskokenationallibraryarchive.org/digital-heritage/apollonia-piña-interview
[28] Ibid.
[29] Ibid.

The years 2020 and 2021 were extremely difficult for the Muscogee (Creek) Nation. COVID-19 stole many Mvskoke people from families, communities, churches, and ceremonial grounds. Relatives, friends, leaders were here one day and gone the next. Churches were left without pastors, ceremonial grounds without a Mekko (Chief), Henehv (Second Chief), Heles-hayv (Medicine Man), and Tvstvnvkes (Warriors), and a Tribal college without its president.

With strong emotion and sadness on the topic of human loss in the Muscogee (Creek) Nation, Ms. Butler states:

> I know that the Nation has been impacted tremendously. I don't know the exact number of how many people, but I know that just from our office perspective and our jobs and roles, we had emergency cleanups for cemeteries every week because families needed assistance for funerals. And the Tribe offers programs that help dig graves for people and citizens, and those increased exponentially so much so that they couldn't even do the regular work that they were supposed to be doing. It was all focused on cemetery and funeral preparations. I know that we have had cultural knowledge and cultural keepers of our knowledge, knowledge bearers, traditional people, fluent speakers, church folks—I mean every aspect of our Tribe has been impacted. I see people on the news talk about, only one percent of people die from COVID, so let's just move on. Well, in our community, one percent is a lot of people. And we know every single person.[30]

Mvskoke Elder, and ceremonial ground member, Roman Powell states:

> I didn't realize it until they had the oak tree ceremony, and a list of all these ceremonial people that passed away. These were just ceremonial people. These were all our, I would say, upper echelon. All these were men of position at the ground. There's a lot of wisdom, a lot of advice that has passed on. We don't get to go back and talk to them again.[31]

Mvskoke citizen, Cebon Kernell speaks about the number of friends and colleagues he lost to COVID-19:

---

[30] RaeLynn Butler, interview by Midge Dellinger.

[31] Roman Powell, interview by Midge Dellinger, November 14, 2022, Tulsa, Oklahoma, transcript, *A Twenty-First Century Pandemic in Indian Country: The Resilience of the Muscogee (Creek) Nation Against COVID-19*, Muscogee (Creek) Nation National Library and Archives, https://mvskokenationallibraryarchive.org/digital-heritage/roman-powell-interview

But I think I was in the area of somewhere like twenty-seven or twenty-eight. I had to start writing them down, of the names of people that I had personally known. Not just acquaintances, Oh, so-and-so, so-and-so. People that would say, 'Cebon' (Mvskoke word for 'boy'), shake my hand. I've ate with them. I've prayed with them.[32]

In 2022, interviews were gathered from front line medical workers; those who experienced first-hand the horrors and devastation of COVID-19 to human health and life, and who worked tirelessly, putting their own lives at risk to care for the sick and dying. It is important to note that beginning in 2021, it was difficult to find medical personnel willing to talk about their experiences with the pandemic. This is very telling in how COVID-19 physically and mentally impacted medical workers in the Muscogee Nation and around the globe (Fig. 7.3).

Mvskoke citizen and Physician Assistant Kelsey Two Bears remembers:

We're going out to cars, using throwaway stethoscopes, things like that, taking things out to them, checking oxygen in the car. And that really, I know it kept me safe because I never got sick, not only COVID, but I didn't get anything for that time. I was seeing COVID patients all the time. I worked in the walk-in clinic, so we were actually seeing those patients outside at that point. I truly feel that Creek Nation did an excellent job. And they didn't panic. They were very cool, calm, collected throughout the whole thing, so I thought they did a really great job handling everything.[33]

Amy Portillo, a Mvskoke citizen and Emergency Room nurse working in a large urban hospital remembers the panic felt by co-workers, once COVID-19 arrived at their medical facility, she recalls:

---

[32] Cebon Kernell, interview by Midge Dellinger, February 27, 2023, Okmulgee, Oklahoma, transcript, *A Twenty-First Century Pandemic in Indian Country: The Resilience of the Muscogee (Creek) Nation Against COVID-19*, Muscogee (Creek) Nation National Library and Archives, https://mvskokenationallibraryarchive.org/digital-heritage/cebon-kernell-interview

[33] Kelsey Two Bears, interview by Midge Dellinger, February 27, 2022, Tulsa, Oklahoma, transcript, *A Twenty-First Century Pandemic in Indian Country: The Resilience of the Muscogee (Creek) Nation Against COVID-19*, Muscogee (Creek) Nation National Library and Archives, https://mvskokenationallibraryarchive.org/digital-heritage/kelsey-two-bears-interview

Fig. 7.3 "Tribute to the Healthcare Warriors in Indian Country During COVID-19." Credit: Johnnie Diacon, 2020

Especially there were some that were pregnant. And there was a couple that resigned. They were like, "I just don't want to risk my pregnancy, my family. And we were like, "Understandable." There was some panic among some of them, especially with the PPE [Personal Protective Equipment] shortage. We had to reuse our N95s for three days. There were nurses that would break down and cry because they were like, "You know, you're risking my life." And so, it—in the beginning, it really took a toll on everyone."[34]

Mvskoke citizen and Secretary of Veterans Affairs Grover Wind, who served as Chaplain in the early days of COVID-19, remembers the extreme difficulty of seeing patients die alone and the struggle of medical personnel who became the dying's last human connection on earth. He recalls:

[34] Amy Portillo, interview by Midge Dellinger, August 9, 2022, Okmulgee, Oklahoma, transcript, *A Twenty-First Century Pandemic in Indian Country: The Resilience of the Muscogee (Creek) Nation Against COVID-19*, Muscogee (Creek) Nation National Library and Archives, https://mvskokenationallibraryarchive.org/digital-heritage/amy-portillo-interview

I would get a call. It might be at ten o'clock at night. Can you come to the hospital? The nurses need you. And again, we would go in, and we'd pray.[35]

The COVID-19 experiences of medical professionals were harsh and unexpected, yet the rest of the world looked to them for health and well-being. The world should remember and be grateful for their service.

In 2020, Mvskoke artist Johnnie Diacon sheltered in place, and like millions of people, kept an eye on the news, where he recalls seeing images of the coronavirus. He remembers:

That little orb with the little red dots all over it.[36]

Compelled by the virus molecule and pandemic events across Indian Country, Mr. Diacon created a series of COVID-19 paintings. His painting, "Kvlonv Ennokvn (Coronavirus)," which in the Mvskoke language translates to "corona sickness," shows the virus molecule floating around an elderly Mvskoke couple. This painting conveys the sense of an invisible "Invader coming into our land,"[37] a reference to the history of the Mvskoke and settler encroachers on Mvskoke lands. Other paintings in the series are titled "Tribute to the Healthcare Warriors in Indian Country During COVID-19, 2020," and "Going for Groceries in the Time of the Pandemic."

As a final interview question, the forty narrators were asked to provide words of wisdom for surviving and finding life again after such a catastrophic event.

Muscogee (Creek) Nation Chief James Floyd (2016–2020) offers:

Memory is one good thing to have here because look at Muscogee (Creek) people and what we do recall from our past. We still talk about the removal and the things that were endured by our people but how that strengthened

---

[35] Grover Wind, interview by Midge Dellinger, December 10, 2021, Tulsa, Oklahoma, transcript, *A Twenty-First Century Pandemic in Indian Country: The Resilience of the Muscogee (Creek) Nation Against COVID-19*, Muscogee (Creek) Nation National Library and Archives, https://mvskokenationallibraryarchive.org/digital-heritage/grover-wind-interview

[36] Johnnie Diacon, interview by Midge Dellinger, March 17, 2022, Tulsa, Oklahoma, transcript, *A Twenty-First Century Pandemic in Indian Country: The Resilience of the Muscogee (Creek) Nation Against COVID-19*, Muscogee (Creek) Nation National Library and Archives, https://mvskokenationallibraryarchive.org/digital-heritage/johnnie-diacon

[37] Ibid.

us. I think recalling what we've gone through and using our knowledge to help us in the future is going to be very important. And so it kind of gets back to the history of our people and kind of studying what we've had to endure before, how we dealt with it, how we overcame it, how we went back in and built our society and how that sustained us.[38]

Mvskoke citizen and artist, Carly Treece believes:

You have to find joy in every day. Even with the anxieties of it. You have to look, and you have to find things that bring you joy; gardening, painting, dancing in your living room silly, and masking up and listening to your science professionals. That's how you survive it. Taking care of your community, helping.[39]

Cherokee citizen and MCN Behavioral Health Department Project Director Tyler Stone shares:

I would encourage future generations to learn about their history and their ancestors and appreciate the sense of resiliency that they had which allows us to be here today. That I have the blood of somebody who was forcefully removed from their homeland is in my blood today. And sometimes I forget about how huge that feels. That my ancestors went through so much, and that blood is in me today. And you get that sense of resiliency from that and that appreciation of how you're here today.[40]

---

[38] Chief James Floyd, interview by Midge Dellinger, March 16, 2021, Tulsa, Oklahoma, transcript, *A Twenty-First Century Pandemic in Indian Country: The Resilience of the Muscogee (Creek) Nation Against COVID-19*, Muscogee (Creek) Nation National Library and Archives, https://mvskokenationallibraryarchive.org/digital-heritage/chief-james-floyd-interview

[39] Carly Treece, interview by Midge Dellinger, December 21, 2022, Tulsa, Oklahoma, transcript, *A Twenty-First Century Pandemic in Indian Country: The Resilience of the Muscogee (Creek) Nation Against COVID-19*, Muscogee (Creek) Nation National Library and Archives, https://mvskokenationallibraryarchive.org/digital-heritage/carly-treece-interview

[40] Tyler Stone, interview by Midge Dellinger, November 4, 2022, Tulsa, Oklahoma, transcript, *A Twenty-First Century Pandemic in Indian Country: The Resilience of the Muscogee (Creek) Nation Against COVID-19*, Muscogee (Creek) Nation National Library and Archives, https://mvskokenationallibraryarchive.org/digital-heritage/tyler-stone-interview

Mvskoke citizen Laura Stewart advises to:

> Not give up hope and to keep loving each other.[41] People are resilient. You know, we find a way. And we'll find our way out of this.[42]

In her closing interview statement, Rebecca Barnett encourages:

> Take care of yourself. Stay clean. You know, my grandma used to tell me, she used to say never be dirty, in mind, in heart, in body. And there's ways, you know, to get through pandemics. Be ready for it. Help each other. Love each other.[43]

Mrs. Barnett remembers her traditional Mvskoke grandmother telling her,

> that love was the most precious thing. And she said long as you have that for people, you'll make it through anything. She used to tell me, if you got love, you have God. That's what they need to know.[44]

## Conclusion

As this chapter reveals, the ability to overcome tremendous adversity remains powerfully intact among Mvskoke descendants of the twenty-first century.

In testament to the Mvskoke understanding of life and living, Mvskoke citizen Jay Fife shares:

> So, in challenging times, it's important to remember that, "aye mahvs", which in our language means, "Keep going." So, I hope that no future generations of Muscogee people have to go through another global pandemic. But in an event that it does happen, just reflect on the importance of love, of family, of kinship, of land, of space, of time. You have to keep going and

---

[41] Laura Stewart, interview by Midge Dellinger, October 1, 2021, Tulsa, Oklahoma, transcript, *A Twenty-First Century Pandemic in Indian Country: The Resilience of the Muscogee (Creek) Nation Against COVID-19*, Muscogee (Creek) Nation National Library and Archives, https://mvskokenationallibraryarchive.org/digital-heritage/laura-stewart-interview

[42] Ibid.

[43] Rebecca Barnett, interview by Midge Dellinger.

[44] Ibid.

that's what our Muscogee people did. They kept going. And that's all that matters for us as Mvskokvlke. As long as we keep going, we're going to be all right.[45]

From a Mvskoke youth perspective, Gabrielle Noriega offers this:

I'd say just keep going. Be strong and just know everything will be okay in the end. Just keep striving for better for yourself no matter what is thrown at you. Sometimes Creator's just trying to see how far you can bend before you break, so just keep going.[46]

COVID-19 appeared around the globe as a ramrod of sickness, death, and chaos. It robbed its victims of wellness and life. Many survivors live as if the COVID-19 pandemic never happened. Others now approach life with a new attitude and respect for the power and potential of things unseen and unknown, such as a microscopic virus eager to snuff out everything humans take for granted, including human existence. Either way, life continues post-pandemic. The world has moved on, but what does the world remember and what are its lessons learned? The trauma, turmoil, and acts of resilience by all who experienced the COVID-19 pandemic deserve their place within its historical narrative. Such historical inclusivity is imperative so that a complete and authentic story of the pandemic lingers in public memory.

And, what can the pandemic experiences of Indian Country teach us about life, living, and survival? When the world was turned upside down by the COVID-19 pandemic, and seemingly no one was paying attention to its impact on Indian Country, the people of the Muscogee (Creek) Nation did as they have always done in times of trauma and turmoil, they resorted to their own acts of resilience and survival. And they *remembered*. They remembered the suffering and sacrifice of Mvskoke ancestors, and just as

---

[45] Jay Fife, interview by Midge Dellinger, February 21, 2022, Tulsa, Oklahoma, transcript, *A Twenty-First Century Pandemic in Indian Country: The Resilience of the Muscogee (Creek) Nation Against COVID-19*, Muscogee (Creek) Nation National Library and Archives, https://mvskokenationallibraryarchive.org/digital-heritage/jay-fife

[46] Gabrielle Noriega, interview by Midge Dellinger, December 17, 2021, Okmulgee, Oklahoma, transcript, *A Twenty-First Century Pandemic in Indian Country: The Resilience of the Muscogee (Creek) Nation Against COVID-19*, Muscogee (Creek) Nation National Library and Archives, https://mvskokenationallibraryarchive.org/digital-heritage/gabrielle-noriega

importantly, they remembered their ancestors' words of encouragement, to not look back, keep looking forward, and keep moving forward.

It is essential to remember that the peoples indigenous to the lands now called the United States have existed since time immemorial, experiencing the ebb and flow of life, including the many traumas inflicted through settler oppression and domination. So when considering the many attributes of Indigenous peoples and their place on Mother Earth, it is their innate wisdom, courage, tenacity, and ability to survive that keeps them everpresent. And it is a perpetual and ever mindful connection to who they have been, who they are today, and who they will always be that allows them to remain unwavering in their journey ever-forward.

> Visit the Muscogee (Creek) Nation National Library and Archives to learn more about the Mvskoke and their experiences with the COVID-19 pandemic. www.mvskokenationallibraryarchive.org.
> *In memory of all Mvskoke who have lost their lives to COVID-19.*

**Competing Interests Declaration** The authors have no conflicts of interest to declare that are relevant to the content of this chapter.

PART III

# Students, Innovative Learning, and Community Building

Throughout the United States, the pandemic posed major challenges at all levels of education. Adjusting to stay-at-home orders and distance learning was universally difficult, but particularly for Indigenous families and students who had limited Internet access, as well as for those attending college who were often isolated from critical support networks. Places of higher learning can be alienating places for many Indigenous people in the best times, much less during pandemic quarantines. Understanding the involved perils, Indigenous and non-Native instructors, support staff, and student groups devised new ways to facilitate learning and personal well-being.

Based on oral interviews conducted with participants from multiple Native nations, Amoneeta Beckstein and Tapati Dutta's opening chapter documents the lived experiences of Native college students during the pandemic. Multiple themes emerge, on the one hand, emphasizing the emotional traumas students suffered, as well as their feelings of helplessness and anger, and, on the other hand, revealing how they leaned on each other and drew strength from their cultural identities to endure the ordeal. The participants and authors also share valuable guidance for academic institutions needing to better serve Indigenous students in times of both calm and crisis.

The Mentoring and Encouraging Student Academic Success program at Utah State University serves as a model for how institutions can indeed serve Native students well in difficult times. In the second entry, Daniel Piper, Melissa Tehee, Racheal Killgore, and Erica Ficklin describe how their program team responded to very stressful times by innovating ways to sustain the Native campus community, including through virtual talking circles. "Together, we found ways to bring in laughter and cultural practices," explains Tehee. "We found new ways to weave culture and higher education and better the system we live, learn, and work in."

Next, Chelsea Mead tells of cooperative efforts by instructors, students, and staff at two Midwestern universities to continue revitalizing the Ojibwe language. Losing fluent Elders to COVID-19 further threatened the language, as did obstacles shutdowns posed for learners. These "language warriors" responded by successfully transitioning their instruction fully online and delivering customized "sense of belonging" care packages. These efforts facilitated language learning and served many nontraditional and long-distance learners for the first time. In the process, peoples' spirits were lifted and a powerful sense of community was instilled.

In the closing chapter of this section, Kelly Berry, in a storyteller's voice, explains how he also experienced the importance of community amid the pandemic, in his case while in the role of a "reluctant leader," guiding Elder faculty in adapting to online teaching at Riverside Indian School. Under the most trying circumstances, and in mind of the traumas past generations of Native American youth experienced in those same hallways, Berry and the school faculty accomplished a smooth and quick transition. They found ways to work together productively and harmoniously through determined efforts, shows of mutual respect, and much-needed moments of laughter.

These are all stories of dedicated educators and students tapping their personal and communal strength to adapt and innovate in order to meet an immediate crisis. In doing so, they transformed ways Indigenous people would teach and learn in the post-pandemic future.

CHAPTER 8

# Lived Experiences of Native American College Students During the COVID-19 Pandemic

## Amoneeta Beckstein and Tapati Dutta

The COVID-19 pandemic affected every aspect of life. College students were impacted[1] and many may continue experiencing negative consequences. It is predicted to affect higher education for many more years,[2] possibly even for generations, and these effects will be disproportional for some groups.[3] COVID-19 seems to have emphasized the disparities felt

---

[1] Aleksander Aristovnik, Damijana Keržič, Dejan Ravšelj, Nina Tomaževič, and Lan Umek, "Impacts of the COVID-19 pandemic on life of higher education students: A global perspective," *Sustainability* 12, no. 20 (2020): 8438.

[2] Giorgio Marinoni, Hilligje Van't Land, and Trine Jensen, "The impact of Covid-19 on higher education around the world," *IAU global survey report* 23 (2020): 1–17.

[3] Jillian Kinzie, and James Cole, "Education disrupted: Students beginning college during the COVID-19 pandemic," *New Directions for Higher Education* 2022, no. 199 (2022): 27–40.

A. Beckstein (✉) • T. Dutta
Fort Lewis College, Durango, CO, USA
e-mail: amoneeta@fortlewis.edu; tdutta@fortlewis.edu

© The Author(s), under exclusive license to Springer Nature Switzerland AG 2024
F. King, W. Davies (eds.), *COVID-19 in Indian Country*,
https://doi.org/10.1007/978-3-031-70184-9_8

by Indigenous peoples worldwide that were already present for years due to effects of colonization.[4] Some Native American college students might be particularly at risk of negative academic and mental health consequences.[5] For example, Native American students saw a decline in their ACT scores during the pandemic.[6] On the other hand, Native college students have shown extreme *reziliency*[7] and survivance during these times.[8] This chapter highlights how Native American college students experienced inequities during the pandemic, much like their ancestors have experienced negative consequences for generations. However, similar to their ancestors, they have also demonstrated unique strengths and survivance skills.

College students in general suffered in numerous ways during the pandemic and students of color, including Native Americans, seem to have been affected disproportionately.[9] Indeed, high percentages of college students of color experienced challenges with their academic performance

---

[4] Sarah de Leeuw et al., "With Reserves: Colonial Geographies and First Nations Health," *Annals of the Association of American Geographers* 102, no. 5 (2012): 904–911, doi: https://doi.org/10.1080/00045608.2012.674897.

[5] Tara Hembrough, and Misty Cavanagh, "Covid-19, stress factors of Native American and Caucasian college students, and implementing classroom dialogues," *International Journal of Instruction* 15, no. 4 (2022): 515–534.

[6] Jeff Allen, "Examining the COVID-19 Pandemic's Impacts on Native American Students' College and Career Readiness. ACT Research. Technical Brief," *ACT, Inc.* (2022).

[7] Annjeanette E. Belcourt-Dittloff, "Resiliency and risk in Native American communities: A culturally informed investigation," PhD diss., (University of Montana, 2007). Note: The alternative spelling of resiliency was used since some have argued that resiliency may look different among Native Americans than other groups.

[8] Erika Derkas, "Disrupting Native Invisibility, Dismantling Settler Colonial Racism and Enhancing Educational Outcomes for Indigenous Students," *The COVID-19 Crisis and Racial Justice & Equity: Addressing the Twin Pandemics* special issue, *Journal of Higher Education Management* 36, no. 1 (2021): 82.

[9] Apurvakumar Pandya and Pragya Lodha, "Mental health consequences of COVID-19 pandemic among college students and coping approaches adapted by higher education institutions: A scoping review," *SSM-Mental Health* 2 (2022): 100122; Markus Lundström, "Young in pandemic times: a scoping review of COVID-19 social impacts on youth," *International Journal of Adolescence and Youth* 27, no. 1 (2022): 432–443; Lia M. Daniels, Lauren D. Goegan, and Patti C. Parker, "The impact of COVID-19 triggered changes to instruction and assessment on university students' self-reported motivation, engagement and perceptions," *Social Psychology of Education* 24, no. 1 (2021): 299–318.

and progress during the pandemic;[10] for example, they had greater challenges transitioning to the study from home format and having access to the needed technology.[11] They also experienced more mental health challenges and abuse and were at greater risk of both housing and food insecurity and lack of Internet access than other students.[12]

We conducted a broad literature review of psychology and public health databases as well as Google Scholar, which revealed very little empirical research that has been conducted addressing Native American undergraduate student experiences during the pandemic. Even less is grounded in qualitative methodologies. Other studies acknowledge the general lack of

---

[10] Sherry Davis Molock and Benjamin Parchem, "The Impact of COVID-19 on College Students from Communities of Color," *Journal of American College Health* 70, no. 8 (2021): 2399–2405, doi: https://doi.org/10.1080/07448481.2020.1865380.

[11] Krista M. Soria, Brayden J. Roberts, Bonnie Horgos, and Katie Hallahan, "Undergraduates' Experiences During the COVID-19 Pandemic: Disparities by Race and Ethnicity," *SERU Consortium, University of California - Berkeley and University of Minnesota* (2020): Retrieved from the University of Minnesota Digital Conservancy, https://hdl.handle.net/11299/218339

[12] Molock and Parchem, "The Impact of COVID"; Soria et al., "Undergraduates Experiences"; Allen, "Examining the COVID-19 Pandemic's Impacts on Native American Students' College and Career Readiness"; Débora Petry Moecke, Travis Holyk, Madelaine Beckett, Sunaina Chopra, Polina Petlitsyna, Mirha Girt, Ashley Kirkham et al. "Scoping review of telehealth use by Indigenous populations from Australia, Canada, New Zealand, and the United States," *Journal of Telemedicine and Telecare* (2023): 1357633X231158835; Candi Running Bear, William PA Terrill, Adriana Frates, Patricia Peterson, and Judith Ulrich, "Challenges for rural Native American students with disabilities during COVID-19," *Rural Special Education Quarterly* 40, no. 2 (2021): 60–69; cmaadmin (EDU), "The Digital Divide for Tribal College Students—COVID, Cares Act, and Critical next Steps," Diverse, last modified November 14, 2022. https://www.diverseeducation.com/podcasts/podcast/15108265/the-digital-divide-for-tribal-college-students-covid-cares-act-and-critical-next-steps; Byron Tsabetsaye (Diné), "Internet and Technology Access during the COVID-19 Pandemic: A Chronological Account and Approach to Helping Native American Students in the Navajo Northern Agency," NASPA: Student Affairs Administrators in Higher Education, accessed August 31, 2023, https://www.naspa.org/blog/internet-and-technology-access-during-the-covid-19-pandemic-a-chronological-account-and-approach-to-helping-native-american-students-in-the-navajo-northern-agency; Olya Glantsman et al., "Risk of Food and Housing Insecurity among College Students during the COVID-19 Pandemic," *Journal of Community Psychology* 50, no. 6 (2022): 2726–45, doi: https://doi.org/10.1002/jcop.22853.

representativeness of Native American participants.[13] Exploring their lived experiences can not only shine light on real stories but also highlight some of the strengths and *reziliency* factors of Native Americans during the pandemic.[14] Indeed, some Native college students appeared to have leaned on their cultural heritages to help cope with the crisis.[15] Although one study looked at underrepresented graduate students' lived experiences during the pandemic, it only contained one Native student. And another study only considered the lived experiences of Native American Elders.[16] A third focused on the lived experiences of college students from the Kumeyaay Tribe but was not related to the COVID-19 pandemic.[17]

To compliment these existing studies and bring to light the important lived experiences of Native college students, this study interviewed individuals who attended college during the pandemic to explore what themes emerged from their experiences. On the one hand, we anticipated that the injustices and disparities due to the long history of colonization and intergenerational trauma that other researchers have found[18] would be present. While on the other, we anticipated that themes of *reziliency*, survivance, and community support would also emerge.[19]

---

[13] Kelly M. Correia et al., "Education Racial and Gender Disparities in Covid-19 Worry, Stress, and Food Insecurities across Undergraduate Biology Students at a Southeastern University," *Journal of Microbiology & Biology Education* 23, no. 1 (2022), doi: https://doi.org/10.1128/jmbe.00224-21.

[14] Rosalind Reid, "Native American Communities Battling Covid-19 Draw on Strengths," CASW, Last modified June 15, 2021, https://casw.org/news/native-american-communities-battling-covid-19-draw-on-strengths/

[15] McKenzie Allen-Charmley, "Native American College Students Found Strength in Their Heritage That Helped Them Get through the Pandemic," CNBC, last modified August 11, 2021, https://www.cnbc.com/2021/08/11/native-american-students-found-strength-in-their-heritage-during-covid.html

[16] Bridget A. Walsh et al., "Historically Underrepresented Graduate Students' Experiences during the COVID-19 Pandemic," *Family Relations* 70, no. 4 (2021): 955–72, doi: https://doi.org/10.1111/fare.12574; Bo Xie et al., "Native American Elders' Experiences during the COVID-19 Pandemic: Case Studies," *Innovation in Aging* 5, no. Supplement_1 (2021): 883, doi: https://doi.org/10.1093/geroni/igab046.3214.

[17] R.R. Ramos, "Exploring the Lived Experience of Kumeyaay College Graduates," PhD diss., (Bethel University, 2021), Spark Repository. https://spark.bethel.edu/etd/750

[18] Blume, *Colonialism and COVID-19*.

[19] Belcourt-Dittloff, *Resiliency and risk*; Rachel E.Wilbur and Joseph P. Gone, "Beyond resilience: A scoping review of Indigenous survivance in the health literature," *Development and Psychopathology* (2023): 1–15; Gone and Trimble, "American Indian Enduring Disparities."

## Methods

This study was approved as exempt by the college's Institutional Review Board (IRB-2023-27). We attempted to use a phenomenological approach[20] which recognizes that our participants' realities are constructed by them based on their lived experiences and data emerges from interaction with the researcher.

### *Researcher Positionality and Reflexivity*

The research team consisted of two Assistant Professors. We introduce ourselves below.

*Amoneeta*

I identify as a cisgender male Indigenous American professor and counseling psychologist. Previously, I conducted some limited research about Native Americans affected by the pandemic.[21] I tried to engage in reflexivity (reflecting on my own values, beliefs, and assumptions that might affect the research) during the current study to try to reduce the effects of pre-existing experience that might have biased the results.

*Tapati*

I identify as a cisgender female, Asian-Indian social scientist and inclusion strategist professor of public health. Previously, I conducted a mixed-methods study among Native American students exploring their COVID-19 vaccine perceptions and prevention behavior.[22] I coauthored

---

[20] Joanne Mayoh and Anthony J. Onwuegbuzie, "Toward a Conceptualization of Mixed Methods Phenomenological Research," *Journal of Mixed Methods Research*, 9, no. 1 (2015): 91–107. https://doi.org/10.1177/1558689813505358; C. Willig, *Introducing Qualitative Research in Psychology, Adventures in Theory and Method* (Open University Press, 2008).
[21] Amoneeta Beckstein, How Indigenous Peoples of North America Are Coping with Covid-19, last modified October 6, 2020, https://www.psychreg.org/indigenous-peoples-of-north-america-covid-19/
[22] Tapati Dutta, "College Student COVID-19 Vaccination Prevalence and Context: A 'Pulse' Survey Conducted Before and After Formal Statewide Rollout," in APHA 2022 Annual Meeting and Expo, APHA (2022, November).

a paper highlighting how "storytelling" was utilized in a Native American-serving college as an effective pedagogic method during COVID-19.[23] I also engaged in reflexivity during the current study.

### Study Design

The study included self-identified Native American undergraduate students enrolled in college between Spring 2020 and Spring 2022. Students were recruited in March 2023 through fliers, class announcements, emails to a Native American student club, and to the college's psychology and public health student listservs, and through a priori relationships we had with our students.

A seven open-ended question, semi-structured interview guide was developed and used to facilitate the interviews.

### Participants

Eight self-identified Native Americans who were students during the pandemic participated. We did not ask about tribal enrollment, although the majority did indicate being enrolled members on their own accord when asked for their tribal identity. There were four that identified as Diné (Navajo), two as Diné and Zuni, one as Cheyenne River Sioux, and one as Isleta and Taos Pueblos. The majority were female ($n = 7$) while the remaining participant was male ($n = 1$). Ages ranged from 20 to 31 ($M = 23.9$). To protect their anonymity and confidentiality, participants' real names were not recorded nor associated with any of their data. They were asked to choose a pseudonym or if they did not choose their own, then a name was randomly chosen and assigned.

---

[23] Tapati Dutta and Camille Keith, "Evolution of storytelling pedagogy in global health course at a US Native American-Serving Nontribal Institution from Fall 2019 to Spring 2023," *Frontiers in Public Health* 11 (2023);

Tapati Dutta, Beth Meyerson, Jon Agley, Priscilla Barnes, Catherine Sherwood-Laughlin, and Jill Nicholson-Crotty, "A Qualitative Analysis of Vaccine Decision-Makers' Conceptualization and Fostering of 'Community Engagement' In India," *Journal for Equity in Health* 19, no. 1 (2020): 1–14, https://doi.org/10.21203/rs.3.rs-29175/v4

### Data Collection

Amoneeta conducted eight interviews from March to May 2023 via Zoom. Amoneeta explained the research objectives and mentioned confidentiality. Verbal informed consent was sought from each interviewee along with asking if they had read the implied consent form. None of the students had any questions and all consented verbally. Participants were informed that they could withdraw from the study at any time and were also offered free debriefing with either of the researchers or with the campus counseling center. All interviews were conducted in English and lasted approximately 40–50 minutes.

### Data Analysis and Reporting

All the interview recordings were transcribed by Zoom and saved on a shared online folder that required two passwords to access. We listened to the interviews and cleaned the transcriptions.

To improve the rigor of the analysis and interrater reliability, we each first independently reviewed and manually coded half (four) of the interviews based on broad themes that we observed.[24] Thereafter, we discussed the emerging themes and any discrepancies until we reached consensus. We appeared to have adequate interrater reliability since many of our themes for many sections of data were similar. Thereafter, we both revisited the transcripts, and each coded them using the newly agreed upon code book.

## Results

Not all the data fit neatly into categories and there were naturally overlaps. Some student comments fit into multiple themes and were coded as such. There were also many comments that did not fit the general themes of the chapter that were excluded from the coding but still contained rich data. Below we list the themes, and then we share some direct quotes as examples of each to give voice to the students' direct lived experiences.

The final set of themes consisted of the following broad domains, each of which had several interrelated sub-themes:

---

[24] We used a color tool in Microsoft Word to highlight the different codes.

I. *Positive Responses*

   (a) Collectivistic coping/Sense of community
   (b) Culture as treatment/Opportunity to reconnect to culture
   (c) *Rezilience*/Survivance/Positive coping/Peritraumatic growth

II. *Negative Impacts*

   (a) Differences/Changes due to COVID-19
   (b) Historical trauma/Injustices
   (c) Uncomfortable effects on mental health

III. *College-Specific Student Experiences*

   (a) Learning challenges
   (b) Positive actions the college took
   (c) Recommendations for what the college could have handled better/could do in the future

## *Positive Responses*

The first main theme that emerged was related to how all the students expressed actually benefiting from the circumstances surrounding the pandemic. They all discussed ways that they had opportunities to focus on areas that had some positive influence on their lives in general and their mental health and well-being. Under this main theme, three subthemes emerged.

### *Collectivistic Coping/Sense of Community*

The first subtheme was based on how the students described experiences of coping collectivistically through interrelated relationships, often with other Native American people. As part of this theme, they also discussed ways of dealing with the pandemic circumstances through connecting with and feeling a sense of community with their Native American friends, family, extended family, and broader community. All eight students brought up examples of this subtheme.

For example, Laya discussed the broader Native community-based support she saw:

> ...they were passing out food and supplies, or PPE out to different communities, to Elders, or those who needed it within communities also, like

those food trucks for food distribution, or PPE distribution, and they saw, like so many communities come together doing that.

Ray, on the other hand, talked about the broader Native community that she found supportive at her college during the pandemic which helped keep her from dropping out:

> …when I came here [to college] I definitely found, like community with a Native population, that I probably wouldn't have gotten anywhere else… finding a community in the Indigenous community, definitely made it more unique, as opposed to just going to some other college and trying to fit in…
> [Later in the interview, she says]: I definitely think the community aspect was a huge part, and why I came back actually. And the Native students on this campus are great.

Similarly, Tori brought up the Native community on campus as a positive support during the pandemic:

> …having that Native American population here was helpful to know that there's a lot of Native students here who are in the same boat as you… if I went to school like somewhere that was predominantly white, I would have felt more excluded.

Others emphasized family support. For example, David said, "I had a lot more connection with my family at that time." Laya also referred to how the mutual support given and received from her family was helpful to cope: "…we're very family oriented, so I feel we needed a ton of support from our families as well… But for us our family is our aunties, our uncles, our cousins, our cousins' kids, and it's just like one whole giant group." Jamiah discussed how going home to her family helped both her and her family reduce stress: "…what really helped was just being able to go home and be with family instead of like worrying about them and having them worry about us."

Kyiah emphasized how friends were important to that collectivistic coping and how she learned to value them more:

> …just appreciating the friendships I have with my friends, because, like, people were just passing away from COVID, and you really didn't know who was next. And so, I guess, just seeing my friends again, which is something to be more appreciative, and to take our friendship more seriously.

Tori also shared how her Native American friends helped her cope positively with the pandemic:

> I feel like it was just being friends with, like the other Native students, too... if I was friends with non-Native students, they wouldn't understand the things that I would be experiencing, or what I'm coming from, or why I would have to travel all the way back home for a vaccine rather than just getting it here.

*Culture as Treatment/Opportunity to Reconnect to Culture*
The second subtheme was also positive in nature. This subtheme was endorsed by all the students. It consisted of comments that seemed to indicate that many of the students appreciated opportunities to reconnect with their traditional Native culture, learn more, and via that reconnection improve their well-being during the uncertain times of the pandemic.

David described how recognizing his Native roots helped him worry less, "...as a Native person, I was less worried than like non-Indigenous people... We're supposed to be here. This is sacred so." He also mentioned how prayer helped reduce mental health symptoms: "we got to pray a lot during this time." Kyiah also spoke of burning cedar and engaging in prayer with her family, praying that the pandemic would end, and their family would not get sick. Amber also frequently mentioned praying a lot. The way she described using *culture as treatment* overlapped with the previous subtheme of collectivistic coping:

> ...we built that kinship like through *K'é*, that is our relations, so through that we step together and we pray together, and we gathered different herbs and boiled sage—drank sage every day.

Gwen also talked about using prayer often and also how her Native faith helped her have confidence that things would turn out well, "...just like praying every day, and knowing, like our Creator, is protecting us and stuff." Jamiah talked about participating in a traditional ceremony, a sweat lodge that her family built during the pandemic, as particularly helpful to reduce both physical and mental health symptoms related to COVID-19. She said, "...just being able to kind of go back to our roots [was] really, really cool. And it was like really effective." Later she said it was "our self-medication, I would think, like our self-therapy."

Tori touched on having the opportunity to learn from Elders during the pandemic, "...for them to teach us those certain values or beliefs, or cult... like traditions." Kyiah also found the time spent with family during the pandemic as an opportunity to decolonize herself and engage in practices that brought her closer to her culture like beadwork and time in nature:

> It also gave me the opportunity to learn more of my language... And I think I also saw the opportunity to learn more of our culture, and just stopping like assimilation and learning how to pray and do certain ceremonies and stuff like that...

Both Ray and Gwen described how they were able to more connect with their culture at college. Ray discussed how being involved with Native campus clubs, spending time at the Native support center, and generally being around other Natives "allowed me to find, like my own identity as a Native American student." Amber also brought up that falling back on culture gave her community strength and reinforced their Indigenous identity. Later, Ray went on to mention that the campus provided "...a lot of different opportunities to smudge outside at different open, outside events..." Gwen experienced something similar through her academic work:

> ...coming up here I learned a lot more about stuff that I was interested in, which is exactly that intergenerational trauma and colonization in accordance to my Native side, and I originally did a couple of research projects on boarding schools and colonization...

*Resilience/Survivance/Positive Coping/Peritraumatic Growth ("Experience of Significant Positive Change Arising from the Struggle with a Major Life Crisis"[25])*
The third subtheme was just as powerfully positive. All the students endorsed this theme by bringing up different examples that spoke to their and their communities' Indigenous strengths that helped them cope with and even grow during the pandemic.

---

[25] Lawrence G. Calhoun, Arnie Cann, Richard G. Tedeschi, and Jamie McMillan, "A Correlational Test of the Relationship between Posttraumatic Growth, Religion, and Cognitive Processing," *Journal of Traumatic Stress* 13, no. 3 (2000): 521–527.

Amber described the history of trauma and disparities in her community that have resulted in becoming *rezilient* and how that *reziliency* helped them get into a "survival state of mind again" to cope during the pandemic. Similarly, the history of survivance of his ancestors gave David confidence that he would make it through this pandemic which "makes me feel like just more confident or stronger or something." He went on to say, "it definitely helped me to get through school." Others connected this theme to their academics as well. Tori talked about, despite everything being very different, doing well in several classes after they went online. She was grateful that she was able to navigate the changes and complications and was "really able to work around things" while recognizing that other Native students might not have had it as easy as her.

As mentioned before, Ray was able to grow in her Native identity which helped her not drop out. Similarly, Jamiah said, "being able to do more things that brought out your personality kind of for me was like a really positive thing." She had more time for hobbies, and she found out that she was good at "basically just finding out more about myself." The time when the college was closed and students studied from home gave Laya and Kyiah more time to slow down and engage in meaningful activities such as being in nature, exercising, walking the dog, meditating, and appreciating the pause that let Mother Nature rest. Laya described having more of a sense of balance: "…it kind of made me think that maybe this happened because we needed to stop and actually breathe… to rest, like that kind of balance from what we've been doing for years." Gwen also described having a greater understanding and acceptance of the circumstances as having a greater purpose.

Jamiah also saw positives of living through a pandemic from the perspective of being a psychology and public health student due to the parallels with what she was learning. For example, it shifted her mindset about mental health: "It kind of really opened up my eyes to be more aware of people around me rather than just like myself." She also expressed that there was more awareness and acceptance generally regarding mental health among Natives.

### *Negative Impacts*

The next broad theme was related to some of the uncomfortable, sometimes labelled negative effects of the pandemic on mental health and well-being. Native students and their communities had to cope with negative impacts such as abrupt and sometimes ongoing changes, the continuing and exacerbated effects of intergenerational trauma, the threat and actual loss of traditional cultures, and harmful influences on mental health.

*Differences/Changes Due to COVID-19*
The first subtheme related to the sudden and then often ongoing, sometimes very drastic changes that occurred that shifted the students' lives. Seven of the eight students discussed this theme. It included things like social distancing, virtual learning and socializing, travel and movement restrictions, Native communities closing to outsiders, reducing the spread guidelines, isolation from loved ones, stopping normal lives, testing, mask wearing, reduction in resources and funds, and more. These COVID-19-induced changes had to be adapted to and coped with and sometimes students had to grieve their previous lives lost.

Many Native communities imposed strict travel restrictions, curfews, and even closures to try to reduce the spread of COVID-19. Ray described the restrictions on her reservation: "It definitely hurt because we weren't able to celebrate, and it definitely was a very different environment than what I was used to growing up." Jamiah also talked about strict restrictions and mandates in her reservation but said that it bothered her that some of her community did not take it seriously, especially in light of the high numbers of cases among Native peoples.

Some students brought up how the restrictions interrupted their ability to collectively connect with their people. Laya, for example, said: "I actually didn't go home to the reservation… [it] felt like for almost two years." Kyiah had a similar experience:

> Because my family is a type to have dinners all the time, and just being among family, and so not seeing them like every other weekend, was, was pretty hard, and the only way to communicate with them by phone.

As opposed to the previous subtheme of being able to reconnect with traditional culture, some students also experienced reduction in the same. Gwen expressed it well: "All our traditional ceremonies and all of our traditional ways of going about like our daily lives, all were on hold." Laya also experienced this:

> ….me and my fiancé's families would hold regularly family functions. Some of them were ceremonial and so I feel like we were almost forced in a way not to be able to practice some of these only because of all the restrictions

were there and all the CDC recommendations. And so, I feel like that made it harder, because we could not go to the ceremonies, or whatever, like all our traditional things to recenter ourselves or to be in a good place. And throughout this whole thing we weren't able to do that and I feel it made it hard to focus as well.

Similarly, two other students described fears and experiences of losing their traditional Native culture. This was mostly through comments about losing the wise Elders who hold the knowledge, wisdom, language, traditions, etc.

Jamiah pointed out that "a lot of the people who did kind of pass away were like the Native speakers. I felt like in our culture, we lost a lot more." Tori's comments exemplified this even further:

> The Elders being like a vulnerable population, our Elders, were the ones who are more fluent in our language, and also who are more, I guess, immersed into our culture and our traditions, and so for them to be getting COVID, or to be like dying and being a part of those statistics, it was kind of disheartening to think that well, there goes our language and there goes our culture.

*Historical Trauma/Injustices*

The next subtheme was related to Native Americans' long history of being colonized and exploited and how that history interacted with the contemporary circumstances of the pandemic. All eight students mentioned this theme in some way. Sometimes students discussed how that history contributed to modern disparities that caused more hardship for Native Americans than some other groups. More than half the students brought up the fact that lack of resources such as running water, electricity, nearby medical facilities, and Internet, etc., may have contributed to disproportionate negative consequences for Natives, particularly those on reservations. Other students mentioned underlying diseases and discrimination and racism all making Natives more vulnerable. Many connected these disparities and circumstances to the colonial history. As Tori brings up, "COVID really hit the minority population a little hard, especially the like lower SES family... like Native people, is how we didn't have the resources."

Tori talked about how in her community...

> ...some families on the rez didn't have money to get masks, hand sanitizers, or anything like that. You could really see like that different advantage... [We] weren't given like PPE. Instead, we are given like body bags, and it was kind of like, I guess a slap in the face, too, and just, yeah, really, just colonization... Just a lack of resources with the hospital. We didn't have the proper equipment.

Tori also talked about distrusting non-Native people to give her the COVID-19 vaccine. She connected that to colonization history, "The smallpox, or something like that... the blankets that were given to Native people... I guess that's where the distrust came." Laya also talked about the death rate on her reservation and connected that to "all the times the U.S. Government came in and purposely spread disease."

Laya also considered vaccines being offered to her community very early on as using Native people as guinea pigs. Somewhat similar to Tori and Laya, Ray was distrustful of the vaccines in general, especially when they were offered to her Tribe before other groups, due to...

> ...like history wise and being colonized is that Natives usually are the first to kind of be, you know, end quote, tested on trial runs and things like that... in alignment with some unethical things that have happened in the past of using Native folks as guinea pigs.

David further explained about this mistrust:

> ...people don't know why Native people don't trust medical professionals, medical facility, and teaching people about instances where, like the US Government and the medical community has wronged Native people.

The seven students who were associated with the Diné Nation all talked about how their Nation was particularly affected more negatively than many other groups in America. David said:

> COVID was a big thing on the Navajo [Diné] Nation; it like tore through the whole community... It just reminded us of a lot about like diseases running through Native communities and tearing through them. And it happens a lot in history... on the news... it was just mostly Native people are dying.

## Uncomfortable Effects on Mental Health

While students all spoke of *positive coping*, all eight students also endorsed this next *uncomfortable sub*theme. This was the most common subtheme with the greatest number of mentions by the students overall. They all discussed examples of how the pandemic increased various mental health symptoms and behaviors that they had to cope with. Together they brought up symptoms of grief, anxiety, panic, isolation, loneliness, fear ("really scary"), it being "rough" and "hard," sadness (using terms like "heartbreaking" and "disheartening"), anger, helplessness, stress, worry (especially about their family and community), annoyance, demotivation ("really discouraging"), difficulties concentrating, emotional dysregulation, imbalance, disharmony, relationship issues, addictive behaviors, role strain, struggles to adjust/adapt, and suicidal ideation, and completed suicide in their communities. Several also brought up challenges with barriers to support, help, and treatment.

The students expressed that the pandemic affected them personally and their families and communities in terms of mental health. Ray stated, "I would say mental health issues were definitely at the forefront... every aspect in my life was really like, affected." This is also exemplified by Tori's reflections:

> It really took a toll on my mental health, and just seeing those numbers specifically to the Navajo [Diné] Nation, was very heartbreaking, and it made me like very depressed that I didn't want it—keep watching the numbers grow.

The collective nature of Native culture was also interwoven through this subtheme with the students expressing concern for their families, Elders, vulnerable groups, and communities. This can be seen in comments like Laya's: "I feel sometimes it was hard just watching all these different communities suffer" and Gwen's: "...it kind of did take a toll on every community member." Laya brought up later in the interview that "it was still difficult, because I just didn't have that connection with being able to go home." Jamiah also stated that the pandemic "...affected, I feel like, my whole community in a lot of ways."

While other subthemes highlighted adaptive coping, this one brought up maladaptive coping. Laya admitted that "...here in town I coped kind of negatively, using substance abuse, mainly alcohol."

## College-Specific Student Experiences

The next main theme was related to the students' experiences specifically as Native American college students during the pandemic. This included discussions about many various challenges they faced to continue their educations, positive things the students observed or heard about their college doing, and recommendations about things that the college could have done better or could do in the future under similar circumstances.

### Learning Challenges

This subtheme showed how higher education shifted during this time and highlighted the challenges experienced by this group of Native American students. Six of the eight students brought up this subtheme. Different factors were brought up such as the shift to virtual learning, being distracted or not able to focus, some faculty and family not being understanding, lack of appropriate study space, or lack of Internet where the student lived.

Kyiah shared, "It was kind of hard for me to pay attention 'til the end of the lecture and I started not to fall behind, but kind of like slack off on my homework… I had that distraction of being home and like being lazy." Some students described how academics might not have been top priority compared to concerns for family, community, vulnerable Elders, and humanity. Tori said, "…maybe some students just thought like, well, my family is more important. So, I should go and take care of them, and try to take care of my grandpa and grandma." Similarly, Amber described one of her friends contracting COVID-19 during their finals: "Being there for them was my highest priority before being a student and getting through my finals."

Others mentioned the challenges of balancing important life domains with school, especially with the overlapping domains. Jamiah said, "[It was] pretty hard trying to juggle school, and then my personal life" which ended up influencing her to take a year off school. Native students had unique challenges as they struggled balancing the two worlds of Westernized education and their more traditional Indigenous home life. For example, some talked about professors not understanding the challenges unique to Natives and their worldviews. And at the same time some of their families did not seem to understand the pressures and expectations the students had from their university (e.g., expecting them to help take care of the farm animals and participate in ceremony). It seems that Jamiah was not the only Native student who either took time off or dropped out of university during those times. Gwen almost did not start college during the pandemic "just because of the fear of COVID and the fear of not being back home." Laya brought up:

> I haven't seen any statistics on how many Native American students dropped out during that time, but I can imagine it was quite a few only because a lot of them were in areas where, like I said, they have no running water, they don't have electricity, they don't have access to high-speed internet.

Many students expressed the lack of access to Internet to complete their academic work as one of the challenges among those who went back to their reservations during the lockdown periods. They spoke of having to drive long distances just to submit homework. Kyiah's experience was not uncommon:

> It was really hard for me, because I asked for extensions for majority of my finals because I didn't have access to Internet and plus my family—both of my parents are working—and so the vehicles are gone right there.

*Positive Actions the College Took*
The next subtheme was related to institutional actions students either experienced, observed, or heard that they believed supported the success, retention, and well-being of Native American students. All the students mentioned at least one thing related to this subtheme. They mentioned physical support like giving students the option to stay in the dorms during lockdown times or to go home; and financial and technology support (e.g., offering hotspots and laptops to students in need). In terms of academics, students mentioned that the college was flexible with grades and initially changed to a pass/fail system instead of letter grades. Once students went back to campus, the college engaged in safety measures to reduce the risk of the virus such as setting up outdoor tents to study and requiring masks and COVID-19 testing. They also mentioned the college helping with *collective coping* by organizing Native events and providing traditional foods and encouraging traditional/*culture as treatment* coping.

Some students appreciated that the college seemed to make efforts to specifically support Native American students. For example, some students mentioned that the college provided counseling hours in the Native

American support center on campus. They also said the college offered Native American specific support groups. Furthermore, students mentioned Native clubs and events. Gwen mentioned, "I did see a lot of the Native American clubs doing a lot of activities, and the school promoting them... Those were definitely put out as resources for people to reach out to and stuff like that."

Some students brought up the fact that the school sometimes did support the idea of a previous subtheme, *culture as treatment*. Gwen appreciated when some professors used a Land Acknowledgment in ways that honored Native students and "how the school lets you like sage your room." Jamiah also observed that the college "encourage[d] Native students to kind of like cope in a way, like their traditional methods, like workshops how to build traditional attire and stuff like that." She saw this as helping students "get back in touch with their cultural values and stuff like that." Amber also observed that the college understood "the different cultures, their beliefs... more of accepting our culture and beliefs."

*Recommendations for What the College Could Have Handled Better/ Could Do in the Future*

This last subtheme included recommendations that the students had for their specific college and for colleges in general in terms of supporting Native American students in light of the COVID-19 pandemic and future pandemics or other crises. They discussed actions the institution could have done better and also suggestions for the future. All the students had constructive suggestions for enabling Native college students' success and well-being. They brought up ideas like being flexible, for faculty and staff to be more culturally knowledgeable and sensitive, offering more services (especially ones that are Native culture informed), and bringing in traditional healers and practices. They also brought up housing options for students to continue to stay on campus, having more funding to specifically support Natives, offering financial support, offering free counseling, and hiring more Native mental health professionals. Next, students mentioned it would be helpful if the college created community, checked in more with students, and had greater understanding of Natives' collectivistic, inter-relational nature.

Ray emphasized the importance of creating opportunities for using *culture as treatment:* "I think some of the key things is just that opportunity for ceremony and prayer and things like that." Amber also discussed supporting students to...

...fall back more towards their culture and their spirituality... for the students who believe, like, are more traditional, bringing in traditional practitioners to help them to get on their level and connect and help them in that way and through prayers and songs which will help their mental well-being.

Ray also recommended intentionally helping Native Americans create community:

...like an upper classman, with a first year coming in and just pairing them up, whether it be first based off major or residence hall... if I had someone who I—people say that look like me, representation or things like that, it definitely would have helped navigating...

Kyiah's response resonated with Ray's:

Put out programs for groups. They could have done it online; like Native students coming together and just talking about it, or telling stories because if they did, then I think they need to do a better job of showing it to the Native Americans. I would sure like to join in and just talk about this stuff.

Similarly, Gwen would have appreciated counselors who are culturally competent to work with Native American college students:

Finding therapists that are culturally acquainted. I tried the counseling services myself and the therapist that I got wasn't spiritually acquainted and I had to go try other therapists. Maybe giving the option for culturally attuned therapists.

David suggested that there needs to be more understanding by the college and others about the adverse effects of colonial history and multigenerational trauma:

Making sure that people are seen, they know their history, and the "correct history." To really understand people's experiences and historical trauma, and then their individual day-to-day experiences... like in the modern day, white people—I'm sorry—not Indigenous people are racist towards me in my everyday life, and that makes it hard for me still.... not as a token person or historical figure, but as just a regular human being. So, I feel like teaching that history, and then explaining, like daily experiences as well, is really important just to make that connection with Native people stronger.

## Discussion

It is hard to generalize these eight students' experiences to others, especially given the small sample size that represented very few tribes and mostly included female students. Another limitation is related to the fact that many of these themes aligned with the interview questions, so it is possible that some of the students' answers were influenced by researcher bias. Furthermore, when analyzing the data, researcher bias may again have influenced our decisions to pay attention to particular data points or to relate them to particular themes. However, many of the themes that emerged align with previous literature demonstrating how these student experiences reflect greater conversations regarding COVID-19 in Indian Country specifically and society in general.

There were definitely stories of challenges that highlight some of the disparities in social indicators of health and the negative effects of colonization (particularly *uncomfortable mental health* symptoms) found in previous literature.[26] These students' stories lend more evidence that COVID-19 seems to have emphasized the disparities felt by Indigenous peoples worldwide that were already present for years due to the effects of colonization.[27] These students' experiences further corroborate other Indigenous people's experiences of being marginalized and having their needs inadequately addressed during those times.[28] Many of the students in this study were from the Diné Nation; their experiences fit with others that have documented how that Tribe was particularly negatively impacted with severe mental and physical health consequences.[29]

The challenges the current students described were contrasted with positive stories of survivance, cultural strengths, culture as treatment,

---

[26] Joseph P. Gone and Joseph E. Trimble, "American Indian and Alaska Native Mental Health: Diverse Perspectives on Enduring Disparities," *Annual Review of Clinical Psychology* 8, no. 1 (2012): 131–60. https://doi.org/10.1146/annurev-clinpsy-032511-143127; Arthur W. Blume, *Colonialism and the COVID-19 Pandemic*, Springer International Publishing, 2022.

[27] de Leeuw et al., "With Reserves."

[28] Kerrie Pickering, Eranga K Galappaththi, James D Ford, Chandni Singh, Carol Zavaleta-Cortijo, Keith Hyams, J Jaime Miranda, et al., "Indigenous Peoples and the COVID-19 Pandemic: A Systematic Scoping Review," Abstract, *Environmental Research Letters* 18, no. 3 (2023): 033001. https://doi.org/10.1088/1748-9326/acb804

[29] Haoying Wang, "Why the Navajo Nation Was Hit so Hard by Coronavirus: Understanding the Disproportionate Impact of the COVID-19 Pandemic," *Applied Geography* 134 (2021): 102526, doi: https://doi.org/10.1016/j.apgeog.2021.102526.

decolonization, and hope. These themes are also in line with previous literature.[30] In fact, it appears that Native people disproportionately have suffered *and* survived many different pandemics over the years.[31] The way these students leaned into their cultures and positively grew from that is similar to what others have documented.[32] The positive stories included here break the mainstream invisible, deficit narrative about Native Americans.[33]

Some important, possibly universal-type themes mentioned here might be helpful in better understanding Native American college students generally. Universities that enroll Indigenous students (likely most if not all), university faculty, staff, and mental health professionals might benefit from these students' stories to help improve Native specific, culturally appropriate interventions, support, relationships, and infrastructure. Really *hearing* Native college student voices and infusing and normalizing Native culture, values, and traditions in higher education can positively enhance Native college students' educational experience and likelihood of success.[34] Decolonization and Indigenous knowledge and ways of being can contribute to giving the interdependent world hope as we move forward from this pandemic and face new challenges.[35] Naturally, much more research is needed. Longitudinal qualitative and quantitative, decolonized studies are needed that examine the lived experiences of a much broader section of the Native American population.

This study adds to the overall narrative of how Indian Country experienced COVID-19. It can help pave the way for future scholarship and interventions that highlight Native American college students' voices. Such research, education, and practice should frame issues from Native American perspectives to improve not only Indigenous lives but all of

---

[30] Blume, *Colonialism and COVID-19*; Belcourt-Dittloff, *Resiliency and risk*; Wilbur and Gone, "Beyond resilience"; Arthur W. Blume, *A new psychology based on community, equality, and care of the earth: An indigenous American perspective* (Bloomsbury Publishing USA, 2020); Derkas. "Disrupting Native Invisibility"; Mallencharmley, "Native American College Students."

[31] Wang, "Why the Navajo Nation Was Hit so Hard."

[32] Mallencharmley, "Native American College Students."

[33] Derkas, "Disrupting Native Invisibility." Tapati Dutta, Jon Agley, Yunyu Xiao, Lilian Golzarri-Arroyo, and Sumayyah Ali. "Students' COVID-19 vaccine behaviors, intentions, and beliefs at a US Native American-Serving Nontribal Institution (NASNTI)." *BMC Research Notes* 16, no. 1 (2023): 175.

[34] Derkas, "Disrupting Native Invisibility."

[35] Blume, *Colonialism and COVID-19*.

Creation.[36] We are eternally grateful to each and every one of these eight students for sharing their time and personal lived experiences to help universities and others better understand Native college students and what they went through during the COVID-19 pandemic. We hope that their narratives of lived experiences will help universities and others improve so that future generations of Native college students feel more supported and culturally affirmed to improve their chances of academic success and having meaningful lives that honor their ancestors and the seven generations to come.

**Competing Interests Declaration** Amoneeta Beckstein received a startup research grant from Fort Lewis College that contributed to funding this study. Tapati Dutta has no competing interests to declare that are relevant to the content of this chapter.

---

[36] Blume, *A new psychology.*

CHAPTER 9

# Navigating the Unknown: Lessons Learned from Sustaining Indigenous Community in Higher Education During the COVID-19 Pandemic

*Daniel Piper, Melissa Tehee, Racheal Killgore, and Erica Ficklin*

INTRODUCTION

We are a group of Native and non-Native faculty and students who have been involved in the Mentoring and Encouraging Student Academic Success (MESAS) program for Native American students at Utah State University. The MESAS program launched in 2018 and continued to grow for two academic years. Unfortunately, in 2020 the program was confronted by the pandemic. During the pandemic, education in Native communities became a challenge with the lack of access to high-speed

---

D. Piper (✉) • M. Tehee • R. Killgore • E. Ficklin
Utah State University, Logan, UT, USA
e-mail: daniel.piper@usu.edu; melissa.tehee@usu.edu; racheal.killgore@usu.edu; erica.ficklin@usu.edu

© The Author(s), under exclusive license to Springer Nature Switzerland AG 2024
F. King, W. Davies (eds.), *COVID-19 in Indian Country*,
https://doi.org/10.1007/978-3-031-70184-9_9

Internet, technology, and online curriculum.[1] However, the most difficult aspect of the pandemic was the loss of family members and loved ones, which reverberated throughout the lives of Native students. In the face of such difficulty at our own institution, the MESAS team remained active in our efforts to sustain Indigenous community on campus. Santa Clara Pueblo scholar Gregory Cajete underscores community as the centerpiece of Indigenous education:

> Community is therefore, the primary setting for traditional Indigenous education. It is inherently holistic since community engages the whole person. It provides the context in which the affective dimension of education unfolds—where emotions develop and are shaped and redefined. Community is where learning and sharing knowledge happens.[2]

Drawing on Cajete's definition of community we ask: how do we sustain Indigenous community in higher education during challenging times, particularly at predominately white institutions (PWI) where historically the needs of Native students have often gone overlooked?

We explore this question by telling our own stories as faculty and students working in the MESAS program.

## The Talking Circle

In this chapter, we use the concept of the talking circle as a framework for sharing our stories. We draw on the work of Patricia Barkaskas and Derek Gladwin who have used the talking circle as a pedagogical tool in Indigenous education.[3] According to Barkaskas and Gladwin, the talking circle is grounded in situated relatedness, respectful listening, and reflective witnessing. We engage these principles in our relationships to one another as colleagues, but also to you as the reader, inviting you to listen

---

[1] US Department of the Interior, Office of Congressional and Legislative Affairs, "Covid-19 Impact on Native Education," April 28, 2021, accessed online, https://www.doi.gov/ocl/covid-19-impact-native-education

[2] Gregory Cajete, *Indigenous Community: Rekindling the Teachings of the Seventh Fire* (St. Paul, MN: Living Justice Press, 2015), 23.

[3] Patricia Barkaskas and Derek Gladwin, "Pedagogical Talking Circles: Decolonizing Education through Relational Indigenous Frameworks," *Journal of Teaching and Learning* 15, no. 1 (2021): 20–38.

to our reflections. What follows is an overview of the MESAS program, our individual stories, and some of the central lessons we have learned throughout our experiences working in this program during the pandemic.

## The Mentoring and Encouraging Student Academic Success (MESAS) Program

The Mentoring and Encouraging Student Academic Success (MESAS) program emerged out of the need to support Native American students at Utah State University (USU), a land grant university with over 30 campuses throughout the state. One of those campuses is in Blanding, Utah, less than 40 miles outside of the Navajo Nation. The USU Blanding campus has a significant Native student population and is designated as a Native American Serving Non-Tribal Institution (NASNTI). The main USU campus is in Logan, Utah, over six hours away from USU Blanding. Historically many Native students from USU Blanding have transferred to the Logan campus to complete four-year degrees not available in Blanding.

To assist students with this transition, the MESAS program was created out of a collective effort on behalf of both Blanding and Logan faculty to strengthen the pathway to the main campus and to create more support for Native students at Utah State University. To fund this program, faculty such as Dr. Al Savitzky, Dr. Melissa Tehee, and Curtis Frazier were involved in the successful submission of a grant to the Howard Hughes Medical Institute (HHM) Inclusive Excellence initiative.

The MESAS program consisted of activities for students that could create a sense of community. This included weekly talking circles, full time staff and faculty, a Native American on-campus Living Community, and a cultural competence course (known as TEACH) available to USU faculty and staff. The Tohi Lab (*tohi* being the Cherokee word for wellness) oversaw the development and implementation of weekly talking circles. This was initiated by Dr. Melissa Tehee and staffed by doctoral students, Racheal Killgore and Erica Ficklin. Briana Kaufman was hired in 2019 as the MESAS Coordinator of Programs and Daniel Piper was hired in spring 2020 as the MESAS Faculty Advocate. In the first two years, the program was gaining momentum, but early 2020 presented a new series of challenges with the onset of COVID-19. Navigating these challenges was difficult, yet we worked to move the program forward and support students, doing our best to sustain community.

## Daniel Piper

My name is Daniel Piper and I am from Northern Utah. I am of settler heritage, on my maternal side being associated with two family groups who arrived in Northern Utah at the turn of the twentieth century from Sweden and Scotland. I was raised with little knowledge of Native communities. My perspective shifted when, as a young adult, I started working as a student mentor in Title VI Indian Education programs. Through guidance from colleagues and friends, I pursued higher education and a career working to support language and culture-based education for Native students and communities.

I joined the MESAS program in August 2020 in the role of Faculty Advocate. This was an incredibly challenging time, and the pandemic impacted my ability to meet students in this new role. Quickly I started to recognize the toll the pandemic was having on students. As COVID-19 spread on the Navajo Nation, many students lost family members and relatives. It was very difficult to hear, and see, the impact of loss cascade into students' academic engagement. I had to become creative with how to engage students. In collaboration with MESAS staff, we developed a variety of virtual activities and community events. This included Zoom activities each month. Briana and I would provide snacks for pick up at our offices and encourage students to jump on Zoom for our events.

Attendance fluctuated as Zoom fatigue wore on. The last thing students often wanted to do was get back on Zoom after a day of classes. We tried to keep in regular contact with students through email and a monthly newsletter. Even though students were not always attending our events, they made comments about seeing our emails and it made them feel good knowing we were there if they needed us. When students did attend the challenges they faced became apparent while they joined on Zoom from their car, or isolated in their dorm rooms.

Each week, the Tohi Lab held their virtual talking circles. This became one of the main pathways to maintain contact with students. Every week students would jump on Zoom to talk with one another, process their emotions, play virtual games, talk about classes, and maintain relationships. This ongoing connection ensured that students had a community despite what was going on in their home lives.

In his definition of community, Gregory Cajete underscores the important role of relationality in Indigenous education.[4] In Indigenous educa-

---

[4] Cajete, *Indigenous Community*.

tion, good relationships create a network of people that students turn to when they need support. Throughout the pandemic, we strived to let students know we were there if they needed us. Maintaining those relationships with students through the talking circles and events allowed us to continue the MESAS program throughout the pandemic.

Because institutions of higher education were not historically designed for Native students, community is an *active* process on our part. That means we must create spaces, locations, and pathways for Indigenous community connection inside of a university setting. Doing so requires developing good relationships among our colleagues, students, and knowing our individual roles and responsibilities in our Indigenous university community. Today we are still living with the ghost of the pandemic. However, our students' resilience and determination is what has driven them—and us—forward. As we heal from the pandemic, we continue to do the important work of creating and sustaining Indigenous community within our university.

*Melissa Tehee*

O-si-yo wa-du-li-si di-hi dah-wah-doh. I am a citizen of the Cherokee Nation and an associate professor in psychology at Utah State University. I am a first-generation college student, and I am thankful to my ancestors who have guided me to American Indian mentors throughout my journey in higher education. They taught me about myself, my culture, and how we could engage with the education system with an Indigenous worldview.

Higher education is presented as an acultural, universal approach to education. However, educational inequities are built into the institution of education as differing worldviews, values, beliefs, ways of knowing and learning are not even considered. I am thankful to those who demonstrated culturally sustaining and revitalizing education and modeled pushing back on the institution to make room for Native American students.

The experiences of Native students in higher education, mine included, motivated me to seek more systematic changes, starting where I live and work. This is how Dr. Al Savitzky and I began asking for changes at Utah State University and also seeking funding to demonstrate the benefits of such changes. The Howard Hughes Medical Institute awarded us an Inclusive Excellence grant aimed at institutional change and provided the needed resources for us to build the MESAS program for Native students at USU.

Toward our goal of institutional change, we developed and delivered cultural competence professional development training for those interacting with Native students. We (the Tohi Lab) co-created a five-hour training, with 1 hour asynchronous modules delivered weekly and a final in-person module. The in-person session was based on contact theory to be sure that those taking the training were interacting with people diverse from them, including Native people on our campus, including many of the facilitators from the Tohi lab. This also provided space to build community across diverse backgrounds. It was an opportunity for us to get out of our offices and classrooms and connect with others—across departments and colleges, which does not happen very often.

In the fall of 2019, we started our first full year of the MESAS program, we were hiring members to fill our team, the Native American Living and Learning Community (NALLC) was underway, we had trained around 150 USU community members to work with Native students, and we had many activities in the works. We brought Native students together around a fire for stories and s'mores. Students came to my house to carve pumpkins, and for many students, it was their first time carving pumpkins. Toward the end of the semester, when students were feeling homesick, we gathered for a family style dinner at my house. We had gone to the gardener's market to enjoy breakfast burritos and gone ax throwing. Racheal and Erica were holding weekly talking circles at the NALLC. And then we started hearing about people getting sick in different parts of the world, and before we could process what was happening, it was here.

Many of our Native students headed back to their familial homes as things got worse and social isolation was being encouraged because they would not have the same support and community in the residence halls. Those who were exposed to COVID-19 while living on campus were isolated for two weeks in an almost empty dorm room without their personal items that bring comfort, as no one knew in which ways the virus was spreading. Our university put together a care team and they were bringing those students in isolation food at every meal, coordinating with their professors, and checking in with them daily, but there was still the physical isolation.

The Navajo Nation declared a public health state of emergency on March 11, 2020, which was in place until June 15, 2023. At the time it was unknown how long this crucial phase of the pandemic would last, and many of our Diné students went home to be with family. The interdependent nature of those of us with Indigenous worldviews are connected with our values of family and reciprocity and by going home, the students could both provide support and care for their families as well as receive support in ways they do not or would not experience on campus.

These world views contributed to higher adherence of mask wearing and such, because we are always thinking of others, and we would not make an individual choice to put others at risk. It is also these worldviews that kept us physically distanced longer. Students' options were additionally complicated by the lack of high-speed Internet and devices needed to connect remotely in rural and reservation locations. On the Navajo Nation, students with cars would drive to their local chapter houses, satellite campuses, or businesses with free Wi-Fi and were doing their homework and joining classes and meetings from their car.

We were all carrying so much stress, through shifting all classes over to online and reconceptualizing how we were going to continue our research projects—for me some of which were in K-12 classrooms that we were following for the year. The Tohi grad students had to figure out how to continue providing therapeutic services to their clients remotely while still meeting criteria from licensing boards. The demands went on and on. We were holistically exhausted—mentally, emotionally, physically, and spiritually.

One of my graduate students and I lived less than two blocks from each other, but navigating how to potentially meet in person was too tiring and we continued to meet over Zoom. I was already using Zoom a lot, but everything moved full time to that platform. Like many, I did not have a workspace set up at home, so I was working on my laptop non-stop, more hours than a person should work in a day, every day, while sitting on a couch or at the table, but all the options were ergonomically poor—leading me to some debilitating physical issues.

In addition, my house was a natural gathering place at times, but I live in an intergenerational household, like many Native families, and one of my family members has elevated risk factors, including already being on supplemental oxygen. So, the questions became, how do we maintain community with those we are physically distanced from—and the more complicated questions—how do we build relationships and community with new students? As Native people, we come from resilient ancestors, and we figured out creative ways to connect.

Many people came together to provide students on the Navajo Nation with Wi-Fi hotspots, led by Kristian Olsen at the USU Blanding Campus. Curtis and Theresa Frazier of USU Blanding Campus provided an opportunity for students to help gather and deliver supplies to families in the Navajo Nation through the Navajo Strong project, started by Bud Frazier. We built a MESAS "course" in our learning management system to help everyone connect and send resources and announcements. We held support circles and beading circles to communicate over a video platform while not talking about work.

We delivered the cultural competence training to faculty, grad student researchers, housing and advising staff. When the pandemic began, not only did we change the format of the in-person sessions to Zoom, we changed what we talked about to include aspects discussed in this chapter, such as limited connectivity and Wi-Fi and how the values of family and community are enacted within Native families.

We in MESAS held our annual convention for the Society of Indigenous Psychologists virtually. We were very intentional to find ways to come together in the virtual space and connect with the land, provide space and time for rest, respite, and healing, connect with spiritual practices, prayers, songs, storytelling, creating, engaging in cultural art, and connecting with our ancestors.

Together, we found ways to bring in laughter and cultural practices. Over time, as people had more access to virtual options, we were able to hold different types of events. Sarah Deer spoke virtually, and we held space for Native students from all campuses to have a more intimate discussion with her. The USU Blanding campus worked with many students and community members and figured out how to hold a virtual Powwow. MESAS started the annual Indigenous knowledge symposium, which has now become a cornerstone of Indigenous programs at USU, sharing these knowledges well beyond USU.

By coming together, we learned and supported each other through the uncertainty and developed many meaningful ways to connect across distance to share and learn from each other. We found new ways to weave culture and higher education and better the system we live, learn, and work in.

### *Racheal Killgore*

My name is Racheal Killgore and I am a member of the Navajo Nation. My maternal clan is Kinyaa'áanii (Towering House) and I am born for Bilagáana (white people). I am originally from Gallup, New Mexico, and I am currently a doctoral student in the Combined Clinical and Counseling

Psychology program at Utah State University. Since starting graduate school, I have had the privilege of working closely with our Native college students in the MESAS program. My engagement with students begins during the fall semester and carries forward through the early summer months. I am available to students via text and phone calls, in addition to in-person gatherings. An important way I connect with students throughout the year is through weekly talking circles I co-facilitate. Prior to COVID-19, which limited options for connecting, talking circles were in-person gatherings that students welcomed with anticipation. Conventionally, participants are seated in a circle and each participant has an opportunity to impart perspectives, stories, and reflections in the shared space.

The listeners refrain from interrupting the sharer or expressing disagreement or judgment. Instead, participants adopt a posture of learning from others and engage in active listening. The inclusive and respectful environment that this format fosters allows participants to contribute in an open and authentic fashion. Talking circles are a wonderful way to learn about what the students value and who they are as individuals while also strengthening community and connection. Finding belongingness can be challenging, even elusive, in university settings, in part because of the cultural clash that exists between our own set of beliefs and values and those of the Western academic world. This can evoke feelings of isolation and have significant consequences for academic outcomes and personal well-being.

When the COVID-19 pandemic struck, it had considerable repercussions not only for Native communities but for our Native students while exacerbating the existing challenges they faced at their educational institutions (e.g., finding belongingness). As higher education institutions across the nation were forced to shift to a mostly online format, this shift had consequences for our students (e.g., increased anxiety, the loss of in-person support systems, and a rise in social isolation). We recognized the need to continue providing talking circles in a consistent manner to ensure that our students received support and a sense of belongingness within the university setting. We had concerns regarding Internet connectivity or access to technology as we began to offer weekly talking circles on a virtual platform.

Students were given the option of joining talking circles through video connection or calling in using their mobile device/landline. The online platform presented unique challenges, for instance, previously we had incorporated cultural activities into talking circles, such as a beading circle or sharing a meal together, but these were more challenging to accomplish during the pandemic due to safety concerns. Though we were not able to always incorporate certain cultural activities as we once did, we worked diligently to hold a space where the students felt comfortable to freely share the things they felt compelled to share. We found that virtual talking circles facilitated wonderful group discourse, insights, and significantly contributed to the development of a strong support system for students.

Several topics surfaced throughout the months of virtual talking circles. The conversations centered on reflections and experiences of the pandemic. Students expressed fear about the virus, its spread, and the impact it was having on their relatives and communities. They were concerned about the possibility of contracting COVID-19 and spreading it to the most vulnerable members of their families. Participation in these conversations was helpful to students because the emotional weight they carried was often interwoven with feelings of fear and uncertainty about the future, and by sharing their concerns in the circle the intensity of their fears felt lighter. Others who had returned home but also held full-time status discussed how these different roles sometimes collided. Upon returning home, balancing their studies and student role with the expectations of their family role (e.g., daughter, son, and grandchild) became difficult.

They found themselves negotiating a liminal space—a point of transition where they shifted back and forth into their roles, pulled by competing demands and not fully able to embrace either set of commitments. They grappled with finding a delicate balance between the two. Those listening to the shared stories offered nods of understanding and support by being present through acknowledgment and reflective practices. This response had a profound impact; those who shared their struggles also shared their sense of relief that others had listened and acknowledged their stories, their struggles. Initially, some students hesitated to share. Perhaps this was due to uncertainty about how their stories might be received, uncertainty about how to begin, or perhaps it was the initial strangeness of a virtual space—so unlike being physically present. However, acceptance, supportive remarks, kindness, or helpful suggestions from the circle provided students with the encouragement to open up and continue sharing, increasing their level of comfort within the circle over time.

Other topics commonly shared by students almost every week were related to sleep hygiene (e.g., getting adequate sleep, dysregulated sleep schedule) and increasing effective coping strategies for stress. Facilitators proposed bringing in presenters (i.e., doctoral psychology students) to provide information and help students tackle these matters, and the students were receptive. Subsequently, students conversed about what they gained and how they would incorporate what they learned. Other raised topics of interest were financial aid resources and obtaining letters of recommendation and references. It was an honor to write letters for students or assist them in the process of securing letters as they applied for future employment or pursued scholarships or other opportunities.

Sometimes due to the strain that came from the pandemic or just the usual drag that often arises toward the end of a semester, motivation would wane. The talking circles served as a valuable resource to draw inspiration from one another, and to rediscover their commitment to their dreams and goals. The students recognized that they held similar experiences in that they all struggled at times, had fears, insecurities, and hopes. Virtual talking circles provided fertile ground to broach difficult subjects and experiences, to share joyful moments and accomplishments, and to shed tears and laughter.

In fact, humor was a frequent companion in our circles. Humor proved to be instrumental early in our talking circles when facilitators were building rapport with the students, and they were getting to know one another better. It also proved to sustain the good relationships our group cultivated throughout the year, reaffirming the sense of belongingness experienced by members and enhancing social support among the group. Furthermore, it encouraged our circle to openly discuss those topics that are considered more sensitive, allowing a place to not only be vulnerable, but to find some healing in a culturally appropriate way.

I remain close with many of the students who participated in the talking circle. Several have graduated, most have moved on to the next chapter of their life, and many will drop me a text now and then describing where their life has taken them thus far. As we embark on another year of talking circles, I look forward to the interactions I will have with the students and the relationships we will build.

*Erica Ficklin*

I am Erica Ficklin, a proud member of the Tlingit and Oglala Lakota. I am currently a doctoral student in the Combined and Clinical Counseling Psychology Program at Utah State University. I have worked in the

MESAS program as a member of the Tohi Lab and co-facilitated weekly talking circles with students. Many of the students in the MESAS program grew up on reservations, which meant that many of their family and close friends were living on the reservation during the COVID-19 pandemic. This meant that many of our students were deeply worried about their family members while they pursued higher education. Several students reported feeling torn about where they should be during the pandemic. Should they be at the university, focusing on their studies, or should they be with their communities?

Many Native students pursue higher education for the purpose of bringing their learned skills back to their communities. Because of this, the students had to balance their purpose for pursuing an education in the first place with what their communities needed at that specific time. This balancing was made more difficult by the sheer distance between home and the university for many students, which required at least a day's worth of driving. Several students did not own cars, which made travel that much more difficult, particularly when family emergencies arose. Thus, the decision to be at the university was not made lightly.

The numbers regarding mortality rates and risk for medical complications are terrifying in and of themselves, but the real nightmare was the grief, loss of close family members and friends, and lack of adequate medical care that Native communities lived with. Native students faced inordinate challenges while they tried to pursue their degrees. College comes with several challenges in relatively normal times. Undergraduate students deal with high levels of stress, anxiety, and depression.[5] Evidence shows that COVID-19 exacerbated these concerns, with rates of major depressive disorder doubling and rates of generalized anxiety disorder nearly doubling.[6] Some evidence shows that Indigenous communities were disproportionately impacted by these worsening mental health conditions.

---

[5] Ann Macaskill, "Undergraduate mental health issues: The challenge of the second year of study," *Journal of Mental Health* 27, no. 3 (2018): 214–221.

[6] Igor Chrikov, Krista M. Soria, Bonnie Horgos, and Daniel Jones-White, "Undergraduate and graduate students' mental health during the COVID-19 pandemic." *UC Berkeley: Center for Studies in Higher Education*, (2020), accessed online, https://escholarship.org/uc/item/80k5d5hw

Indigenous persons were more likely to be considered at a high risk for suicide during the COVID-19 pandemic.[7] Researchers found that historical trauma could contribute to the sensitivity to distress during the pandemic. However, these researchers also found that social support interacted with the effects of historical trauma, meaning that having social support helped Indigenous persons feel less distressed.[8] This is where we saw the benefits of the MESAS program. Racheal and I met with the students weekly for talking circles, which gave students a chance to come together and share what they were going through.

There were some changes to these talking circles from prior years. We met virtually instead of in person, but we still had the opportunity to share time together. I was so happy to see the students attend the talking circles in spite of the numerous demands they had on their time. It gave us all a chance to laugh, support one another, and have some relief from the stress caused by the catastrophes in the world. I believe these talking circles were as helpful to us, as the facilitators, as they were for the students. Every time we came together, I left feeling supported and hopeful.

Because of the high mortality rates among Native communities, Native college students were more likely to have family members who died or were suffering due to COVID-19. I saw this unfortunate truth in the Native students I worked with. In addition to the exacerbated mental health concerns wrought by COVID-19, these students were deeply concerned for their family members. Several disclosed having difficult feelings about pursuing their education while their family members could be at risk for serious medical complications.

Food insecurity also became a serious concern. Our university, thankfully, has resources that supply some food to students in need. However, these quantities of food were still too low to consistently provide enough nutrition to the students. Because of this, the students in the MESAS program were working long hours. Several students worked night shifts despite having to attend classes during the day. Working the night shift

---

[7] Kevin M. Fitzpatrick, Casey Harris, and Grant Drawve, "How bad is it? Suicidality in the middle of the COVID-19 pandemic," *Suicide and Life-Threatening Behavior* 50, no. 6 (2020): 1241–1249.

[8] Neha A. John-Henderson and Annie T. Ginty, "Historical trauma and social support as predictors of psychological stress responses in American Indian adults during the COVID-19 pandemic," *Journal of psychosomatic research* 139 (2020): 110263.

interfered with their ability to get restful sleep. This left them feeling exhausted and stressed, but they were unable to change their work hours because it would interfere with their classes. They were unable to seek out other employment or cut back on their hours because they needed to pay their bills, purchase books and necessary materials for school, and, as previously stated, food. In addition, many students were dedicated to supporting their families in whatever way possible, particularly since they were so far from home. The students sent money home to their families as their way of contributing. Despite these challenges, these students worked hard in their courses and continued to progress toward their degrees.

Overall, I was struck by the resilience of our students in the MESAS program. I heard them talk about unbelievable stressors in their lives that made pursuing an education more difficult. These students faced food insecurity, mental health concerns, grief, stress, long working hours, and more during the COVID-19 pandemic. Still, they persevered. The students succeeded in their classes, applied for and received scholarships, sent money to their families, and built meaningful relationships in their lives. They focused on their cultural values and teachings to guide them through rather difficult decisions. The students were absolutely incredible in their pursuits and as they followed their values. I felt uplifted and hopeful every time I was able to spend time with them. Being around them made me feel that I, too, could persevere through the challenges. Each of these students deeply touched my life.

## Lessons Learned and Moving Forward

### *Maintaining Connection*

What we learned from our time working in the MESAS program during the pandemic was the important practice of maintaining communication, outreach, and connection to students. Reflected in Racheal and Erica's experiences as talking circle facilitators, students were dealing with stressful and difficult times. The talking circles became an opportunity for students to process this stress, share, connect, and deal with the unknown happening around them.

Faculty and students worked to maintain our relationships with students, knowing that we would be together in person at some point in time. Through our individual and collective work, we pursued a goal of sustaining Indigenous community at our university, while navigating the difficulty of the pandemic. This allowed us to ensure that the MESAS program did not dissipate during this time, rather it aided the university in creating more space and support for Native American students on campus.

### *New Tools and Technologies*

The pandemic changed our pedagogy and practices in a variety of ways. We lost, but we also gained new skills and perspectives. This came in the form of virtual platforms and creating new spaces online to connect with students. Many young people find themselves in an ever expanding technological world. The pandemic forced us to learn and adapt to this new world, through which we gained new skills. These skills also allowed us to connect with our wider USU community across the state, and forge new relationships with staff and faculty at other campuses. We did this largely through an annual Indigenous Knowledge Symposium, where over 300 attendees gathered on Zoom to hear from Native scholars.

### *How Do We Sustain Indigenous Community in Higher Education in Challenging Times?*

In Cajete's definition of community, he highlights the importance of relationality. Reflected in our stories are experiences of relationality in practice, connecting to one another to create and sustain Indigenous community in a university setting. This distinguishes Indigenous higher education from that of the mainstream—we move toward a relational framework that supports students' well-being and academic success. We balance the personal and the professional as we are often deeply invested in the future of Native education and the well-being of Native students.

So, how do we sustain Indigenous community in higher education in challenging times? In essence, we argue that relationality is at the core of sustaining Indigenous community in the face of the unknown. Although the pandemic is over, we continue to be confronted with its ghost and face other challenges such as the anti-diversity rhetoric in higher education. We must remain together and strong. Gregory Cajete has used the corn cob as a metaphor for community; each kernel representing an individual as they support and lean on one another to for strength.⁹ It is our hope that the reflections and stories we have shared illuminate ways of relationship building and creating community in your own work. *Ahéhee', Gunalchéesh, Wado, Thank you.*

**Competing Interests Declaration** The program discussed in this chapter was funded by Howard Hughes Medical Institute (HHMI) Inclusive Excellence Initiative [GT11074].

---

⁹ Gregory Cajete, "A Pueblo Story of Sustainability," filmed October 2015 in Albuquerque, New Mexico. TED video, 10:25, accessed online, https://www.youtube.com/watch?v=5_nxJMhSlOg

CHAPTER 10

# Maawanji'idiwag: They Come Together

### Chelsea M. Mead

## COVID-19 AND LANGUAGE EFFORTS AT LARGE

The experience of COVID-19 is multi-layered and varies greatly depending on individual, communal, and national contexts. Each Indigenous nation/community experienced COVID-19 differently, but collectively the data shows that Indigenous peoples across the globe were "the most harshly affected" communities.[1] In the United States, the Kaiser Family Foundation along with government and medical organizations began identifying the fact that American Indian/Alaskan Native and Native Hawaiian/Pacific Islanders had higher risks for contracting COVID-19 due to a range of historic and present-day factors.[2] In certain states, such

---

[1] José Francisco Calí Tzay, "Report of the Special Rapporteur on the Rights of Indigenous Peoples," United Nations General Assembly, July 20, 2020, A/75/185, https://undocs.org/en/A/75/185

[2] Heather A. Howard-Bobiwash, Jennie R. Joe, and Susan Lobo, "Concrete Lessons: Policies and Practices Affecting the Impact of Covid-19 for Urban Indigenous Communities in the United States and Canada," *Frontiers in Sociology* 6 (2021); Samantha Artiga and Kendal Orgera, "COVID-19 Presents Significant Risks for American Indian and Alaska

C. M. Mead (✉)
Minnesota State University, Mankato, MN, USA
e-mail: chelsea.mead@mnsu.edu

© The Author(s), under exclusive license to Springer Nature Switzerland AG 2024
F. King, W. Davies (eds.), *COVID-19 in Indian Country*,
https://doi.org/10.1007/978-3-031-70184-9_10

as Arizona and New Mexico, Indigenous deaths from COVID-19 showed noteworthy disparities indicating a significant number of deaths in individuals 55 and older.[3] Minnesota, the state in which this case study occurs, fared similarly in demonstrating health equity disparities.

Researchers early in the pandemic period found evidence of excess mortality among Minnesota American Indian populations. For example, a team of researchers from the University of Minnesota found that from March 1 to November 25, 2020, Minnesota's American Indian population saw "nearly 100 more deaths than what would have occurred on average during the same time period over the last three years."[4] In October 2020, CBS News Minnesota reported that recent state Department of Health data showed Indigenous Minnesotans experiencing COVID-19 case rates four times their white counterparts, and they were six times more likely to be hospitalized from COVID-19.[5] A year later, Minnesota Public Radio reported that the most recent data showed Native Americans in Minnesota had "contracted COVID-19 at two to three times the rate of white Minnesotans."[6]

While the impact of COVID-19 varied between the seven Anishinaabeg and four Dakota nations in Minnesota, each loss substantially impacted language and cultural revitalization efforts. COVID-19 has proved to be particularly dangerous for Elders who often serve as language keepers, spiritual leaders, and sources of strength for their communities. With their passing, communities lost not only knowledge of the language but also

Native People," *Kaiser Family Foundation*, May 14, 2020, accessed August 1, 2023, https://www.kff.org/coronavirus-covid-19/issue-brief/covid-19-presents-significant-risks-for-american-indian-and-alaska-native-people/

[3] National Congress of American Indians, "Submission of the National Congress of American Indians to the United Nations Special Rapporteur on Indigenous Issues," United Nations General Assembly, June 19, 2020, accessed August 1, 2023, https://www.ohchr.org/en/calls-for-input/report-impact-covid-19-rights-indigenous-peoples

[4] Nicole Martin Rogers, et al., "American Indians in Minnesota Experience Worse Covid Impacts Than Reported," *Star Tribune,* December 15, 2020, https://www.startribune.com/american-indians-in-minnesota-experience-worse-covid-impacts-than-reported/573402071/?refresh=true

[5] "COVID Hospitalization Rate for Indigenous Minnesotans 6 Times Higher Than White Residents," CBS Minneapolis (WCCO), October 15, 2020, https://www.cbsnews.com/minnesota/news/covid-hospitalization-rate-for-indigenous-minnesotans-6-times-higher-than-white-residents/

[6] Dan Kraker, "Indigenous Communities See Rise in COVID-19 Cases," Minnesota Public Radio News, October 22, 2021, https://www.mprnews.org/story/2021/10/22/indigenous-communities-see-rise-in-covid19-cases

stories, and historical knowledge of Native history, community, and place. For example, the Mille Lacs Band lost several fluent speakers and Elders from the pandemic. Prior to COVID-19, 25 fluent speakers of Ojibwe were identified in the Mille Lacs community. Six of these Elders died during the pandemic, resulting in a twenty percent death rate among its first speakers.[7] The Red Lake Nation, for example, experienced the loss of Eugene Stillday, Sr. He was a respected Elder and speaker who worked to support the Ojibwe language through community initiatives, language camps in the summers, and the Ojibwe Language Dictionary housed by the University of Minnesota.[8] Against the backdrop of loss, tragedy, and the many challenges of the pandemic, Indigenous language warriors, learners, teachers, and communities "did what Indigenous peoples have always done in the face of danger and hardship: persist."[9]

Prior to COVID-19, most of the Indigenous language work in the United States took place in person.[10] Over the years, I have been fortunate to participate in a few virtually held Ojibwe language opportunities, but their availability was often unpredictable and limited. Some digital tools existed prior to COVID-19 to support Ojibwe language learning efforts but these were often introductions to the language or not readily available and affordable. With the safety concerns of the pandemic, especially for the Elders, in-person language tables, classes, and immersion efforts ground to a halt. Ceremonies, community events, and opportunities to be together paused with an uncertain return date. In the United States, governors issued stay at home orders. Social distancing and masking became policy and practice. These responses to the pandemic fostered a transition to online networking and connections even more.

The experiences highlighted in this chapter are among thousands shared by Indigenous language teachers and learners during the pandemic. Language warriors turned to social media to facilitate language promotion, use Indigenous languages to discuss COVID-19, and offer trainings

---

[7] Dan Gunderson, "'Our Hearts are Heavy': Covid-19 Deaths of Tribal Elders Leave a Void," *Minnesota Public Radio News*, April 9, 2021, https://www.mprnews.org/story/2021/04/09/our-hearts-are-heavy-covid19-deaths-of-tribal-elders-leave-a-void

[8] "Eugene Stillday, Sr.," *Red Lake Nation News*, December 15, 2020, https://www.redlakenationnews.com/story/2020/12/15/obituaries/eugene-stillday-sr/94448.html

[9] Kari A.B. Chew, "#KeepOurLanguagesStrong: Indigenous Language Revitalization on Social Media During the Early Covid-19 Pandemic," *Language Documentation & Conservation* 15, (2021): 239.

[10] Chew, "#KeepOurLanguagesStrong," 239.

to support language learning, the creating and sharing of language resources, and to disseminate information about Indigenous Language revitalization (ILR) and COVID-19.[11] Language work, as it always has been, remained "an enduring source of strength, comfort, and wisdom" during COVID-19.[12] This case study focuses on how ILR efforts at two Midwestern universities were impacted by COVID-19 and how the faculty, students, staff, and community members involved in the Ojibwe language programs at the institutions navigated the pandemic together.

Similar to other academics and community members writing on language revitalization, I am both a scholar and practitioner. I am a guest in Indigenous language revitalization efforts as a White settler-colonist. I grew up in Potawatomi lands in Southern Michigan. Today, I live and work in Minnesota in Dakota homelands. At my university, I am a professor of American Indigenous Studies, History, and Linguistic Anthropology. I am also a student of Ojibwemowin and have been for the past 20 years. My Ojibwemowin language journey began in a college classroom as an undergraduate student in Michigan, continued via online and through self-study during graduate school in Arizona, and more recently has continued in-person and online throughout Michigan and Minnesota. I have been blessed over the years to learn from several fluent speakers, Elders, and teachers. As a university professor, I have sought out opportunities and ways to create and support Indigenous spaces with students in our institution. One avenue has been the creation of a unique partnership with a sister institution so students could learn Ojibwemowin. In this case study, I refer to "we" or "our" because the reality is that the Ojibwe classes formed an important community. The "we" refers to myself, Anton Treuer, Dennis Jones, students at both campuses, staff members, Elders and guest speakers, and community members connected to the Ojibwe language classes at both institutions.

This project and how we navigated the pandemic is the focus of this chapter. Any errors or mistakes are completely my own. My research efforts and interviews began two years prior to the COVID-19 pandemic, but like all things touched by the virus, this project adapted and mutated to the changing conditions of life. From 2019 until 2022, I conducted over 30 interviews with student participants taking the Ojibwe language

---

[11] Chew, "#KeepOurLanguagesStrong," 239.
[12] Kari A.B. Chew, et al., "Persistence in Indigenous Language work during the COVID-19 pandemic," *AlterNative* 18, no. 4 (December 2022): 597.

classes and faculty, staff, and administrators who supported our collaboration. We applied for and received two MinnState Multi-Campus Collaboration Grants to support our partnership and opportunities for our students. With College of Education colleagues at Minnesota State University, Mankato (MNSU), I also applied for and received funding from a Governor's Educational Emergency Relief Grant which provided some funding connected to the collaboration.

During these years, I was also an enrolled student in the Ojibwe courses. I completed the Intermediate Ojibwe series in 2019–2020 and the Advanced Ojibwe offerings plus the Teaching Ojibwe course in 2021–2022. While I wrote and pursued grant funding for our collaboration, and coordinated the MNSU side of the classes and the sense of belonging items, Anton Treuer taught the language in such a way that students felt their humanity acknowledged, supported, and welcomed. He also facilitated the opportunities for students to gather at drum ceremonies and community-based events. He truly made our little community possible. If you want to gain a sense of what taking a class with Anton is like, I encourage you to read two of his recent books: *The Cultural Toolbox* and *The Language Warrior's Manifesto*. In every interview, students commented on his excellence as an educator and his ability to create a space that helped students feel connected and seen. His belief that we have all "been given a unique set of gifts" and we are the ones our "ancestors were praying for and waiting for through the generations" carries strongly in his teaching.[13]

## Pre-COVID-19 Context

At my home institution of Minnesota State University, Mankato, we offer both Indigenous heritage languages on campus for our students (i.e., Dakota and Ojibwe language). Given our university's location in the Dakota homelands of Southern Minnesota, fellow American Indigenous Studies (AIS) faculty and I prioritized establishing the Dakota classes on campus first before developing offerings in Ojibwemowin. The AIS program originally offered Dakota language in one of the Dakota communities in the early 2010s. In 2015, we were able to offer the course physically on campus. Three years later, we offered our first Elementary Ojibwe

---

[13] Anton Treuer, *The Cultural Toolbox: Traditional Ojibwe Living in the Modern World* (St. Paul: Minnesota Historical Society Press, 2021), 186.

classes via a partnership with Bemidji State University (BSU) and Dr. Anton Treuer.

BSU is located in Northern Minnesota. The university and the town's names come from the Ojibwe word bemijigamaag. The school has the proud distinction of being home to the first collegiate Ojibwe language program in the United States, back in 1971. Students can earn a minor in Ojibwe or complete a Certificate in Instruction of Ojibwe in addition to their Indigenous Studies degrees. Dr. Anton Truer is the instructor of Ojibwemowin at BSU and is a renowned scholar of the language, Indigenous history, and equity work. He and I met several years prior to our partnership when I was conducting some of my early research on the histories of collegiate Ojibwe language programs. After Dakota classes were secured at my home institution, I reached out to Anton and started a conversation about a partnership.

Our institutions formulated an agreement where MNSU students would attend Anton's Ojibwe classes via telepresence and MNSU would contribute to the instructor costs on a per student basis. At that time, our campuses used Cisco, the leading conferencing software of the time, and Zoom was nowhere near our mental landscape. Dr. Treuer and I knew each other from my other research on Indigenous language programs. BSU already had experience offering the classes via ITV from a short collaboration with a Minnesota community college and with Onamia high school in Mille Lacs, Minnesota. In the early years of the partnership, only the high school students and an individual distance learning student attended the classes with us. From the beginning of our partnership in fall 2018, I attended and facilitated the tech support for the Elementary Ojibwe class which met four days a week for a 50-minute class session. Although my time was not factored into my credit load as an instructor, attending the class was extremely beneficial for my own practice and growth as a language learner. We also began to build an Ojibwe language community at MNSU with extra study sessions and gatherings to practice the language.

That following spring during the 2018–2019 academic year, Anton and I personally funded and coordinated an opportunity for students to attend drum ceremony together in Mille Lacs. Students were able to meet Anton in person and listen to Ojibwe being spoken by Elders and community leaders. Additionally, after receiving Institutional Review Board approval, I began interviewing students, staff, faculty, and administrators about the collaboration. My research focus was, at that time, to understand the experience of the partnership from a students' perspective. I also sought to document and share the process we had gone through to set up the collaboration so others may have a blueprint to establish something similar at their own institutions.

Over the 2019 summer and into the next academic year, I conducted interviews and recorded autoethnographic notes and observations as a participant in the classes. That summer Anton and I also applied for and were awarded a Multi-Campus Collaboration Grant offered by our university system office. The grant included funding to take a large group of students to two language conferences and other professional development opportunities. We entered the 2019–2020 academic year and the second year of our partnership excited about the grant and how the funding would assist us in getting students together for more experiential learning.

That fall, we successfully brought students together for a weekend gathering at BSU that included sharing meals, using the language in public venues together, and attending drum ceremony at the White Earth Nation where students listened to fluent Elders speaking the language. For a significant number of students, Native and non-Native, this was the first time they had attended drum ceremony and/or heard Ojibwe being spoken outside of the classroom space. Students and faculty left the gathering excited for our next trip. In Spring 2020, we planned to attend the Anishinaabemowin Teg Conference which was being held on the Canadian side of Sault Ste. Marie at the tip of the Michigan mitten. For many students, this would be their first time traveling internationally. In the Fall and early portion of the 2020 Spring semester, I worked with students to apply for and get their passports ready for the trip.

The new spring semester started with the partnership thriving, students attending class together on each campus, and meeting over telepresence. I continued attending the classes with students and holding study sessions on Wednesdays when we did not formally meet. By February, I was starting to work on the paperwork for the trip to Canada. I remember hearing some discussion of a sickness in the news during this time, but I did not become aware of it in any real capacity until late February and early March. On February 28, the Chancellor of our MinnState system announced a suspension of all international travel. Our spring break ran from March 9 to 13 that year. The weekend before the start of break, I flew to Michigan to attend a family event. By the time I returned to Minnesota on the March 9, I was increasingly hearing conversations about COVID-19 on the news. On March 11, 2020, the World Health Organization declared

COVID-19 a pandemic[14] and two days later the president of the United States declared a nationwide emergency.[15] By the end of the week, the university system chancellor announced that MinnState institutions would be moving to online or alternative delivery options. Spring breaks were extended so that faculty could transition their courses. All out-of-state business travel was also suspended. In many ways, this was the start of the COVID-19 pandemic experience for college students and faculty.

My grant funded reservations and transportation arrangements to attend the Indigenous Language Institute's three-day conference in New Mexico were canceled. Each day, there seemed to be new emails from the chancellor, the university presidents, and our deans. The governor of Minnesota, Tim Walz, also issued several emergency executive orders during this time which closed "places of public accommodation" and issued a "stay at home" order which directed workers to work from home if possible and listed categories of "critical service exemptions" that allowed workers in those areas to travel to work and home.[16] During this period, I sent and received emails from students in my various classes, including students in the Ojibwe offerings. When classes resumed on March 30, the Ojibwe classes were held on Zoom with every student attending virtually from their own unique spaces.

## The Early Days of the Pandemic

When I reflect on this time period of the early days of the pandemic, what strikes me the most is how easily our students adapted to being online together and how critical our community was to the students. When I interviewed students from the Spring 2019 classes who transitioned from ITV in the classroom to meeting fully online, they shared that it was not much of a challenge. In fact, more than one student shared that the Ojibwe

---

[14] Dr. Tedros Adhanom Ghebreyesus, "WHO Director-General's Opening Remarks at the Media Briefing on Covid-19—11 March 2020," World Health Organization, March 11, 2020, accessed August 28, 2023, https://www.who.int/director-general/speeches/detail/who-director-general-s-opening-remarks-at-the-media-briefing-on-covid-19%2D%2D-11-march-2020

[15] Proclamation No. 9994, 85 Fed. Reg. 15337 (March 13, 2020).

[16] Minnesota Executive Order No. 20-20 (March 25, 2020), https://mn.gov/governor/assets/3a.%20EO%2020-20%20FINAL%20SIGNED%20Filed_tcm1055-425020.pdf

classes handled the transition best compared to their other courses. "I think we handled it the best because we were already doing an online thing…it kinda still feels like we're going through the ITV thing" a student said.[17] Multiple students mentioned that they found the Zoom environment more intimate and appreciated the chat feature but ultimately expressed a desire to return to the ITV format when safe to do so.

The teaching delivery of the classes did alter slightly in the early pandemic in that Anton was now teaching from home via his computer, but the delivery of content remained largely the same. Because we were using ITV, Anton had previously utilized word documents to support his verbal delivery of content. All participants could engage with the same word document screen or the video of him as he delivered instruction. When moved fully online, that mode of instruction stayed the same and everyone joined via their own computer. Some students struggled to have reliable access to Internet or computers to join class, but Anton or I worked with those students to address the challenges. In many ways, our Ojibwe classroom was the one space that did not have substantial upheaval for the students. In fact, even more so than before COVID-19, the Ojibwe classroom was a piece of connection, community, and caring in a time of strife. As one student explained, it was "the one thing I could reliably count on."[18]

With state-mandated stay at home orders, travel suspended, and everyone trying to navigate the continuous upheaval of the pandemic, our grant activities shifted gears. We could no longer take students to conferences, but we knew we wanted to connect the students together. We ordered long-sleeve shirts for the students with our university logos on each upper shoulder sleeve corner. On the front left chest perched a yellow American goldfinch, the spiritual keeper of ojibwemowin, and the word ojibwemotawishin which translates to "speak Ojibwe to me." I packaged and mailed these shirts to each students' preferred address.

For some of the local MNSU students, I dropped the packages off at their residence and we did a social distancing exchange where I texted them that the package was outside, and we waved at each other. One student made a heart with their hands and brought it to their chest in a love gesture after picking their package up at their door. When discussing the care packages later, students shared that the gift package:

---

[17] Zachary Houle, Ojibwe class student, in discussion with author, April 2020.
[18] Mitchell Holmberg, Ojibwe class student, in discussion with author, May 2021.

provided some happiness in this dark time right now…a little ray of sun…it's been rough. Especially with certain other things like besides school stuff, personal stuff. So, to get something to show we're all in this together…it's a high school musical kind of situation. It's nice.[19]

Another student who received their shirts in the mail shared:

They were definitely a mood lifter. Especially in such hard times with the stay-at-home order. I know it's kind of difficult to stay home cooped up in the house 24/7. Waking up in the morning and seeing that there's this package on my front step. I was like "oh my goodness" and I go to open it up and just being able to like wear that proudly…it just lifted up my spirits a lot.[20]

The fact that we sent the students these shirts toward the end of the semester was a pick me up when students were beginning to burn out on their classes. One student shared that it was a real morale booster for them, and they were touched that "someone's thinking about me. It makes me feel connected still."[21] As we wrapped up that first semester with COVID-19, I couldn't help but wonder if students would return in the Fall if classes were still fully online. In pre-COVID-19 interviews with BSU students, the majority expressed that they would not take the classes if offered online.

## THE MIDDLE MONTHS OF THE PANDEMIC

The reality was that we did not return to normal. By August, COVID-19 was the third leading cause of death in the United States.[22] On August 19, the Centers for Disease Control and Prevention released a press release confirming that Native American and Alaskan Natives as a group were at a higher risk for severe COVID-19 outcomes than other racial and ethnic

---

[19] Houle.
[20] James (pseudonym), Ojibwe class student, in discussion with author, April 2020.
[21] Anonymous Student, Ojibwe class student, in discussion with author, April 2020.
[22] "CDC Museum Covid-19 Timeline," Centers for Disease Control and Prevention: David J. Sencer CDC Museum, last reviewed, March 15, 2023, https://www.cdc.gov/museum/timeline/covid19.html#:~:text=March%2011%2C%202020,declares%20COVID%2D19%20a%20pandemic

minorities.[23] In June that summer, George Floyd was murdered by police officers in Minneapolis, Minnesota, only a few hours away from our respective locations. Black Lives Matter protests occurred across our state. Some cities instituted city-wide curfews. BLM protests also erupted across the country as the outrage at this systematic violence resonated with people and anti-racist peoples. In the fall, we returned to the virtual classroom more shaken than we had left it, but also less numb than we were before.

With the pandemic still in full swing, both of our institutions, like many across the country, delivered instruction primarily in online formats. Some "hyflex" courses were offered where instruction was delivered in-person by the instructor and on Zoom simultaneously by connecting the classroom to Zoom. Students could attend in-person in the classroom, online via Zoom, or through a combination of both. Our institutions established mask mandates and social distancing protocols across the campuses. Classrooms were updated with new Zoom technology and cameras, but the Ojibwe classes continued to be offered as online only in that first year back. As the pandemic continued from summer and into that fall, ceremonies, Indigenous community events, and gatherings were still largely on hold, canceled, or postponed across Indian country. Many students on both of our campuses elected to attend college from home virtually instead of returning to campus that year. Still, there was a desire and need for connection and community.

Many of the students who had completed classes in the previous year continued their studies with the next level of Ojibwe instruction. Some students who had previously taken a break from school came back to the classes given the virtual delivery. Together, each class formed new communities of learners/speakers. One of the new benefits of holding the Ojibwe classes fully virtual was that learners from around the United States and Canada were able to enroll in the class alongside MNSU and BSU students.

The Fall 2020 class differed from previous offerings because it now had current and retired faculty members, K-12 educators, social service professionals, and students from other institutions beyond our initial partnership enrolled in the courses. Several of the non-traditional students were

---

[23] "CDC Data Shows Disproportionate Covid-19 Impact in American Indian/Alaskan Native Populations," Centers for Disease Control and Prevention, last reviewed August 19, 2020, https://www.cdc.gov/media/releases/2020/p0819-covid-19-impact-american-indian-alaska-native.html/

already working in institutions and organizations that served Indigenous students. The opportunity to learn or improve their language skills in Ojibwemowin immediately benefited the youth and colleagues they worked with.

One of the non-traditional students who joined the class was Chris Bergman, a retired archeologist, who wished to learn the language so he could use it with a friend who is also a speaker. When discussing his experience in the classes he shared that his mom had passed away from COVID-19 that previous spring. Inspired by his sister-in-law's practice of finding gratitude even during the struggles of COVID-19, he found himself thinking "I bet you this year, because of the tragedy of COVID, there's going to be online classes. Maybe instead of COVID always being a tragedy, maybe there are some good things to come out of it."[24] Later in our conversation he reflected, "When I think about it, this was a really fun exciting year for me. I learned a lot. Anton Treuer is one of the finest teachers I've ever encountered, and I have taught in universities... For me, one of the great joys has been this class."[25]

Another non-traditional student who joined the class was an Anishinaabeg graduate student completing a degree at an East Coast Ivy League institution. For their language requirement, they sought out Ojibwe language opportunities. When discussing their experience, they reflected that:

> Normally, we wouldn't all be able to attend without the Zoom era....There are mothers in this class. There are elders. There are older students working full time jobs and I think the way in which Anton approaches teaching is one that can encompass this kind of broad range of life experiences and where people are at.[26]

Student interviews from pre-COVID-19 also consistently shared these sentiments about the nature of the course. Repeatedly, they commented that the space was "very welcoming" and a "forgiving" environment that focused on growth and learning instead of points.

While the classes pivoted, so did our grant efforts. Despite the stay-at-home order and travel restriction being lifted for state employees in

---

[24] Christopher Bergman, Ojibwe class student, in discussion with author, May 2021.
[25] Bergman.
[26] Joseph Zordan, Ojibwe class student, in discussion with author, May 2021.

September, traveling with students was still limited due to the need to socially distance. To foster more connection and outreach across the different levels of classes and the communities at large, we held a weekly online language table in Zoom. Prior to COVID-19, advanced language students at BSU held an in-person language table. At MNSU, I often facilitated a study session for students as well. When COVID-19 first hit, we disbanded those efforts out of necessity. In Fall 2020, with grant funding, we were able to move the language table to a virtual gathering and hire a mix of three students from MNSU and BSU to facilitate the language table. In addition to students, we also had community members join us in those evenings to practice, learn, and share the language with each other.

Like the previous semester, we also mailed "sense of belonging" kits to our students to foster a stronger sense of physical connection. This time, the kits were more substantial than they had been in the previous spring. We mailed boxes full of Ojibwe language books, study supplies, snacks, Ojibwe materials (hats, bags, etc.) purchased from Ojibwe businesses, university items such as lanyards and water bottles, and three-quarter zip sport-tek jackets with the same design as the previous shirts.

When all the students had received their boxes, we coordinated days to wear our shirts together and took photos of our digital gathering. The boxes arrived close to the end of semester and were designed to give students a boost as they went into their final exams. One student shared that "it kind of felt like Christmas. There was a family feel there…when everyone was getting their presents to open and share and enjoy."[27] These "sense of belonging" boxes were shipped across the United States and Canada to reach the diverse group of students in the classes.

As we moved forward into Spring 2021, the new students returned, and the community continued to grow in the language. Periodically, multiple students would wear the "sense of belonging" items on the same day, and it was a positive reminder of our community. "We knew the crowd was gathering again tomorrow and now we had gifts to share…it made this class special, and I've taken a lot of classes," a student said.[28] Another student shared that their family members would often wear the shirt because they liked it so much and family members would like one, too, if extra were available. The books, hats, and other materials from the fall boxes

---

[27] Jerry Lazare, Ojibwe class student, in discussion with author, May 2021.
[28] Lazare.

were often distributed and shared by the students with their friends and family members.

Whereas we had connected with the community via a virtual language table in the Fall, in the Spring semester, we focused on hosting a winter storytelling event. For the event, we were fortunate to have Ojibwemowin language professor and author Pebaamibines (Dennis Jones) join Anton in sharing Ojibwe winter stories in the language for the event. Pebaamibines also had one of his language mentees assist with the storytelling. Over 880 individuals registered for the event and over 500 attended. Participants logged on from the United States, Canada, and Europe. The event was a night of global community interested and passionate about Ojibwe language and culture.

To my knowledge, at least one other Anishinaabeg organization in Minnesota also hosted virtual Ojibwe story gatherings that year, but I am confident there were at least a few. At one event I attended, I casually surveyed the videos of fellow participants. I observed individuals, parents, grandparents, aunts, and uncles tuned in. Many individuals had little ones sitting with them to hear the stories. These events were multi-generational, much like our classroom spaces were. They were community centered and community grounded, a few short hours to dial into the language and its medicinal effects.

With the success of the MNSU/BSU storytelling event, we sought more ways to connect our students to Elders. Ojibwe classes, especially Anton's classes, are so much more than just a language class. They involve cultural understandings, history, stories, and humor. Given the restrictions on most community opportunities for students to interact with Elders, we invited Pebaamibines to spend time in both of the Ojibwe classes taught that semester as an "elder-in-residence." Across three months, he regularly virtually visited the classes to share stories, answer student questions, and support their learning of the language. During certain sessions, he offered ceremony for the students and provided guidance on how to spiritually support their own learning.

The Ojibwe classes have always been a welcoming environment. With the pandemic, though, students were facing new challenges in their lives. Many of us, myself included, lost loved ones and cherished Elders during the pandemic. We often could not attend services due to social distancing and various protocols. In these moments of grief, students often shared these challenging experiences in our classrooms and sometimes sought advice on how to navigate them as Anishinaabeg or non-Native peoples.

During an interview, a student highlighted this holistic and supportive class environment:

> If someone's having a bad day, we talk about it. If something comes up, we talk about it. A story gets told. Those moments make it feel like we're really there together even if it's in that Zoom space…building that community in that group and allowing things to just be in that space and also focusing on the content and learning but not so focused on that, that we lose the being human together in that space.[29]

As the end of the Spring 2021 semester approached, we again shared group photos of us together on Zoom in our Ojibwemowin jackets and shirts. Any students who had newly joined or returned to the classes were mailed sense of belonging kits and the partnership jackets or shirts. As we moved into summer, a group of intermediate students independently led a virtual language circle with fellow students. They wished to continue their community and practice the language with each other outside of school. By that point, several individuals had received their first COVID-19 vaccines and there was a growing hope that we might be able to return, in part, to the classroom safely in the next academic year. Distance learning students expressed their desire to continue attending via Zoom as well.

## Steps Towards the "New Normal"

When we returned for the 2021–2022 school year, the pandemic was still active. Our universities continued to offer hyflex course delivery with students taking classes both in person and/or virtually. Mask mandates were determined by the transmission levels in the county of the school. Vaccination clinics and testing clinics were available on the MNSU campus with campuses encouraging students to get vaccinated. Anton returned to the classroom that semester but offered the course as a hyflex option. I was on sabbatical for that year but continued to coordinate the class for MNSU by finding a room, handling scheduling, working with the bookstore, and meeting with students. I also joined the classes virtually.

As part of my sabbatical plan, I enrolled in the Advanced Ojibwe sequence and other required courses to complete BSU's Certificate in the Instruction of Ojibwe language. The long-distance non-traditional

---

[29] Timb Mannuzza, Ojibwe class student, in discussion with author, May 2022.

learners from the previous year returned at the intermediate level and new long-distance learners joined the Elementary Ojibwe. The classes also included a few students who attended in-person at both of our institutions. Once again, we had a diverse range of students, working professionals, and community members in the classroom.

During this specific academic year, our classrooms truly represented a community in that we had newborns to Elders participating. We had a student become a grandparent, students becoming aunts and uncles, and a student give birth to their third child. I attended class with my newborn nephew sleeping in my arms. I rocked him as I spoke and listened to Ojibwe with my fellow classmates. Together, we celebrated achievements and supported each other during our challenges. One student expressed that "there was just so much to celebrate. Everyone celebrated everybody in a family-like way. It was all very human…It's just human…it's like not being in school…like not being in class. It feels like a community."[30]

In December, we expanded our community even further by hosting a three-day in-person language summit at BSU'S American Indian Resource Center. Masking and social distancing practices were still in place, but we were finally able to meet in person again. The MNSU students and I drove the four hours to BSU together in a car and we all wore masks. The summit involved flying distance-learning students to join us in Bemidji. Five language speakers, including Elders, joined us for a day of language presentations and cultural experiences together. The students who were unable to join in person were Zoomed into the event and their fellow classmates facilitated their engagement via portable laptops that moved with student groups to various presentations. At one point in the weekend, students played bagese, the bone dish game, together. The students attending digitally were given rounds in the game just like the in-person participants. Virtual players either used their own bagese sets or a student in-person took a turn for them. One of the students had their young child with them who also joined in the game. As I watched everyone taking turns around the room, cheering big wins, and teasing each other, I couldn't help but feel the joy in that space. It perfectly encapsulated our community.

On the second day of the summit, after a nice dinner together at a local restaurant, we returned to the American Indian Resource Center (AIRC) on BSU's campus where Pebaamibines and two of his language assistants along with Dustin Burnette and Anton told Ojibwe stories in the

[30] Lazare.

language. The event was hosted in-person and virtually. We had over 1400 people register and had to coordinate an overflow YouTube stream when the Zoom hit the maximum number of participants. In person, we filled the AIRC. Elders, fellow speakers and learners from the community, and a range of interested individuals came to hear the language. Children listened to the stories and young ones played in the back. In every sense of the word, from babies to Elders, the community was there. The next morning, our group once again gathered. Anton held a naming ceremony for multiple students with friends and family in attendance. The entire weekend was a gathering for the spirit.

In Spring 2022, we held another similar event for the students to come together. We met in Mille Lacs to tour the Mille Lacs Museum and attend drum ceremony that evening. The following day, we traveled to Bemidji and participated in sugarbush together. Anton graciously hosted students on his family's property for the sugarbush. We shared the Ojibwe story of maple sap, helped haul and boil it as we ate and visited together. During the gathering, we also distributed our last "sense of belonging" kits to the students. In May of 2022, our MCC grant period ended. It was not until a full year later, on May 4, 2023, that the World Health Organization declared an end to COVID-19 as a public health emergency. For the Ojibwe classes, gathering together once more had been the turning point to find a new sense of normal.

## Lessons Learned

This chapter is a small snapshot of how this collaboration and its students navigated COVID-19. The experiences of individuals involved are diverse, varied, and unique to each person. At the same time, learning Ojibwemowin was a glue that kept us coming back to class every day. For some students, it was sustenance for their journey of personal discovery and explorations of their identity. For other students, it was the one classroom where they felt seen and cared about. They knew they could come and bring their whole self to the space. One student who had a family member fighting cancer during the year shared that:

> There are so many days that I was not okay and going to class made me okay. It was a surprise to be so filled up and just connected when you're feeling like you're losing somebody, or you don't know what's going on with somebody you care about. And then to just be in this space where your brain is

still working and you're learning and you're connected and if something does happen to your loved one there's a bunch of people who care...so for me, it was a real lifeline to just be able to come to class and just be myself and learn about myself. Because, when I'm learning the language, I learn about myself. When we have these spaces, it's hard to even put words and understanding around it...[31]

Like fellow educators in Indigenous language revitalization work across Turtle Island, our community responded to the demands and limitations of the COVID-19 pandemic. In the same tradition of resilience and adaptation that has enabled the language to survive pandemics of the past, our little corner of Ojibwe classes and the community built within them persisted and was a source of joy. Gii-nimaawanji'idimin.

**Competing Interests Declaration** The author received two grants that were connected to the work described in the study. However, the study was not specifically funded by the grant. The author has no conflicts of interest to declare that are relevant to the content of this chapter.

---

[31] Karen Branden, Ojibwe class student, in discussion with author, May 2022.

CHAPTER 11

# Using that Good Tech Medicine: An Indigenous Autoethnographic Recount of Teaching and Learning with Elders During COVID-19

*Kelly Berry*

> *The ultimate aim for these poetics and story-telling measures is to allow for more of a personal conversation tone—a further glimpse into my lived experiences, a way to show the reader the careful in-depth analysis of my thoughts, and not just tell them about what occurs on the surface (S.A. Red Corn,* Set the prairie on fire: an autoethnographic confrontation of colonial entanglements *(Doctoral Dissertation, Kansas State University, 2017), K-REx).*
> *—Alex Red Corn*

My name is Kelly Berry, and I am an enrolled citizen of the Apache Tribe of Oklahoma with affiliations to the Kiowa and Choctaw Nations. I come from the Red Tipi Clan of the Kiowa Tribe. I am the son of William Tennyson Berry (Kiowa Apache) and Donna Jo Sambrano (Choctaw)

K. Berry (✉)
Kansas State University, Manhattan, KS, USA

along with my brother (Tennyson Berry II) and one sister (Amanda Michelle Berry). I am the grandson of Philemon Berry (Kiowa Apache) and Leona Berry (Wolf) and the great-grandson of Tennyson Berry (Kiowa Apache), the last principal chief of the Apache Tribe of Oklahoma and Anne Jones Berry.

Colleagues always ask about my two years of service at a federal Indian boarding school and what it was like to teach there. Of all the experiences that stand out, the most significant was during the early days of COVID-19 when leading faculty and staff, especially Elder faculty, in their transition from in-person to online teaching. It was an opportunity to highlight my computer skills, and it also allowed me to enhance my tech savvy leadership skill sets.

I write this chapter with a voice of a reluctant leader, and I am reluctant to call myself a leader because I do not believe it is my place to do so.[1] I have taken leadership courses; I possess leadership certificates, but at no time do I introduce myself as a leader. I was not raised that way. Once you get to know me, you may find that I am quiet and reserved. I am the son of a coach who told me to be a leader by my actions and not my words, so in the early days of COVID-19, I was assisting my colleagues with navigating new forms of technology. What started out as just tutoring about Zoom turned into tutorials of other digital platforms, such as D2L, Moodle, Blackboard, etc.

I write this chapter as someone who has worked, breathed, and served in a contemporary federal Indian boarding school, Riverside Indian School (RIS) in Anadarko, Oklahoma, which was originally called the Wichita Caddo School, founded in 1871. I walked in those halls daily, where trauma, adaptability, and, most importantly, survivance reverberated down the school hallways.

> The picture of the nuns with our children, smh.
> The picture of the priests with our children, smh.
> Was this place for me?

At times, the dissonance created an internal sense of hypocrisy. Even as I worked to support, I served in the same institution that had shamed, intimidated, and ridiculed my ancestors, reminding me of what my family

---

[1] Heather Shotton, "Being of Service to Our People," In *Indigenous Leadership in Higher Education,* eds. Robin S. Minthorn and Alicia F. Chavez (New York, NY: Routledge, 2015), 144.

members endured. My great-grandparents shared little of their experiences of attending what Vine Deloria, Jr. and Daniel Wildcat call Indian survival schools.[2] I knew enough not to ask any of my family members if there were stories from my great-grandparent's time at survival schools. Having been raised traditionally, I was taught this was an invasion of their privacy. Many of my colleagues attended various Indian survival schools, but as much as I want to ask of their experiences,

> I just stay quiet.
> Why trigger a memory?
> Why be disrespectful?

I write this chapter knowing that each day of my service at RIS conjured up the same dark images and stories of what my relatives and ancestors felt walking the halls of a forced assimilation paradigm designed to eradicate my beautiful Kiowa, Apache, and Choctaw cultures. I sometimes found myself standing against walls, reliving the governmental process of stripping students of what it meant and felt to be Indigenous or Kiowa or Apache or Choctaw. I could detail the many horror stories I heard and felt throughout my time at the RIS, but

> Do I need to bring them up here?
> I'll let my relatives rest.
>                              They've been through enough.

I've inherited a direct linkage to the federal Indian boarding schools where Indians were allowed to determine the content but were generally isolated from the process of education.[3] I am the great-grandson of Indian boarding school survivors. Although I knew to ask no questions, I am familiar with a few oral stories that have been passed down through my family of my great-grandparents' experiences. I figure these are the stories that I was meant to hear, as I was told by an auntie that some of the stories are too graphic to share. Of those stories, I know of only one direct quote my great-grandfather gave of his time at Carlisle Indian Industrial School.

> "It was a long train ride."

---

[2] Vine Deloria, Jr. and Daniel R. Wildcat, *Power and Place: Indian Education in America* (Fulcrum Resources, 2001), 82.

[3] Deloria and Wildcat, *Power, and Place*, 82.

I know he was a member of the school's band, and I was told the band played at a president's inauguration, but if you were to ask me beyond those two stories, I would be as quiet as a cricket. But I think back to my great-grandfather's learning of the White language at Carlisle, which served him well as a cultural broker.[4] He served as an interpreter for Plains Apache chiefs during their visits to Washington DC. He seemed to walk a path between the darkness of Indian survival schools and helping chart new presents and futures.

As for my great-grandmother, there are even fewer stories of her experience at Rainy Mountain Indian School. When I say even fewer, the number is as high as zero. All I know of her experiences at this particular boarding school was that she did not have to travel far. It was around twenty miles south of her home in Carnegie, Oklahoma, maybe not as long as my great-grandfather's train ride, but I'm sure their experiences weren't all that different.

What I can tell you is my great-grandparents
survived
and came home.

Many Indigenous students never came home. This dark reality always hits close to home when the news reports come out of grave after grave being located on Indian survival school campuses.

Investigation finds burial sites at 53 federal Indian boarding schools.[5]
U.S. report identifies burial sites linked to boarding schools for Native Americans.[6]
Remains of more than 1000 Indigenous children found at former residential schools in Canada.[7]

---

[4] Margaret C. Szasz, Indian *Education in the American Colonies: 1607–1783* (Lincoln: University of Nebraska Press, 1988), 263.

[5] Moriah Balingit, "Investigation Finds Burial Sites at 53 Federal Indian Boarding Schools," accessed August 30, 2023, https://www.washingtonpost.com/education/2022/05/12/federal-indian-boarding-schools-remains/

[6] Associated Press, "U.S. report identifies burial sites linked to boarding schools for Native Americans," accessed September 2, 2023, https://www.npr.org/2022/05/11/1098276649/u-s-report-details-burial-sites-linked-to-boarding-schools-for-native-americans

[7] Mindy Weisberger, "Remains of more than 1000 Indigenous children found at former residential schools in Canada," accessed September 2, 2023, https://www.livescience.com/childrens-graves-residential-schools-canada.html

I could just say that many Indigenous students survived and came home and leave it like that, but our survival and adaptability involve much more than that. I always wonder what it was like for my great-grandparents and thousands of other Indigenous students to hear European gibberish for the first time. I always wonder how they survived a foreign colonized curriculum predicated on Eurocentric teachings, predicated on erasing their culture, predicated on a paternalistic domination of another culture forced to walk in two worlds and fight for some sort of balance.

> Damn,
> that *Reservation Dogs* boarding school episode (Season 3, Ep.3)
> really
> hit close to home.
> Difficult to think if my great-grandparents were brutalized.
>                        for speaking their Kiowa and Apache languages too.
> But they came home.
> They came home.
> …and here I am,
>                        an extension of their perseverance.
> But my role may have been different from the future they had imagined for me.
> At Riverside, I was the tech guy—the young man who had…
> Tech Medicine,
> The Wizard,
> The Magician,
> The Savior.

So as our families and communities continue to persevere, here I offer my stories of "leading" individuals through their transition with technology during COVID-19. Specifically, I am going to walk through how I centered Indigenous ways of working with Elders while teaching and leading with technology in two overlapping contexts: 1. as an instructor in a series of Elder computer courses offered to the community, and 2. as a tech-savvy teacher working with Elder teachers at Riverside Indian School during the evolution of COVID-19.

In order to understand this transition within a federal Indian boarding school, we must understand cultural ways of knowing and intergenerational trauma not found in predominantly White institutions (PWIs), and that Riverside Indian School has ninety-seven percent Native American staff and faculty. Also, we must understand the nuances of teaching Elders, who represent a population that did not necessarily grow up utilizing teaching technology. This chapter outlines my journey to work with this important population, as a teacher, learner, and reluctant leader through the early days of COVID-19.

## Prelude to COVID-19: Learning to Teach Elders Technology: HOW DO YOU TURN THIS DAMN THING ON?

I recall when I was a shitass running around the pow wows like any other child just having fun and never listening to anyone in authority. My parents, brother, and sister would have to chase me around telling me to behave, but it was my aunt who would catch me and yell at me to sit down. Anytime an Elder was speaking, I was told to sit down and be quiet, as I was told to listen and stay silent out of respect. In our culture, Elders have a wealth of lived experiences and wisdom that we need to respect and learn from. From our Elders, we find wisdom, guidance, reassurance, strength, and courage. We learn important things from them and owe them our constant service.[8] Never did I think that one day, cultural ways would be reversed, and Elders would be listening and learning from me.

My preparation for teaching faculty nuances of online teaching began five years prior while I worked for a tribal nation. Local community Elders made known their desire to learn basic computer literacy. As they looked for an instructor, rumors began to circulate that I had teaching experience and was tech savvy. I remember receiving a phone call inquiring about my interest in teaching an Elder computer course. With four years of university teaching under my belt, I told myself that "teaching is teaching." Or so I thought.

I remember preparing for the first day of the Elder computer class just like any other class I had taught before. But something seemed off, even though I was unable to put my finger on it. The classroom door creaked more than usual; the birds chirped louder than usual; my shoes squeaked more than usual. Ignoring these signs, I walked into the classroom and there sat ten tribal Elders with a fixed stare at every move as I was

---

[8] Shawn Secatero, "Native Educational Sovereignty in Teaching and Leadership (NESTL): The Transformation of Leadership Utilizing a Holistic Corn Pollen Model to Serve All Students at a Research University," In *Unsettling Settler-Colonial Education: The Transformational Praxis Model*, eds. Cornel Pewewardy, Anna Lees, and Robin Zape-Tah-Hol-Ah Minthorn (New York: Teachers College Press, 2017), 39.

preparing to dive into Lesson 1. I walked over to my stool to prepare to start Lesson 1, and all of the sudden I heard multiple voices at once: "Where's the coffee?" "What are we going to learn today?" "How do you turn this damn thing on?"

Caught off-guard, I remember freezing like a deer in the headlights, not knowing how to react. These were Elders. I was supposed to listen. I was supposed to stay quiet. Everything I knew conflicted with me walking into the class, as the teacher, as the leader of this workshop. In the face of the internal and external questions, I walked out of the classroom into the hallway and collected myself. Breathing deeply, I then walked into the classroom to begin lessons and heard loud distinctive Elder voices, "HOLD ON! I'M NOT READY." "YOU'RE ALREADY GOING TOO FAST!" "DO YOU HAVE ANY SNACKS?"

> I remember a voice in my head.
> Don't disrespect Elders.
> Don't ever disrespect the Elders.
> Don't you do that.

As their questions bombarded me, I seriously thought teaching this class was a big mistake. I was not used to students voicing comments so vigorously; honestly, I did not think I would make it through the first class without quitting. I remember one Elder asking to speak to me outside, and he said to me words that I will never forget. "You've never taught Elders before, have you? Kelly, you have to remember that us Elders are ornery, and we'll say things to you to be mean, sometimes to test you, but remember that our culture is based on respect. And also remember that our generation didn't grow up with technology. We'll learn with you, but for some of us, it is difficult to have a younger person teach us when we are supposed to be all-knowing with this bagful of wisdom. If you show them respect; then they will show you respect as well."

> My teaching preparation courses didn't teach me this.
> Teaching Native Elders is a whole different animal.

Taking his words to heart, I walked into the classroom and calmly sat on my stool in front of the Elders and began class in respectful ways. I introduced myself to the class, stating my tribes, my families, and my relations. I should have respected their level of computer literacy and conducted pre-assessments as to where I needed to begin their lessons instead of assuming all knew their way around a computer.

Having grown up with Indigenous teachings, I was always taught by my grandfather and father that Elders deserved the utmost respect. Respect means that you have respect for other people's views and perspectives and what they represent.[9] Many in the class admitted to not having a computer in their household, and many admitted not having good typing skills, but I did not heed their admissions. I assumed they would be able to handle any typing assignments or computer tasks I threw at them, but my assumptions were my disrespect to my Elders.

> I should have introduced myself and my tribes. That's our way of respect.
> I should have asked for their level of computer literacy.
> I should have asked if they needed to go over computer basics.

And that is where we started the computer course—at the basics. I enjoyed each community Elder computer course because of how much time I was able to spend with them teaching computer basics that they needed. In many ways, I am glad I was able to teach the Elder computer courses. Am I a better teacher because of this? Yes, because teaching Elders has allowed for more patience in my classroom management. Teaching Elders taught me that every step in a process is vital in their learning. I learned how to simplify a procedure to where someone who exhibits no computer literacy can understand a fourteen or so step process of adding a video into a power point presentation.

> I was a teacher before the Elder class.
> Now, I am an effective teacher.

## COVID-19 Pandemic: What the Hell Is Zoom? What the Hell Is Blackboard?

When COVID-19 began, I had five years of experience teaching Elders and had been at Riverside less than a week. The institution had in-person instruction, but there were no aspects of online teaching. There was no

---

[9] Robin Starr Minthorn, "Consciously Leading with Ancestors Prayers, and Community in the Heath," In *Indigenous Leadership in Higher Education*, eds. Robin S. Minthorn and Alicia F. Chavez (New York, NY: Routledge, 2015), 182.

Zoom, no Blackboard, no Canvas, nor any other online instructional programs. Many staff at Riverside self-identified as not tech savvy while also admitting they had never heard of Zoom or Blackboard; however, as we were plunged into the COVID-19 experience, nearly overnight these two programs became mandatory in our teaching instruction.

My first day of teaching service at the Indian boarding school gave inklings of how my time would go. "The Elder faculty are going to need a lot of help learning this technology" is a phrase I kept hearing over and over during the first days on the job. "Do you have any experience teaching Elders" is another phrase I kept hearing throughout my first days.

> If they only knew.
> Should I tell them I teach Elders?
> People don't believe me anyways, when I say,
> 5 years teaching Elders.
> 9 Elder computer classes.
> 432 hours teaching computers to Elders.
> I might be qualified.

I surmise that news of my tech savvy-ness had begun to travel the hallways before my arrival. No sooner did I arrive on campus than, like a herd of buffalo, texts, emails, phone calls began to rush in. Some inquired about my technology skill set and familiarity with online teaching. Some inquired about Blackboard and how it works, but there was no, "Hey, congratulations on your new job" or "Glad to have you onboard."

> I wasn't even sure I knew Blackboard anymore.
> Six years is a long time for a hiatus from such nuance.
> I had a feeling YouTube would become my best friend.
> I just hope I didn't bite off more than I can chew …
> telling people, I knew Blackboard.

I could hear the footsteps approaching my classroom. They sounded like it was more than one person coming down the hallway, and I will never forget the first words as the footsteps entered the doorway.

> *So, Mr. Berry, I hear you're the one to help us learn Blackboard and ZOOM?*
> *First of all, what the hell is Blackboard, and second,*
> *what the hell is Zoom?*

No matter the time of the day, every footstep I heard coming down the hall, someone would walk into my classroom with a question about technology. I was pretty accurate, maybe ninety-eight percent of the time. Someone would venture into my classroom and engage in some superfluous conversation designed to mask a question about technology assistance.

> I never once minded the questions, but
> These questions were all too common during my daily routine.
> but
> I couldn't be the only one who knew this technology,
> Could I?

## Building Trust: Moving Forward and Adapting with Elders ... In a Good Way

Indigenous peoples tend to do things differently in how they meet or exchange greetings in ways that may seem out of the norm to those unfamiliar with the culture. Having been raised traditionally, I am cognizant of who is in the room before I begin teaching. If the audience is non-Native, I introduce myself along with my Tribal nation and my titles; if the audience is Native peoples, then I introduce myself along with all my tribal affiliations and my titles. If the audience has citizens from my Tribal nation, then I make sure to say who my families are. This is our way of building trust. Native peoples love to ask who their families are and are not afraid to call them out if they are incognizant of their Indian families.

> Oh, I remember being called out.
> Not a good feeling.
> I might want to brush up on my families.

Chances are if there is a citizen from my Tribal nation in the audience, they will either be related to me or know what families I come from. When I taught the Elder computer courses for a Tribal nation, there were a few students who were either Kiowa or Apache, so my introduction was predicated on a full acknowledgment of who I am.

I introduced myself at the beginning of a Professional Development (PD) at RIS. Many of the faculty were enrolled citizens in the Kiowa Tribe of Oklahoma and/or the Apache Tribe of Oklahoma, and many faculty either knew the families that I come from or members of those families.

Using the same respectful ways, I built trust with the faculty and staff, especially Elders. I needed them to feel comfortable with me as a younger instructor, and I needed the Elders to give me permission to teach them unfamiliar technology.

## The Struggles of Leading Professional Development: COVID-19 Protocols, Internal Tensions, and Crocheting Socks

I remember the exact wording Riverside's principal sent to all staff detailing COVID-19 Protocols.

> *Due to the COVID-19 Virus, please do not gather in crowds.*
> *Please stay in your room if possible and maintain 10 feet of distance from one another.*

I know the policy was out of safety, but to maximize computer learning, I needed to meet with individuals in person. I know I could have walked some staff through Zoom and Blackboard over the phone, but Elders struggled with this. In-person assistance seemed like our only choice. In hindsight,

> I really needed to see their tech skills up close.
> And they needed to trust me.
> Some have chastised me for having a "secret" in person professional development,
> which violated COVID protocols.
> And I knew the risk with COVID.
> But our meeting gave me an idea where Elder faculty were
> with their tech skills.

I never sent out any coded messages or tried to conduct any subterfuge. I simply sent out a text to faculty and invited them to the computer lab for computer tutorials—provided they wear masks and keep a safe distance adhering to COVID-19 safety protocols. Out of fear of catching COVID-19, I didn't think I would have very many faculty show up, but I had about nine, with a mixture of young and Elder, for this so-called secret PD.

They look hungry.
Ready to learn.
I like it.
But the threat of COVID loomed in my consciousness.

For Elder basic computer courses that I had taught previously for a Tribal nation, I had weeks to guide my students in digital literacy; I had weeks for them to feel comfortable and build relationships. I had weeks for them to learn new skill sets; however, COVID-19 accelerated technology learning at RIS to a mere two weeks. I think I intimidated a few Elder faculty, as I made the mistake of saying that after six years of working with Blackboard, I was still learning.

Nothing I could do about it.
But COVID gave me opportunities.
COVID enhanced my technological skill set.
COVID allowed me to flourish as a practitioner.
COVID brought me back to the difficult space of teaching Elders.

There were no slow-paced lectures, no slow-placed tutorials, no slow-placed questions, or answers. Whenever I was asked how long it would take for faculty to learn these processes, my only response was,

The learning process is going to have to be sped up.

RIS students were due back on campus soon. Whereas during the community Elder computer course, we could spend an entire day or two on one lesson and then pick up where we left off the next day; we didn't have a worldwide virus dictating terms of learning. At RIS, COVID-19 necessitated a variety of technology learning at much faster speeds. I told the faculty I can't be there in your class to help once students arrive because I have my own classes to teach. Basically, I said,

You need to learn this.
Wasn't meant to be hateful.
But they needed to know that,
it was either sink or swim once
students came back to campus.

Due to the varied levels faculty exhibited in digital literacy, I spent the better half of the "secret" PD running from computer to computer making sure everyone was on the same page. But that process had contradictory results. The younger, more technology savvy faculty completed each task with ease and speed, while Elder faculty experienced difficulty and exhibited frustration with each task. Younger faculty sat quietly waiting patiently for Elder faculty to catch up.

> Heck, I even had a younger faculty pull out her crochet set.
> and start crocheting socks,
> while she waited for people to catch up.

The crocheting episode served as a catalyst that highlighted the need to change how I did the PD. I could tell that if we continued this way with Elder faculty lagging behind tutorials and the younger faculty having to wait for significant periods of time for people to catch up, then I might just lose the class and have people walk out. I knew the younger faculty would just go to YouTube and learn Zoom and Blackboard, but I was worried about my Elders.

> I didn't want them to feel ashamed.
> I didn't want to become frustrated.
> I needed them to be able to teach on their own.
> We needed a change.

I only conducted one PD before devising an alternative plan to speed up the learning process. I facilitated a plan of one-on-one tutorials in-person. During the group PD, it took some Elder faculty around thirty minutes to learn a task, but during our one-on-ones, the amount of time it took them to learn a process decreased to under ten minutes. I had one Elder tell me,

> *I was afraid to raise my hand for help in front of the younger faculty.*
> *I didn't want them laughing at me.*

I didn't have a set curriculum or outline. Whatever the individual requested assistance with, I provided. At first, it was all about Zoom and Blackboard, but it turned into me hooking up speakers to desktops, how to use a USB drive, how to Facetime on a cell, and sometimes teachers from other disciplines would request my assistance with formatting papers, creating formulas in Excel, and creating flyers in PowerPoint.

## Routine Day: Wizardry Tech Medicine Guy

I could see sticky notes on my desk –

"Need Help,"

"Call Me,"

"Kelly, do you think you can help me. My computer is acting funny."

"ZOOM issues again. Drop by."

Sometimes, it really-truly felt like Groundhog Day.
Trying to make sense or describe my days as best I can.
I'm glad I was great at multitasking, or
My personal work might have suffered.

The number of individuals needing assistance varied from day to day; the individuals who did not leave sticky notes, text messages, emails, or voicemails figured out my routine of venturing down the hallways any time between 8 am to 9 am would wait until I passed by to ask for assistance. Sometimes I would play games and try to sneak by each classroom to see if I could pass by unnoticed. Once, I overheard another teacher on the phone asking if they had seen Mr. Berry because he usually walks down the hallway by now.

    Bond,
    James Bond.
    Kelly,
    Kelly Berry.

This routine stayed the same for weeks into the fall semester. I actually never tired of helping fellow faculty, especially the Elders, as we kept our Indian humor intact during COVID-19.

*Dang! Mr. Berry has those gooooood ways!*
    *Haw! He's got that gooooood Tech Medicine!*

I recall an instance when I was visiting with other faculty, when I received a text message from an Elder needing help with Zoom. As I grabbed my laptop bag and headed to the door, one of the teachers told me to stay for a second because he wanted to do something for me as he went and grabbed his feather duster. He told me to stand in the makeshift circle of chairs the teachers were sitting in and began to fan me off with his feather duster, while trying to sing some kind of 49 song that had no relevance to the "blessing ceremony."

> *Nephew, you do good things around here. We surrrrrrrrrrre do appreciate your help!*
> *I wanna send you off in that gooooood way to help the Elder.*

The whole time he was fanning me off, all the dust from his makeshift feather fan was getting on my shirt and in my face making me sneeze. Each day, there was some kind of joking or laughter going on with the occasional Ayyyyyyyeeeeeee or Ennnnnit, but it was good to laugh considering the frustrations many teachers had in learning modern technology.

For some of us.
Indian humor was our medicine.
In dealing with COVID-19.

COVID-19 actually allowed me to become closer friends with all the faculty, especially the Elders. Eventually, they began referring to me as grandson when they needed assistance.

> *Grandson, I need help with my computer.*

After a few weeks, the assistance requests decreased in frequency, as faculty became familiar with technology using my tutorials, but whenever I received a call for help, I made sure to head their way, but there were days when I had very little to do in my classroom, so I would venture down the hallways to check on every single teacher to make sure they were not experiencing any issues with their technology.

I had a habit of leaving campus during lunch time to grab Subway, McDonalds, Sonic, but the Elders sometimes would feed me as a way to express their appreciation for my technological assistance. I would receive a text from one of the Elders from time to time telling me to drop by on my lunch break. They would hand me a plate of food and tell me to sit and eat with them. Sometimes the plate consisted of frybread with meat and potatoes, meat gravy, meat pies, kidney, or corn soup.

The lunches were good, But.
These were teachable moments for me.

During our lunches together and not worrying about technology, I sat imagining I was around the flickering campfire listening to stories and sometimes songs, just mesmerized by what I would hear from the Elders. I heard oral stories of the Kiowa and Apache histories and deeper meanings that no textbook could provide, mainly because these stories and songs weren't written down. I would hear stories of the old ways of how young men, young warriors would step up and lead in time of need. Some of the Elders referred to my technological assistance as leadership in the same manner that young warriors displayed in the past, but I was just doing it in a different way.

Even though I was raised in the traditional ways of my culture, the Elders taught me knowledge I could use in my teachings. I could bring these oral stories into my classroom and expand my students' bandwidth.

My lunch breaks were transformational.
I ceased being a teacher of technology.
And became a listener and learner. And.
I never knew what I would learn.
I never knew what I would hear.
I always felt like Bilbo Baggins from *The Hobbit*.
I'm going on an adventure.
But.

I am going on an adventure down the same boarding school hallways my relatives and ancestors walked in their forced assimilation. I am walking down the same boarding school hallways where they were forced to have their hair cut; I am walking down the same boarding school hallways where they were forced to learn a foreign language and curriculum, where they heard a language but in the form of gibberish they did not understand.

Some days, my mind would play tricks.
Daydreaming seeing students in 1800s period uniforms.
Being herded to class.
Being told to learn this and that.

But most of all, I am walking down the same boarding school hallways where COVID-19 forced us to confront, adapt, and survive a new type of learning—technology. During COVID-19, I brought two kinds of knowledge with me to RIS: 1. tech knowledge that helped many teachers advance their computer skill sets, and 2. teachings infused with Indigenous knowledge and protocols about how and why to listen to Elders.

I was known by many names throughout my time at Riverside—the Savior, the Tech Magician, He who has tech medicine, but

> I didn't come here to be some sort of savior or whatever.
> I didn't lead because I wanted to.
> I just helped out where I was needed.
> I just hope I was helpful in the end!

**Competing Interests Declaration** The author has no conflicts of interest to declare that are relevant to the content of this chapter.

PART IV

# Art as Survivance

Coping with the pandemic required more than medical interventions. In the presence of overwhelming emotions of fear and loss, Indigenous people needed outlets to express their creative energies and determination to persevere. Some did so through telling stories, writing poetry, or music, while others drew on their established talents in the material arts—as silversmiths, potters, weavers, and painters. Both entries in this section speak of the power of art and craftwork to empower Indigenous peoples who might otherwise have felt helpless and isolated, allowing them to share the joy of creating beautiful things amid the pandemic ugliness.

Gavin Healey's opening chapter features Native American aerosol muralists who, during the pandemic, drew from a muralist tradition "to inform all communities of the persistence and resilience of Indigenous peoples." That tradition, extending back many decades, and including artists like the Kiowa 6 of the 1930s, involves breaking free of confining places to make statements of visual sovereignty in colonized spaces. Aerosol muralists, Healey explains, have also combatted COVID-19 by relaying vital information about safety and well-being to Indigenous audiences.

Christine Ami similarly speaks to the power of art in times of crisis, recounting her efforts to arrange an art instillation at the Arizona State Capitol to emphasize Diné resilience amid the pandemic. In its design this exhibit conveyed *wołí bee*, her people's determination to never surrender in the face of adversity and defeat. In the "dust" of COVID-19 it is "the fog lights, guiding Diné cultural arts and Diné people into an unseen, unknown, yet brilliant future." As do other authors in this volume, Ami also speaks to the difficulties of transitioning educational instruction from in-person to distance learning during the pandemic. The determination of *wołí bee* showed through in this effort as instructors, students, and veteran artists found innovative ways to use technology and cultural arts bundles to stay productive; share their creations and experiences publically and in culturally appropriate ways; and move forward to graduation and distinguished careers.

Whether sprayed in bold colors on public walls or enlivening the austere halls of a state capitol building, Healey and Ami highlight expressions of public art that stand as testaments to Native survivance during difficult times.

CHAPTER 12

# Native American Graffiti and Aerosol Muralism of the Pandemic: Alternative Messaging of Community Well-Being

*Gavin A. Healey*

In 2019, the coronavirus forced galleries, museums, and places of private art to close their doors and start moving the entirety of their work online. This caused a major disruption to the art market[1] and the artists that relied on sales for an income. Art has a fascinating way of reacting to major societal and political disruptions such as a pandemic. In this case, COVID-19

---

I would like to dedicate this chapter to all of my relations during the COVID-19 pandemic, especially my Native relations that gifted me strength, persistence, and compassion during such a difficult epoch in life.

[1] See Léa Saint-Raymond, "'The Show Must Go On'. Ethnography of the Art Market Facing the COVID-19 Pandemic," *Arts* 10, no. 3 (2021): 53, for an incredibly insightful analysis of this disruption with interviews and insider perspectives.

---

G. A. Healey (✉)
Northern Arizona University, Flagstaff, AZ, USA
e-mail: gavin.a.healey@nau.edu

© The Author(s), under exclusive license to Springer Nature Switzerland AG 2024
F. King, W. Davies (eds.), *COVID-19 in Indian Country*,
https://doi.org/10.1007/978-3-031-70184-9_12

encouraged many with graffiti and street art[2] backgrounds to turn to the city streets and contribute their skills concerning information distribution about the evolution of the virus and vaccines in unselfish acts of solidarity to their human counterparts. Aerosol muralism—murals created with aerosol paints (spray paints) and limited other supplies—is still a medium that many graffiti artists engage in for the community without making much, if any, money in comparison to studio work. Indigenous graffiti murals become part of the landscape in reverence for historical ties of Indigenous people to land. The impacts of COVID-19 on Indigenous and Native American[3] communities are still being felt and Indigenous graffiti artists are part of an art community that has painted the landscape to inform all communities of the persistence and resilience of Indigenous peoples during times of the most severe crises.

The following discussion will focus on Native American graffiti artists' contributions to the COVID-19 response in Indian Country through public murals, coupled with how aerosol muralism became a grassroots dialectic for Native communities, urban and reservation, during the COVID-19 pandemic. Instead of working from a deficit model, this discourse will employ an abundance model that appeared from Native American artists' contributions to the COVID-19 response using abandoned and unconventional structures. COVID-19's decimating effects advertently brought global focus to Indigenous communities, especially Native American communities in North America. Indigenous and Native American artists like America Meredith (Cherokee Nation), chief editor of *First American Art Magazine*, observed, "Immediately people flew into action. It was like, 'Okay, what can I do in my skills to help the community.'"[4]

---

[2] "Graffiti" and "street art" are sometimes used interchangeably. The artists I have personally interacted with and most scholars have clearer definitions for each. Graffiti is the act of creating public art with very few utensils and primarily aerosol paints, "spray paint." Street art includes wheat pastes, markers, stickers, etc. alongside aerosol paints. This article focuses primarily on graffiti and aerosol murals.

[3] The term "Native American" references Indigenous peoples of North America, primarily the United States, with the acknowledgement of other terminology and no consensus of a homogenized term for all 574 Federally recognized tribes (Native Nations) in the United States and "First Nations" the preferred term in Canada. "Indigenous" is the chosen term for those peoples and communities with histories, stories, and physical connections to a geographical area and a global connotation. This is always a difficult choice in respectful labeling of a peoples and at all instances tribally specific names will be used.

[4] Meredith qtd. In Sophia Herring, "Indigenous Art Communities Emerged from the Pandemic More Resilient," *The Art Newspaper*, January 3, 2023, https://www.theartnewspaper.com/2023/01/03/indigenous-artists-more-resilient-pandemic

Creating alternative means to communicate information about COVID-19 to community members, aerosol mural installations sought to broaden messaging in the same way that traditional highway billboards conveyed a dialectic of safety and well-being about the virus. This is part of a history in Native aerosol muralism where some artists have used highway billboards to disseminate Native social movements and sovereignty (Fig. 12.1). During the pandemic these murals also functioned as an intergenerational messaging mechanism reaching younger Indigenous citizens where formal billboard messaging might not. The dissemination of aerosol murals across reservation and border-town areas like Shiprock and Fruitland in New Mexico with health clinics dedicated to serving the Navajo Nation displayed how artists were collaboratively communicating well-being to the community. Looking through the transgressive history of graffiti in correlation to a virus that had lethal transgressions on Indigenous peoples exemplifies the confluence Native American aerosol muralism had with COVID-19.

The Navajo Nation became a global "hot spot" for COVID-19 and brought attention to the United States government's failure to live up to

**Fig. 12.1** Jaque Fragua (Jemez), "Idle No More." Mural (2014). Undisclosed location. Image courtesy of Jaque Fragua

its trust and treaty responsibilities to Native Nations.[5] Almost simultaneously, Great Plains Nations like the Cheyenne River Sioux Tribe angered their non-Native American neighbors and politicians by closing their borders and setting up check points to keep outsiders and those with COVID-19 off the reservation, just as the Navajo Nation and Hopi Tribe had done around their reservation borders,[6] instigating debates about the extent to which Native American sovereignty could be employed. As vaccines were developed, strained discussions arose in Native American communities about trusting the efficacy of the vaccines in the same manner as other minoritized and colonized groups in the United States vocalized, with some resisting vaccination because of historical misuse of Western medicine against their community members.[7] While the Navajo Nation was able to obtain vaccination rates higher than most U.S. communities, others like the Osage Nation had a fervent distrust and struggled to get community members to vaccinate.[8] Further examples of Native American populations either accepting or resisting vaccinations proliferated across Indian Country. What became of all the trust and distrust was a multimodal response where Native American graffiti artists used their skillsets to create an alternative means of information dissemination. As everyone in the world found themselves isolated in different ways it was important to have these types of monikers of community togetherness.

Aerosol murals have historically straddled reservation border-towns and appear in semblance with the landscape by conveying messages of cultural ontologies. Border-towns function as a hub for arts as much as they do material and health related activities. These types of spaces also

---

[5] I use the term "Native Nation" to honor the sovereignty of Indigenous communities while acknowledging some identify as "Tribe." When speaking in general terms Native Nation will be used and Tribe used when a community self-identifies as such to honor their inherent sovereignty.

[6] Elizabeth Hidalgo, "Supporting Native American Communities During the Coronavirus Pandemic: Checkpoints, Tribal Sovereignty, and the Implications of McGirt v. Oklahoma," *Houston Journal of Health Law & Policy* 21, no. 2 (2022): 449-482, https://houstonhealthlaw.scholasticahq.com/article/33837

[7] Wilfred F. Denetclaw, Zara K Otto, Samantha Christie, Estrella Allen, Maria Cruz, Kassandra A Potter, and Kala M Mehta, "Diné Navajo Resilience to the COVID-19 Pandemic," *PloS One* 17, no. 8 (2022): e0272089-e0272089,

[8] Louise Red Corn, "Chief Standing Bear: I'm not going to force you to get vaccinated for work," *Osage News*, January 5, 2022.

https://osagenews.org/chief-standing-bear-im-not-going-to-force-you-to-get-vaccinated-for-work/

**Fig. 12.2** Jaque Fragua (Jemez), "People System." Mural (2020). Albuquerque, New Mexico. Image courtesy of Jaque Fragua

speak to outsiders where heavy tourist traffic infuses cross-cultural messaging that can be important in expressions of resilience. One such place is the border-town of Farmington, New Mexico, where vibrant aerosol murals proliferate the city center, many of them Navajo and Native centered. Other murals straddle urban areas like Albuquerque in Fig. 12.2 and Los Angeles in Fig. 12.3 completed by Jaque Fragua[9] in an act of reclaiming Indigenous space—both external and internal—within colonized environments. Both murals are in densely populated urban areas where a multitude of viewership is reminded of Indigenous presence and persistence. In Fig. 12.2, Fragua exemplifies Native American aerosol muralism by carefully mixing the messaging of "people" reminiscent of our shared humanity and "system" as a reminder of the human

---

[9] For more of Jaque's work see Fragua, Jaque. *Low Res: Selected Works 2006-2016* (Mobil Savage Press, 2024) https://www.mobilsavage.com/

**Fig. 12.3** Jaque Fragua (Jemez), "This Is Indian Land." Mural (2016). Los Angeles, California. Image courtesy of Jaque Fragua

operational machinations of sacred landscapes. Figure 12.3, placed in downtown Los Angeles, is also a perfect example of the dialectics that Native aerosol muralism encapsulates, "This Is Indian Land."[10] Fragua is demanding onlookers remember the histories of the land they walk upon, and the Native interconnectedness derived from sacred relationships between human beings, the environment, remembrance, and community well-being. Murals such as Fragua's that are placed on unconventional structures like a construction wall (Fig. 12.3) support a sense of community by infusing imagery that can speak to Native and non-Native audiences in multi-modalities while interacting with voyeuristic tourism activities. Examples such as these speak to the diversity of Native aerosol muralism messaging of resilience and community well-being, especially when combatting a pandemic.

---

[10] See Annis, Amber A. "This Is Indian Land: A Call to Museums in Addressing Mass Incarceration of American Indians." *Museums & Social Issues* 12 no. 1 (2017): 14–25. doi:10.1080/15596893.2017.1289774.

At the beginning of the pandemic, I was teaching and conducting social science research at an American university. COVID-19 adversely impacted many of my mentees, students, and research assistants. The virus swept through their diverse families and communities in a way that was foreign to most everyone. My Indigenous and Native American students exemplified ideals of resilience while communicating to me losing loved ones, feelings of loss, and the hardships of trying to balance university and life responsibilities. As a non-Native mentor, I had always encouraged positionality and the importance of their stories in dismantling systems of power built to control them in some of the same ways COVID-19 was now dictating their human experience. The difficulty as COVID-19 became widespread was that those stories and the support needed from a professional mentor metamorphosized into shared tears, understanding, and flexibility. These mentees, students, and assistants were, and are, a reminder of how important sacred connections of community well-being and sovereignty are in times of crisis.

Upon taking a break from university employment, I ended up working in a Title VI Indian Education program in Omaha, Nebraska, as the pandemic was slowing its spread, and to the trepidation of some, schools were resuming in-person classes. In this program I worked with Native American high school students who primarily grew up and lived in a purely urban environment that were dealing with the same social-emotional impacts that university students were experiencing at the beginning of the pandemic, albeit during an important social-emotional maturation period in their lives. The work in a Title VI program can vary depending on each program's vision, either focusing solely on academic aid, a focus on tribally specific expression and learning, or a blending of both. In Omaha, there was freedom of both, which suited me as an outsider to Umo$^n$ho$^n$ (Omaha), Lakhota (Lakota), Pá$^n$ka iyé (Ponca), Ho-Chunk, and many other Native Nations represented by these students. Anyone who worked in K–12 education during this period will have stories of outbursts, emotional and intellectual strain, and a myriad of both positive and negative experiences with students. What the students in Omaha gifted me was the understanding that what broke these binaries was working on art projects like beading, weaving, leatherworking, and painting. Although based in a traditional craft,[11] in many instances the students visibly and verbally released their

---

[11] Beadwork can be viewed by some as a contemporary Native American craft because until the introduction of glass beads by Europeans there was no such craft, but the community

social-emotional turmoil in constructive ways while working on art projects. Under the leadership of the Elder and Cultural Consultant of the program these students took a break from all the stresses of the pandemic and used art as therapy. Seeing the power of art to dissipate the current traumas of COVID-19 and instead empower these young adults to express themselves in productive ways was proof that art was an outlet for Native American youth to navigate the pandemic. They did so in the same ways that older Native American graffiti artists were using art to remind Native communities that artistic expression is built into their persistence as a people.[12]

The various artistic mediums the Omaha students and their communities engaged in were grassroots remembering of their community histories of perseverance and resilience—histories that are older than colonial intrusions on their way of life where artistic expression has always been present. Observing youths creating art and releasing their stresses while connecting to their past is something that anyone can learn from. Watching students enjoy their own observations of older artworks to dampen the constant reminders of a pandemic was important for their remembering the abundance of Native persistence around them. Students seeing parents and Elders participating with their children and relatives in arenas of art as modes to navigate the pandemic registered an impact on their self-knowing. Obscure mediums like graffiti and street art also provided a means for art as a self-knowing vehicle to encourage collective therapies counteracting feelings of isolation, loss, and existential crisis.

### Native Aerosol Muralism and the Pandemic

The origins of both COVID-19 and graffiti are still being investigated—and debated—with undecided beginnings, it seemed destined that each would lay to bare a lasting imprint on the topography of the world. A divergent evolution took place in each as the virus continued to mutate and graffiti murals began to amplify the public voice. Unlike most other

---

members I worked with consider it a "traditional" craft that has connections to tribally specific expression. The idea that they were working on a "traditional" craft was a motivating factor for some students. With that positive impact I found the "traditional" debate moot and the positive outcome paramount.

[12] I would like to thank Echohawk Lefthand, Steve Tamayo, Danae Woods, and all the students that I worked with in the Omaha Public Schools that gifted me with these life-affirming experiences.

coronaviruses in human history, COVID-19 has had a global reach that impacted most, if not all, human populations. More specifically, Native American communities in North America and Indigenous communities across the globe had not had to deal with this kind of plague since the 1918 influenza pandemic, and prior to that the eighteenth-century genocidal spread of smallpox, propagated by Europeans. The same can be said of graffiti having a long history with no definitive origin, making it an allusive yet conversely a positive tool in conveying meaning, especially in times of public peril.

Cityscapes endure physical changes due to human activity, fueled by shifting social and political discourses. Public art has consistently played a central role in city identity as an integral part of the urban aesthetic. Murals have historically been important community markers infusing color and semiotic messages into the everyday cityscape where, "[Graffiti is] about the semiotic reinterpretation of urban environments ... [it] transforms cities into different kinds of places that carry not only the designs of urban planners but also the redesigns of urban dwellers."[13] A simple internet search for "Indigenous mural pandemic" will yield over two million results, and when "graffiti" is added to that search over 250,000 results appear. The tactics of graffiti muralism appear in glimpses of many kinds of expression depending on the histories of a given group or person, but during the pandemic aerosols murals proliferate addressing that specific topic, along with the issues of wearing protective masks, vaccination, certain policies, etc. creating an alternative public dialectic.

Contemporary graffiti is commonly traced to the American cities New York and Philadelphia where artists began using aerosol paints to create pieces of art on public structures like buildings, subway trains, and locomotives during the 1970s that coincided with the hip-hop movement of the time.[14] The origins of "historical graffiti" is a debated topic and depends on the lens of analysis. In archeological literature, Jennifer Baird and Claire Taylor note the use of graffiti among the Greek and Roman empires over 2000 years ago during antiquity, mapping the historical

---

[13] Alastair Pennycook, "Linguistic Landscapes and the Transgressive Semiotics of Graffiti," In *Linguistic Landscape: Expanding the Scenery*, edited by Elana Shohamy and Durk Gorter, 1st ed. Vol. 9,780,203,930,960 (New York: Routledge, 2009), 302-312.

[14] Gregory J. Snyder, *Graffiti Lives: Beyond the tag in New York's urban underground* (New York: NY University Press, 2009). Snyder explains that much of the analysis on graffiti has been conducted by sociologists adhering to the "broken windows theory" (Snyder 5) fostered by James Q. Wilson and George Kelling.

significance of graffiti found in Pompeii, Egypt, and around the Mediterranean region.[15] In the Western Hemisphere, Dennis Tedlock documented graffiti during the ancient Mayan empire in masonry workrooms.[16] Other ancient petroglyphs and pictographs of Indigenous peoples in North, Central, and South America could fall under the auspice of graffiti depending on the lens in which it is viewed. Links to how important graffiti—historical and contemporary—can be for disseminating information is evolving through the increasing literature addressing the functionality of contemporary Indigenous and Native American aerosol muralism as a connection to petroglyph and pictographic placement. It was, and is, an important topographical component in times of duress like those of COVID-19. As Matthew R. Smith posits, "the radical potential of indigenous graffiti and street art to critique and delegitimize oppressive social conditions forced upon indigenous peoples ... [permits artists to] strategize towards reclamation, renewal, and recovery."[17] This is especially true as more social consciousness is displayed through Indigenous and Native American aerosol murals on cityscapes.

United States reservation border-towns—those located on reservation boundaries and considered part of the state, not reservation—have become important places of convergence for Native American aerosol muralism. The murals are seen by consumer and tourist traffic coupled with commuters of many different walks of life. Native American artists find border-town spaces a popular place to deploy their art to wide viewership and destabilize settler colonial influences on the cityscape. Dean Rader has observed that "the symbolic interplay between Indian art and capitols becomes an incredibly complex canvas on which historical, cultural, political and racial issues get painted in big, broad strokes. The conflict of history (as opposed to the conflict of fantasy) actuates Native public art that facilitates both the contextual and compositional resistance and also cultural and aesthetic engagement."[18]

---

[15] Jennifer Baird and Claire Taylor, eds. *Ancient Graffiti in Context*, Vol. 2 (Routledge, 2010) and Jennifer A. Baird and Claire Taylor, "Ancient Graffiti," In *Routledge handbook of graffiti and street art* (Routledge, 2016), 17-26.

[16] Dennis Tedlock, "Graffiti," In *2000 Years of Mayan Literature* (Berkeley: University of California Press, 2010).

[17] Matthew Ryan Smith, "Indigenous graffiti and street art as resistance," In *Street Art of Resistance*, edited by Sarah H. Awad and Brady Wagoner, Palgrave Studies in Creativity and Culture (Palgrave Macmillan, Cham., 2017), 251-274.

[18] Dean Rader, *Engaged Resistance: American Indian Art, Literature, and Film from Alcatraz to the NMAI*, 1st ed. (Austin: University of Texas Press, 2011), 193.

Fine art and public art in colonized spaces where there is a presumed Indigenous absence are an expressive outlet for Indigenous peoples to signal their presence. This signaling of presence by Indigenous groups and individuals is the practice of visual sovereignty that demarcates objections to dominant colonial ideologies.[19] Using public murals and new tools like aerosol paints are not new movements in Indigenous storytelling. The wordsmith Gerald Vizenor has written extensively on Native survivance that Elizabeth LaPensée suggests "is an indigenous social impact game that honours [original spelling] storytelling and art as self-determined pathways to healing from historical trauma caused by colonization."[20] Native American artists and Native art[21] further narrate survivance and visual sovereignty by continually creating signposts of Native presence in the world. These narratives function as a communal space to explore the well-being of Native American communities instead of the false representations created by dominant cultures or "simulations" of Native Americans.[22] Vizenor believes that Native American literatures, oral traditions, and the spoken word are communal spaces that hold more power than simulations created for Native peoples, "Tribal power is more communal than personal, and the power of the spoken word goes with the stories of the survivors, and becomes the literature of survivance."[23] Native American aerosol murals act as an illustration to the written and spoken word, a complementary narrative of community persistence and well-being that lives in visual communal public spaces. They also break through the barriers that have been installed in some privileged spaces like museums and art galleries.

Just as books can be confined to libraries, various mediums of Native art can be confined to museums and gallery spaces. When Native literature and art are freed from these spaces, the narratives reinvent structure and

---

[19] For an in-depth analysis of visual sovereignty see, Michelle H. Raheja, "Visual Sovereignty," In *Native Studies Keywords* (Tucson: University of Arizona Press, 2015), 25–34.

[20] Elizabeth LaPensee, "Survivance as an Indigenously Determined Game," *AlterNative: An International Journal of Indigenous Peoples* 10, no. 3 (2014): 264.

[21] I choose to use the term Native art instead of "Indian art" to connote artworks produced by Native American artists. This is the term I have heard used most frequently in the contemporary Indian Art world and is possibly a better canonical term due to the problematic etymology of the term "Indian."

[22] Vizenor uses this term and harkens to postmodernist writings.

[23] Gerald Vizenor and A. Robert Lee, *Postindian Conversations* (Lincoln: University of Nebraska Press, 1999), 135.

simulation of Native persistence and well-being in a postmodern play of place. Vizenor furthers this notion by stating, "Alas, surveillance is a modernist separation of tribal imagination and the concoction of the other in ruins of representation. Postindians discover the survivance of their others and double others in libraries."[24] Native American aerosol muralism is a counterpoise to the surveillance of museums and galleries of presumed public space by establishing communal places of civic reflection that were originally Indigenous spaces of presence. Native American aerosol murals create postindian counternarratives that when taken into the public cityscape project community well-being as, "a counterpoise in 'wild knowledge' and language games, an invitation to a 'reflexive nature' that would undermine the trust of presence in translation, representation, and simulations."[25] We find ourselves in a pre-and-post pandemic era where it is necessary to branch out to a multitude of audiences the way Native American aerosol murals have done in unique spaces and places in order to better address Native presence and community well-being.

## Flashpoints in the History of Native American Public Art

The contemporary movement of Native artists creating counternarratives through public art is certainly one of constant debate, but there are a few flashpoints in American history where "contemporary" Native American muralism permeated into colonial spaces.[26] The 1930s proved to be a budding period for Native American muralism as then President Franklin D. Roosevelt's New Deal program and the National Parks Service began commissioning Native artists to paint murals in colonial public spaces. This was an important opportunity for Native studio artists to gain broader exposure with support from public funding. Under Roosevelt's New Deal, a Public Works of Art Project (PWAP) was initiated to fund artists and art

---

[24] Vizenor and Lee, *Postindian Conversations,* 169.

[25] Vizenor and Lee, *Postindian Conversations,* 69.

[26] Diego Rivera's numerous murals are prominent examples of this type of cultural and political messaging. Rivera, a Mexican muralist, whose frescos led to the Mexican mural movement and his numerous murals across the United States are strong examples of culturally relevant muralism. For more on Rivera's work see, Anthony W. Lee, *Painting on the left: Diego Rivera, Radical Politics, and San Francisco's Public Murals* (Berkeley: University of California Press, 1999) and Patrick Marnham, *Dreaming with his Eyes Open: A Life of Diego Rivera* (Berkeley: University of California Press, 1998).

in public spaces. Under the PWAP, the Santa Fe Indian School became a focal point of commissions. A group called the "Kiowa 5," named so because of their tribal affiliation was comprised of five male artists; Spencer Asah (ca. 1905/1910–1954), James Auchiah (1906–1974), Jack Hokeah (ca. 1900/1902–1969), Stephen Mopope (1898–1974), and Monroe Tsatoke (1904–1937). It was later acknowledged that a sole female, Lois Smoky (1907-1981), was originally part of the group that developed what has come to be called the "Kiowa-style" and so the group was contemporaneously re-named the Kiowa 6.[27] Different members of the group were commissioned to paint murals across Oklahoma including in the Anadarko Federal Building and Post Office, being of great significance because the Kiowa 6 all attended St. Patrick's Mission School near Anadarko and the Post Office was originally the Kiowa Indian Agency, a U.S. government entity that controlled economic activity of the Kiowa Tribe.[28] Sixteen murals were painted in the Anadarko Post Office alone and still stand as an important flashpoint in Native American muralism. Mopope and Auchiah were also commissioned to paint murals in the Department of the Interior building in Washington, DC, where a clash of ideology occurred because of paternalistic actions by white overseers who controlled the project funds, while the commissioned Native artists were struggling financially.[29] Public works funding of these murals was a leap forward for Native muralism, but one problem existed—and still exists— they are indoors and in privileged colonial spaces like the U.S. Department of the Interior.

Hopi artist Fred Kabotie (ca. 1900-1986) who also attended the Santa Fe Indian School was also among those that benefited from the PWAP when he was commissioned to paint the Desert View Watchtower at Grand Canyon National Park. As Mary Jane Colter was designing the Watchtower, she approached Kabotie to paint a mural in the Hopi Room and a mural was eventually completed in 1932. Kabotie—like the Kiowa 6—had gained national recognition after a showcase of his work in New York City during the 1920s. Kabotie painted a replica of a kiva mural from

---

[27] See http://plainshumanities.unl.edu/encyclopedia/doc/egp.art.042 for a brief synopsis of the Kiowa 6.

[28] For more on Indian Agencies during this period see Cathleen D. Cahill, *Federal fathers & mothers: A social history of the United States Indian Service, 1869-1933* (Chapel Hill: University of North Carolina Press).

[29] Nicolas G. Rosenthal, "Painting Native America in Public: American Indian Artists and the New Deal," *American Indian Culture and Research Journal* 42, no. 3 (2018): 47-70.

Awatovi depicting a Hopi emergence narrative.[30] His choice to use a kiva mural specifically from Awatovi was noteworthy because kivas are among the—if not the—most sacred spaces for Hopi people and are limited to only those who have gone through extensive ceremonial processes. Awatovi itself has been a contested site both within Hopi and with outsiders. Previous archeological excavation, documenting, and artistic reconstructions were done initially through Peabody museum funding and contained items that were not meant for general consumption.[31] Although there is debate over Kabotie's choices, when combined with the plethora of Kiowa 6 murals and all the prominent locations and abundance of Native murals appearing during the decade, the 1930s was a period of major expansion for Native muralism. These murals were the beginning of a challenge to the deficit models commonly associated with Native Americans. They also became signifiers of visual sovereignty to Native and non-Native audiences. In an interesting contemporary move the National Park Service began restoration of the Kabotie mural in 2015–2019, once again using public funds under an Artplace America grant to fund the restoration.[32] The murals were a movement in educating non-Native audiences and expressions of sovereignty but lacked the freedoms enjoyed by later Native American graffiti and muralism.

Moving forward a little over thirty years, on November 9, 1969, a group of Native American activists called the Indians of All Tribes sailed across the San Francisco Bay and started a movement now called the "Occupation of Alcatraz." During the almost nineteen-month occupation, activists scattered graffiti across Alcatraz Island and the decommissioned prison that sat upon it. They painted signifiers stating, "Indians Welcome," "Indian Land," "You are on <u>Indian</u> Land" (the underline of

---

[30] I purposely use the term "narrative" instead of "story" or "myth" commonly attached to these traditional theories to show respect to the importance of such narratives in the larger vernacular of theological discourse. The later terms have led to common misconceptions that demote the narratives to fables instead of being on par with other high religious texts like the Bible, Koran, etc.

[31] John Otis Drew, "Preliminary Report of the Peabody Museum Awatovi Expedition of 1937," *American Antiquity* 5, no. 2 (1939): 103-114 and Anna J. Osterholtz, "Hobbling and torture as performative violence: An example from the prehistoric Southwest," *Kiva* 78, no. 2 (2012): 123-144.

[32] https://www.nps.gov/articles/conservation-work-at-desert-view-watchtower-concludes-10-04-2019.htm

"Indian" was included in the graffiti), "Red Power," and various other monikers of the resistance movement. The graffiti was placed on top of other U.S. government signage littering the prison with a notable sign originally reading, "Warning—Keep Off—U.S. Govt—Property" where the activists crossed out with bold lines "Warning—Keep Off—U.S. Govt" and replaced it with "Indian" resulting in the sign reading "Indian Property."[33] One of the most striking places the graffiti appeared was on the facilities water tower reading, "Peace and Freedom Welcome—Home of the Free Indian Land." This was a moment of abundance for the transgressive form of Native graffiti muralism. Unlike the PWAP murals, these historical markers were transgressive, outdoors, and were widely shown across news outlets providing a sort of evolution of Native public art. Dean Rader has asserted, "[R]eadings of the paintings on the facades of buildings, on water towers, on walls, and, most provocatively, on other signs asserts that the artist-occupiers also re-created an iconography of resistance that has been part of Native aesthetic production for centuries."[34] In 2012 the National Park Service used federal monies to restore the water tower graffiti long after the forceful removal of the occupiers by the FBI in June 1971.[35]

Social and economic strife led to a reliance on art to convey personhood and presence of Native peoples in the U.S. cultural diorama. What became apparent is those with monies, connections, and power in the social spheres of the U.S. looked to Native public art as important—albeit possibly exotic or appropriated—for non-Native audiences. All combined, these flashpoints connect to what occurred with Native American graffiti muralism and muralists during the COVID-19 pandemic.

---

[33] Carl Nolte, "Alcatraz pays tribute to Indian occupation: American Indians Activists' painted statement is emblazoned on tower once more." *SFGATE* (San Francisco). January 14, 2013. https://www.sfgate.com/bayarea/article/Alcatraz-pays-tribute-to-Indian-occupation-4191169.php

[34] Rader, *Engaged Resistance*, 28-29.

[35] Malia Wollan, "Antigovernment Graffiti Restored, Courtesy of Government," *New York Times* (New York), December 24, 2012. https://www.nytimes.com/2012/12/25/us/alcatraz-american-indian-occupation-graffiti-preserved.html

## STREETS OF WARNING, STREETS OF THANKS

Some Native American aerosol muralists draw upon community histories in their art, and one could argue that we are in a post-graffiti era.[36] Artists themselves are reevaluating terminologies associated with the craft, such as, using the term "Style Writers" instead of graffiti or street artist. The concrete surroundings of modern cityscapes become dynamic artistic canvases for Native American aerosol muralists that connect to environmental elements. Much like Kabotie, Fragua—mentioned above—eloquently touches on this topic stating:

> I, and a lot of other muralists, think the tradition of creating murals is a selfless one and it's also one that connects people. And it can be in a spiritual way, which is how I understood it first growing up with the Kiva walls and seeing it on sacred sites, and I saw them more as living beings, you know, like Kachina dolls are living to me. I, you know when you're impressed from a young age that the walls are living, then you want to make sure that you're not a disruption but that you're a contributor to that life, and that's how I see it. And the way that I can do that is create murals that speak, create murals that talk.[37]

What Fragua also alludes to is a life cycle for these murals. The ephemeral nature of aerosol muralism is an important aspect that harkens back to the 1970s New York and Philadelphia graffiti; it would appear, be cleaned, then disappear, so the goal was to capture images as quickly as possible as Henry Chalfant, Martha Cooper, and others did while befriending graffiti artists of the era.[38] The difference is that during that era there was a popular sense of gaining personal recognition and prestige.[39] This did not take away from graffiti artists recruiting and joining "crews" that were very organized and in which each person played an important role when painting illegally; the painter, lookout, supplier, etc. were all integral to com-

---

[36] Smith references this point of the post-graffiti condition in reference to contemporary Indigenous graffiti and street art.

[37] Jaque Fragua quoted in Gavin A. Healey, "American Indian Graffiti Muralism: Survivance and Geosemiotic Signposts in the American Cityscape" (Ph.D. diss., The University of Arizona, Tucson, 2016), 155, ProQuest (10110992).

[38] Martha Cooper and Henry Chalfant, *Subway Art*, 1st American ed. (New York: Holt, Rinehart and Winston, 1984).

[39] Going "All City" for train graffiti artists (writers) was an important accolade. The reference alludes to painting a subway train that went through all the boroughs of New York City.

pleting a piece, especially in the train yards of New York.[40] Native American graffiti artists also develop crews for non-transgressive murals to showcase stylistic abilities and share space. Native American graffiti artists may be a smaller subset of the larger graffiti world but as Fragua alludes to there are some unique characteristics of this subset.

Ivan Lee painted two iconic murals during the pandemic, one on the Navajo Nation and another off-reservation close to Farmington, NM. Due to Navajo Nation protocols I will refer to the first mural in words only—a high resolution image can be found in photographer Erica Goldring's collection (a link to the image is provided in the footnotes).[41] Lee's mural in Shiprock, New Mexico, speaks directly to the ephemeral nature of Native aerosol murals as signage. Painted on a burned down hardware store synonymous with graffiti of all types Lee used it as a canvas to caution his Diné (Navajo) community about COVID-19. Shiprock is a medical hub for Diné peoples with a health care clinic and some patients traveling great distances across the Navajo Nation for health care services. The structure has since been demolished and no longer exists, so like Fragua suggests that mural had a limited lifespan during the pandemic. Lee was able to connect community persistence and well-being to the life of an aerosol mural while also connecting the tools of graffiti in the respirator commonly worn to avoid the toxic paint aerosols to the Centers for Disease Control suggestion to wear surgical masks. A clever combination of warning and protection in one image.

During the COVID-19 pandemic, it became important to some muralists to work for, and with, their community to bring people together while under extreme duress. The exterior structures of Farmington, New Mexico and the surrounding area also became a canvas for Lee who decided to create alternative messages to formal billboards thanking his Diné community (Fig. 12.4).[42] The mural "We Will Survive" he painted near Fruitvale, NM, outside of Farmington is an homage of thanks to the healthcare workers on the frontlines fighting the pandemic. As mentioned,

---

[40] Henry Chalfant's documentary *Style Wars* (1983) and Craig Castleman, "The Politics of Graffiti," In *That's the Joint!: the Hip-Hop Studies Reader*. 2. ed., edited by Mark Anthony Neal, Murray Forman, and Michael Eric Dyson, 13-22, (New York: Routledge, 2012), both cover this era of graffiti art and the politics fighting against it.

[41] https://www.erikagoldring.com/gallery-image/Places/G0000TtBfVGL6FJU/I0000pmF9H5Ty79Y.

[42] I would like to thank both Ivan Lee and Kayla Jackson for generously agreeing to the use of this art and photograph.

**Fig. 12.4** Ivan Lee (Diné/Navajo), We Will Survive. Mural (2020). Fruitvale, New Mexico. Image courtesy of Kayla Jackson

the Navajo Nation was inundated with COVID-19, from roughly March 2020 to 2021, and this mural reminded other Diné about the persistence of their own citizens in the healthcare fields. The western iconography of the winged rod and dual snakes—a reference to Greek mythology[43]—with the traditional Diné symbols in the backdrop blend together to possibly encourage the idea of Western medicine as an ally instead of a threat. The two human figures adorned with turquoise jewelry suggest that these are Native American and/or Diné healthcare workers. The turquoise jewelry also references the protective nature of the stone in traditional Diné philosophy or at the very least is a relatable iconography to the community. This mural could be viewed as both a "thank you" and inspiration to younger audiences to enter the medical field where there is a systemic dearth of Native practitioners. Having the "We Will Survive" contained within a stylized image of the Earth honors the global Indigenous and

---

[43] Prakash M and Johnny JC, "Things you don't learn in medical school: Caduceus," *J Pharm Bioallied Sci*. April 7, 2015 (Suppl 1): S49-50.

non-Indigenous audiences with the suggestion that the Diné community is not alone or isolated in their COVID-19 issues.

Native American aerosol murals in urban environments can be tools used to illuminate socio-political issues facing Indigenous peoples while also acting as symbols of persistence, well-being, and self-determination in an otherwise subjugated, or muted, public mindset of dominance, "The contemporary storier creates a new nativeness expressing an imaginative reformulation of a specific cultural past by nativizing a present-day social situation."[44] In his untitled Shiprock mural, Lee has engaged this idea of the contemporary storier and documentarian combining the Diné language with English to convey a message of both warning and strength.[45] The person also has their hair in a *Tsiiyéél*, the traditional hair bun of the Diné people that is said to contain prayers. Like many Native aerosol murals there are multiple signifiers which either separately or together form meaning for the community. They are a message to the community that a formal billboard, pamphlet, sign or poster, etc. cannot always convey. Occupying spaces otherwise disregarded or ignored by the community also makes these murals part modern beautification and part alternative dialectic akin to Vizenor's nativizing the cityscape with a focus on issues surrounding COVID-19 in Indian Country.

## Conclusion

Native aerosol murals produced during the COVID-19 pandemic had important implications for Native American presence, resilience, and visual sovereignty. Artists proved that their alternative means of conveying messages about the COVID-19 pandemic in tandem with other modalities of information was an effective means to reach an even larger group of community members. The response to the pandemic by Native American and Indigenous communities may have varied but Native aerosol murals were outlets to promote the abundance of community togetherness needed to combat the deficits caused by COVID-19. As the murals spread across other mediums like news media outlets and social media the messages also

---

[44] Karl Kroeber, "Why it's a Good Thing Gerald Vizenor is Not an Indian," In *Survivance: Narratives of Native Presence*, edited by Gerald Vizenor (Lincoln: University of Nebraska Press, 2008), 25-38.

[45] I would like to thank Erika Goldring (https://www.erikagoldring.com) for providing the photograph for this analysis.

delivered statements on tribal sovereignty. The collaboration between western ideologies and tribal ontologies has not always proven to be copacetic. What aerosol muralism provided is another means to address the harms and celebrate the successes of fighting a pandemic.

The U.S. federal government has been steadfast in impeding tribal sovereignty since formulating laws and policies surrounding Native Nations. State governments consistently infringe on tribal sovereignty in their own ways. Popular media has not always been helpful in properly informing the general non-Native public on issues that infringe on tribal sovereignty. News media outlets are quick to report on a checkpoint established by a Native Nation during the pandemic without taking the care to speak to tribal sovereignty. Alternatively, Native American aerosol muralism and the artists behind it provide a means of expressing tribal sovereignty and promoting community well-being. If the period of intense COVID-19 spread taught anything it was that communities needed to band together. Native American aerosol murals and artists rose to that challenge by contributing with their messages of abundance, perseverance, and resilience through the lens of tribal sovereignty.

**Competing Interests Declaration** The author has no conflicts of interest to declare that are relevant to the content of this chapter.

CHAPTER 13

# Wołí bee: Diné Cultural Arts Amid Pandemics

*Christine Marie Ami*

Click

Opening my email in the late Spring of 2021 one subject line popped out among several unread notifications: "Request to meet w/AZ State Representatives." *Well, nothing more to do with an email from the House of Representatives than to open it*, I thought.

Click

It read: "Representative Jasmine Blackwater-Nygren is requesting to schedule a meeting with you over Zoom to meet with Arizona House Democratic leadership member Rep. Jennifer Longdon." *This could be interesting*, I assumed. I knew Rep. Blackwater-Nygren's grandparents from years before, helping medicine people with ceremonies in Sweetwater, Arizona. With little more context other than the cc'd Navajo Cultural Arts Program, I agreed to meet and then closed the email.

Click

I didn't know it at the time, but *wołí bee* would form the center of my conversation with Rep. Blackwater-Nygren who sought to dress the walls of the Arizona State Capitol Building with Diné resilience. *Wołí bee*, while

---

C. M. Ami (✉)
Diné College, Tsaile, AZ, USA
e-mail: cmami@dinecollege.edu

© The Author(s), under exclusive license to Springer Nature Switzerland AG 2024
F. King, W. Davies (eds.), *COVID-19 in Indian Country*,
https://doi.org/10.1007/978-3-031-70184-9_13

used as a mantra by the Indian Health Service to encourage Diné people to continue "masking up" following the peak of COVID-19, demands much more. *Wolí bee* is a Diné survivance attitude, a chance mindset with immediate action to tackle challenges, even in the face of defeat. In this chance, one that is akin to self-determination rather than happenstance, we find a dare to play with conditions placed upon us by colonization, internal colonization, and as it turns out pandemics much in the same way as Gerald Vizenor's manifestation of survivance:

> I am serious about the use of the word "survivance" rather than survival. Survivance is a condition, not a mere response to domination. Survivance is the end of domination in literature. Life is a chance, story is a chance. That I am here is a chance. This interview is a chance survivance. The advantages of survivance are that it provides a way to accept this condition, reverse what's been imposed on us—and play with it.[1]

It was a chance Representative Blackwater-Nygren was taking in reaching out. It was a chance that I would respond with a plan sourced from the community's determination to continue creating amid destruction. In between this play with the realities placed upon us by COVID-19, the *T'áá awoli bee* Exhibit was born.

Following its temporary duty assignment at the Capitol building, the *T'áá awoli bee* Exhibit is now permanently housed at Diné College's Tsaile Campus on the third floor of the Ned Hatathli Culture Center. The 20 pieces of this exhibit do not merely align with considerations of visual Diné aesthetics or serve as art therapy to cope with our COVID-19 induced environments. Rather, these pieces exude our resilience as Diné people on much deeper levels—levels that we face daily, pandemic or not. The stories which appear in the backspace of this exhibit carry me through a debriefing space as the Navajo Cultural Art Program grant manager during the thrusts of COVID-19. In this dust, *wolí bee* served as the fog lights, guiding Diné cultural arts and Diné people into an unseen, unknown, yet brilliant future.

---

[1] Quoted in Larry McCaffery, "On Thin Ice, You Might as Well Dance: An Interview with Gerald Vizenor," In *Some Other Frequency: Interviews with Innovative American Authors*, edited by Larry McCaffery (Philadelphia: University of Pennsylvania Press, 1996), 293.

## Debriefing with Wołí Bee

I accepted the meeting with Rep. Blackwater-Nygren one month before stepping down from a six-year adventure as the Diné College's Navajo Cultural Arts Program grant manager. The NCAP, as it was fondly called, was created in 2015 from a partnership with the Margaret A. Cargill Philanthropies. Our mission focused on enhancing traditional Diné cultural arts practices. Staff fluctuated in numbers from a one woman show when I picked up the vacant grant manager position to three full time staff with several student interns at the peak of grant funding and organization. Over the course of six years, the NCAP assembled a roster of Diné consultants, adjunct faculty, workshop leaders, and guest speakers over 40 artists deep. Together, we created lecture, workshop, language, and demonstration series as well as academic programming for the Navajo cultural arts certificate, Navajo silversmithing bachelor of fine arts, and Navajo weaving bachelor of fine arts.

While I treasured what the NCAP had come to mean to our Diné community, unsettled levels of institutional support coupled with a 5/5 teaching workload, and daily life as a mother, wife, and livestock steward in the dust of COVID presented a moment of pause. Late May of 2021, I submitted my resignation letter to the NCAP and President's offices. Without fanfare, I quietly scaffolded away from public functions of the program. For two additional years, I lingered a mere Facebook message away for staff, who now needed to affirm managerial skills. I provided suggestions when asked and emotional support when needed—an unpaid consultant of sorts. All the while, I confess, I missed the inner workings of the program, specifically celebrating the successes of the NCAP students. Cohort after cohort, I had watched them grow from inquiring minds, desiring deeper cultural arts connections into confident workshop hosts, juried show artists, and cultural arts instructors.

Yet, the time that I previously dedicated to helping faculty build lesson plans, ensuring supplies were readily available, confirming that workshop leaders were paid, and forging avenues for students to engage with art markets allowed for a much-needed grant manager debriefing period. In this unfolding of experiences, one conversation prior to my resignation stood out. During one of our social distanced chats, moccasin maker and paternal grandfather through clan relations, Brent Toadlena asked how I was doing. I spoke of the death of my *nálí's* (paternal grandparents) from COVID-19. "*Nálí*, all of my grandparents are gone now." Brent, who had

**Fig. 13.1** Brent Toadlena, "Traditional Diné Moccasins." White Latigo, Rust Suede, Sterling Silver and Liberty Half Dollar Buttons. *T'áá awołí bee* Exhibit, Diné College, Tsaile, Arizona. credit: Photography by Matthew Bollinger, 2021

also recently experienced the loss of his paternal grandparents, looked me in the eyes and shared words that hugged me when he couldn't. "*Nálí*, we are each other's *nálí* now. *Wołí bee ánítí*." Brent always has a way to pull me from fatalist thinking back into gratitude made of our own self-determination. That is how I have come to understand *wołí bee*—even in the face of imminent failure, you give it your all. During my debriefing, I thought of all those like Brent who held me up as I held them up. I recognized that I had, indeed, given the NCAP my all. In return, I was gifted with responsibilities to an extended family of Diné artists who exude *wołí bee* both during pedestrian times as well as in the most extreme scenario conceivable: a pandemic (Fig. 13.1).

## Diné Cultural Arts Meet the Monster, COVID-19

Prior to COVID-19, the Navajo Cultural Arts Certificate graduation rates consistently ranked second, immediately behind Diné College's Public Health Certificate. Our Diné community valued the intergenerational transference of knowledge, skills, and business assets associated with our cultural arts at a similar weight to community physical health and social well-being. These student achievements were not the results of mere passive enrollment. Rather, these were the summation of community determination derived from *wołí bee*, a Diné survivance mode that would soon be put to the test. Where the program had previously thrived in face-to-face activities, following the onset of the COVID-19 in March 2020, all the NCAP efforts were geared to support conversions to distance learning environments. Community outreach programs screeched to a halt as academic courses transitioned to one of several distance learning formats: synchronistic live Zoom lessons, asynchronistic recorded posted lessons, or a hybrid of both.

While the cultural arts philosophy, history, and business adjunct instructors guided themselves through this new terrain, the NCAP staff focused heavily on the hands-on workshop classes where students learned the technical proficiencies of weaving, moccasin making, pottery, basketry, and silversmithing. Our staff worked tirelessly to replicate the kinesthetic learning environment of their former face-to-face settings. Classes led by master artists such as Teddy Draper Jr.'s Introduction to Navajo Silversmithing, Harry Walter's Advanced Navajo Moccasin Making, and Ilene Naegle's Intermediate Navajo Weaving used Facebook Messenger, email, and good old phone conversations as supplemental pedagogical tools. It was not only our senior artists continuing the intergenerational transfer of knowledge by adapting to technology, but also tech savvy Diné community members joined our adjunct faculty. The Heard Museum's resident weaver, Velma Craig created an online synchronist Introduction to Navajo Weaving class to continue interest in the budding BFA weaving program and The House of Stamps owner, Lyndon Tsosie with the assistance of his wife and partner, Valerie Joe Zoomed out of his Gallup workshop to continue funneling students into the silversmithing BFA program. Their efforts aided in producing the first Navajo Cultural Arts BFA graduates: Sue V. Begay graduated in December of 2022 with a BFA in Navajo Weaving and Carlon P. Ami II followed in May of 2023 with a BFA in Navajo Silversmithing (Figs. 13.2 and 13.3).

While I labored on the bureaucratic processes associated with these ever-evolving transitions, including applications for COVID-related grants available for the arts, the NCAP staff removed themselves from office detail to serve as production assistants. Throughout the summer of 2020, weekly trips were made to the east to Table Mesa, New Mexico, to record wool processing lessons by esteemed weavers, TahNibaa and Sarah Naataanii. Then, changing directions, trips to Canyon de Chelly, Arizona captured cabbing lessons for Teddy Draper Jr.'s silversmithing classes. When recording and editing became overwhelming, community member Hondo Lewis and his media crew answered the call for aid. The instructors were armed with as much support as the NCAP staff could muster.

There was still one major hurdle to tackle. Many students did not have access to the supplies, tools, and materials that were located on the Tsaile

**Fig. 13.2** Sue V. Begay, "Beauty." Wedge Weave, Natural Wool, Natural Dyes. *T'áá awołí bee* Exhibit, Diné College, Tsaile, Arizona. credit: Photography by Matthew Bollinger, 2021

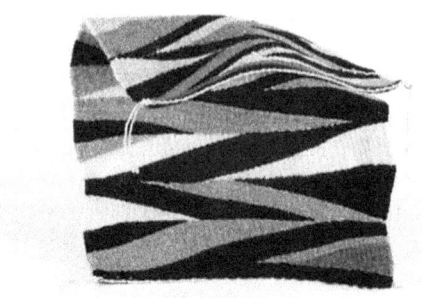

**Fig. 13.3** Carlon P. Ami II, "Ripples." Sterling Silver, Handmade Graduated Beads, Tufa Cast Pendant, Lapis Lazuli Buttons. *T'áá awołí bee* Exhibit, Diné College, Tsaile, Arizona. credit: Photography by Matthew Bollinger, 2021

campus. *We need cultural arts bundles*, I thought to myself thinking about Diné medicine bundles. Traditionally, these sacred packages include precious stones, soils, and paraphernalia. They are gathered for families to care for and, in turn, be cared for. With that concept, the NCAP worked with local suppliers in Gallup, New Mexico like City Electric Shoe Shop, Silver & Turquoise Supply, and The House of Stamps as well as regional and national suppliers such as Rio Grande Jewelry Supply Company and Brown and Brown Wool Company. Together, we built bundles that

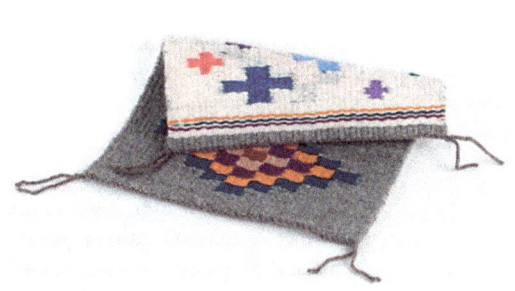

**Fig. 13.4** Tammera Martin, "My Worlds." Commercial Dyed Brown & Brown Wool, Natural Wool, Mixed plant Dyed. *T'áá awołí bee* Exhibit, Diné College, Tsaile, Arizona. credit: Photography by Matthew Bollinger, 2021

included basic tools and materials necessary to not only complete classes but to create workshops in students' homes.[2]

But for reciprocal guardianship to take place, it wasn't just about picking up the bundles, which was done through CDC guidelines. It was about putting the beings to proper use. NCAP students like Tammera Martin, a Navajo Weaving BFA student, did just that. With her bundle created for wool dying studio and distance learning instruction, Tammera acquired natural wool dye skills, credentialing her for a well-deserved position at Gallup's Weaving In Beauty. There she has since earned the nickname "Dye Queen" and now cares for antiquated rugs in need of repair. These bundles did indeed know how to care for us when we cared for them. The NCAP managed through the Summer and Fall semester of 2020 thanks to these bundles and pure community determination (Fig. 13.4).

By Spring 2021, I could foresee a return of our popular Navajo Cultural Arts Week, a celebration filled with lectures, workshops, and a juried exhibit. After a one-year postponement due to the onset of COVID-19, the Navajo Cultural Arts Week resumed virtually with Navajo Cultural Arts Practicum II students at the helm. Triston Black, Ryan Dodson, Willis Tsosie, and Valene Hatalthi devised a schedule in areas of

---

[2] Funding from the American Indian College Fund's Native Arts Enrichment and Expansion Program Distance Learning Grant Opportunity assisted in the creation and distribution of the cultural arts bundles.

leatherwork, wool processing, and stamping. In addition to the workshops, the week's celebrations also included the return of the Ned Hatathli Navajo Cultural Arts Juried Exhibit with the aid of Native American Arts Magazine, who agreed to host the virtual exhibit. In the planning stages, the college's president accepted a request to photograph the student and alumni work. However, as deadlines began to skulk in and communications slowed, Bryan Roessel, a NCAP alumni, stepped up last minute to photograph the forty pieces. Running a few hours off timeline but still determined to showcase our student work, images were uploaded to the Native American Arts Magazine gallery page. By noon, we were LIVE! Anyone could access the virtual exhibit by weblink and see Diné College student artwork side by side with the greatest Native American artists of the twenty-first century. More important, students could see their work in these venues. For some, this would spark the start of their own fine arts show career (Figs. 13.5 and 13.6).

With the Navajo Cultural Arts Week successfully behind us, I could finally analyze data regarding the academic courses. At end of the Spring 2021, the NCAP reported an increase of enrollment during the exclusive distance learning set up. Diné community members from as far away as California, Ohio, and Washington registered for classes. Their appreciation for the online learning structure was apparent. In their final class assessments, statistically significant results revealed a reconnecting with Diné identity and the Navajo Nation as a direct result of our classes. It was a lesson for me as well. I had been hesitant to put our cultural teaching on

**Fig. 13.5** Bryan J Roessel, "Lightning." Sterling Silver, Tufa Cast. *T'áá awolí bee* Exhibit, Diné College, Tsaile, Arizona. credit: Photography by Matthew Bollinger, 2021

Fig. 13.6 Ryan Dodson, "Tobacco Canteen." Sterling Silver, Hand Stamped, Handmade Chain-link, 1860s inspired. *T'áá awołí bee* Exhibit, Diné College, Tsaile, Arizona. credit: Photography by Matthew Bollinger, 2021

a virtual platform. Then and now I still believe that many of our stories and practices are to remain within our sacred mountains. While we could have stopped there at this impasse, *wołí bee anitį* resounded in my head. *I need an advisory circle*, I responded to myself.

With the aid of cultural advisors, the NCAP used the Diné language, live lessons, and strategic storytelling to ensure that connection to our ways of knowing was grounded to the land. This was done not to cultural gatekeep students, but to push them regardless of locale even harder to gain the extra intellectual ways of knowing associated with Diné cultural arts. They met the challenge. Triston Black, Ryan Dodson, and Willis Tsosie would be the first to complete the Navajo Cultural Arts Certificate in a fully online setting. Watching their names during the virtual graduations, I thought to myself, *I don't know if I could have done what they did!*

### T'ÁÁ AWOŁÍ BEE: CONVERSATION SERIES[3]

The theoretical roots of the exhibit that would eventually dress the walls of Rep. Blackwater-Nygren's workplace formally materialized through a collaboration between individuals from the School of Arts and Humanities

---

[3] Diné College Libraries, *Navajo Cultural Arts Program: Conversation Series*, https://lib.dinecollege.edu/NCAP/Conversation-Series, (n.d). The Diné College Libraries houses a digital archive of all the NCAP series on their website. While Navajo Cultural Arts Program YouTube links are referenced within this chapter, if ever those links are broken or found as unretrievable, this link to the Diné College Libraries safeguards these conversations.

and the NCAP. Art historian Dr. Karla Britton along with Diné College's first BFA graduate Kayla Jackson worked with the Indigenous Design + Planning Institute at the University of New Mexico to address a focus on art leadership and community planning on the Navajo Nation.[4] Together we would ask Diné artists to define success in their careers and to postulate the future of Diné art. This series would also keep the growing BFA and Certificate programs in the minds of potential students, serving as a key recruitment tool during the peak of COVID-19.

While still in the brainstorming stage I spoke of this vision with my husband. He mentioned the phrase "*awolí bee*" as a suggested title. It is an older phrase, often evoking memories of parents and grandparents. It has been replaced recently with *yéego* (keep going) and is akin to *t'áá hwo ajitéego* (self-determination). Yet, *wolí bee* is more than going through the motions—it is being stronger in mind. The *T'aa awolí bee* series would be a demonstration of Diné artists' abilities to push our arts not only through surviving the pandemic but into a thriving time despite what would result as one of the deadliest periods in recent Diné history. Twenty-nine established Diné artists agreed to join us from April 2020 through April 2021 for conversations about art, life, COVID-19, and *wolí bee*. Looking back, 29 echoes the infamous 29 gold medal Navajo Code Talker recipient roster. Coincidence? Not intentionally but now it resounds *wolí bee* from a warrior standpoint.

With the schedule set, the NCAP staff and I learned how to host Facebook LIVE through the Zoom interface, utilize social media lighting, and integrate jpeg images during live broadcasts. It was daunting, requiring countless nights of YouTube DIY videos and amassing more technology lingo than I ever envisioned. Originally, the programming was advertised as a "lecture" series. But as soon as we started recording with our first guests, father-son duo, Darrell and Jared Tso, I quickly noticed that our discussions were far beyond a list of questions provided to interviewees. We shared stories, failures, and hopes for art and Diné people. So as the programming continued, I approached our discussions through the Indigenous research method of conversations.[5] In this sense, the Diné

---

[4] Funding from ArtPlace America partially assisted in the *T'áá áwolí bee* Conversation Series initiative.

[5] Margaret Kovach, "Conversation Method in Indigenous Research," *First Peoples Child & Family: An Interdisciplinary Journal* 14, no. 1 (2019): 40-48. Kovach's work provided a flexibility of conversations that allowed for relationality between collaborators beyond a mere semi-structured interview.

artists who joined us held stronger positionalities than mere "interviewees." Rather than an extraction of information, we formed relationships that not only informed the topics at hand, but also constituted our roles as Diné people and created lasting bonds to each other.

Looking back on this first conversation with the Tso potters, I am reminded of the intergenerational teachings that we were gifted. Darrell, who passed away from COVID-19, left more than his legacy with Jared, he left just a bit of that magic with our community through that conversation and all who would take Jared's pottery classes at Diné College, including myself. I enrolled in Jared's pottery classes prior to the COVID's intrusion because pottery was so far from my weaving and silversmithing repertoire. If we were going to continue to offer pottery classes, I had better learn the basics. Little did I know a few months following the classes, my son would need a ceremony requiring pottery. I brought all the works I made during Jared's classes to the medicine people for use. It turns out "the basics" were more than just for curriculum. They were for life and future. I continued to practice what Jared shared as COVID-19 settled in to keep me grounded to the earth and to combat overwhelming anxieties around us. Today, when I see Jared, with his daughter, on the plaza of the Santa Fe Indian Market, happily leaving a sold-out table, I know that *wołí bee* is there with them because they were there with me during the summer of 2020 (Fig. 13.7).

That summer series moved forward to spark conversations with silversmith: Lyndon Tsosie, weavers: Marlow Katoney, Barbara Teller Ornelas,

**Fig. 13.7** Christine Ami, "Running with Mud." Hand Processed Clay, Kiln Fired Pot. *T'áá awołí bee* Exhibit, Diné College, Tsaile, Arizona. credit: Photography by Matthew Bollinger, 2021

and Lynda Teller Pete, painters: Beverly Blacksheep, Tony Abeyta, and Don Whitesinger and photographers: Corey Begay, Hulleah Tsinhnahjinnie, and Raphael Begay. Each artist shared moments in their lives that defined them as Diné artists and Diné people. This included when, mid series, I shattered my orbital bone following a collision with one of our sheep during shearing, appearing on camera with eyepatches and headbands to cover the changing shades of my black eye pre- and post-eye surgery. But more pressingly than injuries associated with day-to-day interactions as a Diné livestock steward, we shared the often-unseen injuries we walk around with and how *wołí bee* helps us through them.

In one of the most passionate of the series conversations, The House of Stamps owner, Lyndon Tsosie revealed his struggles with alcoholism and how silversmithing helped him to overcome them. That battle technique transitioned over into his daily practices of tackling life's challenges. Specifically, when speaking of *wołí bee* in the contemporary, Lyndon references Bruce Springsteen's "Wrecking Ball" and how that song encourages The House of Stamps family to push through adversity:

> Man, you know, there's a song from Bruce Springsteen and it's our anthem song because when we're really when we're down and out, I put that song on. You know there's going to be hard times coming, there's going to be good times coming. Swing that ball at me because I'm going to work as hard as I can to do what needs to be done.... You know, bring that wrecking ball on is all I can say and that's what the word, you know, is that. Bring it on.[6]

In the end, both Springsteen and The House of Stamps crew take it all on—the good and the bad. This explication, as it intersects with *wołí bee,* struck me so deeply that I immediately inserted it into the opening credits of the series to help viewers contextualize the conversations. The mustering of courage to continue with our ways of life, including our artforms, is one of practice, dedication, and chance self-determination through good times and bad.

Nevertheless, at times, life deals you more than one wrecking ball at a time. During the summer of 2020, those wrecking balls pounded without break. COVID-19 hit my family, both at the NCAP and in Sandsprings, Arizona, where my grandparents lived. Jerome Nez, a Navajo Cultural Arts Certificate 2017 graduate who emphasized in silversmithing passed

---

[6] Lyndon Tsosie, "T'áá awołí bee: Navajo Contemporary Arts Lecture Series – Lyndon Tsosie (Navajo Silversmith)," Navajo Cultural Arts Program. April 28, 2020, lecture video, 1:03:01, https://youtu.be/QYlUd0bpg1E.

away in June 2020. He spent his last energies caring for his mother who succumbed to COVID-19 as well. Shawna Johnson, a student in the moccasin making emphasis, passed away in July 2020. She had paused her cultural arts studies to return to the COVID-19 frontline as nurse, contracting the monster herself. Then, just few days before I would host a live Zoom *T'áá awołí bee* conversation with weavers, Barbara Teller Ornelas and Lynda Teller Pete both my grandparents passed away from COVID-19. I confessed to the NCAP Coordinator that I needed a moment to breathe. We switched roles for the day, and she hosted the conversation while I held down the technicalities. By the end of the conversation, the lump in my throat gave way so I could thank the weaving sisters. "*T'áá awołí bee*— it is about the future; it isn't about us. Thank you for reminding me of that," I told them, holding back tears of the prospect.

Thinking of the future, I remembered how youth can be defined by age as well as experience. The NCAP sourced both kinds of elders for our academic programs. Often instructors were younger than students and frequently, nontraditional students, the ones who do not directly start college studies following high school, dared to venture into unknown cultural arts learning paths.[7] This was especially true during the throws of COVID-19, when the nontraditional student enrollment increased due to the distance learning options. Brittany Greymountain, a first-time weaver who attended Velma Craig's online weaving class, was the only Introduction to Navajo Weaving student to submit to the 2021 Navajo Cultural Arts Week Exhibit. I could see how intimidating a juried show could be for first semester students but that didn't stop Brittany. And Tavian Nutlouis, who registered for the silversmithing emphasis of the Navajo Cultural Arts Certificate, did so as a dual credit student. This means, as he worked on his high school requirements, he was simultaneously working on his cultural arts curriculum at Diné College. Challenging? Yes. But that didn't stop him from learning from master artists such as Teddy Draper Jr. (Figs. 13.8 and 13.9).

The Draper classroom mantras of "Don't be lame" and "Up your game" that Tavian often spoke about, reverberated through the Zoom meeting when Teddy joined me in the second to last conversation of the *T'áá awołí bee* series in April of 2021. These calls for action are not personal quests, but rather challenges to our emerging artists in areas of chance, play, and the cultural arts through *wołí bee:*

---

[7] Nontraditional pathways reference when students do not attend college immediately following their high school graduations.

**Fig. 13.8** Tavian Nutlouis, "Ch'ééh Digháhii." Shadow Box Bolo, Sterling Silver, Handmade Bolo Tips. *T'áá awołí bee* Exhibit, Diné College, Tsaile, Arizona. credit: Photography by Matthew Bollinger, 2021

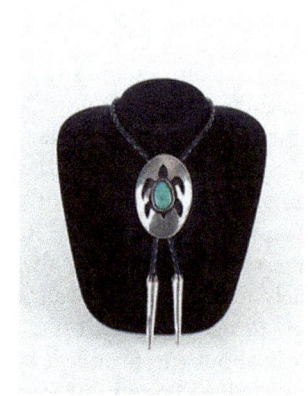

**Fig. 13.9** Brittany Greymountain, "For My Children: Our Robot." Commercial Dyed Brown & Brown Wool, Handspun Wool Warp. *T'áá awołí bee* Exhibit, Diné College, Tsaile, Arizona. credit: Photography by Matthew Bollinger, 2021

'*Aa awołí bee anit'į*—it's just like when my grandma and grandfather used to say that. It's their way of saying that there's going to be a time if you don't learn and you don't push yourself hard now, we won't be here forever and there won't be anybody around to reinforce this in you anymore except yourself.[8]

---

[8] Teddy Draper Jr., "T'áá awołí bee: Navajo Contemporary Arts Lecture Series – Teddy Draper, Jr. (Navajo Silversmith and Painter)," Navajo Cultural Arts Program. April 7, 2021, lecture video, 48:34, https://youtu.be/c8F6lawjCcE

Doing what needs to be done is a hard lesson, one that was taught to Teddy through his own experience of overcoming substance addictions. While the Diné community listened in as silversmithing served as an axis for both accomplished artists in life and business, they also learned how *wołí bee* is a source of motivation from the generations before us. Unlike many who talk about "giving back" to the community, listening intently to Teddy, I realized that we, Diné people, don't give back. "Giving back" is a mere temporal debt paid through western approaches of gratitude reciprocation. Our Diné *wołí bee* strength is found in pulling from what has been gifted to us and giving forward just like our prayers.

Prayers became a focal point in another conversation, this time with NCAP weaving adjunct, TahNibaa Naataanii. For her, transforming words that could easily fall into jargon or mere propaganda into action was key for understanding *wołí bee*:

> [W]hen I think of *T'áá awołí bee,* I feel that those are the efforts of my parents and my grandparents; that the philosophies that they shared and that we need to continue to learn and implement and put into our lives. Like walking in beauty, what does that mean, how many different areas does that consist of, how do we achieve that so you know learning those learning those philosophies and implementing them in our way of life and sharing them with my family in during challenging times, during non-challenging? You know, just because there's a challenge, that doesn't mean that we have to disregard some of those important teachings so I believe that for me *T'áá awołí bee* means to honor those efforts and live by them.[9]

Prayers and words are so significant, but actions count just as much as TahNibaa stresses. We so often hear the Diné mantra "walk in beauty," but how does beauty encompass the challenging times. That is where *wołí bee* roams.

The *T'áá awołí bee* Conversation Series lasted 3 seasons. Following the initial Summer 2020 season, the Fall 2020 and Spring 2021 seasons welcomed accomplished artists such as Bahe Whitethorn Sr., William Wilson, Nonibah Chacon, Nanibaa Beck, Shane Hendren, Peterson Yazzie, Emmi Whitehorse, Kayla Jackson, and JT Willie. Whether it was painter, Emmi Whitehorse speaking both metaphorically and literally about driving into

---

[9] TahNibaa Naataanii, "T'áá awołí bee: Navajo Contemporary Arts Lecture Series – Sarah, TahNibaa, and Winter Rose Naataanii (Weavers)," Navajo Cultural Arts Program. December 2, 2020, lecture video, 1:00:05, https://youtu.be/knxJFuAgvO8

the dawn or jeweler, Nonibaa Beck sharing how Diné traditional art is defined not as a stagnant past but as an ever-changing future, these Diné artists embodied *wołí bee*, in all its struggle. While all the conversations fill a special place in my heart, the last of the series remains as my favorite. In my final major event with the NCAP, I was joined by the NCAP Exhibit Best of Show Winners from 2016–2020: Carlon P. Ami II, Heather Williams, Brent Toadlena, and Brandon Dinae. Together we reminisced about the program and our accomplishments and challenges. My *nálí*, Brent Toadlena, brought together the series sentiments, explaining:

> *T'áá awołí bee*, you are going to struggle. No matter what you try; anything you do; if you are learning something new, you are going to struggle. So, you have to "*awołí bee*" and want it so bad that there is no other option than to just be there to do it and put in the effort. *Awołí bee anit'į ayiila diil ch'iids*, hard work on your hands. Do it.[10]

With those words, we announced the 2021 Best of Show Winner: "Heavy Clouds." This hallowed formed ring with turquoise inlay would take home the last Best of Show Ribbon that I would tender for the NCAP. I left role as the manager of the NCAP with blessings of rain.

## T'ÁÁ AWOŁÍ BEE: THE EXHIBIT

Click

These memories and others flashed before me as I jumped onto the Zoom meeting to listen to Rep. Blackwater-Nygren's team describe an exhibit space in the west and north hallways on the third floor of the House of Representatives Building. They wished to fill the walls with artwork exuding resilience and hoped that the NCAP might have an idea of how to fill those walls. "I have the perfect idea. Let me tell you about *wołí bee*." There I pitched an exhibit inspired by an embodiment of Diné Collegé's students, staff, faculty, and alumni who have maintained and perpetuated Diné cultural arts teachings throughout the COVID-19 pandemic. It had been a project building for some time. Now was the chance time.

---

[10] Brent Toadlena, "T'áá awołí bee: Best of Show Panel," Navajo Cultural Arts Program. April 25, 2021, lecture video, 1:25:45, https://youtu.be/BEao5erui4g?si=PKrels XVZsDcNuCL

The *T'áá awołí bee* Exhibit would encapsulate Diné ways of knowing through a visual format. Our hope was to reinvigorate the use of *wołí bee* and other older phrases spoken by our grandparents, which encourage our Diné people to push through adversity, trauma, and personal walls to find success in whatever manner it may be defined: cultural, economic, familial. In the case of this exhibit, our students, staff, and faculty pushed through the extreme challenges of distance learning during a pandemic to continue the perpetuation of Diné cultural arts. Together we fought through limited or no internet access, learned new technologies for delivering instructional presentations, endured personal trauma, including the deaths of loved ones, and, in several cases, faced COVID-19 ourselves. Our end game was and is to perpetuate our unique Diné ways of knowing the world, even in the face of possible failure.

In the light of *wołí bee*, this exhibit would be dedicated to those who fought this pandemic, specifically two of our students who would watch our battles from another world: Shawna Johnson (moccasin maker) and Jerome Nez (silversmith). This dedication was not done to encapsulate their deaths as a mere tribute. Rather it is a chance reminder. We should not forget that despite the dark moments, beauty is made by way of the creations in this exhibit, before and after. Our cultural arts exist because, even though we know that the process of creating these pieces is difficult and learning the songs and prayers associated with the creation and destruction processes is challenging, we persist. That's *T'áá awołí bee*. That's Diné cultural art; that's what the hallways of the House of Representatives Building would exude: a continuous, never pausing building of the future of Diné art.

With a commitment from the NCAP, I set out to write the proposal seeking additional funding to make this exhibit materialize. Despite my now assumed role as the "former" NCAP grant manager, the Dean of Diné Studies and Education, Dr. Lawrence Isaac and the Dean of Arts and Humanities, Dr. Paul Willeto answered my calls. With a budget set, we sent out invitations to NCAP students, alumni, and staff to submit pieces that were created during the pandemic. Responses were overwhelmingly positive, including a submission of my own work. Encouragement of NCAP staff would be to bring forth the first time my work would stand with my students. I felt intimated in their shadows. Their work and their dedication to the arts humble(d) me. But if the NCAP alumni were trusting me with their work in this exhibit vision, then I could find that confidence too.

Together we entrusted Diné College's BFA Graphic Arts assistant professor Matthew Bollinger, of Bollinger Design Studio LLC, to capture, edit, and portfolio 20 pieces which exuded the *T'áá awołí bee* philosophy. His work was printed and framed by Ms. Gina McGowan from Aficionado Framing in Flagstaff, AZ. The exhibit images were then mounted in the public hall of the Arizona State Capitol Building. In immutable silence, they tirelessly spent a year shouting the *T'aa awołí bee* realities through the hallways of a building where decisions are made directly and indirectly impacting the well-being of Diné community members living hundreds of miles away.

## *Wołí bee*: Back Home, But Did It Ever Leave?

The showing at the Arizona State Capitol Building was never the final destination for this exhibit. Part of the initial discussion with Diné College's Provost, Dr. Geraldine Garrity included arrangements for the *T'áá wołí bee* Exhibit to return home to the Navajo Nation. These voices would continue their work, dressing the walls of the administrative center of Diné College. Gina McGowan once again answered the call, professionally hanging the 20 framed voices throughout the circular hallways on the third floor of the Ned Hatathli Culture Center. Regardless of consciousness, all who enter are now greeted by *wołí bee*. On the surface, they see photos on thick, matte finished giclee paper through the nonreflective glass. This archival paper highlights material images of weavings, jewelry, pottery, and moccasins. They are beautiful and crisp, stoically reminding the community of our rich, unique histories as Diné people. However, within these images are stories of *wołí bee*, non-material ways of knowing that shout from the walls.

My hope is that these images evoke conversations within ourselves and within our families about the roles of Diné art as more than aesthetic labels and arguments between what is traditional and what is contemporary. In that hallway, we engage the play with creation, destruction, and creation once more. My husband, Carlon, often speaks of this pattern in his silversmithing work. For him, it is a testament to Diné people's willingness to destroy what has been created by the Holy People for the purpose of Diné use and aesthetic. For me, as it appears in this exhibit, it's a demonstration of survivance play with pandemics, not only in the form of COVID-19 but also of colonization and internal colonization within Native nations.

Given its home is in an academic setting that is ever changing with waves of administration fluctuations, I don't know how long permanent means for the *T'áá wolí bee* ("Permanent") Exhibit. For now, I enjoy the extra few minutes as I make my way through Ned Hatathli Culture Center. Climbing the stairs to the third floor, I pass through the threshold, make my way around the circular hallway, and listen to the stories of:

Aaron Begay's "Daan"
Brent Toadlena "Traditional Diné Moccasins"
Brittany Greymountain's "For My Children: Our Robot"
Bryan J. Roessel's "Lightning"
Carlon P. Ami II's "Ripples"
Christine Ami's "Running with Mud"
Crystal Littleben's "New Beginnings"
Delia Wauneka's "Sterling Silver Set"
Ephraim Anderson's "Cosmic Gate"
Francis Noble's "Shik'is"
Ilene Naegle's "Wool Sashbelt Plant Hanger"
Kevin Aspaas' "Diné Silverware Set"
Nabahe Hill's "Destruction of Thought"
Ryan Dodson's "Tabacco Canteen"
Sue V. Begay's "Beauty"
Tammera Martin's "My Worlds"
Tavian Nutlouis' "Ch'ééh Digháhii"
Valene Hatathlie's "Lean on Me"
William J. Yazzie's "Tufa Flower Bracelet"
Willis Tsosie's "Ready to Dance".[11]

---

[11] Though not all the exhibit images may have appeared in this chapter, their stories and pieces are proudly shown on the Diné College walls. To every one of those artists, I hear you. Thank you to each Diné College community member and visitor for pausing to hear these voices of *wolí bee*, either via this chapter or passing through the third floor exhibit. To the Navajo Nation's First Lady, Jasmine Blackwater-Nygren, your vision was a *wolí bee* chance. We thank you and your team for that self-determination opportunity. To the Diné College staff, thank you for bringing this exhibit home to the Navajo Nation. To Tori Cody, thank you for your transcription of the *T'áá awolí bee* Conversation Series. To Lydia Fasthorse, *shimá yázhí*, thank you for reading this piece and aiding with the Navajo language orthography. To our brilliant Diné artist mentors, *t'aa iiyisii ahé'hee'*. There is no exhibit that could truly encapsulate what you have taught our students. But this is a humble try. To the Diné College Library team, specifically Rhiannon Sorrell, you certainly outdid yourselves creating a permanent archive for not only the *T'áá awolí bee* Conversation Series, but all the NCAP community outreach virtual programming. For anyone that I may have missed and those who have requested to remain nameless, I hope you forgive me for any lapse in memory at the time of this publishing. Know that you are remembered within the exhibit and without.

BANG! I hear the pounding of silversmithing hammers. WAH! I hear the laughter of instructors who look at oddly sewn moccasins that need to be redone. THUMP, THUMP, THUMP! I feel the pulsations of multiple weaving combs learning the relationship between rain and warp. SQUISH! I feel the freshly collected and soaked clay sourced from our local hills.

SHINE! I remember Shawna's giant smile and Jerome's glasses that he refused to wear. FUTURE! I remember my boys in my belly and strollers, growing up amongst these artists. FIGHT! I remember battles with the functioning of the western institution. WOŁÍ BEE I remember late nights prepping for workshops, exhibits, and classes. CHRISTINE!!!! I remember Facebook Messages informing me of the silversmith building flooding that wet all the *T'áá awołí bee* Exhibit pieces negligently stored on the floor, requiring them to be reprinted, reframed, and repaid for. WOŁÍ BEE I remember the advocating for students, staff, and faculty for literal and creative space. FIGHT! I remember the failures, the shortcomings, the broken relationships with community members. FUTURE! I remember most the students' pride. SHINE!

These conversations depress as I see a student with moccasin making materials waiting for the elevator. I pause to chat with her. She doesn't know me, nor do I know her. I point at her black shoulder bag that has latigo peeking out and I ask her through my mask where she is going. "I am taking a moccasin making class," she tells me, pulling a hide from her bag. I ask her who her instructor is. "Brent Toadlena," she responds. "Tell my *nálí* that his *nálí* says 'hello,'" I smile. I wish her a good class as the elevator doors open to take her to the fifth floor. *Nálí is always grounding me. Woli bee is out there. It doesn't need a classroom, a grant, or an exhibit. But right now, at this very moment, it's ready to head up the elevator,* I think hopefully. The elevator doors close. I turn and head toward the east exit so that I may go home and weave. As I walk out of the survivance hallway, I hear my ancestors hug me, *"Wołí bee aniti, shiyázhí."*

Creation, COVID-19, Creation Endures.

**Competing Interests Declaration** The author has no conflicts of interest to declare that are relevant to the content of this chapter.

PART V

# Motherhood and Family Wellness

The final part of the volume focuses on the urgency of sustaining Indigenous kinship and relationality, especially through women in crises such as the COVID-19 pandemic. Many Indigenous communities stem from matrilineal and matriarchal foundations, which uphold women as the key to the health of their families and people. Native American mothers, in particular, lead in everyday healing work for their kin, Native Nations, and posterity, which they continued to do during the pandemic.

Mary Jo Tippeconic Fox and Aresta Tsosie-Paddock coauthor the chapter, "American Indian Women Combating COVID-19, the House Disruptor," which addresses the impacts of the COVID-19 pandemic on Indigenous women living in urban areas. Many Native American women are heads of households and serve as primary caretakers to their children, and sometimes other family members and/or relatives. As heads of households, Native American women provide not only financial support but also emotional support, discipline, and protection. They serve as central figures to home life. Tippeconic Fox and Tsosie-Paddock consider how Native American women heads of household have experienced disruptions caused by COVID-19, and how they combat the social effects of the pandemic at home with their families and at work. This chapter also explores how Indigenous women, more generally, have navigated through the pandemic, and how COVID-19 has continued to affect their lives.

Chapter 15, "Indigenous Motherhood Resiliency: Adapting Cultural Teachings During COVID-19 Restrictions," by Natahnee Nuay Winder traces the pandemic's disruption of home life from a Native woman's perspective among Indigenous communities across Turtle Island. Government requirements for quarantining and isolation emphasized modeling that prioritized the nuclear family, which challenged Indigenous knowledge systems for new mothers residing away from their communities. Communal ceremonies and gatherings such as naming ceremonies for children were postponed, which prevented them from being introduced to the community and their family. In addition, the closing of colonial borders, such as the Canada-U.S. border for 18 months, furthered the division among Indigenous relatives by preventing them from visiting family and/or participating in condolence ceremonies for their loved ones who went on their spiritual journey. The global lockdown, however, also created a space for individuals to use poetry and other creative forms to help with healing processes for the loss of loved ones, decreasing anxiety and fears during the restrictions, and allowed for reconnecting with oneself, like becoming a new mother. Thus, poetry became a therapeutic space to bridge hearts, create a way for healing, and devise new approaches to Indigenous cultural teachings.

In Chap. 16, "COVID-19 Memory Dreamscapes," a Diné woman delves into the meanings of her dreams and memories, while facing the struggles of single motherhood and a child custody battle during the pandemic. Her connection to land and family intertwines with her dreamscapes, guiding her on a path toward expressing her own voice through writing. Many Native American mothers and women face life challenges caused by a host of violence and abuses, as well as social, legal, and economic inequities and injustices, and the pandemic has exacerbated these issues. Nonetheless, their power of hope and healing saves nations.

CHAPTER 14

# American Indian Women Combating COVID-19: The Household Disruptor

*Aresta Tsosie-Paddock and Mary Jo Tippeconnic Fox*

> *We really see so many communities mobilizing and are really determined to protect each other. This is driven by shared values across tribes such as connectedness, and living in relation to each other, living in relation to all living beings and our lands. And we protect our families, our communities, our elders, our cultural keepers* (This quote is by Victoria O'Keefe, a member of the Cherokee and Seminole Nations. See Rhitu Chatterjee, "Hit Hard by Covid, Native Americans Come Together to Protect Families and Elders," NPR, November 24, 2021, https://www.npr.org/sections/health-shots/2021/11/24/1058675230/hit-hard-by-covid-native-americans-come-together-to-protect-families-and-elders).
> —*Victoria O'Keefe*

---

A. Tsosie-Paddock (✉) • M. J. T. Fox
University of Arizona, Tucson, AZ, USA
e-mail: atsosiepaddock@arizona.edu; foxm@arizona.edu

© The Author(s), under exclusive license to Springer Nature Switzerland AG 2024
F. King, W. Davies (eds.), *COVID-19 in Indian Country*,
https://doi.org/10.1007/978-3-031-70184-9_14

## Introduction

Patricia became ill and was hospitalized in an intensive care unit (ICU) for a month with COVID-19. Once out of the hospital "I had to relearn how to walk [and return to breathing normally]."[1] This quote by Patricia illustrates the extent that COVID-19 disrupted and impacted her life and that of her family.

This study seeks to explore how American Indian women[2] living in urban areas were impacted by the COVID-19 pandemic. The current scholarship primarily focuses on the experiences of Native women residing on Native Nations not in urban areas.[3] The primary purpose of this research is to examine how urban American Indian women as heads of households handled the disruptions caused by COVID-19 at home with their families and at work. Many American Indian women are heads of households and serve as primary caretakers to their children, and perhaps other family members and relatives. As heads of households, American Indian women not only provide financial support, but provide emotional support, discipline, protection, and are central to home life.[4] Moreover, the study asks how American Indian women navigated daily through the pandemic, how COVID-19 continues to impact their lives, what their concerns were throughout the pandemic, and what effects the pandemic had on their lives in its aftermath. This study thus contributes to the sparse COVID-19 scholarship on the experiences of American Indian women living in urban areas.

## Background

Even though COVID-19 statistics do not always provide definitive comparisons between urban and rural Native populations, available evidence indicates that Indigenous peoples in many urban areas were similarly hard

---

[1] Interview with Patricia, June 09, 2023.

[2] The terms American Indian women and Native women are used interchangeably.

[3] The study received approval through the authors' university's institutional review board (IRB).

[4] On the role of Native women with family and community, see J.L. Liddell, C.E. McKinley, H. Knipp, & J.M. Scarnato, "She's the Center of My Life, the One That Keeps My Heart Open: Roles and Expectations of Native American Women," *Affilia* 36, no. 3, (2020):16, DOI: 10.1177/0886109920954409; and Donna Martinez, Grace Sage, and Azusa Ono, *Urban American Indians: Reclaiming Native Space* (Santa Barbara, CA: Praeger Publishers, 2016), 13, 31 and 35.

hit as those residing on reservations. Indian Health Service (IHS) data indicated 30,419 positive COVID-19 tests by July 26, 2020, with the Navajo Nation and Phoenix areas showing similarly high positive test rates above 16 %.[5] In addition, IHS data showed that at least 6766 Indigenous people in urban areas had tested positive for COVID-19 by mid-February 2020.[6]

According to Abigail Echo-Hawk, director of the Tribal Epidemiology Center Urban Indian Health Institute in Seattle, COVID-19 positivity numbers in urban Indigenous communities do not fully capture the reality. "From the limited data that we have, we are seeing a disproportionate impact … our community is seeing and having higher rates of positive COVID tests."[7] However, data specific to urban Indian populations, says Echo-Hawk, is particularly difficult to find despite the fact that they make up an estimated 70 % of the overall American Indian and Alaska Native population.[8]

Compared to the non-Native population, American Indian women's lives have also been disproportionately impacted by COVID-19 in the realm of work, home, and family. The same dynamic has historically

---

[5] Elizabeth D. Hathaway, "American Indian and Alaska Native People: Social Vulnerability and COVID-19," *The Journal of Rural Health* 37, no. 1 (2021): 1, DOI: 10.1111/jrh.12505.

[6] For further information on COVID-19 data, see Casey Kuhn, "Why Indigenous People in Cities Feel Invisible as Pandemic Wears On," *PBS News Hour*, February 23, 2021, https://www.pbs.org/newshour/health/why-indigenous-people-in-cities-feel-invisible-as-pandemic-wears-on; Sarah M. Hatcher, Christine Agnew-Brune, Mark Anderson et al. "COVID-19 Among American Indian and Alaska Native Persons — 23 States, January 31–July 3, 2020." MMWR Morb Mortal Wkly Rep 2020; 69:1166–1169. DOI: https://doi.org/10.15585/mmwr.mm6934e1; Jessica Arrazola, Matthew M. Masiello, Sujata Joshi S, et al. "COVID-19 Mortality Among American Indian and Alaska Native Persons — 14 States, January–June 2020," *Morbidity and Mortality Weekly Report* 69, no. 49 (2020):1853–1856. DOI: https://doi.org/10.15585/mmwr.mm6949a3external-icon; J. Michael Ryan, "Surviving a Pandemic," in *COVID-19: Surviving a Pandemic,* ed. J. Michael Ryan (London: Routledge, 2022), 16. DOI: 10.4324/9781003302698-1; Indian Health Service, Coronavirus (COVID-19) (website), accessed September 30, 2023, https://www.ihs.gov/coronavirus/

[7] Kuhn, "Why Indigenous People in Cities Feel Invisible as Pandemic Wears On."

[8] Kalen Goodluck, "Why the U.S. is Terrible at Collecting Indigenous Data," *High Country News*, December 14, 2020, 4, https://www.hcn.org/articles/indigenous-affairs-interview-why-the-u-s-is-terrible-at-collecting-indigenous-data; Urban Indian Health Institute, "About urban Indians," accessed September 18, 2023, https://www.uihi.org/urban-indian-health/

occurred during other impactful crises, such as pandemics and economic recessions.[9] During these periods, the unemployment rates for American Indian and Alaska Native women and men peaked at 14.4 % and 16.1 %, compared to 7.9 % and 9.6 % for Whites.[10] The household of an American Indian woman who is a single parent and head of household can include children, grandparents or other family members and relatives. During COVID-19, American Indian women heads of households often served in caretaker capacities for those who were impacted by the illness as well as caring for themselves. A recent study of American Indian women's roles describes mothers "as the primary caregivers in the household."[11] Moreover, "mothers were also often portrayed as the 'glue' that held the family together and as playing important roles as role models and leaders in the home."[12] The maternal role as caretakers has been embedded since pre-contact time in caring for the family's emotional and physical well-being, and as leaders within the home, women are important and respected figures.[13]

## Positionality

As researchers, we are uniquely positioned as Navajo Nation and Comanche Nation citizens raised in Native communities, currently working, and living in urban areas, and both experienced having COVID-19. We can relate firsthand to many of the issues expressed by the urban American Indian women interviewees. We also draw on our experience as being part of a Native community through our engagement in previous research and projects where relationships are essentially based on long-term community

---

[9] Jeffrey D. Burnette, "Inequality in the Labor Market for Native American Women and the Great Recession," *The American Economic Review 107*, no. 5 (2017): 426, https://doi.org/10.1257/aer.p20171144; United Nations Department of Economic and Social Affairs, "Indigenous Peoples & the COVID-19 Pandemic: Considerations," accessed September 5, 2023, https://www.un.org/development/desa/indigenouspeoples/wp-content/uploads/sites/19/2020/04/COVID19_IP_considerations.pdf; Willem Thorbecke, "The Impact of the COVID-19 Pandemic on the U.S. Economy: Evidence from the Stock Market," *Journal of Risk and Financial Management* 13, no. 10 (2020): 1-32.

[10] Burnette, "Inequality in the Labor Market for Native American Women and the Great Recession," 426.

[11] Liddell et al., "She's the Center of My Life, the One That Keeps My Heart Open: Roles and Expectations of Native American Women," 14.

[12] Ibid.

[13] Ibid.

kinship. Our relationships are through our rapport and knowledge with community members who reside in urban communities or elsewhere off Native Nations, which allows us to network as insiders, positioning us to locate participants who are willing to assist with this research. Because participant trust is important, our positionality may have been a factor in participants deciding whether to engage in this study.

## METHODS

In the face of multiple piercing hardships and trauma, Native people found themselves moving forward from the egregious impacts of COVID-19 toward well-being and survival. The conceptual framework of resilience and survivance is applied to the study. Utilizing the lens of resilience exemplifies how participating Native women living in urban areas navigated through the COVID-19 pandemic in their work and family life with persistence. Resilience is often associated with Indigenous people's ability to overcome challenges, yet too often "indigenous people are not given credit for being able to combat, survive, and persist through novel diseases."[14] Lindsay Montgomery writes that resiliency denotes the "dynamic and ongoing process of reorganization within micro- and macro-systems that helps individuals thrive and even increase capacity in the face of adversity."[15] The notion of resilience recognizes the capacity of many people to do well, and display strength, in the face of hardships, trauma, and scarcity.[16]

In conjunction with resilience, survivance, a term coined by Anishinaabe scholar Gerald Vizenor provides the lens of Indigenous experiences as having an "active sense of presence."[17] Native life stories illustrate people being actively engaged and present while facing hardships, enabling them to survive by not allowing tragedy to defeat them, thus demonstrating

---

[14] Lindsay M Montgomery, "A Rejoinder to Body Bags: Indigenous Resilience and Epidemic Disease, from COVID-19 to First 'Contact'," *American Indian Culture and Research Journal* 44, no. 3 (2020): 66, https://doi-org.ezproxy4.library.arizona.edu/10.17953/aicrj.44.3.montgomery

[15] Montgomery, "A Rejoinder to Body Bags," 67.

[16] Laurence J. Kirmayer, Stéphane Dandeneau, Elizabeth Marshall, Morgan Kahentonni Phillips, and Karla Jessen Williamson, "Rethinking Resilience from Indigenous Perspectives," *Canadian Journal of Psychiatry* 56, no. 2 (2011): 85.

[17] Gerald Robert Vizenor, *Manifest Manners: PostIndian Warriors of Survivance* (Hanover: University Press of New England, 1994), vii.

resilience.[18] American Indians in urban communities live and thrive with an "active presence."[19] Survivance can transpire through stories of "overcoming and thriving in the face of physical, cultural, and spiritual assaults"[20] This is demonstrated here by a study participant named Mary, who is Catholic and did not rely on tribal beliefs and values, but did remember stories and beliefs she heard from her grandmas and aunties and others when she was growing up which helped her deal with the pandemic.

Our recruiting method utilized the snowball method or referral method, and personal outreach to potential participants who shared or were willing to share their COVID-19 experience during or after the pandemic.[21] Potential participants were contacted by email or phone to inform them about the purpose of the study and invite them to participate. Upon further communication, we provided more details about the study and were able to recruit five participants. Three urban American Indian women declined for several reasons.

Semi-structured interviews[22] were all completed through Zoom due to travel distance and to reduce the risk of COVID-19 contraction as the

---

[18] Rachel E. Wilbur, and Joseph P Gone, "Beyond Resilience: A Scoping Review of Indigenous Survivance in the Health Literature," *Development and Psychopathology* (2023): 12, doi:10.1017/S0954579423000706.

[19] Martinez, Sage, and Ono, *Urban American Indians: Reclaiming Native Space*, 23-24.

[20] Wilbur and Gone, "Beyond Resilience: A Scoping Review of Indigenous Survivance in the Health Literature," 12.

[21] The snowball method was used to recruit participants that could be considered vulnerable and hidden populations. "Snowball sampling is a highly effective recruitment strategy that enables the researcher to gain access to vulnerable populations that are otherwise difficult to reach." See Wendy M. Edmonds, "Snowballing ... #Prayforme: A Qualitative Study Using Snowball Sampling," *Sage Research Methods Cases Part 2* (London: Sage Publications Ltd., 2023), 6, https://doi.org/10.4135/9781526491039

[22] We used qualitative methodology to study individual lived experiences through in-depth analysis of these interviews. Semi-structured interview questions were employed for the study. The set of questions emphasized their experience with COVID-19. We purposely followed the order of the semi-structured questions with each participant along with follow up questions to seek more details if we thought it was necessary to collect comparable types of data from each participant. Chilisa indicates that the questionnaire's "sequence of questions is not the same for every participant as it depends on the process of the interview and answer from each individual participant." If they consented to participate, they completed a consent form. Upon their consent, we provided them with several interview dates and made sure they had access to Zoom for a virtual interview. Most importantly, we provided each participant with counseling contact information if they felt they needed to speak to someone about their COVID experience. The participants all consented and expressed the importance of sharing their pandemic experience. Bagele Chilisa. *Indigenous Research Methodologies* (Thousand Oaks, Calif.: SAGE Publications, 2012), 205.

participants already had some level of traumatic experiences with the contagion.[23] During the interviews, we made field notes of any surrounding distractions and difficulties with the Zoom connection, virtual interview locations, key terms, and follow up questions.[24]

After transcribing the interviews, we analyzed the transcriptions both together and independently to identify main themes and subthemes. We transcribed and analyzed the coding and allowed the themes to emerge. In addition to content analysis, we did a comparative analysis of semi-structured questions and participant responses for any differences that we might have missed.

## American Indian Women Interviewees

The five American Indian women in this study were given the pseudonyms of Mary, Nora, Terri, Nancy, and Patricia to protect their identities. All five lived in urban areas in Arizona, New Mexico, Nevada, or Montana.[25] Mary is a working mom with eight children. Nora is married and a mom to two boys and teaches at a public university. Terri is a single graduate student and mom to grown daughters. Nancy is a single mom to three young children and works full-time and is a graduate student, and Patricia is a single mom to two grown sons and teaches at a research university. Four of the five women contracted COVID-19 and one woman had symptoms but was told to stay home and quarantine without being tested.

---

[23] For further information about adjusting to the pandemic environment of virtual data gathering using Zoom which created "a need for innovation in qualitative data collection" and forcing us to look at approaches to qualitative inquiry, see Christian Williams, *Virtual Qualitative Interviews on Grief and Loss: Benefits, Challenges, and Considerations* (London: Sage Publications Ltd., 2022), 4, https://doi.org/10.4135/9781529603187

[24] The settings for the virtual interviews were the participants' home or work. We did not specify where the locations should take place but let the participants decide. The locations chosen were perhaps places where they felt comfortable, safe, and supported. We interviewed four participants from their homes and one from their work. There were two minor interruptions or distractions during the interviews either by family members or work colleagues, or weak connections. Data gathering concluded with recorded interviews which were transcribed. As PIs, we listened to the audio recording prior to transcribing to make sure the interviews were successfully recorded from beginning to end. While transcribing, we listened to the recordings several times to make certain the transcriptions were aligned with the interviews.

[25] Of the five American Indian women we interviewed, two were married and three were single. They were of various tribal backgrounds—Diné, Tohono O'odham, Aaniiih, and Paiute.

## Exposure to COVID-19

The exact date of exposure to COVID-19 varied for the five women, but the four who definitely contracted COVID-19 did so between 2020 and 2022. Mary felt she was exposed to COVID-19 because she and her family were homeless living in their cars after losing their rental house. The exposure to COVID-19 could have been anywhere since she and her family were homeless. Mary worked in a conservative state where masks were not required. She did try to wear a mask but once she got to work, she removed it. Some of her co-workers contracted COVID-19. Once Mary and her family started feeling ill, they got tested. The tests were positive, so they all quarantined in a hotel.

Nora and her family felt they contracted COVID-19 at her son's kindergarten school event where people seemed to be "kind of relaxed, but we were never 'relaxed' about COVID-19."[26] Nora and her family were wearing masks at the event. Not aware that they were exposed to COVID-19, Nora and her family traveled to her niece and nephew's graduation where they visited with her family. When they returned home, her oldest son started coughing, and Nora thought it was from swimming the night before. COVID-19 then spread to her youngest son and then to her and her husband. She felt like she had been in an accident given her aches and pain. Once home, she received a message from her son's school that "we had been exposed to COVID-19."[27] Her extended family never got COVID-19. Nora administered home tests, and her family received drive-through testing where they all tested positive for the disease.

Terri could not identify where she was exposed to COVID-19, but she had a daughter who worked in a nursing home as a nurse. Terri quarantined herself once she developed symptoms and called her healthcare provider who told her to stay home unless she had severe symptoms. Her immediate family did not get COVID-19.

Nancy caught the virus from her son who was sick for two weeks in 2020. She took him to the hospital twice where they tested him for everything. This was before COVID-19 tests were available, and he kept testing negative for the flu. He could not move and could barely breathe. In 2022, Nancy and all three of her children got COVID-19. Her daughter was five years old, and her oldest son was ten years old.

---

[26] Interview with Nora, June 20, 2023.
[27] Interview with Nora, June 20, 2023.

Patricia became ill and was hospitalized in an intensive care unit (ICU) for a month. She does not know when or where she contracted COVID-19, but she had children (a son and daughter-in-law) working in the health field and who lived with her. The daughter-in-law mentioned she had been exposed, and she locked herself in her room. Her son and daughter-in-law both became ill, but their symptoms were more subtle, and they got a hotel room to protect Patricia. However, she still caught COVID-19.

## THEMES

The interview data was collected and coded identifying themes among the narratives. The following themes of protection, daily lives, support, beliefs/values, and lasting impacts emerged from the analysis of the data, along with certain subthemes such as relationships, kinship, and vulnerability.

### *Protection*

To protect their families was of upmost importance for all the women interviewed as caregivers and providers. They practiced a variety of protective measures including wearing masks, getting COVID-19 boosters, sanitizing, quarantining, self-testing, and seeking online medical advice and support from professionals, family, friends, and colleagues. In addition, they stocked up on food and supplies for their families during the pandemic.

Mary and her family of eight quarantined for fourteen days when they all tested positive for COVID-19, staying in two hotel rooms due to losing their rental house and becoming homeless. In addition, they wore masks even though it was not mandated in her state.

Nora implemented protective measures to deal with COVID-19 before and once they were exposed to the virus. She kept her house clean as a protective measure and made sure everyone in her family had the COVID-19 boosters and wore masks.

Terri implemented protective measures to deal with her COVID-19 symptoms by staying home and working in her garden to fight off negative thoughts about COVID-19 and its possible impact on her family. Her daughter who worked in healthcare stayed away to protect her mother. Terri stayed in touch with her family, Tribe, and community through Facebook and felt bonded to them.

Nancy did not have protective measures in place, believing that "we couldn't control it. It was going to happen anyways, and we didn't go anywhere during the entire pandemic." She cleaned everything but did not wear masks in the house. Nancy took her family back home to Nevada to be around additional family members.

Patricia wore masks and in fact she was making masks for family members and healthcare workers before she contracted the virus herself. She bought cleaning supplies to keep her home clean, wiped things down in the house and mopped the floors, and was careful about touching things. Her son and daughter-in-law worked in healthcare, and they were careful to remove their clothes before coming into the house, took showers, and washed their clothes right away. Patricia and her son and daughter-in-law did their best to avoid exposure to COVID-19 around each other. They were extra careful and kept everything sanitized. Once Patricia got out of the hospital, she moved in with her oldest son and his family while she recovered.

### *Daily Lives*

The five interviewees as heads of households took responsibility for helping their families by adjusting and adapting to the disruptions of their daily lives during COVID-19. The impact on daily life and routines were profound for the women and their families. These disruptions included quarantining in one place, limited travel for food and supplies, wearing masks, and administering COVID-19 tests. Having food delivered, the inability to work or attend school in person, taking Zoom classes, and not meeting work deadlines were added disruptions. The incapacity to see extended family caused concerns about their welfare resulting in communicating with them by Zoom, phone, and social media when possible. Taking extra care of one another, having to move residences and find places to rent, updating COVID-19 vaccines, and not taking risks were additional impacts for the urban American Indian women and their families.

Mary, her husband, and son continued to work until they tested positive for COVID-19 and had to quarantine. Mary's daughter tried to go to school for a while, as she was a sophomore in high school, but she eventually dropped out. She was not able to learn over Zoom, and she got behind and did not go back to school. They all sheltered in their hotel rooms trying to recover. Cooking was the hardest task for Mary but otherwise while quarantined they would wake up and shower just like they did before

COVID-19. When Mary and her family tested positive for COVID-19, they went shopping to get food and other necessities in bulk before quarantining.

Nora contracted COVID-19 at the end of a semester. She was not teaching at the time, but she missed deadlines for proposals and book chapters because she could not work. Nora was in too much pain to think; COVID-19 impacted her thinking abilities, smell, and taste. She and her family just laid around because everything was hurting. They took ibuprofen, hot baths, and tried Theraflu. Nora tested positive for two weeks, and everyone else in her family tested negative after five days. Nora's kids bounced back fine, and their symptoms were not as bad as their parents'. It was summertime so they managed. It was hard being sick. Nora had food delivered or had her husband go out and get food. She froze a lot of food, and they drank smoothies. Nora felt she was hostage to COVID-19 and that she was trapped in her house. Once the semester started, Nora implemented university policies for COVID-19 with her classes.

Terri became depressed and saw a counselor who she communicated with over the phone. She was trying to complete her requirements for a master's degree, and Terri felt the pressure to do so. She said her thesis "kind of helped save me."[28] Terri was fearful for her adult daughter because she was a nurse at a nursing home and had to go to work completely encased in a white face mask, gloves, and suit. She stated: "Everyday it was very important that we touch base with my daughter and tell her we loved her."[29] Terri worked in her garden, listened to music, and meditated to deal with negativity, and she reconditioned a bike. In addition, she talked to her counselor on the phone, and she tried hard to eat right. For exercise, she avoided the community pool but did use her bike.

Nancy worked remotely and went to school online. She tried to maintain her work and school assignments as best she could through online platforms although she was not able to do anything for two weeks; she spent those weeks on the couch. Nancy had her mom fly in to take care of her and her family so she could manage her school and work. Eventually, she moved back to her Tribal community.

Patricia's son and his family had her move in with them after she left the hospital fearing she might contract COVID-19 again since her other son was still working with COVID-19 patients as a nurse. Her grandchildren

[28] Interview with Terri, July 03, 2023.
[29] Interview with Terri, July 03, 2023

were not in school, and they helped her heal. She got to know her grandchildren better which strengthened their relationship. Patricia was in ICU for a month and unconscious for two weeks. It was a scary time for Patricia and her family. Her sons were just happy that she recovered. The doctors wanted to intubate her, but her sons opposed it. She believes this was the result of her son being a nurse and the knowledge he had. Yet, her sons had to make decisions which they normally would not. It impacted them as they worried whether their mother would survive. When she woke up, her family had put posters and pictures of her dog, sewing machine, grandkids, and their drawings in her room because they were afraid Patricia would not know where she was. Once out of the hospital "I had to relearn how to walk [and return to breathing normally]."[30] She was fortunate to be able to work with her employer to return to work after recovering from COVID-19. Prior to contracting COVID-19, Patricia made sure the house was sanitized and everyone wore a mask and gowns for those in her family that worked in hospitals. She taught classes on Zoom. After she moved in with her son and his family after contracting COVID-19 and being hospitalized, visitors were restricted, and they were cautious about where they went to stay away from people. She exercised by getting outdoors and helping with chores as well as helping with her son's children. When she returned to work after having COVID-19, she taught seven-week courses over Zoom, which was a very full day.

*Support*

The urban American Indian women interviewed received support—mental, spiritual, and physical—from a variety of sources including family, colleagues, friends, tribes, community, and professionals. Additional support was received from spiritual leaders, caretakers, pets, work, school, and through physical activities. As heads of their households, it was vital to the women to support their families' and their own needs to successfully get through the pandemic. Kinship and relationships were essential forms of support.

Mary came from a big family and was the oldest in the family. She remarked: "I didn't check up on them (her siblings) when I was well so why would I check up on them when I am sick."[31] However, they did ask

---

[30] Interview with Patricia, June 09, 2023.
[31] Interview with Mary, June 16, 2023.

if she needed anything, but she told them "we're good."³² She and her family brought their own stuff and paid for their own hotels. "We didn't get help from any programs if there were any."³³ She had no knowledge of any assistance programs. Her Tribe did not support her as she was living off the reservation. Yet, the Tribe did provide cases of water. Due to their urban residence, they did not benefit from Tribal resources. Work peers knew her family members were sick and offered to help, but she did not want them to come over and always said no, "we're good."³⁴

Nora's friends would leave food at the door, providing them food cards and supplies for her family. She was unable to see her extended family while her family had COVID-19. Although she missed them, Nora did not want them to catch COVID-19.

Terri belonged to several communities. She would Zoom into church on Sundays, had a pipeline to her Tribal Nation, and was able to keep up with all the gossip: "when you know Indians, Indians let you know what's happening."³⁵

One friend, who was like Nancy and also a mother, would talk to her daily through the pandemic and post-pandemic. She was supportive, and if advice was needed on what to do through COVID-19, Nancy called her. Nancy's mom came to help and stayed for two weeks but did not get COVID-19, and she cooked and cleaned. Her Tribe provided tests and care packages during the pandemic.

Patricia's sons were there for her and made a difference as well as other family members. Her oldest son, daughter-in-law, and her family were helpful especially when she was released from the hospital. Family and community members would drop off cases of hydration drinks, food, masks, and cleaning supplies. It was also helpful to talk to other family members and relatives over the phone. She especially appreciated the time she spent with her grandchildren forming stronger bonds with them.

### *Beliefs/Values*

Traditional and non-traditional beliefs/values helped the Native women deal with COVID-19. They relied on cultural teachings, religion and

---

[32] Interview with Mary, June 16, 2023.
[33] Interview with Mary, June 16, 2023.
[34] Interview with Mary, June 16, 2023.
[35] Interview with Terri, July 03, 2023.

spirituality, predetermined destiny, traditional medicines, and identity to survive the pandemic. They also relied upon prayer, meditation, foretold traditional teachings, and maintaining a positive attitude as mechanisms to persist during disruptive times.

Mary is Catholic and did not rely on tribal beliefs and values, although, as previously noted, she did recall stories and beliefs she heard from her grandmas and aunties and others when she was growing up. She left home at 15 and she is soon to be 50. No relatives stepped in to help her. Her Tribe did nothing for her, and she had to do it on her own. Mary attended school off the reservation and converted to Catholicism, yet she tried to the best of her ability to instill Tribal values in her children. However, her children want nothing to do with their own people and are assimilated because they never lived on the reservation. Moving back to the reservation post-pandemic has been hard for the kids because of the drugs, alcohol, poverty, and depression that exist in their Tribal community. Her children were not used to living amid these social-economic issues since they were not concerns for them in their urban environment.

Nora felt her strength came from kinship, and she kept thinking of protecting her kin, especially Elders. She did not want to pass COVID-19 to someone else. "What stuck out is that I wanted it to be K'é[36] and kinship and just relationality is the way we need to think about each other and protect each other."[37] She kept kinship in the front of her mind as she read posters and websites about COVID-19.

Terri stated that her brothers and sister do not see each other every day, but they are connected, and if anything happens, she said she just picks up the phone. On her mother's side, they are Quechan from Yuma who are also a part of Terri's community that she can phone. Her brother lives down the street. Being connected to her family and coming from a very special place on the Nation is important to her. She and her people are from a distinct spiritual place on Indigenous lands utilized by medicine people where they communicate in metaphysical ways. It reminds her of the Levites in the Bible. All three of her brothers are ministers and are sounding boards for many people to help heal in their daily lives. "Just

---

[36] K'é is defined as clan system/clan relationships/kinship, see, Evangeline Parsons-Yazzie, Margaret Speas, Jessie Ruffenach, and Berlyn Yazzie, *Diné Bizaad Bináhoo'aah: Rediscovering the Navajo Language: An Introduction to the Navajo Language*, 1st ed. (Flagstaff, Arizona: Salina Bookshelf, 2007), 411.

[37] Interview with Nora, June 20, 2023.

knowing they are near is healing to me."[38] Terri meditated to help build resilience.

Nancy believes in tribal medicines and wanted to use her natural medicines more, but she used them in moderation during the COVID-19 pandemic because she was taking Tylenol. She did not want to overdose her children or get them sick. She tried to balance traditional and nontraditional medications to care for her children, but it was a scary time.

Patricia thought of the Navajo concept, T'áá hwó'ají t'éego t'éíyá (*it's up to you*),[39] which motivated her to focus on healing especially when the doctors told her to try to become stronger. "I was going through the healing process of making myself physically stronger; that is what came into my mind. Also, lots of prayers with the concept of being grateful and relations or K'é[40] not only in this universe. COVID, as an illness has its own life, in some ways just being able to acknowledge the illness."[41] She further remarked that "I guess culturally, the question I ask myself is 'why did COVID happen?' As a people in a region or maybe globally, did we do something wrong? Why did it happen? And not only that, but what are the Elders saying? Did some of our Elders foretell this? I don't know, so those are things that I think about sometimes."[42] Patricia relates COVID-19 to her Diné beliefs and viewpoints of balance and harmony, the belief that when one's environment or surrounding is out of balance, it can result in a form of negativity; to keep harmony everything must balance each other.

### *Lasting Impacts*

COVID-19 left lasting impacts on the Native women interviewed pertaining to kinship (family), relationships, trust, health, and overall viewpoints on life and perceptions of themselves. Some have become overprotective, continue to wear masks, take better care of themselves, mistrust vaccines

---

[38] Interview with Terri, July 03, 2023.

[39] The concept of T'áá hwó'ají t'éego t'éíyá (*it's up to you*) is taught and expressed throughout one's lifetime, especially to young Diné people to achieve goals or milestones. Spelling can vary due to dialect, see "T'áá hó'ájitéégóó t'éíyá," Navajo Word of the Day, accessed Dec.15, 2023, https://navajowotd.com/word/taa-hoajiteegoo/

[40] Evangeline Parsons-Yazzie, Margaret Speas, Jessie Ruffenach, and Berlyn Yazzie, *Diné Bizaad Bináhoo'aah: Rediscovering the Navajo Language: An Introduction to the Navajo Language*, 411.

[41] Interview with Patricia, June 09, 2023.

[42] Interview with Patricia, June 09, 2023.

and western medicine, mistrust outsiders in general, appreciate family more, and have more empathy. Two of the women have long COVID-19 with a loss of smell, taste, and brain fog. COVID-19 has resulted varyingly in stronger family bonds, breakup of marriages, new relationships, and the loss of relatives. Their plans regarding future COVID-19 boosters similarly vary.

After Mary became homeless, she lost her mother to COVID-19 when she returned to the reservation and had no place to live. Her grandfather also died from COVID-19. Mary does not plan to take the COVID-19 boosters in the future. After she recovered from COVID-19, Mary returned to her Tribal community where her children who were raised in an urban area are finding adjusting to reservation life difficult. COVID-19 also impacted her marriage, and she is now divorced and in a new relationship. Mary now says she does not trust people due to the experience with COVID-19. She does not look at things through rose-colored glasses anymore. Mary's situation and homelessness illustrates how racism and sexism are challenges many American Indian women deal with in mainstream urban society.

COVID-19 has had a lasting impact on Nora. She has become very protective of her family and takes precautions like still wearing masks and keeping up with COVID-19 shots. Often, Nora and her family are the only ones still wearing masks. She feels like she took a risk by attending her son's school event where her family was exposed to COVID-19. This was a hard choice for her because she did not want her family to miss this important event for her son. Nora continues to have some difficulty focusing (known as brain fog) and has been prescribed medication by her doctor and continues using sanitizing habits. She also has more empathy and understanding for her students and their experiences with COVID-19. As of 2023, she continues to put a COVID-19 statement in her syllabi for classes. Family and especially her dad are just more important to her after seeing the loss of lives to COVID-19. Nora continues to test whenever her family gets a cough or does not feel well. Nora says, "It's a regular practice for them."[43]

Terri realizes that she needs to "stop being so strong woman-ish and realize how susceptible I am."[44] Terri continues to be cautious. She states

---

[43] Interview with Nora, June 20, 2023.
[44] Interview with Terri, July 03, 2023.

that "even if I think I have a plan and I may carry out the plan there may be something missing in the plan I don't see."[45] Terri eats better now, but she doesn't know if her taste buds have returned. Foods taste different now. Terri has realized that being a strong person did not protect her from the impacts of COVID-19. She needs to develop relationships and community within an urban environment to better care for herself and her family.

Nancy claims that "I wouldn't say it's [COVID] changed my perspective because I've always had an understanding that everything always happens the way that it's supposed to and, two that death isn't the end all so I mean it was sad to see a lot of our family members go and a lot of our friends go but I tried to maintain that knowledge that everything was already decided when they were born."[46] This quote reflects Nancy's traditional Tribal values and beliefs that were passed on to her from Elders, family, and spiritual leaders. Nancy still uses sanitizers especially on her children. She is undecided if she will continue to take the COVID-19 boosters if it becomes an annual thing because Nora does not take flu shots.

Patricia experienced the most serious case of COVID-19 of all interviewees. Her hospitalization and recovery from the virus have made Patricia more conscious of her health and taking care of herself, noting that "I think part of that is not taking things for granted, taking care of myself and being more in-tune with myself, just being more present."[47] She plans to take COVID-19 boosters in the future and take better care of herself. This is what she will do differently given her experience with COVID-19. Patricia stated, "maybe be more mindful but then again you don't really think about these things until you have …in my case being in ICU and having lost consciousness for a couple of weeks, and waking up unable to walk, unable to really eat and taking only three steps felt exhausting and I feel like my lungs was going to burst, just even being afraid of heights from like two feet, I couldn't believe it!"[48] COVID-19 changed Patricia's perspective on caring for herself; she now exercises and eats healthier, and Patricia does not take life for granted.

---

[45] Interview with Terri, July 03, 2023.
[46] Interview with Nancy, July 03, 2023.
[47] Interview with Patricia, June 09, 2023.
[48] Interview with Patricia, June 09, 2023.

## Conclusion

The findings show that all five American Indian women living in urban areas were impacted by COVID-19; it disrupted their lives and those of their families. This was especially impactful for urban American Indian women because their extended families were often not available for support or for the women to take care of. This provided additional stress and worry for these women because of the cultural importance of family. COVID-19 made the women value family more and realize the importance of caring for them and themselves better. Throughout the pandemic, the women showed resilience in the face of numerous challenges, but they also realized their susceptibility no matter how strong they were. They combated, survived, and persisted to protect their families and themselves by creating coping mechanisms to deal with COVID-19. They did not back away from the situation and showed their determination to deal with COVID-19 as heads of their household and caregivers of their families by providing financial support, physical care, emotional support, discipline, and protection. The women came through the disruption of COVID-19 stronger and better equipped to deal with the future challenges by relying on relationships, spirituality, kinship, identity, and traditions. It changed their outlook and helped them develop practices and confidence to deal with unplanned situations such as the pandemic in an urban setting that is not always supportive of American Indians, especially Native women.

The themes of protection, impacts of COVID-19 on daily lives, support, beliefs and values, and the lasting impacts of COVID-19 encompassed the responses to the questions asked. The subthemes of kinship and relationships were especially relevant for the interviewees as they cared for their families and realized their importance to their lives. "What stuck out is that I wanted it to be k'é[49] and kinship and just relationality is the way we need to think about each other and protect each other."[50] Focusing on urban American Indian women's experiences during the pandemic provides a voice from an often-invisible population, and it adds to the limited scholarship on COVID-19 and American Indian women. The results of this study show urban American Indian women carrying on traditional

---

[49] Parsons-Yazzie, *Diné Bizaad Bináhoo'aah: Rediscovering the Navajo Language: An Introduction to the Navajo Language*, 411.

[50] Interview with Nora, June 20, 2023.

roles as caregivers by feeding, nurturing, protecting, and managing their families and households as their female ancestors did before them.

As COVID-19 is predicted to continue as a health issue, these stories of resilience and survival of urban American Indian women provide real life examples of strength and fortitude as they sought to protect and care for their families. However, the pandemic also made the women realize their vulnerability, as Terri remarked, "stop being so strong woman-ish and realize how susceptible I am."[51]

**Competing Interests Declaration** The authors have no conflicts of interest to declare that are relevant to the content of this chapter.

---

[51] Interview with Terri, July 03, 2023.

CHAPTER 15

# Indigenous Motherhood Resiliency: Adapting Cultural Teachings During COVID-19 Restrictions

*Natahnee Nuay Winder*

> *Children are one the greatest gifts a person can receive from the Creator. I thank the Creator every day for you and your sister. You are blessed with your son. Children are our most influential teachers.*
> —*Mom*

Máykh/Pehnaho. Nia natepinnia'a Natahnee Nuay Winder, citizen of the Tsaidüka Tribe of Nevada. I come from an intertribal lineage of Tsaidüka, Kooyooe Ticutta or Cui Ui Ticutta on my mother's side; I am Nuucic, Diné, and Black on my father's side. I grew up on the homelands of the Nuunu'agaat(ü) in what is currently called Colorado. I acknowledge that I am an uninvited guest on the unceded traditional territories of the səlilwətaʔɬ, kʷikʷəƛəm, Sḵwx̱wú7mesh Úxwumixw, and xʷməθkʷəy̓əm on which I work. I have lived and traveled extensively through the Great

N. N. Winder (✉)
Simon Fraser University, Burnaby, BC, Canada
e-mail: nwinder@sfu.ca

© The Author(s), under exclusive license to Springer Nature Switzerland AG 2024
F. King, W. Davies (eds.), *COVID-19 in Indian Country*,
https://doi.org/10.1007/978-3-031-70184-9_15

Basin, Southwest, and Plains regions of Turtle Island between the two reservations. I was privileged to be raised and immersed in my culture and ceremonies, surrounded by my maternal and paternal family members. My family fostered a strong Newe₁ and Nuucic identity. During my childhood and adolescent years, I lived with my parents in Southern Ute territory throughout the school year, and during the summers, I traveled to Pyramid Lake to stay with my maternal grandparents and relatives and then to Albuquerque, Duckwater, and Ignacio to visit my paternal family. I describe my education as being braided because it is a combination of mixed learning: institutional education, traditional learning more based in nature, culture, and ceremony curated by family and community, as well as a creative education based in art and beauty: photography, painting, poetry. When I began my post-secondary education, institutional learning took over. However, now I can take the braided education and utilize all of the parts in my work. It allows me to reflect upon my life's turning points by adding pieces of my childhood, adolescence, womanhood, and motherhood like different colored strands instead of fabric. I use memory, research, wisdom, traditions, and so importantly, emotions and acts of love. So many of the teachings in this braided knowledge of motherhood have been passed from woman-to-woman and generation-to-generation in my family and community. This process of "braiding brings forth love and transformation–intergenerationally and across the veil of Spirit and matter" to share, reflect, and tell a story through life seasons about motherhood in the time of COVID-19.[1]

Due to my pursuit of education, I lived throughout Turtle Island as an Indigenous transplant. However, I honored my family and community by frequently visiting home to contribute to our ceremonies and social gatherings during my academic breaks. Currently, I am an assistant professor who resides in a city away from my community and traditional territory; I still travel home regularly. Maintaining and rejuvenating connections to one's family, community, and ancestors are a foundation of our existence as Indigenous people, as well as a way to uphold the responsibilities that were given to us by the Creator. When I had my son, I felt the ancestral pull to support him with traditional teachings. My partner and I

---

[1] Kimberly Todd and Maria Vamvalis, "Puncturing, Weaving, and Braiding: Integrating Spiritual Knowing in Education," in *Ignite: A Decolonial Approach to Higher Education Through Space, Place and Culture* eds. Laura M. Pipe and Jennifer T. Stephens, (Wilmington, DE: Vernon Art and Science Inc., 2023): 230.

continued to braid our lives by going between the territories of Duckwater Shoshone, Paiute, and Ute with our son (Tau'a). It has always been important to me that our son be a contributing member of the community. The summer months of 2020 were filled with excitement from family and community members who eagerly awaited my son's arrival and introduction to the world.

On March 11, 2020, shortly after his birth, the World Health Organization declared that the devastating impact of the coronavirus disease 2019 (COVID-19) was officially a pandemic.[2] COVID-19, a highly infectious severe acute respiratory illness, was spreading from person-to-person through droplets: coughs, sneezes, and even conversations. The virus also led to and heightened cardiovascular, gastrointestinal, and neurological diseases and often led to death.[3] Furthermore, the COVID-19 pandemic forced countries to close their borders and restrict travel, which interrupted Indigenous family and community celebrations, including birth and naming ceremonies. The Canada-U.S. border restricted non-essential travel on March 21, 2020, to protect their citizens and prevent the spread of the virus.[4] Unable to return home for an undetermined amount of time, we, as first-time parents, forged a new path for our son to find a way to create and maintain connections to our family and community.

This chapter interweaves storytelling, poetry, and photography to give voice to my journey of becoming a new mother during the height of the COVID-19 pandemic. I also revisit a season in my life before my son was born when I learned that motherhood might be impossible for me. The chapter is woven as a braided, creative non-fiction essay where I peel open layers of my journey, including my desire to learn the Ute and Shoshone languages as an adult beginner with hopes that I will be able to teach my Tau'a to be fluent in the language of our ancestors. The design of this piece encourages the reader to partake in the self-learning of Ute and

---

[2] World Health Organization, "Who Director-General's Opening Remarks at the Media Briefing on COVID-19 – 11 March 2020," World Health Organization, accessed 18 June 2023, https://www.who.int/director-general/speeches/detail/who-director-general-s-opening-remarks-at-the-media-briefing-on-covid-19%2D%2D-11-march-2020

[3] Faith Sekercioglu and Nicholas D. Spence, "Introduction," in *Indigenous Health and Well-Being in the COVID-19 Pandemic*, eds. Nicholas D. Spence and Faith Sekercioglu, (London and New York: Routledge Taylor and Francis Group, 2023): 1.

[4] Tanji Armenski et al. "StatCan COVID-19: Data to Insights for a Better Canada Crossing the Border During the Pandemic: 2020 Review," Statistics Canada, accessed 2 May 2023, https://www150.statcan.gc.ca/n1/pub/45-28-0001/2021001/article/00007-eng.htm

Shoshone by utilizing the provided glossary to move back and forth between the chapter and the definitions. Hopefully this opens a small window into this process, to see what it is like to pronounce new words and learn and help revitalize an Indigenous language. Finally, it will discuss how my relationships with family, friends, and community were, are, and can be maintained during a crisis like the pandemic. I explain why these relationships are foundational to the growth of my ohaa. As a first-time mother, I had to learn how to adapt my cultural teachings. My partner and I had to figure out a new way to introduce our Tau'a to family and community. The pandemic had created an environment where paitenee like my Tau'a experienced asti'i, tsaan suankan and tukku kammankan from their relatives virtually. We were unable to travel and visit with family. We missed out on holding a family feast to celebrate our Tau'a's first laugh, first steps, first hugs and kisses. Many milestones of our Tau'a took place over Zoom. The closing of borders made life solitary, but also popularized the virtual space for communicating with relatives on a different pathway to teach paitenee to be good relatives. I caution readers to pause and breathe during the next section as it might bring back memories of loss and obstacles created from the pandemic, and many Indigenous women had pregnancy challenges during this uncertain time, especially those whose pregnancies are woven with experiences of grieving the loss of relatives occurring at the same time.

## Focusing on the Nuclear Family

The COVID-19 pandemic quietly and violently shuttled in a new form of colonization by prioritizing the nuclear family unit. For many, the pandemic came to symbolize micro ruptures in many Indigenous communities. Families were asked to separate themselves, quarantined away from relatives and others who did not reside with them. Devastating impacts also included the heavy loss of matriarchs, beloved family and community members, and Elders. In no way am I minimizing the importance of public health guidelines put forth by the Public Health Agency of Canada or the Centers for Disease Control and Prevention. However, it is important to be aware that the COVID-19 pandemic uncovered three neoliberal narratives that are currently "in the process of collapsing: individualism as the solution to social problems, the economic supremacy of capitalism, and the nuclear family form as a privatized model of self-sufficiency."[5] These three neoliberal narratives impacted each Indigenous community differently. The pandemic enforced patriarchy, increased gender inequality, amplified the barriers of inequality among underrepresented and vulnerable groups, created an upsurge in intimate partner violence, restricted the movement between households, and placed limitations on how many individuals were to be included in one's bubble of contact.[6] Additionally, Indigenous women who became mothers and who resided away from their communities during the pandemic had to embrace the sociological construct of the nuclear family. I am using the most recent notion of the nuclear family as children who reside in a single household versus the outdated hegemonic concept where the family is a heterosexual married unit.[7] Indigenous households are often composed of extended family as well: grandparents, cousins, aunts, uncles, and other relatives who play significant roles in a child's development. Unable to receive external support from multiple households and family on the reservation, many urban Indigenous families recreated their familial network with friends, neighbors, and colleagues to create communities similar to their reservation.[8]

---

[5] Daniel Ian Rubin and Faith Agostinone Wilson, *A Time of Covidiocy: Media, Politics, and Social Upheaval* (Leiden, The Netherlands: Brill, 2021), 1.

[6] Brad Boserup, Mark McKenney, and Adel Elkbuli, "Alarming Trends in US Domestic Violence During the COVID-19 Pandemic," *The American Journal of Emergency Medicine* 38 no. 12 (2020): 2753–55. https://doi.org/10.1016/j.ajem.2020.04.77; Anastasia Kourti et al., "Domestic Violence during the COVID-19 Pandemic: A Systematic Review," *Trauma, Violence, & Abuse* 24, no. 2 (2023): 719–45. https://doi.org/10.1177/15248380211038690; Braden Leap, Marybeth Stalp, and Kimberly Kelly, "Reorganizations of Gendered Labor during the COVID-19 Pandemic: A Review and Suggestions for Further Research," *Sociological Inquiry* 93, no. 1 (2023): 179–200. https://doi.org/10.1111/soin.12488

[7] Faith Agostinone-Wilson, *Marxism and Education Beyond Identity: Sexuality and Schooling*, 1st ed. (New York: Palgrave Macmillan, 2010). https://doi.org/10.1057/9780230113558; Brigitte Berger, *The Family in the Modern Age: More Than a Lifestyle Choice*, 1st. ed. (New Brunswick, NJ: Transaction Publishers, 2002). https://doi.org/10.4324/9781315132006

[8] Hilary N. Weaver and Barry J. White, "The Native American Family Circle: Roots of Resiliency," *Journal of Family Social Work* 2, no. 1 (1997): 72. https://doi.org/10.1300/J039v02n01_05

## Cultural Upbringing Reflection

Each Indigenous Nation has their own unique holistic teachings to equip and prepare women for womanhood and motherhood and to equip their community members with the requisite skills and knowledge to be contributing members.[9] Indigenous women have an irreplaceable role as carriers of Indigenous knowledge and traditions and bringing life into the next generation. They link others to the spirit world by bringing the unborn generation of children to the natural world. Indigenous women's perspectives are based on various interconnections that are rooted in established relationships with place, spiritual beings, humans, and the environment.[10] Indigenous mothers and aunties are responsible for passing these teachings onto younger generations so they can be contributing members of their Indigenous nations. Indigenous women who have children resist colonization by passing on traditional teachings and knowledge to their children.[11] Indigenous children are considered gifts from the creator. My mother believed in this and told my sister and me that we were the greatest gifts she ever received. She constantly thanks me for gifting her with a grandson. I grew up with the worldview that Indigenous women are the backbones of their families and of the community. Because they are the knowledge keepers and the carriers of life, they are responsible for gifting traditional names and upholding cultural teachings like being helpful to others, being accountable to one's Indigenous relatives, their Nation, and other-than-human relatives. They provide support to the whole of creation.

I was raised to honor and respect how Indigenous women are sacred because they are carriers of paa and have a sacred connection to paa especially since the baby's first home is the womb. The womb's amniotic fluid is mostly water and keeps the growing baby healthy by providing cushioning, aiding with muscle and bone development, and keeping the umbilical

---

[9] Gregory Cajete, *Look to the Mountain: An Ecology of Indigenous Education* (Durango, CO: Kivakí Press, 1994).

[10] Isabel Altamirano-Jiménez and Nathalie Kermoal, "Introduction," in *Living on the Land: Indigenous Women's Understanding of Place*, eds. Nathalie Kermoal and Isabel Altamirano-Jiménez, (Edmonton, AB: Athabasca University Press, 2016): 9.

[11] Amy Shawanda, "Anishinaabe Motherhood: The Act of Resistance by Resurging Traditional Teachings and Pedagogies," (PhD Dissertation, Trent University, 2022), 3. ProQuest Dissertations & Theses A&I, http://proxy.lib.sfu.ca/login?url=https://www.proquest.com/dissertations-theses/anishinaabe-motherhood-act-resistance-resurging/docview/2624693294/se-2

cord strong for proper delivery of food and oxygen.[12] Paa plays a significant role in our bodies. The adult body consists of 55–65% water, and developing babies' bodies contain about 70–90% water.[13] Water is fundamental to the life and growth of the baby, as well as its mother. There is a deep connection to the feminine energies within the cosmos which link women to the Creation of the Earth, the moon, and the water.[14] The values and responsibilities connected to the Earth's teachings have been instilled in my nana pa̲itenu with my mom and in conversations with my late gagu'u. These teachings and responsibilities were further reinforced by participating in ceremonies and social gatherings, which I will expand upon later in this chapter. It is also important to acknowledge the roles that Indigenous males have in fostering the growth of young Indigenous girls. One of my role models, the late Chichigavach(i), played a huge role in my upbringing, and I considered him to be my uncle, and one of my greatest teachers during my youth and adolescent years. My father went in-and-out of my family during my life, so Uncle often filled that role.

Chichigavach(i) was a substance abuse counselor and a protector of Indigenous sovereignty and rights. He was also an Indigenous land and water protector. Some of Uncle's notable contributions were his participation as a security guard in the 1978 Longest Walk, protecting the fishing rights, protesting the Denver Columbus Day parade, and founding the American Indian Movement Chapter in Portland. Chichigavach(i) also established a community Run Against Drugs, a Mother's Day Brunch for all women and girls in the community, and an annual New Year's Sobriety Walk on the Rez to encourage others to begin the new year in a healthy way. One of my favorite memories and teachings from Uncle was at the annual Mother's Day Brunch. He always began with a prayer circle, and he stated how men have the responsibility to be providers and to protect

---

[12] Emily D. Fitzsimmons and Tushar Bajaj, "Embryology, Amniotic Fluid." National Library of Medicine, StatPearls Internet, accessed May 6, 2023, https://www.ncbi.nlm.nih.gov/books/NBK541089/

[13] M.H. Beall, J.P.H.M. van den Wijngaard, M.J.C. van Gemert, and M.G. Ross, "Amniotic Fluid Water Dynamics," *Placenta* 28, no. 8-9 (2007): 816–23, https://doi.org/10.1016/j.placenta.2006.11.009

[14] Kim Anderson, *Life Stages and Native Women: Memory, Teachings, and Story Medicine* (Winnipeg, MB: University of Manitoba Press, 2011); Kim Anderson, "Giving Life to the People: An Indigenous Ideology of Motherhood," In *Maternal Theory: Essential Readings*, ed. Andrea O'Reilly, (Bradford, Ontario: Demeter Press, 2007), 761–81. http://www.jstor.org/stable/j.ctt1rrd94h.49

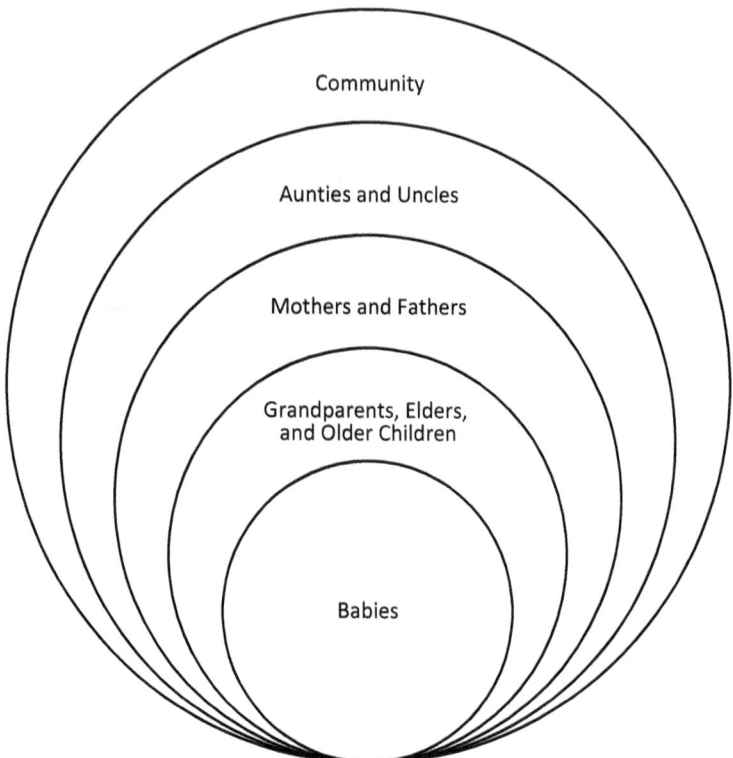

**Fig. 15.1** Traditional kinship system. Credit: Natahnee Nuay Winder

Indigenous women because they carry the responsibility of creating and nurturing life. This teaching for both boys and younger men also served as a reminder to women and girls. Social gatherings are significant for Indigenous peoples because they foster "a deep sense of responsibility for the cultural survival of their people."[15] The annual gatherings hosted by Uncle created a traditional kinship system as described in Fig. 15.1 where children were taught about their expectations in family and community.

Similar to other Indigenous nations, each person in the family and community helps to support and raise a child as outlined in Fig. 15.1;

---

[15] Wilma Mankiller, *Every Day Is a Good Day: Reflections by Contemporary Indigenous Women* (Golden, CO: Fulcrum Pub., 2004), 95.

children are understood to be gifts from the Creator. At the center of the kinship system are babies since they will sustain the futures of the family and community. Grandparents, Elders, and other children are the next teachers, providing support. The next three circles ebb and flow, working together to support the nation through hunting and harvesting, gathering of medicines, attending, and curating various ceremonies, and assisting with the formal processes of education and other responsibilities. The pandemic temporarily dismantled the traditional kinship system for those residing away from their family and community. Many Native Americans struggled to interact with each other, and it became difficult to receive or accept help raising children. Teaching the next generation also became a challenge and many resorted to virtual means of connecting and offering emotional support for educational purposes. Less was available for babies in this respect.

Becoming a mother during COVID-19 felt like climbing a steep mountain climbing several treacherous routes. This became the first season of my motherhood journey. Below is my personal fertility story which begins with navigating a painful terrain filled with uterine fibroids. I share this rocky path to shed light on fertility/infertility obstacles that could impact other Indigenous women, especially those who have experienced fibroids while trying to become pregnant. This section could be difficult to read for women who have faced similar challenges. Hopefully this discourse opens a dialogue for individuals who need support and helps to create safe space for intimate conversations about fertility challenges before, during, and after pregnancy. I returned to journaling as a form of self-therapy in the fall of 2009, which is when I received very uncertain and devastating news.

## Tama'riyu 2009

During a routine check-up, the physician surprisingly asked if I was pregnant. I laughed and said it would be a miracle if I were. This was how I learned about my fibroid. After the diagnosis, I spent endless hours researching uterine fibroids on the Internet: their causes, symptoms, and how to get rid of them. I felt frustrated and angry like a pressurized tea kettle ready to explode; my fibroids were so large that they required I visit a specialist. I ended up getting three different medical opinions. One physician actually advocated for a hysterectomy so he could study this mass in my uterus. I tried to hold back my tears as I was faced with the possibility of having my uterus removed before I had even had the chance to become pregnant.

> I can't believe it. I feel devastated. My chance of being a mother is hanging by a thread. Today, my heart sank into an abyss. Sorrow knowing, I might not be able to carry my own child. The doctor said I have an unusually large fibroid. The infertility specialist told me that he wanted to study my fibroid because of its size, and he said it with so much excitement that his eyes sparkled. Tears filled my eyes and I tried to hold them back from flooding my face, the breaking of a dam. I left the office horrified; my eyes swollen because I had cried so hard. The physician referred me to a fertility specialist who prescribed me medication to reduce the fibroid's size. This treatment will last several months, and then I'll be scheduled to have them removed. But the fibroids are so massive that the surgeon said they didn't know what type of surgery they would have to perform on my uterus until they opened me up.

I weave in a poem that I wrote about my experience with uterine fibroids and undergoing surgery. Prior to the myomectomy surgery, I was prescribed medication to shrink the fibroid, and during these three months, I experienced several menopausal symptoms like hot flashes. The myomectomy was my best chance of decreasing the fibroid's size and increasing my chances of carrying a child. When the surgery was complete, my surgeon reported that he had removed two grapefruit-sized masses.

Will I Carry My Own?

> For as long as I could remember I looked forward to being a mother someday.
> Holding a soft, precious, tiny hand in the palm of my hand that I would place on my heart.
> Hearing toddler feet scurry across the hallway.
> As I lay on the surgery table, an immense sadness and frustration enters my mind.
> My dream of motherhood might be torn apart.
>
> 50/50 chance is what I am told.
> 50/50 chance of being a mother.
> 50/50 chance that my womb will carry.
> 50/50 chance of being sterilized.
>
> My fibroid took up my whole uterus cavity.

I didn't have time to process missing out on motherhood.
The words, "the ultrasound didn't prepare us to remove a fibroid this large."
"You have a 50/50 of having a hysterectomy."
The next time that I wake up I'll find out if I can carry my own baby.

50/50 chance is what I am told.
50/50 chance of being a mother.
50/50 chance that my womb will carry.
50/50 chance of being sterilized.

Will I carry a child of my own?
Will I be a foster mom?
Will I be an adoptive mom?
50/50 chance is what I am told.
50/50 chance of being sterilized.

When I first found out I was pregnant with my son, my mind flashed back to my fibroidectomy. I remembered how I felt about the uncertainty, the possibility of such abrupt changes in my life. I had been raised not to say negative things about myself and my life, but I felt conflicted with my traditional teachings because I was fearful of having a miscarriage. My first trimester was scary and challenging. I was in and out of the emergency room due to light bleeding, and the ultrasound identified that the other fibroids were invading my uterine cavity. My unborn son and the fibroids were in a constant competition. Yet, I remained positive and talked constantly to my family, to my growing son, and to the Creator. I prayed for strength and courage.

## Yepani$_1$ 2019

Yepani$_1$ brought many changes into my life. I was in the middle of my second trimester, entering my second year of teaching at Simon Fraser University, serving on committees, finishing the last couple chapters of my dissertation, and teaching a new course while trying to remain balanced and healthy. I am thankful for the patient students who took my classes as I dealt with pregnancy brain fog. One student felt overjoyed during lecture when they noticed my son was kicking. The class would laugh and pause to watch the trembles on my belly. This class was small, and I focused on relationship building, which is why the comfort level surrounding my pregnancy existed. I continued to pray my son would be healthy and strong, and that he wouldn't be impacted by the growing fibroid. These concerns were shared in a letter I wrote to him regarding my hopes for his future:

> Dear Son,
> You are so strong and will beat this. Everyone in the family is praying for you and can't wait to meet you. Your Daddy and I have been talking for days about how you kicked him as he hugged me. You are so playful already. We do not want you to feel scared. Mommy loves you so much, and I can't wait to hold you in my arms. Daddy loves singing to you each morning. I love talking to you throughout the day and going for walks with you and Daddy around campus. My students are also thrilled when you let everyone know that you are awake and paying attention during my lectures and in our small group discussions. I am working hard to finish dissertating before you arrive. I can't wait to meet you, see your eyes, hold you, kiss you, and give you a huge hug.

I continued to think positively about the birth of my son. I redirected my negative thoughts about the complications and the fibroid. The fibroid seemed to represent a foreign force trying to colonize my uterine cavity, my body, my heart, and my son. I began to think about the resiliency of all the women in my family and about the future: how would I be as a new mother, the person responsible for developing my son's character and teaching him cultural values, history, and what his responsibilities would be throughout his life. During my pregnancy I felt more creative than I ever had been. I crafted a poem to be read with Fig. 15.2 to capture the sacred role of Indigenous motherhood, another braided strand that carries connections between generations and retells the histories of our people and how to foster these values.[16]

> Tau'a, you are our tapaitoaihkanna
> You chose my womb as your first home. Your little growing body, surrounded by ancestral and familial love, warmth, good energy, and our good thoughts for your arrival. We made you a feast of buffalo meat, corn, squash, beans, and oven bread.
>
> Tua'a, we honor and thank you for picking us to be your mother, father, and blessing the family with this gift of you.

---

[16] Robin Zape-tah-hol-ah Minthorn, "Indigenous Motherhood in the Academy, Building Our Children to Be Good Relatives," *Wicazo Sa Review*, 33, no. 2 (2018): 62–75.

**Fig. 15.2** Connecting with our medicines

> Each morning I rise before the sun emerges over the mountain tops, and its rays pierce through the Cedar trees to offer tobacco to Mother Earth. Prayers nourish your growth and create a connection to family members living far away, as well as our ancestors and Creator.
> Tau'a, we honor and thank you for picking us to be your mother, father, and blessing the family with the gift of you.
> An earthquake had torn through my heart…and I felt the ground part…a fibroid! Fibroids started invading your home trying to colonize it.
> But we prayed for your health and wellbeing. We asked our family members on earth and those in the spirit world to pray for you, too. We prayed for protection and safety. This foreign object would not harm you.
> Tau'a, we honor and thank you for picking us to be your mother, father, and blessing the family with the gift of you.

Tau'a, I talked to you each day and sang a newe hupia$_1$. Your Tso'o$_1$ taught me these songs as a child so I could sing them to you. Tau'a, you are our tap<u>ai</u>to<u>ai</u>hkanna. Tso'o$_1$ was a fluent speaker of Shoshone. She carried and passed on these songs from our ancestors. Every time we speak newe taikwappeh, our ancestors and relatives' hearts sing with joy. Tau'a, you will be the first generation in our family to speak our ancestral tongue.

Tau'a, we honor and thank you for picking us to be your mother, father, and blessing the family with the gift of you.

Tso'o$_1$ is a survivor of the boarding school. They prevented her and our people from speaking our ancestral language, trying to assimilate us. We were robbed from being fluent because it was safer to learn English and the ways of the white man.

Tso'o$_1$ was a fierce woman who held on to our teachings and pushed us to pursue our dreams despite her having been trapped in constant survival mode. The old ones said boarding school tried to change our people. Many suffered many forms of abuse, and some lost the ability to speak, they lacked parenting skills, the ability to cope in healthy ways. Tso'o$_1$ shared her experiences from this institution with us. I will tell you the truth when you are older, Tau'a.

Tau'a, we honor and thank you for picking us to be your mother, father, and blessing the family with the gift of you.

Tso'o$_1$ taught us numerous things from making oven bread and knit sweaters to singing traditional newe hupia$_1$. Even though, she didn't pass on newe taikwappeh, she held fast to our sacred prayers, songs, and some phrases. Sometimes Tso'o$_1$ newe taikwappeh was fuzzy for her and felt like the ground was thawing when she recalled words. These long pauses to remember newe taikwappeh is a breaking point to break the colonizers chains and begin anew in our family.

Tau'a, you will be the first generation in our family to speak our ancestral tongue. We are revitalizing and learning newe taikwappeh for you, Tau'a so we can pass it on to you. Tepitsi tsaa napuihten tau'a, you are the lineage of our family. You resemble a new path for our people as we continue healing from the trauma of boarding school.

Tau'a, we honor and thank you for picking us to be your mother, father, and blessing the family with the gift of you. You are the new fire in our lives, our tap<u>ai</u>to<u>ai</u>hkanna.

The sacred role of motherhood ties so intricately to the cultivation of relationships with family and community which are essential and central to Indigenous lifeways. My becoming a mother meant that I was responsible for transmitting not only our family history but also the history of our community. During my pregnancy, I reflected a lot on what I would teach my tau' and how I would establish connections to his grandparents and family members and introduce him to the community since he has an intertribal heritage. The following section discusses the impacts of COVID-19 on my family and how it changed the dynamic of introducing my ohaattsi tau'a into the world.

## Tǒmǒ 2020

The Canadian government implemented a policy requiring all travelers to quarantine and isolate. My tuwach(i) was born during the height of the pandemic during the tǒmǒ of 2020. Creator blessed my piyan, namich(i), yaachin, and tatawayvin with the gift of time. They were able to visit us in the hospital before the governments shut down. As I've stated, relationships are essential and central to Indigenous lifeways. Parents and their newborn babies are constantly establishing connections to their parents, grandparents, relatives, and to their community to foster growth and maintain ties to their culture, language, and homelands. My piyan was able to assist us with our first 30-day customs. The initial 30 days for the aanuruwach(ü) and the new family are vital. In Ute culture, parents must withhold eating meat, drinking cold beverages, and forgo sweets.[17] Mothers do not cut their hair, touch their faces, and they should receive assistance combing their hair for hygienic purposes. During the first month of life and parenthood, the first three spheres of the traditional kinship model come to visit the new family and provide support with cooking and cleaning to aid with the new adjustments as well as keeping aanuruwach(ü) away from illness.

Bonding between parents and newborn during the first thirty days is also vital. Aunties, uncles, grandparents, and other children are observing and preparing for ceremonies like the naming to take place.[18] These

---

[17] Lynda Grove-d'wolf, *The Life and Times of a Ute Woman* (Createspace Independent Pub., 2014).

[18] Natahnee Winder, "Post-secondary Education (PSE) Indigenous Students' Perspectives: Sharing Our
 Voices on How We Fit into Residential School (RS) History of Canada and the United States Using Photovoice" (PhD Dissertation, University of Western Ontario, 2020). ProQuest Dissertations & Theses A&I, http://proxy.lib.sfu.ca/login?url=https://www.proquest.com/dissertations-theses/post-secondary-education-pse-indigenous-students/docview/2714874142/se-2

traditional newborn baby gatherings were non-existent for us due to the pandemic. My pivan's time with us was cut short because she had to vacate Canada prior to the border closure. The following poem, *Önöönik(i)*, expresses my experience introducing our tuwach(i) to family and the events following his birth (Fig. 15.3):

Önöönik(i)

A flood of emotions when I heard your first cry, I felt
Immersed in unconditional love, it consumed my heart, body, and spirit
You had entered the world quickly through C-section
Önöönik(i)

Full head of black, straight hair with beautiful patches
Skin-to-skin with Daddy until I recovered
the longest 60 minutes of my life being away from you
Önöönik(i)

Grandma brought you gifts from the family
Blue Pendleton blanket, beaded moccasins, clothes
Flux of calls and texts, family checking in on us
Önöönik(i)

Respiratory infections are increasing around the world.

**Fig. 15.3** *Önöönik(i)*

"Leave or be prepared to stay where you're at for an indefinite period of time"
Grandma left quickly, no time to process, COVID-19 is here
Exhausted, just keep writing, back to work, just keep writing

Clogged milk duct
Just keep writing, just keep writing
Zoom meetings with supervisor then video chats with family just keep writing,
Where did the days go? Where did the nights go?

Restrictions to leave and enter Pyramid Lake
Building closures at Southern Ut
Loss of Elders…Great-grandma passed
My world will never be the same
More loss across Turtle Island

November 8, 2021 all ports open
2020 had been a blur: dissertation writing, sleep deprivation
We survived
Finally, we get to go back the rez but nothing is the same
Grandma is in the spirit world like so many relatives, others
Önöönik(i)

The majority of 2020 I spent on Zoom, participating in numerous meetings. I defended my Ph.D. dissertation on November 26, 2020; my son was eleven months old. It was a difficult time for my family; we lost my grandma, and many individuals from our community. The closure of the Canada-U.S. border prevented me from attending my grandma's service, my uncle's service, and many others for community members. I was processing massive amounts of loss, grief, excitement, and growth as a mother, partner, relative, and academic. I relied heavily on phone calls and video calls with family and friends. My partner and I blossomed as parents, supporting each other in our careers. I was blessed my grandma got to see our son when he started walking, and she would laugh when he would pop his head up to see her on the laptop screen. We feasted when he hit his milestones and shared stories and laughter with family over Zoom. We spent 2020 and 2021 going for walks around the neighborhood, praying, and offering tobacco. Eventually we were able to go home and support the family and the community on the Rez by returning to ceremonies and embracing loved ones.

## Tach(a) 2023

This chapter is written to acknowledge significant seasons in my life that had momentous impacts and are pivotal moments of self-learning, change, patience, and love. The global pandemic also created a space for individuals such as myself to utilize writing, journaling, and other creative forms to help with healing over the loss of loved ones, to help decrease anxiety and fear, and to allow for reconnecting with oneself in different ways, like becoming a new mother. Poetry became a therapeutic space to bridge my heart to others; it assisted me in my healing and provided me with a new approach to my cultural learnings and teachings. Poetry, photography, and storytelling were a way to maintain Indigenous relationships and adapt cultural teachings for children while we were under strict governmental restrictions. Highlighted here is the resiliency it takes to face challenges while being separated from one's tribal community as a new mother during the time of COVID-19. I incorporated Ute and Shoshone words throughout the chapter because I am learning the language so my son can one day be fluent. New mothers need physical support and love from family after the birth of a child; this was unavailable to me and to many during the pandemic. Building community was strained for new Indigenous mothers. Once the border reopened, we traveled back as soon as we could to introduce our son to the rest of the family and our community. The impacts of COVID-19 are still lingering. It is my hope we can open up a discussion and identify support for Indigenous mothers who are away from their communities for an extended period of time.

Glossary of Traditional Names

| | |
|---|---|
| Cui Ui Ticutta | Cui-ui eaters |
| Diné | Navajo |
| Kooyooe Ticutta | Pyramid Lake Paiute |
| Kʷikʷəƛəm | Kwikwetlem |
| Sḵwx̱wú7mesh Úxwumixw | Squamish |
| Səlilwətaʔɫ | Tsleil-Waututh |
| Xʷməθkʷəy̓əm | Musqueam |

Glossary of Terms for Shoshone

| | |
|---|---|
| Aisen tsaan | Thank you. |
| Gagu'u | Grandmother |
| Nana pa̱itenu | Mother & daughter relationship |

| | |
|---|---|
| Nia natepinnia'a | My name is. |
| Newe$_1$ | Person |
| Newe hupia$_1$ | A Shoshone song |
| Newe taikwappeh | Shoshone language |
| Ohaa | Baby or infant |
| Ohaattsi | Newborn |
| P<u>a</u>itenee | Children |
| Pehnaho | Hello |
| Tau'a | Son |
| Tap<u>a</u>ito<u>a</u>ihkanna | Sunlight |
| Tsaan suankan | Means to think well about, love, like, and feel good about. |
| Tsaidüka | Duckwater Shoshone |
| Tso'o$_1$ | Great-grandmother |
| Tukku kammankan | to care /to cherish/feel for |
| Paa$_3$ | Water |
| Yepani$_1$ | Fall/autumn. |

Glossary of Terms for Ute

| | |
|---|---|
| Aanuruwach(ü) | Newborn |
| Asti'i | To love or to care for someone. |
| Chichigavach(i) | Strong |
| Máykh | Hello |
| Namich(i) | Younger Sister |
| Nuucic | Ute people in Southern Ute dialect |
| Nuunu'agaat(ü) | Ute people in Ute Mountain dialect |
| Önöönik(i) | Fresh Start |
| Paa | Water |
| Piyan | Mother |
| Tama'riyu | Springtime |
| Tatawayvin | Father-in-law |
| Tach(a) | Summer |
| Tòmo | Winter |
| Tuwach(i) | Son |
| Yaachin | Mother-in-law |

**Competing Interests Declaration** The author has no conflicts of interest to declare that are relevant to the content of this chapter.

# CHAPTER 16

# COVID-19 Memory Dreamscapes

*Shaina A. Nez*

In the wake of a global pandemic, I remember dreaming about skeletons, bones, and its hollow emptiness. I remember shimá's first reaction using the word "bááhádzid" to mean danger. This word in the Navajo language can also be transcribed to assume that the real danger is harmless, but you should take extra precautions. Navajo author, Tiana Bighorse, describes wars over land as bááhádzid to mean *don't bother with it…it's just the same as an enemy…it kills people.* Ironically, in that moment, shimá is talking to me while placing silver, tiny teardrop-shaped, bezel, what I like to call thin silver strips with teeth on one end, onto a square silver sheet. Mother is a silversmith carrying a legacy since her maiden name Harvey was once known as a family-owned business in Lukachukai, Arizona. Mother was making cluster-styled rings, as she placed the last teardrop bezel onto the plate, it looked like a skeleton too. Picture a cluster-styled ring with no stones inside the hollow spaces.

When Gallup's closure and stay-at-home order was issued, I was living in Mentmore, New Mexico, a couple of miles to the west of that city. During this time, I was facing a custody battle and it felt like the end of my world was closing in. This fear frightened me more than the thoughts of

S. A. Nez (✉)
Diné College, Shiprock, NM, USA
e-mail: shainez@dinecollege.edu

© The Author(s), under exclusive license to Springer Nature Switzerland AG 2024
F. King, W. Davies (eds.), *COVID-19 in Indian Country*,
https://doi.org/10.1007/978-3-031-70184-9_16

my demise from the pandemic. Though I was behind closed doors, I felt exposed still and alone in the world of single motherhood. To keep my mind preoccupied, I tried celebrating the fact that I earned an MFA in Creative Nonfiction from the Institute of American Indian Arts. But even that particular accomplishment already seemed so far away and the virtual space only ever made me feel happy-go-lucky. My future didn't appear to be clear to me. While my graduating peers were celebrating their first book deals and querying literary agents, I was more worried about my child custody case. Hailee was with her dad in Colorado, and her traveling to see him bi-weekly wasn't my preferred choice given that the pandemic threatened her safety. Before sunset, I remember Googling, searching basic dream interpretations about skeletons. They told me if a skeleton was hiding in my dream that my unbearable truths may soon come out or that I'm deliberately cutting off my true feelings and talents in real life.

I take that back, I tried living in the present tense at the time and honing in my literary aesthetic as best as I could. To rid myself of the icky feelings of the child custody case, I went back to my inner child at age ten re-learning my relationship with nahasdzáán shimá. My first relationship was with the land, and they encouraged me to run. Before dawn, shizhé'é would wake me up to run with him. Father was a former state champion in basketball and at the time I wanted to be just like him: attend Holbrook High School, stay at Tiis Yaa Kin residential hall, and run cross-country and play basketball. Which I did, but after graduating high school and experiencing college, running became secondary since I was of age to smoke tobacco and club-hop on weekends. I let the social scene take over in my undergraduate years, but I still would run miles on the treadmill or up hiking trails in Durango greeting Dibé Nitsaa. Running kept me accountable as an individual, there were no excuses, and I couldn't manipulate the time, pace, or endurance. I remember coughing up and squeezing the sides of my abdomen—this gesture reminded me of a childhood friend who became the fastest cross-country runner on our team and the sweetest soul. We were in the same grade, played the same sports, and became sisters for life—I often wondered about her, where she was, and whether she gave up the street life for good. But I wish I was more firm with her as a sister should be. I wish I could have told her to come with me to Holbrook High School; that we could start anew but the Chinle desert was her sanctuary. On mile three, I was on the opposite side of Mentmore and while I ran alongside the road, I was greeted by reservation pups and brown men who thought it was wise to try and stop me. I carried rocks and pepper spray with me dare I say waiting for another face to try and test me. The land told me to restructure my life and to honor my intellectual abilities by being conscious and giving myself grace. The land also told me to start a reconnection with relatives on my journey of life, the lifeline of Sa'ah Naaghai Bik'eh Hozhóón.

While the Black Lives Matter movement continued to fight for justice for George Floyd Jr., I thought about him in a unified, relational aspect. George Floyd Jr. was an African American man who was murdered while in police custody in Minneapolis, Minnesota, on May 25, 2020. "I can't breathe," echoes on the television and phone screens everywhere, and I'm reminded of the simplest epitome of breath. In this moment, I paused my anxieties about the child custody case, my writing life, and my future. This man's life mattered—if all of the world could've paused with me, we would understand relationality and autonomy. In this space, his memory lives on. In this space, I'm reminded of the continuing injustices against African Americans in the United States.

My dreams about skeletons continued.

One day I received a notification via Submittable that I was a finalist for the 2020 Eliza So Fellowship for my submission, *Sun Child*. During my MFA, I wrote letters to my daughter as I was navigating single motherhood. At the time, I was adamant about writing as a way to remember our own familial teachings and values from both maternal and paternal sides. I remember instilling my own fears of not knowing enough language, culture, and history, that I must prioritize Hailee's curriculum at home with the help of her grandparents. Unfortunately, she will only know them and not her Nalis. Her dad reassured me that she will learn about her nali asdzáán's last moments in Ignacio, Colorado, to get in proper touch with her bilagáana side, but she will never know nali hastiin who lives in Maricopa County. In *Sun Child*, I opened with her creation story in Albuquerque, New Mexico. In this chapter, I'm honoring my mother and oldest sister who stayed by my side during the birth. I'm honoring the moment I endured a C-section and when a hospital intern fainted at the scene. I later write about the importance of prayer and when I learned to pray for myself as a sign of embracing my soon-to-be maternal power. These words carried me into understanding power, autonomy, and human agency. When I applied to the MFA, I did so because shicheii came to me in a dream visiting Hailee's crib-side and pronouncing my name loud enough for me to wake up and wish to see his smiling face again. I grieve and continue to grieve, though it's not the Diné way, as a reminder of my rejected and denied agency as his granddaughter.

When shimá and shizhe'é finish the cluster-styled rings, I take one and slip it across my pointer finger examining its perfection. The sleeping beauty turquoise now fills in the hollow spaces with breaths of life. None of us contract COVID, but in the next year I will soon be quarantined in Farmington, New Mexico, during Super Bowl LV. I'm not going to mention how many hearts we buried that year, but I will give them space here:

With this time, the land told me to re-center my stories; that I was the storyteller and should give my truth some grace. My stories have been neglected since the day I graduated with my MFA, one thousand and three-hundred and seventy-eight days and maybe even longer, I abandoned them. I often heard the phrase 'to surrender on the page, bleed on the page,' but yet I couldn't bring myself to hear, see, feel, taste, or touch my own stories. I began absorbing all the pain, grief, and turmoil during COVID. These feelings were drowning, and I had to create a boundary in order to keep them above water. My heart once linked to tó and I counted about how many of us roamed this Earth aimlessly looking for thirst. Thirst pinned me down in euphoria telling me to take some more and that I would be okay. I'd open my mouth just enough for it to enter my senses and periphery. My pain could be felt in my neck hump. I don't have the best posture, my height not being too short or tall, and I could never stand up straight enough. I link the millions of stories I've ever heard and place the weight of it on my neck hump indicating I'm a Navajo woman who didn't have a Kinaałda ceremony. I'm a Navajo woman who didn't have her hair tied properly in a Navajo bun, and I'm a woman who didn't wear jewelry naturally even if my mother was a silversmith. These intrusive thoughts live in the space between my strength, wisdom, and future womb. When I stand up straight now, the neck hump disappears, and I wake from a decade-old loop of nostalgia and self-criticism.

My grief trickles downstream along the Chuska Mountains. In undergrad, I longed for a sense of home that I no longer have back in Lukachukai; I started to feel like an outsider the longer I was away in school. I thought about how the universe tends to deal a hand of cards and hope that I don't carry an ace with me. This rabbit hole of grief once surrendered my chances of living in the present tense, but I continue to honor my ancestors even when my therapist told me I might be diagnosed with bereavement. My turmoil once could not be contained; it was a version of a Navajo story about when First Man and First Woman discovered puss, lice, and poverty that live among the beauty. When I centered hopelessness, I knew that I needed to revisit the foundational stories that kept me alive in the present tense. I remember during the MFA, my residency leader told me to pick a tense and stay with it throughout the piece, but at the time I didn't know that I was still living in-between the present and past tenses. My hollow space needed rekindling in this COVID-19 memory dreamscape.

**Competing Interests Declaration** The author has no conflicts of interest to declare that are relevant to the content of this chapter.

CHAPTER 17

# Conclusion

*Farina King and Wade Davies*

COVID-19 has disproportionately affected Native Americans since the silent intruder broke the confines of Indian Country. Swiftly, the virus infiltrated gatherings, churches, flea markets, ceremonies, and especially family living spaces. Why Indigenous peoples were affected by the virus to such an extreme can be narrowed down to colonialism, and for Indigenous peoples throughout generations, remembering serves as an act of resistance. This work highlights inequities, preexisting challenges, legacies of history, failures of trust and responsibility, and problems communicating and coordinating with the federal government, states, localities, and tribal nations. These are all themes Tanana, Towersap, and Frazee underscore in their respective chapters.

COVID-19 caused the deaths of people from all walks of life, but especially those experiencing comorbidities, and particularly Elders. Native Elders are the culture bearers and language keepers as they preserve

F. King
The University of Oklahoma, Norman, OK, USA
e-mail: farinaking@ou.edu

W. Davies (✉)
The University of Montana, Missoula, MT, USA
e-mail: wade.davies@mso.umt.edu

heritage and impart wisdom they received from their ancestors to future generations. On the ground, Native Nations, as well as Native American programs at local schools and universities, have compensated, as best they can, for the gaps in knowledge left by the devastating loss of Native Elders to the pandemic, including by expanding preexisting Indigenous language programs.

For over 20 years, the University of Oklahoma's (OU) Sam Noble Museum has sponsored the Oklahoma Native American Youth Language Fair (ONAYLF), which was initiated and has been sustained by a critical mass of Native American language first-speakers from several communities of the thirty-nine Native Nations in Oklahoma. ONAYLF has become one of the largest Native American language fairs in the world with over a thousand participants from throughout Oklahoma and Indian Country. Many of the language first-speakers are Elders, such as Geneva Woomavoyah Navarro (Comanche) and Quinton Roman Nose (Cheyenne), who have supported the fair for years along with assuming significant roles in their communities and Native Nations as educators, as well as culture and knowledge carriers.

In 2023, OU dedicated the Native Language Fair Honor Fund to the many Elders who made the fair possible, specifically acknowledging those who had died from COVID-19-related causes. Fund organizers shared images of photos, names, and tribal affiliations of those pandemic victims who were first-language speakers. These Elders came from many different Native Nations, and some had been among their people's few remaining fluent speakers. Much of their knowledge was irreplaceable, but many Native Nations of Oklahoma and their relatives throughout Native America are nevertheless fighting to sustain and save their languages. They believe that their very identity and existence as Native people depend on their languages and the knowledge embedded in them. In a September 2023 press release from ONAYLF's new endowment fund, Jason Salsman (Muscogee/Creek) emphasized these points: "It's knowledge that absolutely can't be found anywhere else on earth. ... You can scour the globe. And it's specific to this area and this culture. So to lose that is devastating."[1]

---

[1] Jason Salsman cited in press release, "New endowment fund established to support preservation of Native American languages," September 14, 2023, accessed online May 29, 2024 via *Native Oklahoma Magazine*, https://www.nativeoklahoma.us/new-endowment-fund-established-to-support-preservation-of-native-american-languages/

17 CONCLUSION    289

The ONAYLF and Native American language and education programs rely on community Elders who are the most respected teachers and leaders. The endowment fund seeks to support the resilience of Native American communities and remember beloved ones lost during one of the darkest moments in recent history. Most importantly, the fair and language revitalization work continue the legacy of what first-language speaker Elders stood for, reminding people as Abigail Echo-Hawk did with her healing dress made from body bags that hope heals. First language-speakers like Cherokee educator Durbin Feeling hoped for a day when their posterity would learn and speak their Indigenous languages. Feeling's hope lives on with the opening of the Durbin Feeling Language Center named in his honor in Tahlequah, Cherokee Nation, in 2022, and the reauthorization of the Durbin Feeling Language Preservation Act in 2024.[2]

This edited volume has shared stories of despair and hardship as well as stories that speak to Native Americans' unwavering hope during and after the COVID-19 pandemic. An overreaching theme throughout the work has been inspired by Gerald Vizenor's survivance theory, which posits that Indigenous people have persisted in the face of colonial oppression; that they are not solely victims of colonizers but rather have played active roles in historical narratives. These authors have demonstrated the many ways that Native Americans have maintained this determined presence in the face of this recent threat to their existence, whether by working to maintain the vitality of their languages or otherwise promote their people's physical, mental, social, and cultural wellbeing.

Among the silver linings Native Americans grasped hold of amid the tragedy and chaos, the COVID-19 pandemic prompted a digital revolution wherein billions of dollars from government and private industries were redirected to promote digital technologies. From telehealth to e-commerce, the pandemic changed the way many people connected, and

---

[2] Chuck Hoskin, Jr., "Durbin Feeling Language Center Starts a New Chapter in Cherokee Language Revitalization," November 20, 2022, accessed online May 30, 2024, https://nativenewsonline.net/opinion/durbin-feeling-language-center-starts-a-new-chapter-in-cherokee-language-revitalization; and Lindsey Bark, "CN reauthorizes Durbin Feeling Language Preservation Act," *Cherokee Phoenix*, January 26, 2024, accessed online May 29, 2024, https://www.cherokeephoenix.org/news/cn-reauthorizes-durbin-feeling-language-preservation-act/article_8473a2ec-bbcc-11ee-a891-e3c85df28315.html

Native Americans were no exception. Platforms like Zoom, Microsoft Teams, Slack, as well as e-learning platforms, and streaming services like Netflix and Disney+ expanded services available to Native communities, providing them powerful new tools for communicating, learning, and celebrating their languages and cultural ways. Since the pandemic, Disney+ has expanded its services to include the Diné bizaad (Navajo language) dubs of *Finding Nemo* and *Star Wars: A New Hope*. In 2022, the streaming service also announced it would offer an Arapaho dub for *Bambi*. *Prey*, an installment of the *Predator* franchise that was dubbed entirely in Comanche, became available on Hulu. Many Native Americans were taken by surprise when Disney+ announced that most of an episode, "What If… Kahhori Reshaped the World?" of the *What If* series, was written in the Mohawk language with Akwesasne Mohawk consultants such as Doug George-Kanentiio.[3] Instead of having a program dubbed from English to a Native American language, Season 2, Episode 6 was written in a Native American language and dubbed into English, among other languages.

Online platforms like the First Nations Development Institute's Native Language Immersion Initiative, Indigenous Language Institute, as well as different YouTube Channels have increased their offerings for Indigenous language learning. Zoom, which was not well-known prior to the pandemic, has become more than just a way for students to learn and attend lectures, or for conducting business meetings. It continues to be used now as a means to connect Indigenous language speakers and learners across Native America, and promises to continue serving this function into the future. The COVID-19 pandemic like previous waves of attack on Indigenous peoplehood and existence sparked Indigenous ingenuity, often called "Indigenuity."[4] Multiple authors in Part III of this volume speak to the power of "Indigenuity" in the ways that many, though certainly not all, educators and students successfully adapted to distance technologies in order to continue learning and connecting, including through innovations like virtual talking circles.

---

[3] Ava Pukatch, "Season 2 of Marvel's 'What if…?' includes episode mostly in Mohawk language," *All Things Considered*, NPR, December 28, 2023, accessed online May 30, 2024, https://www.npr.org/2023/12/27/1221890957/season-2-of-marvels-what-if-includes-episode-mostly-in-mohawk-language

[4] See, for example, Caroline Wigginton, *Indigenuity: Native Craftwork and the Art of American Literatures* (Chapel Hill: University of North Carolina Press, 2022).

As the COVID-19 pandemic wreaked havoc, Indigenous peoples demonstrated both survivance and "Indigenuity" in other ways as well, thereby discovering other silver linings. Amid the fears, losses, and profound dislocations, they carved out spaces to heal and to create. Both Ami and Healey write about the power of art and poetry as therapy, and the innovative ways Indigenous peoples channeled the power of creativity to heal themselves as artists and communicate messages of healing and hope to their broader communities.

Narratives from this work also reveal ways Native peoples maintained existing communities and forged new ones during the pandemic. Native Nations experienced kindness and empathy in the way of community support from both Native and non-Native entities. They relied on government aid, "sense of belonging" care packages, and other programs and innovations, which mitigated the effects of the virus. Several chapters refer to the significance of families and communities in individual health and wellness. Nez, Tsosie-Paddock, Tippeconnic Fox, and Winder similarly address motherhood, and the vital roles mothers and women have played as protectors and healers despite the overwhelming challenges they faced.

This work not only places the pandemic in historical context, but also helps readers comprehend the gravity of this moment, and how it was felt by Indigenous peoples who experienced it in real time—these authors included. All these contributors hope to help future generations better understand the context in which people made tough choices and did what they thought best for themselves and their communities. We hope that this knowledge will contribute to systemic changes and improved strategies so that this kind of disaster will not disproportionately target Indigenous peoples again in the future.

For all that this volume offers as a source for understanding this moment and plotting a better course forward, meeting these objectives must also depend on other scholars, now and in the future, providing vantage points we have not or cannot offer. These should include studies focusing on other Indigenous communities from throughout the Americas and overseas, not as well represented here, and how their pandemic stories may correlate or contrast with those told in this volume.

We have emphasized the value of studies in the moment (or near the moment) but further scholarship five, ten, or more years in the future will be revealing in other ways. Benefitting from hindsight and additional data, these scholars will inevitably evaluate federal, state, tribal, and local responses to COVID-19 quite differently than have we. They will assess which public health measures and medical services proved most effective and what social, physiological, and economic costs these may have incurred for Native communities and individuals, weighed against the benefits gained. Future scholars will also assess whether emergency federal measures to meet the moment through injections of funding for the IHS and improved access to clean water will break the pattern of the past or, yet again, prove fleeting and inadequate.

In lieu of waning media attention, these studies will also help maintain public focus on the chronic inequities that enflamed this pandemic across Indian Country, lest a lost sense of urgency translate, again, into apathy. Future studies must also evaluate the long-term returns on the innovative practices described in this volume, through which Indigenous peoples maintained communities, languages, artistry, and learning. Will all these innovative measures prove ephemeral as well or translate into orthodox strategies for sustaining the wellbeing of Native communities—as standard tools of survivance? What too, will be the long-term effects of this pandemic for the IHS, as well as on the nature and vitality of tribal-administered healthcare and the ways tribal governments advocate for their peoples in times of crisis? How may it continue influencing ways people will teach and learn both traditionally in-person and aided by evolving technologies? What will be the long-term consequences for people's mental and spiritual wellbeing as the traumas wrought by this pandemic ripple through time?

An Assiniboine Elder, Lawrence Wetsit, of the Fort Peck Assiniboine and Sioux Tribes noticed how his Native Nation "lost one person a day on average" to COVID-19 between October and November 2020. Because many of the deaths were Elders, Wetsit explains looking back, it was "like taking a number of pages of their [people's] textbook and ripping it out and throwing it away."[5] Wetsit reminds everyone that Indigenous cultural teachings and languages have and will continue to instill hope "that things will get better." Considering the innovations and technologies during the pandemic, especially with Native American language practice and preservation, Wetsit senses how "our people realize that our culture can be

---

[5] Lawrence Wetsit cited in Sara Reardon, "Native American Use Technology to Keep Traditions, Language Alive During Pandemic," *KFF Health News*, February 9, 2021, accessed online May 30, 2024, https://kffhealthnews.org/news/article/native-americans-use-technology-to-keep-traditions-language-alive-during-pandemic/

changed a little bit without great harm."[6] As all the contributors of this volume have witnessed and can attest, we remember, and still experience deeply, the sorrow, pain, and loss of the COVID-19 pandemic that affected Native Americans at disproportionate rates. But so too have we witnessed the strengths Indigenous people have drawn from their ancestors and relatives to persevere in hopes for the future and cycles of healing yet to come.

[6] Wetsit cited.

# Bibliography

25 U.S.C. § 1601.
207 U.S. 564 (1908).
Adams, David Wallace. *Education for Extinction: American Indians and the Boarding School Experience, 1875–1928*. Lawrence: University Press of Kansas, 1995.
Adams, Mikaëla M. "#COVIDintheSouth: Social Distancing in the Age of Assimilation: The Influenza Pandemic of 1918–1920 in Indian Country." The Center for the Study of the American South, University of North Carolina, Chapel Hill. April 16, 2020. accessed online, https://south.unc.edu/2020/04/16/covidinthesouth-social-distancing-in-the-age-of-assimilation/.
Agostinone-Wilson, Faith. *Marxism and Education Beyond Identity: Sexuality and Schooling*, 1st ed. New York: Palgrave Macmillan, 2010.
Ahmad, Farida B., Jodi A. Ciseski, Jiaquan Xu, and Robert N. Anderson. "COVID-19 Mortality Update—United States, 2022." *CDC Morbidity and Mortality Weekly Report*, accessed online January 8, 2024, https://www.cdc.gov/mmwr/volumes/72/wr/pdfs/mm7218a4-H.pdf.
Allen, Jeff. "Examining the COVID-19 Pandemic's Impacts on Native American Students' College and Career Readiness. ACT Research. Technical Brief." *ACT, Inc.* (2022).
Allen-Charmley, McKenzie. "Native American College Students Found Strength in Their Heritage That Helped Them Get through the Pandemic." CNBC, last modified August 11, 2021, https://www.cnbc.com/2021/08/11/native-american-students-found-strength-in-their-heritage-during-covid.html.

Altamirano-Jiménez, Isabel, and Nathalie Kermoal. "Introduction," In *Living on the Land: Indigenous Women's Understanding of Place*, eds. Nathalie Kermoal and Isabel Altamirano-Jiménez, 3–18. Edmonton, AB: Athabasca University Press, 2016.

Alvord, Lori Arviso, and Elizabeth Cohen Van Pelt. *The Scalpel and the Silver Bear: The First Navajo Woman Surgeon Combines Western Medicine and Traditional Healing*. New York: Bantam Books, 2000.

Anderson, Kim. *Life Stages and Native Women: Memory, Teachings, and Story Medicine*. Winnipeg, MB: University of Manitoba Press, 2011.

Anderson, Kim "Giving Life to the People: An Indigenous Ideology of Motherhood," In *Maternal Theory: Essential Readings*, ed. Andrea O'Reilly, 761–81. Bradford, Ontario: Demeter Press, 2007.

Arias, Elizabeth, et al. *Provisional Life Expectancy Estimates for 2021*, Vital Statistics Surveillance Report. 2022, accessed online, https://www.cdc.gov/nchs/data/vsrr/vsrr023.pdf.

Aristovnik, Aleksander, Damijana Keržič, Dejan Ravšelj, Nina Tomaževič, and Lan Umek. "Impacts of the COVID-19 pandemic on life of higher education students: A global perspective." *Sustainability* 12, no. 20 (2020): 8438.

*Arizona v. California*, 373 U.S. 546, 598 (1963).

*Arizona et al. v. Navajo Nation et al.*, no. 21–1484, slip op. (S. Ct. Jun. 22, 2023).

Armenski, Tanji, et al. "StatCan COVID-19: Data to Insights for a Better Canada Crossing the Border during the Pandemic: 2020 Review." Statistics Canada, accessed 2 May 2023, https://www150.statcan.gc.ca/n1/pub/45-28-0001/2021001/article/00007-eng.htm.

Arrazola, Jessica, Matthew M. Masiello, Sujata Joshi S, et al. "*COVID-19 Mortality Among American Indian and Alaska Native Persons — 14 States, January–June 2020.*" *Morbidity and Mortality Weekly Report* 69, no. 49 (2020):1853–1856.

Arrington, Leonard J. "The Influenza Epidemic of 1918–1919 in Southern Idaho." *Idaho Yesterdays* 32, no. 3 (September 1988): 19–29.

Artiga, Samantha, and Kendal Orgera. "COVID-19 Presents Significant Risks for American Indian and Alaska Native People." *Kaiser Family Foundation*, May 14, 2020, accessed August 1, 2023, https://www.kff.org/coronavirus-covid-19/issue-brief/covid-19-presents-significant-risks-for-american-indian-and-alaska-native-people/.

Associated Press. "U.S. report identifies burial sites linked to boarding schools for Native Americans," accessed September 2, 2023, https://www.npr.org/2022/05/11/1098276649/u-s-report-details-burial-sites-linked-to-boarding-schools-for-native-americans.

Atkins, Liz, and Vicky Duckworth, eds. *Research Methods for Social Justice and Equity in Education*. Cham, Switzerland: Palgrave Macmillan, 2019.

Baird, Jennifer, and Claire Taylor, eds. *Ancient Graffiti in Context*, Vol. 2. Routledge, 2010.

Baird, Jennifer A., and Claire Taylor. "Ancient Graffiti." In *Routledge handbook of graffiti and street art*, Routledge, 2016.

Balingit, Moriah. "Investigation Finds Burial Sites at 53 Federal Indian Boarding Schools," accessed August 30, 2023, https://www.washingtonpost.com/education/2022/05/12/federal-indian-boarding-schools-remains/.

Bark, Lindsey. "CN reauthorizes Durbin Feeling Language Preservation Act." *Cherokee Phoenix*, January 26, 2024, accessed online May 29, 2024, https://www.cherokeephoenix.org/news/cn-reauthorizes-durbin-feeling-language-preservation-act/article_8473a2ec-bbcc-11ee-a891-e3c85df28315.html.

Barkaskas, Patricia, and Derek Gladwin. "Pedagogical Talking Circles: Decolonizing Education through Relational Indigenous Frameworks." *Journal of Teaching and Learning* 15, no. 1 (2021): 20–38.

Barnett, Rebecca. Interview by Midge Dellinger, October 30, 2021, Tulsa, Oklahoma, transcript, *A Twenty-First Century Pandemic in Indian Country: The Resilience of the Muscogee (Creek) Nation Against COVID-19*, Muscogee (Creek) Nation National Library and Archives, https://mvskokenationallibraryarchive.org/digital-heritage/rebecca-barnett-interview.

Barry, John. *The Great Influenza: The Story of the Deadliest Pandemic in History*. Penguin Books: New York. 2005.

Beall, M.H., J.P.H.M. van den Wijngaard, M.J.C. van Gemert, and M.G. Ross. "Amniotic Fluid Water Dynamics." *Placenta* 28, no. 8–9 (2007): 816–23.

Beaver, Second Chief Del. Interview by Midge Dellinger, June 6, 2022, Okmulgee, Oklahoma, transcript, *A Twenty-First Century Pandemic in Indian Country: The Resilience of the Muscogee (Creek) Nation Against COVID-19*, Muscogee (Creek) Nation National Library and Archives, https://mvskokenationallibraryarchive.org/digital-heritage/second-chief-del-beaver-interview.

Beckstein, Amoneeta. How Indigenous Peoples of North America Are Coping with Covid-19, last modified October 6, 2020, https://www.psychreg.org/indigenous-peoples-of-north-america-covid-19/.

Belcourt-Dittloff, Annjeanette E. "Resiliency and risk in Native American communities: A culturally informed investigation." PhD dissertation, University of Montana, 2007.

Ben, Cyrus cited in Martha Hostetter and Sarah Klein. "Learning from Pandemic Responses Across Indian Country," September 30, 2020, *Advancing Health Equity*, The Commonwealth Fund, accessed online January 31, 2024, https://www.commonwealthfund.org/publications/2020/sep/learning-pandemic-responses-across-indian-country.

Bennett, Sukee. "American Indians have the highest Covid vaccination rate in the US." *Nova*, July 6, 2021, accessed online January 8, 2024, https://www.pbs.org/wgbh/nova/article/native-americans-highest-covid-vaccination-rate-us/.

Berger, Brigitte. *The Family in the Modern Age: More Than a Lifestyle Choice,* 1st ed. New Brunswick, NJ: Transaction Publishers, 2002.

Bergman, Christopher, in discussion with Chelsea M. Mead, May 2021.
Blake, Justin and Sarah Deer. *Introduction to Tribal Legal Studies*. Lanham, MD: AltaMira Press, 2010.
Blume, Arthur W. *A new psychology based on community, equality, and care of the earth: An indigenous American perspective*. Bloomsbury Publishing USA, 2020.
Blume, Arthur W. *Colonialism and the COVID-19 Pandemic*. Springer International Publishing, 2022.
Boserup, Brad, Mark McKenney, and Adel Elkbuli. "Alarming Trends in US Domestic Violence During the COVID-19 Pandemic." *The American Journal of Emergency Medicine* 38 no. 12 (2020): 2753–55.
Boyd, Amanda D. and Dedra Buchwald. "Factors That Influence Risk Perceptions and Successful COVID-19 Vaccination Communication Campaigns with American Indians." *Science Communication* 44, no. 1 (February 2022): 130–139.
Brady, Benjamin R. and Howard M. Bahr. "The Influenza Epidemic of 1918–1920 among the Navajos: Marginality, Morality, and the Implications of Some Neglected Eyewitness Accounts." *The American Indian Quarterly* 38, no. 4 (Fall 2014): 459–91.
Branden, Karen, in discussion with Chelsea M. Mead, May 2022.
Brown, Jeremy. *Influenza: The Hundred-Year Hunt to Cure the Deadliest Disease in History*. Simon & Schuster: New York. 2018
Bureau of Indian Affairs. *Federal Indian Boarding School Initiative Investigative Report* 21 (citing S. Rep. No. 91–501, at 143 (1969)).
Burki, Talha. "COVID-19 among American Indians and Alaska Natives." *The Lancet Infectious Diseases* 21, no. 3 (2021): 325–26.
Burnette, Jeffrey D. "Inequality in the Labor Market for Native American Women and the Great Recession." *The American Economic Review* 107, no. 5 (2017): 425–29.
Butler, RaeLynn. Interview by Midge Dellinger, April 17, 2021, Tulsa, Oklahoma, transcript, *A Twenty-First Century Pandemic in Indian Country: The Resilience of the Muscogee (Creek) Nation Against COVID-19*, Muscogee (Creek) Nation National Library and Archives Oral History Collection, https://mvskokenationallibraryarchive.org/digital-heritage/raelynn-butler-interview.
Cahill, Cathleen D. *Federal fathers & mothers: A social history of the United States Indian Service, 1869–1933*. Chapel Hill: University of North Carolina Press.
Cajete, Gregory. *Indigenous Community: Rekindling the Teachings of the Seventh Fire*. St. Paul, MN: Living Justice Press, 2015.
Cajete, Gregory. *Look to the Mountain: An Ecology of Indigenous Education*. Durango, CO: Kivakí Press, 1994.
Calhoun, Lawrence G., Arnie Cann, Richard G. Tedeschi, and Jamie McMillan. "A Correlational Test of the Relationship between Posttraumatic Growth,

Religion, and Cognitive Processing." *Journal of Traumatic Stress* 13, no. 3 (2000): 521–527.

Calloway, Colin. *The Indian History of an American Institution: Native Americans and Dartmouth.* Dartmouth College Press: Hanover, NH.

Cameron, Catherine M., Paul Kelton, and Alan C. Swedlund, eds. *Beyond Germs: Native Depopulation in North America.* Tucson: University of Arizona Press, 2015.

Castleman, Craig. "The Politics of Graffiti." In *That's the Joint!: the Hip-Hop Studies Reader.* 2. ed., edited by Mark Anthony Neal, Murray Forman, and Michael Eric Dyson, 13–22. New York: Routledge, 2012.

CDC. "Health Disparities in HIV, Viral Hepatitis, STDs, and TB." accessed online January 8, 2024, https://www.cdc.gov/nchhstp/healthdisparities/american-indians.html.

CDC. "Hospitalization, and Death by Race/Ethnicity," accessed online https://www.cdc.gov/coronavirus/2019-ncov/covid-data/investigations-discovery/hospitalization-death-by-race-ethnicity.html.

"CDC Data Shows Disproportionate Covid-19 Impact in American Indian/Alaskan Native Populations," Centers for Disease Control and Prevention, last reviewed August 19, 2020, https://www.cdc.gov/media/releases/2020/p0819-covid-19-impact-american-indian-alaska-native.html/.

"CDC Museum Covid-19 Timeline," Centers for Disease Control and Prevention: David J. Sencer CDC Museum, last reviewed, March 15, 2023, https://www.cdc.gov/museum/timeline/covid19.html#:~:text=March%2011%2C%20 2020,declares%20COVID%2D19%20a%20pandemic.

Chalfant's, Henry documentary *Style Wars* (1983).

Chatterjee, Rhitu. "Hit Hard by Covid, Native Americans Come Together to Protect Families and Elders." *NPR*, November 24, 2021, https://www.npr.org/sections/health-shots/2021/11/24/1058675230/hit-hard-by-covid-native-americans-come-together-to-protect-families-and-elders.

Chew, Kari A.B. "#KeepOurLanguagesStrong: Indigenous Language Revitalization on Social Media during the Early Covid-19 Pandemic." *Language Documentation & Conservation* 15, (2021): 239–266.

Chew, Kari A.B., et al., "Persistence in Indigenous Language work during the COVID-19 pandemic," *AlterNative* 18, no. 4 (December 2022): 594–604.

Chilisa, Bagele. *Indigenous Research Methodologies.* Thousand Oaks, Calif.: SAGE Publications, 2012.

Chrikov, Igor, Krista M. Soria, Bonnie Horgos, and Daniel Jones-White. "Undergraduate and graduate students' mental health during the COVID-19 pandemic," *UC Berkeley: Center for Studies in Higher Education*, (2020), accessed online, https://escholarship.org/uc/item/80k5d5hw.

cmaadmin (EDU). "The Digital Divide for Tribal College Students – COVID, Cares Act, and Critical next Steps." Diverse, last modified November 14, 2022, https://www.diverseeducation.com/podcasts/podcast/15108265/the-digital-divide-for-tribal-college-students-covid-cares-act-and-critical-next-steps.

Cohen's Handbook of Federal Indian Law, chapter 1 (2012).

Cooper, Martha, and Henry Chalfant. *Subway Art*, 1st American ed. New York: Holt, Rinehart and Winston, 1984.

Correia, Kelly M., et al. "Education Racial and Gender Disparities in Covid-19 Worry, Stress, and Food Insecurities across Undergraduate Biology Students at a Southeastern University." *Journal of Microbiology & Biology Education* 23, no. 1 (2022), https://doi.org/10.1128/jmbe.00224-21.

Cothran, Boyd. *Remembering the Modoc War: Redemptive Violence and the Making of American Innocence*. Chapel Hill: University of North Carolina Press, 2014.

"COVID Hospitalization Rate for Indigenous Minnesotans 6 Times Higher Than White Residents," CBS Minneapolis (WCCO), October 15, 2020, https://www.cbsnews.com/minnesota/news/covid-hospitalization-rate-for-indigenous-minnesotans-6-times-higher-than-white-residents/.

Crepelle, Adam. "Tribes, Vaccines, and COVID-19: A Look at Tribal Responses to the Pandemic." *Fordham Urban Law Journal* 49, no. 1 (2021): 31–64.

Crosby, Alfred. *America's Forgotten Pandemic: The Influenza of 1918*. Cambridge University Press: New York. 1989.

Daniels, Lia M., Lauren D. Goegan, and Patti C. Parker. "The impact of COVID-19 triggered changes to instruction and assessment on university students' self-reported motivation, engagement and perceptions." *Social Psychology of Education* 24, no. 1 (2021): 299–318.

Davies, Wade. *Healing Ways: Navajo Health Care in the Twentieth Century*. Albuquerque: University of New Mexico Press, 2001.

DeJong, David H. *"If You Knew the Conditions": A Chronicle of the Indian Medical Service and American Indian Health Care, 1908–1955*. Lanham, MD: Lexington Books, 2008.

Dellinger, Linda. Interview by Midge Dellinger, January 27, 2021, Tulsa, Oklahoma, transcript, *A Twenty-First Century Pandemic in Indian Country: The Resilience of the Muscogee (Creek) Nation Against COVID-19*, Muscogee (Creek) Nation National Library and Archives Oral History Collection, https://mvskokenationallibraryarchive.org/digital-heritage/linda-dellinger-interview.

de Leeuw, Sarah, et al. "With Reserves: Colonial Geographies and First Nations Health" *Annals of the Association of American Geographers* 102, no. 5 (2012): 904–11, https://doi.org/10.1080/00045608.2012.674897.

Deloria, Vine Jr., and Daniel R. Wildcat. *Power and Place: Indian Education in America*. Fulcrum Resources, 2001.

Denetclaw, Pauly. "Final COVID restrictions lifted on Navajo Nation," *Indian Country Today*, May 9, 2023, accessed online January 31, 2024, https://www.nhonews.com/news/2023/may/09/final-covid-restrictions-lifted-navajo-nation/.

Denetclaw, Wilfred F., Zara K. Otto, Samantha Christie, Estrella Allen, Maria Cruz, Kassandra A. Potter, and Kala M. Mehta. "Diné Navajo Resilience to the COVID-19 Pandemic." *PloS one* 17, no. 8 (August 2022), accessed online, https://doi.org/10.1371/journal.pone.0272089.

Derkas, Erika. "Disrupting Native Invisibility, Dismantling Settler Colonial Racism and Enhancing Educational Outcomes for Indigenous Students." *The COVID-19 Crisis and Racial Justice & Equity: Addressing the Twin Pandemics* special issue, *Journal of Higher Education Management* 36, no. 1 (2021): 82–92.

Diacon, Johnnie. Interview by Midge Dellinger, March 17, 2022, Tulsa, Oklahoma, transcript, *A Twenty-First Century Pandemic in Indian Country: The Resilience of the Muscogee (Creek) Nation Against COVID-19*, Muscogee (Creek) Nation National Library and Archives, https://mvskokenationallibraryarchive.org/digital-heritage/johnnie-diacon.

DigDeep: Navajo Water Project. "About the Project," accessed online, https://www.navajowaterproject.org/project-specifics.

Diné College Libraries, *Navajo Cultural Arts Program: Conversation Series*, https://lib.dinecollege.edu/NCAP/Conversation-Series.

Dowd, Gregory Evans. *Groundless: Rumors, Legends, and Hoaxes on the Early American Frontier.* Baltimore: Johns Hopkins, 2015.

Draper, Teddy, Jr. "T'áá awołí bee: Navajo Contemporary Arts Lecture Series – Teddy Draper, Jr. (Navajo Silversmith and Painter)," Navajo Cultural Arts Program. April 7, 2021, lecture video, 48:34, https://youtu.be/c8F6lawjCcE.

Drew, John Oti. "Preliminary Report of the Peabody Museum Awatovi Expedition of 1937." *American Antiquity* 5, no. 2 (1939): 103–114.

Duran, Eduardo. *Healing the Soul Wound: Counseling with American Indians and Other Native Peoples.* New York: Teachers College Press, 2006.

Dutta, Tapati. "College Student COVID-19 Vaccination Prevalence and Context: A 'Pulse' Survey Conducted Before and After Formal Statewide Rollout," in APHA 2022 Annual Meeting and Expo, APHA (2022, November).

Dutta, Tapati, and Camille Keith. "Evolution of storytelling pedagogy in global health course at a US Native American-Serving Nontribal Institution from Fall 2019 to Spring 2023," *Frontiers in Public Health* 11 (2023).

Dutta, Tapati, et al. "A Qualitative Analysis of Vaccine Decision-Makers' Conceptualization and Fostering of 'Community Engagement' In India." *Journal for Equity in Health* 19, no. 1 (2020): 1–14, https://doi.org/10.21203/rs.3.rs-29175/v4.

Echo-Hawk, Abigail, cited in Cecilia Nowell. "They Asked for PPE and Got Body Bags Instead—She Turned Them Into a Healing Dress." *Vogue*, February 4, 2021, accessed online, https://www.vogue.com/article/body-bag-native-ribbon-dress.

Edmonds, Wendy M. "Snowballing ... #Prayforme: A Qualitative Study Using Snowball Sampling," *Sage Research Methods Cases Part 2*. London: Sage Publications Ltd., 2023, https://doi.org/10.4135/9781526491039.

Ely, Daniell M. and Anne K. Driscoll. "Infant Mortality in the United States: Provisional Data from the 2022 Period Linked Birth/Infant Death Rate." *NVSS Vital Statistics Rapid Release*, no. 33 (November 2023), accessed online January 8, 2024, https://www.cdc.gov/nchs/data/vsrr.vsrr033.pdf.

Emerson, Marc A. and Teresa Montoya. "Confronting Legacies of Structural Racism and Settler Colonialism to Understand COVID-19 Impacts on the Navajo Nation." *American Journal of Public Health* 111, no. 8 (August 2021): 1465–69.

"Eugene Stillday, Sr." *Red Lake Nation News*, December 15, 2020, https://www.redlakenationnews.com/story/2020/12/15/obituaries/eugene-stillday-sr/94448.html.

Faulds, Joseph. "In Memoriam: Mitakuye Oyasin," April 19, 2021, Tahlequah, Oklahoma.

Fenn, Elizabeth A. "Biological Warfare in Eighteenth-Century North America: Beyond Jeffrey Amherst." *The Journal of American History* 86 (March 2000): 1552–1580.

Fife, Jay. Interview by Midge Dellinger, February 21, 2022, Tulsa, Oklahoma, transcript, *A Twenty-First Century Pandemic in Indian Country: The Resilience of the Muscogee (Creek) Nation Against COVID-19*, Muscogee (Creek) Nation National Library and Archives, https://mvskokenationallibraryarchive.org/digital-heritage/jay-fife.

Finley, Laura. "State Crime, Native Americans and Covid-19." *State Crime Journal* 10, no. 1, (2021): 45–60.

Fitzsimmons, Emily D., and Tushar Bajaj. "Embryology, Amniotic Fluid." National Library of Medicine, StatPearls Internet, accessed May 6, 2023, https://www.ncbi.nlm.nih.gov/books/NBK541089/.

Fitzpatrick, Kevin M., Casey Harris, and Grant Drawve. "How bad is it? Suicidality in the middle of the COVID-19 pandemic." *Suicide and Life-Threatening Behavior* 50, no. 6 (2020): 1241–1249.

Fixico, Donald. *Bureau of Indian Affairs*. Landmarks of the American Mosaic. ABC-CLIO, LLC: Santa Barbara, 2012.

Floyd, Chief James. Interview by Midge Dellinger, March 16, 2021, Tulsa, Oklahoma, transcript, *A Twenty-First Century Pandemic in Indian Country: The Resilience of the Muscogee (Creek) Nation Against COVID-19*, Muscogee (Creek) Nation National Library and Archives, https://mvskokenationallibraryarchive.org/digital-heritage/chief-james-floyd-interview.

Fort Bridger Treaty of July 3, 1868. 15 Stat. 673.

Foxworth, Raymond et al. "COVID-19 Vaccination in American Indians and Alaska Natives—Lessons from Effective Community Response." *The New England Journal of Medicine* 385, no. 26 (2021): 2403–06.

Gadarian, Shana Kushner, Sara Wallace Goodman, and Thomas B. Pepinsky. *Pandemic Politics: The Deadly Toll of Partisanship in the Age of COVID*. Princeton, NJ: Princeton University Press, 2022.

Ghebreyesus, Dr. Tedros Adhanom. "WHO Director-General's Opening Remarks at the Media Briefing on Covid-19–11 March 2020." World Health Organization, March 11, 2020, accessed August 28, 2023, https://www.who.int/director-general/speeches/detail/who-director-general-s-opening-remarks-at-the-media-briefing-on-covid-19%2D%2D-11-march-2020.

Gillson, Stefanie L. and David A. Ross. "From Generation to Generation: Rethinking 'Soul Wounds' and Historical Trauma." *Biol Psychiatry* 86, issue 7 (October 2019): 19–20, accessed online February 1, 2024, https://www.ncbi.nlm.nih.gov/pmc/articles/PMC7557912/#R3.

Glantsman, Olya, et al. "Risk of Food and Housing Insecurity among College Students during the COVID-19 Pandemic." *Journal of Community Psychology* 50, no. 6 (2022): 2726–45, https://doi.org/10.1002/jcop.22853.

Gomez, Melissa del Carmen. "How COVID-19 is Affecting Indigenous Communities." *Voices of Gen-Z*, July 26, 2020, accessed online, https://www.voicesofgenz.com/post-1/how-covid-19-is-affecting-indigenous-communities.

Gone, Joseph P., and Joseph E. Trimble. "American Indian and Alaska Native Mental Health: Diverse Perspectives on Enduring Disparities." *Annual Review of Clinical Psychology* 8, no. 1 (2012): 131–60. https://doi.org/10.1146/annurev-clinpsy-032511-143127.

Goodluck, Kalen. "Why the U.S. is Terrible at Collecting Indigenous Data." *High Country News*, December 14, 2020, https://www.hcn.org/articles/indigenous-affairs-interview-why-the-u-s-is-terrible-at-collecting-indigenous-data.

Grove-d'wolf, Lynda. *The Life and Times of a Ute Woman*. Createspace Independent Pub., 2014.

Gunderson, Dan. "'Our Hearts are Heavy': Covid-19 Deaths of Tribal Elders Leave a Void." *Minnesota Public Radio News*, April 9, 2021, https://www.mprnews.org/story/2021/04/09/our-hearts-are-heavy-covid19-deaths-of-tribal-elders-leave-a-void.

Hall, Clyde, interview on June 4, 2021.

Handsel, Jennifer. Interview by Midge Dellinger, January 27, 2023, Tulsa, Oklahoma, transcript, *A Twenty-First Century Pandemic in Indian Country: The Resilience of the Muscogee (Creek) Nation Against COVID-19*, Muscogee (Creek) Nation National Library and Archives Oral History Collection, https://mvs-kokenationallibraryarchive.org/digital-heritage/jennifer-handsel-interview.

Hansen, Lani, *Mvskoke Media*, "A Third of all Oklahoma COVID-19 Deaths are happening on the MCN Reservation," accessed online August 29, 2023, https://www.mvskokemedia.com/a-third-of-all-COVID-19-deaths-are-happening-on-the-mcn-reservation/.

Harjo, Laura. *Spiral to the Stars: Mvskoke Tools of Futurity*. Tucson: University of Arizona Press, 2019

Harjo-Moffer, Melissa. Interview by Midge Dellinger, June 29, 2021, Okmulgee, Oklahoma, transcript, *A Twenty-First Century Pandemic in Indian Country: The Resilience of the Muscogee (Creek) Nation Against COVID-19*, Muscogee (Creek) Nation National Library and Archives, https://mvskokenationallibraryarchive.org/digital-heritage/melissa-harjo-moffer-interview-part-two.

Hatcher, Sarah M., et al. "COVID-19 Among American Indian and Alaska Native Persons—23 States, January 31–July 3, 2020. *Morbidity and Mortality Weekly Report* 69, no. 34 (2020): 1166–69.

Hathaway, Elizabeth D. "American Indian and Alaska Native People: Social Vulnerability and COVID-19." *The Journal of Rural Health* 37, no. 1 (2021): 256–59.

Healey, Gavin A. "American Indian Graffiti Muralism: Survivance and Geosemiotic Signposts in the American Cityscape." Ph.D. dissertation, The University of Arizona, Tucson, 2016.

Heaton, John W. "Bad Medicine": The Shoshone-Bannock Rejection of the First Fort Hall Reservation Boarding School, 1880–1900." *Idaho Yesterdays*, 51, no. 1 (Spring/Summer 2010).

Hedgpeth, Dana. "Native American tribes were already being wiped out. Then the 1918 flu hit." *The Washington Post,* January 27, 2020, accessed online January 8, 2024, https://www.washingtonpost.com/history/2020/09/28/1918-flu-native-americans-coronavirus/.

Hein, HannaLore. "Idaho's Response to the 1918 Influenza Pandemic: ISHS Briefing Paper No. 1." Idaho State Historical Society, August 31, 2020.

Hembrough, Tara, and Misty Cavanagh. "Covid-19, stress factors of Native American and Caucasian college students, and implementing classroom dialogues." *International Journal of Instruction* 15, no. 4 (2022): 515–34.

Herring, Sophia. "Indigenous Art Communities Emerged from the Pandemic More Resilient," *The Art Newspaper*, January 3, 2023, https://www.theartnewspaper.com/2023/01/03/indigenous-artists-more-resilient-pandemic.

Heth, Charlotte. "Overview." In *The Garland Encyclopedia of World Music*, 366–373.

Hidalgo, Elizabeth. "Supporting Native American Communities during the Coronavirus Pandemic: Checkpoints, Tribal Sovereignty, and the Implications of *McGirt v. Oklahoma*." *Houston Journal of Health Law & Policy* 21, no. 2 (2022): 449–482, https://houstonhealthlaw.scholasticahq.com/article/33837.

Hill, Chief David. Interview by Midge Dellinger, June 1, 2022, Okmulgee, Oklahoma, transcript, *A Twenty-First Century Pandemic in Indian Country: The Resilience of the Muscogee (Creek) Nation Against COVID-19*, Muscogee (Creek) Nation National Library and Archives, https://mvskokenationallibraryarchive.org/digital-heritage/chief-david-hill-interview.

Hill, Latoya and Samantha Artiga. "Health Coverage among American Indian and Alaska Native and Native Hawaiian and other Pacific Islander Peoples." *KFF*, November 30, 2023, accessed online January 8, 2024, https://www.kff.org/racial-equity-and-health-policy/issue-brief/health-coverage-among-american-indian-and-alaska-native-and-native-hawaiian-and-other-pacific-islander-people/.

Holmberg, Mitchell, in discussion with Chelsea M. Mead, May 2021.

Hoskin, Chuck Jr. "Durbin Feeling Language Center Starts a New Chapter in Cherokee Language Revitalization," November 20, 2022, accessed online May 30, 2024, https://nativenewsonline.net/opinion/durbin-feeling-language-center-starts-a-new-chapter-in-cherokee-language-revitalization.

Hoss, Aila and Heather Tanana. "Upholding Tribal Sovereignty and Promoting Tribal Public Health Capacity during the COVID-19 Pandemic," in S. Burris, et al., eds., *Assessing Legal Responses to COVID-19*. Boston: Public Health Law Watch, University of Utah College of Law Research Paper No. 391, 2020, accessed online January 8, 2024, https://ssrn.com/abstract=3675940.

Houle, Zachary, in discussion with Chelsea M. Mead, April 2020.

Howard-Bobiwash, Heather A., Jennie R. Joe, and Susan Lobo. "Concrete Lessons: Policies and Practices Affecting the Impact of Covid-19 for Urban Indigenous Communities in the United States and Canada." *Frontiers in Sociology* 6 (2021).

Indian Health Care Improvement Act, 25 U.S.C. § 1602.

Indian Health Service. "About IHS," accessed online, https://www.ihs.gov/aboutihs/.

Indian Health Service. *Annual Report to the Congress of the United States on Sanitation Deficiency Levels for Indian Homes and Communities.* 2019, 4, accessed online, https://www.ihs.gov/sites/newsroom/themes/responsive2017/display_objects/documents/FY_2019_RTC_Sanitation_Deficiencies_Report.pdf.

Indian Health Service. Coronavirus (COVID-19) (website), accessed September 30, 2023, https://www.ihs.gov/coronavirus/.

Indian Health Service. *FY 2021 Annual Report of Sanitation Deficiency Levels* (Nov. 16, 2021), accessed online, https://www.ihs.gov/sites/dsfc/themes/responsive2017/display_objects/documents/FY_2021_Appendix_Project_Listing.pdf.

Indian Health Service. "Mortality Disparity Rates, 2009–2011." accessed online January 8, 2024, https://www.ihs.gov/newsroom/factsheets/disparities/.

Indian Health Service, et al., *Criteria for the Sanitation Facilities Construction Program*, 1–1. 1999, accessed online, https://www.ihs.gov/sites/dsfc/themes/responsive2017/display_objects/documents/Criteria_March_2003.pdf.

Indian Sanitation Facilities Construction Act of 1959, Pub. L. 86–121.

John-Henderson, Neha A., and Annie T. Ginty. "Historical trauma and social support as predictors of psychological stress responses in American Indian adults during the COVID-19 pandemic." *Journal of psychosomatic research* 139 (2020): 110263.

Kernell, Cebon. Interview by Midge Dellinger, February 27, 2023, Okmulgee, Oklahoma, transcript, *A Twenty-First Century Pandemic in Indian Country: The Resilience of the Muscogee (Creek) Nation Against COVID-19*, Muscogee (Creek) Nation National Library and Archives, https://mvskokenationallibraryarchive.org/digital-heritage/cebon-kernell-interview.

KFF. "COVID-19 Cases, Deaths, and Vaccinations by Race/Ethnicity as of Winter 2022." accessed online January 8, 2024, https://www.kff.org/coronavirus-covid-19/issue-brief/covid-19-cases-deaths-and-vaccinations-by-race-ethnicity-as-of-winter-2022/.

Khazaie, Joubin. "Fanon, Colonial Violence, and Racist Language in Federal American Indian Law." *University of Miami Race and Social Justice Law Review* 12, no. 2 (2022): 297–311.

Kickingbird, Kirke and Everett R. Rhoades. "The Relation of Indian Nations to the U.S. Government." In *American Indian Health: Innovations in Health Care Promotion, and Policy*, edited by Everett R. Rhoades, 61–73. Baltimore, MD: Johns Hopkins University Press, 2000.

King, Farina. "Diné Doctor: A Latter-day Saint Story of Healing." *Dialogue: A Journal of Mormon Thought* 54, no. 2 (Summer 2021a): 81–85.

King, Farina, cited in Brian D. King. "Candlelight vigil mourns lives lost during pandemic, especially Natives." *Tahlequah Daily Press*, April 19, 2021b, accessed online February 1, 2024, https://www.tahlequahdailypress.com/multimedia/when-i-see-you-again/video_0c7dabb6-a12b-11eb-9079-17b58542b2e0.html.

King, Farina. "They Called Her 'Nááníbaa' Or 'She Returns From War.'" COVID-19 Mormon Stories, May 6, 2020, accessed online February 1, 2024, https://research.cgu.edu/mormonism-migration-project/farina-king/.

King, Thomas. *The Inconvenient Indian: A Curious Account of Native People in North America*. Toronto: Doubleday Canada, 2012.

Kinzie, Jillian, and James Cole. "Education disrupted: Students beginning college during the COVID-19 pandemic." *New Directions for Higher Education* 2022, no. 199 (2022): 27–40.

Kirmayer, Laurence J., et al. "Rethinking Resilience from Indigenous Perspectives." *Canadian Journal of Psychiatry* 56, no. 2 (2011): 84–91.

Kourti, Anastasia, et al. "Domestic Violence during the COVID-19 Pandemic: A Systematic Review." *Trauma, Violence, & Abuse* 24, no. 2 (2023): 719–45

Kovach, Margaret. "Conversation Method in Indigenous Research." *First Peoples Child & Family: An Interdisciplinary Journal*, 14, no 1 (2019): 40–48.

Kraker, Dan. "Indigenous Communities See Rise in COVID-19 Cases." Minnesota Public Radio News, October 22, 2021, https://www.mprnews.org/story/2021/10/22/indigenous-communities-see-rise-in-covid19-cases.

Kroeber, Karl. "Why it's a Good Thing Gerald Vizenor is Not an Indian." In *Survivance: Narratives of Native Presence*, edited by Gerald Vizenor, 25–38. Lincoln: University of Nebraska Press, 2008.

Kuhn, Casey. "Why Indigenous People in Cities Feel Invisible as Pandemic Wears On." *PBS News Hour*, February 23, 2021, https://www.pbs.org/newshour/health/why-indigenous-people-in-cities-feel-invisible-as-pandemic-wears-on.

LaPensee, Elizabeth "Survivance as an Indigenously Determined Game." *AlterNative: An International Journal of Indigenous Peoples* 10, no. 3 (2014): 263–75.

Lazare, Jerry, in discussion with Chelsea Mead, May 2021.

Leap, Braden Marybeth Stalp, and Kimberly Kelly. "Reorganizations of Gendered Labor during the COVID-19 Pandemic: A Review and Suggestions for Further Research." *Sociological Inquiry* 93, no. 1 (2023): 179–200.

Lee, Anthony W. *Painting on the left: Diego Rivera, Radical Politics, and San Francisco's Public Murals*. Berkeley: University of California Press, 1999.

Leggat-Barr, Katherine, Fumiya Uchikoshi, and Noreen Goldman. "COVID-19 risk factors and mortality among Native Americans." *Demographic Research* 45, 39 (November 17, 2021): 1208, accessed online, https://www.demographic-research.org/volumes/vol45/39/45-39.pdf.

Le-Morawa, Nam et al. "Effectiveness of a COVID-19 Vaccine Rollout in a Highly Affected American Indian Community, San Carlos Apache Tribe, December 2020–February 2021." *Public Health Reports* 138, sup. 2 (2023): 23s–29s.

Liddell, J.L., C.E. McKinley, H. Knipp, & J.M. Scarnato. "She's the Center of My Life, the One That Keeps My Heart Open: Roles and Expectations of Native American Women." *Affilia* 36, no. 3, (2020): 357–75.

Lundström, Markus. "Young in pandemic times: a scoping review of COVID-19 social impacts on youth." *International Journal of Adolescence and Youth* 27, no. 1 (2022): 432–443.

Macaskill, Ann. "Undergraduate mental health issues: The challenge of the second year of study." *Journal of Mental Health* 27, no. 3 (2018): 214–221.

Madsen, Brigham. *The Northern Shoshoni* Caxton Printers, Ltd: Caldwell, 1980.

Mankiller, Wilma. *Every Day Is a Good Day: Reflections by Contemporary Indigenous Women*. Golden, CO: Fulcrum Pub., 2004.

Mann, Barbara Alice. *The Tainted Gift: The Disease Method of Frontier Expansion*. Santa Barbara, CA: ABC Clio, 2009.

Mannuzza, Timb, in discussion with Chelsea M Mead, May 2022.
Marinoni, Giorgio, Hilligje Van't Land, and Trine Jensen. "The impact of Covid-19 on higher education around the world." *IAU global survey report* 23 (2020).
Marnham, Patrick. *Dreaming with his Eyes Open: A Life of Diego Rivera*. Berkeley: University of California Press, 1998.
Marsh, Kevin. "Influenza in Idaho: How the World's Deadliest Pandemic Shaped the Gem State," June 1, 2020.
Marshall, Anna. Interview by Midge Dellinger, May 5, 2021, Tulsa, Oklahoma, transcript, *A Twenty-First Century Pandemic in Indian Country: The Resilience of the Muscogee (Creek) Nation Against COVID-19*, Muscogee (Creek) Nation National Library and Archives Oral History Collection, https://mvskokenation-allibraryarchive.org/digital-heritage/representative-anna-marshall-interview.
Martinez, Donna, Grace Sage, and Azusa Ono. *Urban American Indians: Reclaiming Native Space*. Santa Barbara, CA: Praeger Publishers, 2016.
Mayor, Adrienne. "The Nessus Shirt in the New World: Smallpox Blankets in History and Legend." *The Journal of American Folklore* 108, no. 427 (Winter 1995): 54–77.
Mayer, Susan M. "Four Pacific Northwest Reservations and the Influenza Pandemic from 1918 to 1919." Master's Thesis. Emporia State University, 2012.
Mayoh, Joanne, and Anthony J. Onwuegbuzie. "Toward a Conceptualization of Mixed Methods Phenomenological Research." *Journal of Mixed Methods Research*, 9, no. 1 (2015): 91–107. https://doi.org/10.1177/1558689813505358.
McCaffery, Larry. "On Thin Ice, You Might as Well Dance: An Interview with Gerald Vizenor." In *Some Other Frequency: Interviews with Innovative American Authors*, edited by Larry McCaffery, 287–309. Philadelphia: University of Pennsylvania Press, 1996.
Memorandum No. 02075, 86 Fed. Reg. 7,491, 7,491 (Jan. 26, 2021).
Meriam, Lewis. *The Problem of Indian Administration: Report of a Survey Made at the Request of Honorable Hubert Work, Secretary of the Interior, and Submitted to Him, Feb. 21, 1928*. Baltimore, MD: The Johns Hopkins Press 1928.
Miller, Ely F., Jacob Neumann, Ye Chen, Abhishek Mallela, Yen Ting Lin, William S. Hlavacek, and Richard G. Posner. "Quantification of early nonpharmaceutical interventions aimed at slowing transmission of Coronavirus Disease 2019 in the Navajo Nation and surrounding states (Arizona, Colorado, New Mexico, and Utah)." *PLOS Global Public Health* 3, no. 6 (June 21, 2023), accessed online, https://doi.org/10.1371/journal.pgph.0001490.
Minnesota Executive Order No. 20–20 (March 25, 2020), https://mn.gov/governor/assets/3a.%20EO%2020-20%20FINAL%20SIGNED%20Filed_tcm1055-425020.pdf.

Minthorn, Robin Starr. "Consciously Leading with Ancestors Prayers, and Community in the Heath." In *Indigenous Leadership in Higher Education*, eds. Robin S. Minthorn and Alicia F. Chavez (New York, NY: Routledge, 2015.

Minthorn, Robin Zape-tah-hol-ah. "Indigenous Motherhood in the Academy, Building Our Children to Be Good Relatives." *Wicazo Sa Review*, 33, no. 2 (2018): 62–75.

Moecke, Débora Petry, Travis Holyk, Madelaine Beckett, Sunaina Chopra, Polina Petlitsyna, Mirha Girt, Ashley Kirkham et al. "Scoping review of telehealth use by Indigenous populations from Australia, Canada, New Zealand, and the United States." *Journal of Telemedicine and Telecare* (2023): 1357633X231158835.

Molock, Sherry Davis, and Benjamin Parchem. "The Impact of COVID-19 on College Students from Communities of Color." *Journal of American College Health* 70, no. 8 (2021): 2399–2405, https://doi.org/10.1080/07448481.2020.1865380.

Montgomery, Lindsay. "A Rejoinder to Body Bags: Indigenous Resilience and Epidemic Disease, From COVID-19 to First 'Contact.'" *American Indian Culture and Research Journal* 44, no. 3 (2020): 65–86.

Mourning Dove and Jay Miller, Editor. *Mourning Dove: A Salishan Autobiography*. University of Nebraska Press: Lincoln, 1990.

Muscogee (Creek) Nation, Executive Branch, FY2020, 2$^{nd}$ Quarter Report (January, February, March), accessed online August 29, 2023a, 6–7, https://www.muscogeenation.com/wp-content/uploads/2022/08/FY20-2nd-Quarterly-Report-Digital-FINAL.pdf.

Muscogee (Creek) Nation, Executive Branch, FY2021, 1$^{st}$ Quarter Report (October, November, December, 2020), accessed online August 29, 2023, 7, https://www.muscogeenation.com/wp-content/uploads/2022/08/FY-2021-1st-Quarterly-Report-Final.pdf.

Muscogee (Creek) Nation, Executive Branch, FY2023, 1$^{st}$ Quarter Report (October, November, December), accessed online August 29, 2023b, 8, https://www.muscogeenation.com/wp-content/uploads/2023/01/FY23-1st-Quarterly-Report.pdf.

Mvskoke Media, accessed online August 31, 2023, https://www.mvskokemedia.com/national-council-passes-citizen-vaccine-incentive/.

Naataanii, TahNibaa. "T'áá awolí bee: Navajo Contemporary Arts Lecture Series – Sarah, TahNibaa, and Winter Rose Naataanii (Weavers)." Navajo Cultural Arts Program. December 2, 2020, lecture video, 1:00:05, https://youtu.be/knxJFuAgvO8.

National Community Reinvestment Coalition. "Racial Wealth Snapshot: Native Americans," accessed online, https://ncrc.org/racial-wealth-snapshot-native-americans/.

National Congress of American Indians. *Reducing Disparities in the Federal Health Care Budget in Fiscal Year 2020 Indian Country Budget Request.* 2019, accessed online, https://www.ncai.org/07_NCAI-FY20-Healthcare.pdf.

National Congress of American Indians. "Submission of the National Congress of American Indians to the United Nations Special Rapporteur on Indigenous Issues." United Nations General Assembly, June 19, 2020, accessed August 1, 2023, https://www.ohchr.org/en/calls-for-input/report-impact-covid-19-rights-indigenous-peoples.

Navajo Department of Health. *Dikos Ntsaaígíí-19 (COVID-19)*, accessed online, https://www.ndoh.navajo-nsn.gov/COVID-19.

Navajo Nation Office of the President and Vice President. "E. Agency Council Rep., President Nez Provides Testimony in Support of Congressional Bills That Will Deliver More Clean Water to Navajo Communities," June 4, 2022, accessed online, https://opvp.navajo-nsn.gov.

NBC News. "'Hit us at our core': Vulnerable Navajo Nation fears a second COVID-19 wave," Aug. 3, 2020, accessed online, https://www.nbcnews.com/specials/navajo-nation-fears-second-covid-19-wave/index.html.

"New endowment fund established to support preservation of Native American languages," September 14, 2023, accessed online May 29, 2024 via *Native Oklahoma Magazine*, https://www.nativeoklahoma.us/new-endowment-fund-established-to-support-preservation-of-native-american-languages/.

Nicole Pasia, Nicole. "When they gave her body bags instead of PPE, she used them to make a healing ribbon dress." *Seattle Times*, April 1, 2021, accessed online, https://www.seattletimes.com/life/when-they-gave-her-body-bags-instead-of-ppe-she-used-them-to-make-a-healing-ribbon-dress/.

Nolte, Carl. "Alcatraz pays tribute to Indian occupation: American Indians Activists' painted statement is emblazoned on tower once more." *SFGATE* (San Francisco). January 14, 2013. https://www.sfgate.com/bayarea/article/Alcatraz-pays-tribute-to-Indian-occupation-4191169.php.

Nooe, F. Evan. *Aggression and Sufferings: Settler Violence, Native Resistance, and the Coalescence of the Old South.* Tuscaloosa, AL: University of Alabama Press, 2023.

Noriega, Gabrielle. Interview by Midge Dellinger, December 17, 2021, Okmulgee, Oklahoma, transcript, *A Twenty-First Century Pandemic in Indian Country: The Resilience of the Muscogee (Creek) Nation Against COVID-19*, Muscogee (Creek) Nation National Library and Archives, https://mvskokenationallibraryarchive.org/digital-heritage/gabrielle-noriega.

Oladipo, Gloria. "Native American communities lashed by Covid, worsening chronic inequities." *The Guardian*, May 13, 2021, accessed online February 17, 2022, https://www.theguardian.com/us-news/2021/dec/13/pandemic-challenges-native-american-communities.

Ortiz, Erik. "Native American health center asked for COVID-19 supplies. It got body bags instead." NBC News, May 5, 2020, accessed online, https://www.nbcnews.com/news/us-news/native-american-health-center-asked-covid-19-supplies-they-got-n1200246.

Osterholtz, Anna J. "Hobbling and torture as performative violence: An example from the prehistoric Southwest." *Kiva* 78, no. 2 (2012): 123–144.

Pandya, Apurvakumar, and Pragya Lodha. "Mental health consequences of COVID-19 pandemic among college students and coping approaches adapted by higher education institutions: A scoping review." *SSM-Mental Health* 2 (2022): 100122.

Parsons-Yazzie, Evangeline, Margaret Speas, Jessie Ruffenach, and Berlyn Yazzie. *Diné Bizaad Bináhoo'aah: Rediscovering the Navajo Language: An Introduction to the Navajo Language*, 1st ed. Flagstaff, Arizona: Salina Bookshelf, 2007.

Pennycook, Alastair. "Linguistic Landscapes and the Transgressive Semiotics of Graffiti." In *Linguistic Landscape: Expanding the Scenery*, edited by Elana Shohamy and Durk Gorter, 1st ed. Vol. 9780203930960 (New York: Routledge, 2009), 302–312.

Pickering, Kerrie, et al. "Indigenous Peoples and the COVID-19 Pandemic: A Systematic Scoping Review." Abstract, *Environmental Research Letters* 18, no. 3 (2023): 033001. https://doi.org/10.1088/1748-9326/acb804.

Piña, Apollonia. Interview by Midge Dellinger, May 25, 2021, Tulsa, Oklahoma, transcript, *A Twenty-First Century Pandemic in Indian Country: The Resilience of the Muscogee (Creek) Nation Against COVID-19*, Muscogee (Creek) Nation National Library and Archives, https://mvskokenationallibraryarchive.org/digital-heritage/apollonia-pi%C3%B1a-interview.

Portillo, Amy. Interview by Midge Dellinger, August 9, 2022, Okmulgee, Oklahoma, transcript, *A Twenty-First Century Pandemic in Indian Country: The Resilience of the Muscogee (Creek) Nation Against COVID-19*, Muscogee (Creek) Nation National Library and Archives, https://mvskokenationallibraryarchive.org/digital-heritage/amy-portillo-interview.

Powell, Roman. Interview by Midge Dellinger, November 14, 2022, Tulsa, Oklahoma, transcript, *A Twenty-First Century Pandemic in Indian Country: The Resilience of the Muscogee (Creek) Nation Against COVID-19*, Muscogee (Creek) Nation National Library and Archives, https://mvskokenationallibraryarchive.org/digital-heritage/roman-powell-interview.

Prakash, M., and J. Carlton Johnny. "Things you don't learn in medical school: Caduceus." *Journal of Pharmacy and Bioallied Sciences*. April 7, 2015 (Suppl 1): S49–50.

Proclamation No. 9994, 85 Fed. Reg. 15337 (March 13, 2020).

Public Law 117–169, Section 50232.

Pukatch, Ava. "Season 2 of Marvel's 'What if...?' includes episode mostly in Mohawk language." *All Things Considered*, NPR, December 28, 2023, accessed online May 30, 2024, https://www.npr.org/2023/12/27/1221890957/season-2-of-marvels-what-if-includes-episode-mostly-in-mohawk-language.

Quintero, Donovan. "The COVID-19 Outbreak in the Navajo Nation." *American Indian: Magazine of Smithsonian's National Museum of the American Indian* 22, no. 2 (Summer 2021), accessed online January 11, 2024, https://www.americanindianmagazine.org/story/the-covid-19-outbreak-in-the-navajo-nation#:~:text=Addressing%20the%20Navajo%20Nation&text=(As%20of%20mid%2DJune%202021,the%20Navajo%20Nation%20have%20died.).

Rader, Dean. *Engaged Resistance: American Indian Art, Literature, and Film from Alcatraz to the NMAI*, 1st ed. Austin: University of Texas Press, 2011.

Raheja, Michelle H. "Visual Sovereignty." In *Native Studies Keywords*. Tucson: University of Arizona Press, 2015.

Ramos, R.R. "Exploring the Lived Experience of Kumeyaay College Graduates." PhD dissertation, (Bethel University, 2021).

Ranlet, Philip. "The British, the Indians, and Smallpox: What Actually Happened at Fort Pitt in 1763?" *Pennsylvania History: A Journal of Mid-Atlantic Studies* 67, no. 3 (Summer 2000): 427–41.

Reardon, Sara. "Native American Use Technology to Keep Traditions, Language Alive During Pandemic." *KFF Health News*, February 9, 2021, accessed online May 30, 2024, https://kffhealthnews.org/news/article/native-americans-use-technology-to-keep-traditions-language-alive-during-pandemic/.

Red Corn, Louise. "Chief Standing Bear: I'm not going to force you to get vaccinated for work." *Osage News*, January 5, 2022, https://osagenews.org/chief-standing-bear-im-not-going-to-force-you-to-get-vaccinated-for-work/.

Red Corn, S.A. *Set the prairie on fire: an autoethnographic confrontation of colonial entanglements*. Ph.D. dissertation, Kansas State University, 2017.

Reid, Rosalind. "Native American Communities Battling Covid-19 Draw on Strengths." CASW, Last modified June 15, 2021, https://casw.org/news/native-american-communities-battling-covid-19-draw-on-strengths/.

Rogers, Nicole Martin, et al., "American Indians in Minnesota Experience Worse Covid Impacts Than Reported." *Star Tribune*, December 15, 2020, https://www.startribune.com/american-indians-in-minnesota-experience-worse-covid-impacts-than-reported/573402071/?refresh=true.

Rosenthal, Nicolas G. "Painting Native America in Public: American Indian Artists and the New Deal." *American Indian Culture and Research Journal* 42, no. 3 (2018): 47–70.

Rowe, Tara A. "Pocatello and the 1918 Spanish Flu." *Idaho State Journal*, April 10, 2020, accessed online, https://www.idahostatejournal.com/opinion/columns/pocatellos-and-the-1918-spanish-flu/article_639ca612-76f6-5ed2-9fda-afdec3e80d6f.html.

Rubin, Daniel Ian, and Faith Agostinone Wilson *A Time of Covidiocy: Media, Politics, and Social Upheaval*. Leiden, The Netherlands: Brill, 2021.

Running Bear, Candi, William PA Terrill, Adriana Frates, Patricia Peterson, and Judith Ulrich. "Challenges for rural Native American students with disabilities during COVID-19." *Rural Special Education Quarterly* 40, no. 2 (2021): 60–69.

Ryan, J. Michael. "Surviving a Pandemic." In *COVID-19: Surviving a Pandemic*, ed. J. Michael Ryan. London: Routledge, 2022.

Saint-Raymond, Léa. "'The Show Must Go On': Ethnography of the Art Market Facing the COVID-19 Pandemic." *Arts* 10, no. 3 (2021): 53.

Shawanda, Amy. "Anishinaabe Motherhood: The Act of Resistance by Resurging Traditional Teachings and Pedagogies." PhD Dissertation, Trent University, 2022.

Shotton, Heather. "Being of Service to Our People." In *Indigenous Leadership in Higher Education*, eds. Robin S. Minthorn and Alicia F. Chavez. New York, NY: Routledge, 2015.

Slane, Joshua, *Mvskoke Media*, "Muscogee (Creek) Nation Declares COVID-19 State of Emergency," accessed August 29, 2023, https://www.mvskokemedia.com/muscogee-creek-nation-declares-COVID-19-state-of-emergency/.

Smith, Libby. "Impact of the Coronavirus and Federal Responses on Indigenous Peoples' Health, Security, and Sovereignty." *American Indian Law Review* 45, no. 2 (2021): 297–326.

Smith, Matthew Ryan. "Indigenous graffiti and street art as resistance." In *Street Art of Resistance*, edited by Sarah H. Awad and Brady Wagoner, Palgrave Studies in Creativity and Culture. Palgrave Macmillan, Cham., 2017.

Snyder, Gregory J. *Graffiti Lives: Beyond the tag in New York's urban underground*. New York: NY University Press, 2009.

Solomon, Teshia G. Arambula, et al. "The Generational Impact of Racism on Health: Voices from American Indian Communities." *Health Affairs* 41, no. 2 (2022): 281–88.

Soria, Krista M., Brayden J. Roberts, Bonnie Horgos, and Katie Hallahan. "Undergraduates' Experiences During the COVID-19 Pandemic: Disparities by Race and Ethnicity." *SERU Consortium, University of California – Berkeley and University of Minnesota* (2020): Retrieved from the University of Minnesota Digital Conservancy, https://hdl.handle.net/11299/218339.

Soweka, Robin. Interview by Midge Dellinger, April 26, 2022, Okmulgee, Oklahoma, transcript, *A Twenty-First Century Pandemic in Indian Country: The Resilience of the Muscogee (Creek) Nation Against COVID-19*, Muscogee (Creek) Nation National Library and Archives, https://mvskokenationallibraryarchive.org/digital-heritage/robin-soweka-interview.

Spruhan, Paul. "Guardians of Tribal Tradition: Litigation in the Navajo Nation," *Litigation* 43, no. 3 (2017): 31–33.

Stewart, Laura. Interview by Midge Dellinger, October 1, 2021, Tulsa, Oklahoma, transcript, *A Twenty-First Century Pandemic in Indian Country: The Resilience of the Muscogee (Creek) Nation Against COVID-19*, Muscogee (Creek) Nation National Library and Archives, https://mvskokenationallibraryarchive.org/digital-heritage/laura-stewart-interview.

Stone, Tyler. Interview by Midge Dellinger, November 4, 2022, Tulsa, Oklahoma, transcript, *A Twenty-First Century Pandemic in Indian Country: The Resilience of the Muscogee (Creek) Nation Against COVID-19*, Muscogee (Creek) Nation National Library and Archives, https://mvskokenationallibraryarchive.org/digital-heritage/tyler-stone-interview.

*Superintendents Annual Narrative and Statistical Reports from Field Jurisdictions of the Bureau of Indian Affairs, 1907–1938*. MI0II microfilm. Washington, DC: National Archives and Records Service, 1975.

Szasz, Margaret C. *Indian Education in the American Colonies: 1607–1783*. Lincoln: University of Nebraska Press, 1988.

Tanana, Heather, et al. *Universal Access to Clean Water for Tribal Communities*. 2020, accessed online, https://tribalcleanwater.org/wp-content/uploads/2021/09/WTI-Full-Report-4.20.pdf.

Tedlock, Dennis. "Graffiti." In *2000 Years of Mayan Literature*. Berkeley: University of California Press, 2010.

Terry, Shawn. Interview by Midge Dellinger, June 24, 2021, Tulsa, Oklahoma, transcript, *A Twenty-First Century Pandemic in Indian Country: The Resilience of the Muscogee (Creek) Nation Against COVID-19*, Muscogee (Creek) Nation National Library and Archives Oral History Collection, https://mvskokenationallibraryarchive.org/digital-heritage/shawn-terry-secretary-health-interview.

Theobald, Brianna. *Reproduction on the Reservation: Pregnancy, Childbirth, and Colonialism in the Long Twentieth Century*. Chapel Hill: The University of North Carolina Press, 2019.

Thorbecke, Willem. "The Impact of the COVID-19 Pandemic on the U.S. Economy: Evidence from the Stock Market." *Journal of Risk and Financial Management* 13, no. 10 (2020): 1–32.

Sandoval, Hastin Tlo'tsi hee (Old Man Buffalo Grass) recorded by Aileen O'Bryan in November 1928 in Aileen O'Bryan, *The Diné origin myths of the Navaho Indians [transcribed] by Aileen O'Bryan*. Washington, DC: *Bulletin* of the Smithsonian Institution, Bureau of American Ethnology, 1956, 84.

Secatero, Shawn. "Native Educational Sovereignty in Teaching and Leadership (NESTL): The Transformation of Leadership Utilizing a Holistic Corn Pollen Model to Serve All Students at a Research University." In *Unsettling Settler-Colonial Education: The Transformational Praxis Model*, eds. Cornel Pewewardy, Anna Lees, and Robin Zape-Tah-Hol-Ah Minthorn. New York: Teachers College Press, 2017.

Sekercioglu, Faith, and Nicholas D. Spence. "Introduction." In *Indigenous Health and Well-Being in the COVID-19 Pandemic*, eds. Nicholas D. Spence and Faith Sekercioglu. London and New York: Routledge Taylor and Francis Group, 2023.

Toadlena, Brent. "T'áá awołí bee: Best of Show Panel," Navajo Cultural Arts Program. April 25, 2021, lecture video, 1:25:45, https://youtu.be/BEao5er ui4g?si=PKrelsXVZsDcNuCL.

Todd, Kimberly, and Maria Vamvalis. "Puncturing, Weaving, and Braiding: Integrating Spiritual Knowing in Education" in *Ignite: A Decolonial Approach to Higher Education Through Space, Place and Culture* eds. Laura M. Pipe and Jennifer T. Stephens, 215–34. Wilmington, DE: Vernon Art and Science Inc., 2023.

Tohe, Laura. "Hwéeldi Bééháníih: Remembering the Long Walk." *Wicazo Sa Review* 22, no. 1 (Spring 2007): 77–82.

Trafzer, Clifford E. *Strong Hearts and Healing Hands: Southern California Indians and Field Nurses, 1920–1950*. Tucson: The University of Arizona Press, 2021.

Treaty between the United States of America and the Navajo Tribe of Indians, Sept. 9, 1849, 9 Stat. 974 (ratified Sept. 24, 1850).

Treece, Carly. Interview by Midge Dellinger, December 21, 2022, Tulsa, Oklahoma, transcript, *A Twenty-First Century Pandemic in Indian Country: The Resilience of the Muscogee (Creek) Nation Against COVID-19*, Muscogee (Creek) Nation National Library and Archives, https://mvskokenationallibraryarchive.org/digital-heritage/carly-treece-interview.

Trennert, Robert A. *White Man's Medicine: Government Doctors and the Navajo, 1863–1955*. Albuquerque: University of New Mexico Press, 1988.

Treuer, Anton. *The Cultural Toolbox: Traditional Ojibwe Living in the Modern World*. St. Paul: Minnesota Historical Society Press, 2021.

Tsabetsaye, Byron. "Internet and Technology Access during the COVID-19 Pandemic: A Chronological Account and Approach to Helping Native American Students in the Navajo Northern Agency." NASPA: Student Affairs Administrators in Higher Education, accessed August 31, 2023, https://www.naspa.org/blog/internet-and-technology-access-during-the-covid-19-pandemic-a-chronological-account-and-approach-to-helping-native-american-students-in-the-navajo-northern-agency.

Tsosie, Lyndon. "T'áá awołí bee: Navajo Contemporary Arts Lecture Series – Lyndon Tsosie (Navajo Silversmith)." Navajo Cultural Arts Program. April 28, 2020, lecture video, 1:03:01, https://youtu.be/QYlUd0bpg1E.

Tulsa Health Department, accessed online August 31, 2023a, https://www.tulsa-health.org/news/tulsa-health-department-reports-first-case-COVID-19.

Tulsa Health Department, accessed online August 31, 2023b, https://www.tulsa-health.org/news/tulsa-health-officials-confirm-first-COVID-19-death-oklahoma.

Two Bears, Kelsey. Interview by Midge Dellinger, February 27, 2022, Tulsa, Oklahoma, transcript, *A Twenty-First Century Pandemic in Indian Country: The Resilience of the Muscogee (Creek) Nation Against COVID-19*, Muscogee

(Creek) Nation National Library and Archives, https://mvskokenationallibraryarchive.org/digital-heritage/kelsey-two-bears-interview.

Tzay, José Francisco Calí. "Report of the Special Rapporteur on the Rights of Indigenous Peoples." United Nations General Assembly, July 20, 2020, A/75/185, https://undocs.org/en/A/75/185.

United Nations Department of Economic and Social Affairs. "Indigenous Peoples & the COVID-19 Pandemic: Considerations," accessed September 5, 2023, https://www.un.org/development/desa/indigenouspeoples/wp-content/uploads/sites/19/2020/04/COVID19_IP_considerations.pdf.

Urban Indian Health Institute. "About urban Indians," accessed September 18, 2023, https://www.uihi.org/urban-indian-health/.

U.S. Bureau of Labor Statistic. "Unemployment rate for American Indians and Alaska Natives at 7.9 percent in December 2021," January, 26, 2022, accessed online January 8, 2024, https://www.bls.gov.opub/ted/2022.

U.S. Commission on Civil Rights. *Broken Promises: Continuing Federal Funding Shortfall for Native Americans* (2018), accessed online, https://www.usccr.gov/files/pubs/2018/12-20-Broken-Promises.pdf.

U.S. Congress. *Addressing the Urgent Needs of Our Tribal Communities: Hearing before the House Committee on Energy and Commerce*, 116th Congress, 2020a.

U.S. Congress. *Addressing Tribal Needs Through Innovation and Investment in Water Resources Infrastructures through the U.S. Bureau of Reclamation: Hearing on Energy and Water Development Appropriations for 2022 Before the House Committee on Appropriations and Subcommittee on Energy and Water Development*, 117th Congress, 2021.

U.S. Congress. *Hearing on An Unequal Burden: Addressing Racial Health Disparities in the Coronavirus Pandemic Before the Select Subcommittee on the Coronavirus Crisis*, 116th Cong. 3–6 (2020b) (written testimony of Fawn Sharp, President of the National Congress of American Indians).

U.S. Department of the Interior, Office of Congressional and Legislative Affairs. "Covid-19 Impact on Native Education," April 28, 2021, accessed online, https://www.doi.gov/ocl/covid-19-impact-native-education.

U.S. Global Change Research Program. "Tribes and Indigenous Peoples." In Fourth National Climate Assessment, Volume II: Impacts, Risks, and Adaptation in the United States, 572–603. 2018.

U.S. Government Accountability Office, GAO-18-309, *Drinking Water and Wastewater Infrastructure: Opportunities Exist to Enhance Federal Agency Needs Assessment and Coordination on Tribal Projects*. 2018.

U.S. Water Alliance and Dig Deep. *Closing the Water Access Gap in the United States: A National Action Plan*. 2019.

Van Hook, Charles J. "Hantavirus Pulmonary Syndrome—The 25th Anniversary of the Four Corners Outbreak." *Emerging Infectious Diseases* 24, no. 11 (November 2018): 2056–2060.

Vizenor, Gerald. *Manifest Manners: Narratives on Postindian Survivance*. Lincoln: University of Nebraska Press, 1999.
Vizenor, Gerald, and A. Robert Lee. *Postindian Conversations*. Lincoln: University of Nebraska Press, 1999.
Walker, Mark. "Pandemic Highlights Deep-Rooted Problems in Indian Health Service." *New York Times*, September 29, 2020, accessed online, https://www.nytimes.com/2020/09/29/us/politics/coronavirus-indian-health-service.html.
Walls, Melissa, et al. "Stress Exposure and Physical, Mental, and Behavioral Health among American Indian Adults with Type 2 Diabetes." *International Journal of Environmental Research and Public Health* 14, no. 9 (2017): 1074.
Walsh, Bridget A., et al. "Historically Underrepresented Graduate Students' Experiences during the COVID-19 Pandemic" *Family Relations* 70, no. 4 (2021): 955–72, https://doi.org/10.1111/fare.12574.
Wang, Haoying. "Why the Navajo Nation Was Hit so Hard by Coronavirus: Understanding the Disproportionate Impact of the COVID-19 Pandemic." *Applied Geography* 134 (2021): 102526, https://doi.org/10.1016/j.apgeog.2021.102526.
Weaver, Hilary N. and Barry J. White. "The Native American Family Circle: Roots of Resiliency." *Journal of Family Social Work* 2, no. 1 (1997): 67–79.
Weisberger, Mindy. "Remains of more than 1,000 Indigenous children found at former residential schools in Canada," accessed September 2, 2023, https://www.livescience.com/childrens-graves-residential-schools-canada.html.
Wigginton, Caroline. *Indigenuity: Native Craftwork and the Art of American Literatures*. Chapel Hill: University of North Carolina Press, 2022.
Wilbur, Rachel E., and Joseph P. Gone. "Beyond resilience: A scoping review of Indigenous survivance in the health literature." *Development and Psychopathology* (2023): 1–15.
Williams, Christian. *Virtual Qualitative Interviews on Grief and Loss: Benefits, Challenges, and Considerations*. London: Sage Publications Ltd., 2022.
Willig, C. *Introducing Qualitative Research in Psychology, Adventures in Theory and Method*. Open University Press, 2008.
Wind, Grover. Interview by Midge Dellinger, December 10, 2021, Tulsa, Oklahoma, transcript, *A Twenty-First Century Pandemic in Indian Country: The Resilience of the Muscogee (Creek) nation Against COVID-19*, Muscogee (Creek) Nation National Library and Archives, https://mvskokenationallibraryarchive.org/digital-heritage/grover-wind-interview.
Winder, Natahnee. "Post-secondary Education (PSE) Indigenous Students' Perspectives: Sharing Our Voices on How We Fit into Residential School (RS) History of Canada and the United States Using Photovoice." PhD Dissertation, University of Western Ontario, 2020.

Wollan, Malia. "Antigovernment Graffiti Restored, Courtesy of Government." *New York Times* (New York), December 24, 2012, https://www.nytimes.com/2012/12/25/us/alcatraz-american-indian-occupation-graffiti-preserved.html.

World Health Organization. "Who Director-General's Opening Remarks at the Media Briefing on COVID-19 – 11 March 2020." World Health Organization, accessed 18 June 2023, https://www.who.int/director-general/speeches/detail/who-director-general-s-opening-remarks-at-the-media-briefing-on-covid-19%2D%2D-11-march-2020.

Xie, Bo, et al. "Native American Elders' Experiences during the COVID-19 Pandemic: Case Studies." *Innovation in Aging* 5, no. Supplement_1 (2021): 883, https://doi.org/10.1093/geroni/igab046.3214.

Yellow Horse Brave Heart, Maria et al. "Historical Trauma among Indigenous Peoples of the Americas: Concepts, Research, and Clinical Considerations." *Journal of Psychoactive Drugs* 43, no. 4 (2011): 282–90.

Young, Allie, cited in Colton Shone and Nathan O'Neal. "How the Navajo People are using culture to fight back against 'Covid Monster.'" Center for Health Journalism, September 15, 2020, accessed online January 27, 2024, https://centerforhealthjournalism.org/our-work/reporting/how-navajo-people-are-using-culture-fight-back-against-covid-monster.

Zordan, Joseph, in discussion with Chelsea M. Mead, May 2021.

# Index[1]

**A**
Abeyta, Tony, 230
Alabama (state), 97
Albuquerque, NM, 85, 203, 262, 283
Alcatraz Island (occupation), 212
Alvord, Lori Arviso, 80
American Indigenous Studies, *see* Native American and Indigenous Studies
Ami, Carlon P., 229, 237, 291
Ami, Carlon P. II, 223, 224, 234, 237
Ami, Christine, 197, 198
Anadarko, OK, 180, 211
Anderson, Ephraim, 237
Andrew W. Mellon Foundation, 102
Anishinaabe Anishinaabeg, 17, 162, 172, 174, 245
  *See also* Ojibwe
Apache Tribe of Oklahoma, 179, 180, 188
Arizona (state), 247
  and capitol building, 219, 236
  and House of Representatives, 219
*Arizona v. Navajo Nation* (2023), 31
Art and artists, 199, 219–238
  and exhibits, 197, 225, 231, 235
  and galleries, 209, 226
  and graffiti muralism, 207, 213
  and Kiowa 6, 197
  and murals, 200, 200n2, 208, 210, 211, 215, 218
  and painters/paintings, 113, 114, 197, 205, 213, 214, 214n39, 230, 233, 262
  and pottery, 223
  and silversmithing, 221, 223, 230, 231, 233
  and weaving, 205, 221, 223
  *See also specific artists*
Artplace America, 212, 228n4
Asah, Spencer, 211
Aspaas, Kevin, 237
Auchiah, James, 211
Awatovi, AZ, 212

[1] Note: Page numbers followed by 'n' refer to notes.

© The Author(s), under exclusive license to Springer Nature Switzerland AG 2024
F. King, W. Davies (eds.), *COVID-19 in Indian Country*,
https://doi.org/10.1007/978-3-031-70184-9

## B

Baird, Jennifer, 207
Ballard, Jim, 53
Barkaskas, Patricia, 146, 146n3
Barnett, Rebecca, 107, 115
Beaver, Del (Second Chief), 106
Beck, Nanibaa, 233, 234
Begay Raphael, 230
Begay, Aaron, 237
Begay, Corey, 230
Begay, Sue V., 223, 224, 237
Bemidji State University (BSU), 166, 167, 170, 173–176
Ben, Cyrus (Chief), 5
Benally, Jeneda, 39
Benally, Nathan, 77
Bergman, Chris, 172
Biden, President Joseph, 2, 39
Bighorse, Tiana, 281
Black, Triston, 225, 227
Black Lives Matter (BLM), 171, 283
Blacksheep, Beverly, 230
Blackwater-Nygren, Jasmine (AZ Representative), 219–221, 227, 234, 237n11
Blanding, UT, 147
Boarding schools, *see* Education
Body bags, 1–3, 18, 19, 135, 289
Bollinger, Matthew, 222, 236
Bosque Redondo (Fort Sumner, Hwééłdi), 29
Bridges, G.M., 61
Britton, Karla, 228
Bureau of Indian Affairs (U.S.) (Office of Indian Affairs), 54, 82
Burials and cemeteries, 100, 101, 110
Burnette, Dustin, 176
Butler, RaeLynn, 74, 104, 110

## C

Cajete, Gregory, 146, 148, 159
Canada, 167, 171, 173, 174, 182, 200n3, 264, 275–277
Canyon de Chelly, AZ, 223
Carlisle Indian School, 181
Carnegie, OK, 182
Carter Seminary, 67
Casinos (closings), 14
Catholicism, 254
Centers for Disease Control and Prevention (CDC), 3, 36, 91, 134, 170, 215, 225, 264
Ceremonies, 47, 130, 139
 *See also* Specific Indigenous Nations
Chacon, Nonibah, 233
Chalfant, Henry, 214
Changing Woman, 80n10
Cherokee
 and Cherokee Nation, 26, 73, 76, 149, 200
 United Keetoowah Band of, 73, 76
 *Cherokee Nation v. Georgia* (1831), 26
Cheyenne River Sioux, 126, 202
China, 78, 93, 106
 and Wuhan, 93
Choctaw
 and language, 67
 tribe, 5, 6, 6n17, 8, 14, 21, 25–35, 38–41, 49, 52, 58, 62, 64, 77, 110, 119, 135, 141, 185, 186, 200n3, 202, 202n5, 205, 218, 236, 239, 241, 242, 245, 249, 252–254, 288, 291, 292
Church of Jesus Christ of Latter-day Saints, 92
Colonialism
 colonization and "settler colonialism," 208
 effects of, 140, 141
 *See also* Decolonization
Colorado (state), 261, 282, 283
Colter, Mary Jane, 211
Colville Indian Reservation, 46
Comanche Nation, 244
Community
 collective coping, 128–130
 value/values of, 15, 73, 152

Cook, A.L., 52
Cooper, Martha, 214
Coronavirus Aid, Relief, and Economic Services Act (CARES), 7, 14
Courts and cases, 26, 30, 31
  U.S. Supreme Court cases, 26
  *See also specific cases*
COVID-19
  and "brain fog", 256, 271
  case (infection) rates of, 56
  and comorbidities (pre-existing conditions), 3, 9, 76, 287 (*see also specific diseases*)
  fears of, 138, 189
  and lockdowns/shutdowns/stay-at-home orders, 5, 14, 41, 72, 77, 119, 120, 138, 163, 168–170, 172, 240, 281
  and long COVID, 2, 256
  mortality rates (deaths) of, 6, 7, 10, 12, 36, 46, 50, 56n46, 57, 58, 91, 92, 105, 135, 156, 157, 163
  public perception of, 125 (*see also* Media coverage)
  and testing, 18, 133, 138, 248
  and timeline of spread, 218
Craig, Velma, 223, 231

**D**
Dakota, 162, 164–166
  and language, 162, 165
Dawes Act (General Allotment Act), 49
Decolonization, 65–72, 142
Dellinger, Linda, 103
Deloria, Vine, Jr., 181
Department of the Interior (US), 211
Diabetes, 9, 36, 71, 76
Diacon, Johnnie, 96, 100, 112, 113
Dick, Alexandria, 86
Dick, Florence, 75–78, 80, 83–87
Dinae, Brandon, 234
Diné College, 220–222, 224–229, 231, 232, 234, 236, 237n11
*Disney+*, 290
Doctor, *see* Physicians
Doctrine of Discovery, 25
Dodson, Ryan, 225, 227, 237
Draper, Teddy, Jr., 223, 231
Durbin Feeling Language Center, 289
Durbin Feeling Language Preservation Act (2024), 289

**E**
Echo-Hawk, Abigail, 1, 18, 19, 243, 289
Economies (tribal), 14
  and pandemic disruptions, 3, 14, 91, 105
Edmo, Ladd, 41
Education, 222–223, 262, 271
  and boarding schools, 49, 51, 59, 181
  and college students, 121, 142
  and computer literacy, 184–186
  and curriculum, 79
  disruptions of, 50, 132–133, 171, 180
  and innovative teaching, 17
  and school closings, 56, 58, 61
  and student challenges, 17, 122, 137, 153
  and student scholarships, 142
  and student support/mentoring, 148
Elders
  losses of, 69, 277
  respect and values for, 163, 186
  roles of, 120, 288
Environmental Protection Agency (EPA), 40
Epidemics, *see* COVID-19; Influenza

**F**
Facebook, 221, 249
Families (kinship)
  and separations, 17, 60, 82
  and support networks, 265
  values (definition) of, 66, 76, 130, 252, 268
Farmington, NM, 203, 215, 284
Faulds, Joseph, 87
Feeling, Durbin, 289
Ficklin, Erica, 119, 147, 155–158
Fife, Jay, 115
Floyd, George, 171
Floyd, James (Chief), 113
Food (nutrition and malnutrition)
  and food deserts, 9
  and food insecurity, 123, 157, 158
  and food sovereignty, 15
  and fry bread, 66
  and traditional foods, 138
  *See also* Gardening
Fort Bridger (Treaty of), 49
Fort Hall, 21, 22, 42, 47–50, 53, 54, 56, 57, 59, 62, 63
Fort Lewis College, 143
Fragua, Jaque, 201, 203, 204, 214, 214n37, 215
Frazier, Bud, 152
Frazier, Curtis, 147
Fruitvale, NM, 215, 216
Funston (Camp), 45

**G**
Gallup, NM, 77, 152, 223–225, 281
Gardening, 114
Garrity, Geraldine, 236
General Allotment Act, *see* Dawes Act
George-Kanentiio, Doug, 290
Georgia (state), 97
Gladwin, Derek, 146

Grand Canyon National Park, 211
  and Desert View Watchtower, 211
Greymountain, Brittany, 231, 232, 237

**H**
Hall, Clyde, 58
Handsel, Jennifer, 104
Hantavirus, 3n6
Harjo, Laura, 19
Harjo-Moffer, Melissa, 108
Haskell Institute, 45
Hatalthi, Valene, 225
Healing and healers (Indigenous)
  and Indigenous beliefs and practices, 108
  *See also* Physicians
Health and health care
  and data collection/data sovereignty, 6, 127
  and disparities/inequities, 3, 4, 6, 7, 11, 21, 32, 34–36, 162
  and statistics, 7, 47, 50, 55
Health education, 91
Heard Museum, 223
Hendren, Shane, 233
Hill, David (Chief), 105–107
Hill, Nabahe, 237
Ho-Chunk, 205
Hokeah, Jack, 211
Hopi
  and kachina dolls, 214
  and kivas, 212
Hospitals
  and accessibility, 71
  and capacities, 91, 100
  and rates of admission, 186
House of Stamps, 223, 224, 230
Housing (conditions)
  Indigenous architecture, 105, 228, 236

and multi-generational, 8
and overcrowding, 8
Howard Hughes Medical Institute (HHMI), 147, 149, 160
Hulu, 290

## I
Idaho (state), 21, 41, 46, 47, 50, 54, 55, 62, 63
Incomes, *see* Socioeconomic status
Indian Health Care Improvement Act (IHCIA) (1976), 33
Indian Health Service (U.S.) (IHS)
  and contract care, 8
  and funding hygiene and handwashing, 2, 9, 37, 59, 63
  history of, 5
  and response to COVID-19, 7, 220, 243
  *See also specific facilities and services*; Water
Indian law (federal), 25, 26
Indian Removal Act, 97
Indian Self-Determination and Education Assistance Act (1975), 33
"Indigenuity," 290, 291
Influenza, 9, 11, 12, 41–64, 81, 82, 207
  and the 1918–1920 pandemic, 41–64, 81, 207
Infrastructure Investment and Jobs Act (IIJA) (2021), 39
Institute of American Indian Arts (IAIA), 282
Institutional Review Boards (IRBs), 125, 166, 242n3
Insurance (health), 8
Internet, *see* Technology (digital); Zoom (use of)
Isaac, Lawrence, 235

## J
Jackson, Kayla, 215n42, 216, 228, 233
Jemez Pueblo, 77, 201, 203, 204
Joe, Valerie, 223
Johns Hopkins Center for American Indian Health, 92
*Johnson v. M'Intosh* (1823), 26
Johnson, Shawna, 231, 235
Jones, Dennis, 164, 174

## K
Kabotie, Fred, 211, 212, 214
Kaiser Family Foundation, 161
Kansas (state), 45
Katoney, Marlow, 229
Kaufman, Briana, 147
Kernell, Cebon, 110
Killgore, Racheal, 119, 147, 152–155
King, Thomas, 2
Kinship, 258
  *See also* Families (kinship)
Kiowa, 179, 181, 183, 188, 194
Kiowa Apache, 179, 180
Knife Chief, Charles, 86
Kumeyaay, 124

## L
Lakota, Oglala, 87, 205
  *See also* Cheyenne River Sioux
Language
  learning, 120, 163, 164, 264, 278, 290
  retention, 15
  revitalization, 15, 164, 178, 264, 289 (*see also Specific languages*)
LaPensée, Elizabeth, 209
Lapwai, ID, 47
Lawrence, KS, 45

Lee, Ivan, 215–217, 215n42
Lessard, Kerry Hawk, 13
Lewis, Hondo, 223
Littleben, Crystal, 237
Logan, UT, 147
Longdon, Jennifer, 219

## M
Margaret A. Cargill Philanthropies, 221
Martin, Tammera, 225, 237
Masking and mask mandates, 5, 14, 114, 163, 171, 175, 220
Maternal care/health/pregnancy, 1, 3–9, 11–13, 15, 18, 21, 23–44, 47, 49, 50, 52–55, 55n42, 59–64, 68, 71, 75–77, 80, 82, 83, 89–94, 97, 99–102, 105, 106, 111–113, 122, 123, 125, 126, 126n23, 128, 130, 132, 133, 136, 139, 141, 142, 150, 156–158, 162, 177, 201, 202, 215, 222, 239, 249, 255, 257, 259, 264, 269, 271–273, 275, 291, 292
McGowan, Gina, 236
Media coverage, of COVID-19, 98
Medicine (Indigenous), 7, 254, 255
and herbal remedies, 47 (*see also* Healing and healers (Indigenous))
Mental health, 9, 68, 77, 100, 122, 123, 128, 130, 132, 133, 136, 139, 141, 142, 156–158, 156n6
*See also* Suicide
Meredith, America, 200
*Meriam Report* (1928), 33, 37, 54
Michigan (state), 164, 167
Mille Lacs Band, 163
Miller, H.H., 55
Minnesota (state), 162, 164, 166–168, 171, 174, 283

Minnesota State University, 165
Missing and Murdered Indigenous Women (MMIW), 19
Montana (state), 247
Montgomery, Lindsay, 245
Monument Valley (UT), 73
Mopope, Stephen, 211
Motherhood, 84, 242, 244, 266, 282
and child custody, 240, 281
roles of, 272, 274
*See also* Maternal care/health/pregnancy
Muscogee (Creek)
and ceremonies, 110
and Department of Health, 99–101, 105
and Historic and Cultural Preservation Department, 74, 98, 101, 102, 104
and Muscogee (Creek) Nation, 95–117

## N
Naataanii, Sarah, 223
Naataanii, TahNibaa, 233
Naegle, Ilene, 223, 237
National Park Service (U.S.) (NPS), 212, 213
Native American and Indigenous Studies (and subdisciplines) (NAIS), 15, 17, 164, 165
Native Language Fair Honor Fund, 288
Navajo (Diné)
and Code Talkers, 228
court system, 31
creation/origin story of, 81
and Cultural Arts Program, 219, 221
and Diné Bikéyah, 75, 77, 79, 83
and language (Diné bizaad), 89, 91, 290

and Long Walk, 29 (*see also* Bosque Redondo (Fort Sumner, Hwééłdi))
and Navajo Nation, 3n6, 4–6, 5n11, 9, 12, 14, 15, 21, 23–25, 29–31, 35–38, 74, 76, 77, 89–93, 147, 148, 150–152, 201, 202, 215, 216, 226, 228, 237n11, 243, 244 (*see also* Diné College)
Navarro, Geneva Woomavoyah, 288
Ned Hatathli Culture Center, 220, 236, 237
Nevada (state), 247, 250
New Deal (Great Depression), 210
*See also specific New Deal agencies*
New Mexico (state), 29, 152, 162, 168, 201, 203, 215, 216, 223, 224, 247, 281, 283, 284
New York (city and state), 5, 15, 207, 211, 214, 215
Nez, Jerome, 230, 235
Nez, Johnathan (President), 25
Nez Perce, 47
  Nez Perce Reservation, 47
Noble, Francis, 237
Noriega, Gabrielle, 116
Nursing homes, 77, 85, 86, 248, 251
Nutlouis, Tavian, 231, 232, 237
Nutrition and malnutrition, *see* Food (nutrition and malnutrition)
Nuucic, 261, 262

O
Office of Indian Affairs and Indian Service, *see* Bureau of Indian Affairs (U.S.) (Office of Indian Affairs)
Oglala Lakota (Sioux), 155
Ohoychisba, 66

Ojibwe, 163–169, 169n18, 171, 173, 174, 176–178
  and language, 120, 163–166, 172–175
  *See also* Mille Lacs Band; Red Lake Nation; White Earth Nation
O'Keefe, Civtoria, 241
Oklahoma Native American Youth Language Fair (ONAYLF), 288, 289
Oklahoma (state), 73, 74, 82, 82n14, 95, 98, 99, 104, 106, 180, 182, 211, 288
Oljato, UT (Navajo Nation), 93
Olsen, Kristian, 151
Omaha, NE, 205, 206
Oral history, *see* Muscogee (Creek); Oral traditions (stories)
Oral traditions (stories)
  importance of, 97
  perseverance of during COVID-19, 107
Ornelas, Barbara Teller, 229, 231
Osage Nation, 202

P
Paiute, 247n25, 263
Pandemics, *see* COVID-19; Influenza
Pawnee, 86
  Pawnee Nation, 1
Pebaamibines (Dennis Jones), 164, 174, 176
Personal protective equipment (PPE), 18, 81, 112, 128, 129, 135
Pete, Lynda Teller, 230, 231
Physicians, 11, 32, 33, 47, 50–53, 58, 70, 73–75, 77, 80, 83, 86, 89, 93, 252, 255, 256, 269, 270
Piña, Apollonia, 109
Piper, Daniel, 119, 147–149
Plumbing, *see* Water

Pneumonia, 9, 45, 50, 52, 62
Pocatello, ID, 49, 54
Poetry and poets, 79, 197, 240, 262, 263, 278, 291
Ponca, 205
Portillo, Amy, 111
Powell, Roman, 110
Powwow, 14, 152
Pratt, Richard Henry (Capt.), 50
Pregnancy, 266, 269, 272, 275
  *See also* Maternal care/health/pregnancy
Public Health Agency (Canada), 264
Public messaging and outreach
  and signage and billboards, 17, 217
  *See also* Art and artists; Health education
Public Works of Art Project (PWAP), 210, 211, 213
Pueblo peoples, 77
  *See also specific Nations*
Pyramid Lake, 262, 277

**Q**
Quarantines
  lockdowns, 5, 14, 77, 138, 240
  shutdowns, 72, 120
  and stay-at-home orders, 5, 119

**R**
Racism (racial bias), 68, 69, 79, 134, 256
Rader, Dean, 208, 213
Rainy Mountain Indian School, 182
Red Corn, Alex, 179
Red Cross, 46, 46n16
Red Lake Nation, 163
Religion, *see* Specific Indigenous Nation

Removal (policy of), 11
Respirators, 64, 215
Riverside Indian School (RIS) (Wichita Caddo School), 120, 180, 181, 183, 188, 190, 195
Roessel, Bryan, 226, 237
Roman Nose, Quinton, 288
Roosevelt, Franklin D. (President), 210

**S**
St. Patrick's Mission School, 211
Salsman, Jason, 288
Salt Lake City, UT, 92
San Carlos Apache Tribe, 13
Sandsprings, AZ, 230
Sanitation, 21, 23, 25, 34, 35
  *See also* Sanitation Facilities Construction Program(SFCP); Water
Sanitation Facilities Construction Program (SFCP), 32, 34, 35, 39
Santa Clara Pueblo, 146
Santa Fe Indian School, 211
Santa Fe, NM, 229
  and Indian Market, 229
Sault Ste. Marie, MI, 167
Savitzky, Al, 147, 149
Schools, *see* Education
Seattle Indian Health Board, 1, 2, 18
Seattle, WA, 243
Sells, Cato, 55
Shiprock, NM, 201, 215, 217
Shoshone (Duckwater), 263
Shoshone-Bannock tribes, 12
Shutdowns/lockdowns, *see* COVID-19
Simon Fraser University, 271
Smallpox, 6, 10, 11, 45, 50, 52, 53, 135, 207

Smith, Matthew R., 208
Smith, Phillip, 73, 74, 83, 90
Smoky, Lois, 211
Snyder Act (1921), 33
Socioeconomic status, 9, 14, 199
　communities, 1, 6, 8, 31
South Dakota (state), 14
Soweka, Robin, 108
Specific indigenous nations, 253
Springsteen, Bruce, 230
Stay-at-home orders, *see* COVID-19
Stewart, Laura, 115
Stillday, Eugene, Sr., 163
Stone, Tyler, 114
Stories and storytelling, *see* Oral
　traditions
Students, 271
　*See also* Education
Suicide, 9, 136, 157
Supreme Court (US), *see* Courts
　and cases
Survivance, 17, 122, 124, 132, 141,
　180, 197–198, 209, 210, 220,
　222, 236, 238, 245, 246, 289,
　291, 292
　definition of, 17, 209, 220, 245,
　　289, 291
Swine flu (2009), 42

T
Table Mesa, NM, 223
Tahlequah, OK, 73, 76, 77, 82,
　82n14, 83, 86, 289
Taylore, Claire, 207
Technology (digital), 8, 62, 70, 72,
　119, 123, 134, 137, 138, 146,
　151, 153, 169, 207, 235,
　269, 277
　and computer software, 190
　*See also* Education; Zoom

Tedlock, Dennis, 208
Tehee, Melissa, 119, 120,
　147, 149–152
Terry, Shawn (Secretary), 105, 106
Testing, *see* COVID-19
Texas (state), 71
Toadlena, Brent, 221, 222, 234,
　234n10, 237, 238
Tohe, Laura, 79
Transportation, 8, 37, 82, 91, 168
　and road closures, 133
Trauma (generational/historical), 28,
　36, 68, 70, 128, 134–135, 140,
　157, 209
Treaties, 6, 21, 25, 29, 30, 32, 35,
　38–40, 202
Treece, Carly, 114
Treuer, Anton, 164–166, 165n13, 172
Tribal health initiatives, 13, 82
Truchot, Hazel, 59, 59n55, 64
Truchot, Louise, 43, 48, 58–59, 64
Trump, Donald (President), 4
Tsaidüka Tribe, 261
Tsaile, AZ (Navajo Nation), 222–225,
　227, 229, 232
Tsatoke, Monroe, 211
Tsinhnahjinnie, Hulleah, 230
Tso, Darrell, 228, 229
Tso, Jared, 228
Tsosie, Lyndon, 223, 230
Tsosie, Willis, 225, 227, 229, 237
Tuba City, AZ, 75
Tuberculosis, 9, 11, 47, 50, 52, 57
Two Bears, Kelsey, 111

U
University of Minnesota, 162, 163
University of New Mexico, 228
University of Oklahoma (OU), 288
Urban populations, 46, 242, 243, 258

U.S. Army, 45
U.S. federal government
  and Indigenous policies, 11
  and trust responsibilities, 25, 30–32, 35, 38, 40, 61
  See also Courts and cases; *specific agencies*; *specific statutes*; Treaties
Utah Navajo Health System (UNHS), 75, 77, 90
Utah (state of), 147
Utah State University (and MESAS program), 119, 145, 147
Ute (Southern), 262

**V**
Vaccines, 135
  and attitudes, 74, 125
  and development of, 12, 93
  and Pfizer, 92
  and rates of, 12
  and vaccination campaigns, 13
Vizenor, Gerald, 17, 209, 209n22, 210, 217, 220, 245, 289

**W**
Walter, Harry, 223
Walz, Tim, 168
Washington (state), 1, 3, 46, 226
Washington, D.C., 182, 211
Water
  and accessibility, 21, 23
  and indoor plumbing, 8–9, 23
  and quality, 40
  quantification of, 30, 31
  and water rights, 30, 31

  See also Sanitation Facilities Construction Program (SFCP)
Wauneka, Delia, 237
Wetsit, Lawrence, 292
Wheeler, Henry, 51, 53, 55–60, 62, 63
White Earth Nation, 167
Whitehorse, Emmi, 233
Whitethorn, Bahe, Sr., 233
Wildcat, Daniel, 181
Willeto, Paul, 235
Williams, Heather, 234
Willie, JT, 233
Wilson, William, 233
Wind, Grover, 112
*Winters v. United States* (1908), 30
*Worcester v. Georgia* (1832), 26
World Health Organization (WHO), 3, 167, 177, 263
World War I, 43n4, 48
Wright, John, 50

**Y**
Yazzie, Peterson, 233
Yazzie, William J., 237
Yellow Horse Brave Heart, Maria, 28
Young, Allie, 81

**Z**
Zoom (use of), 17, 127, 148, 151, 152, 166, 168, 169, 171–173, 175, 177, 180, 186–189, 191, 192, 219, 223, 228, 231, 246, 246n22, 247, 247n23, 250, 252, 253, 264, 277, 290
Zuni, 126

GPSR Compliance
The European Union's (EU) General Product Safety Regulation (GPSR) is a set of rules that requires consumer products to be safe and our obligations to ensure this.

If you have any concerns about our products, you can contact us on

ProductSafety@springernature.com

In case Publisher is established outside the EU, the EU authorized representative is:

Springer Nature Customer Service Center GmbH
Europaplatz 3
69115 Heidelberg, Germany

www.ingramcontent.com/pod-product-compliance
Lightning Source LLC
LaVergne TN
LVHW021335080526
838202LV00004B/187